Sensible Flesh

Sensible Flesh

On Touch in Early Modern Culture

Edited by Elizabeth D. Harvey

PENN

University of Pennsylvania Press
Philadelphia

10   9   8   7   6   5   4   3   2   1

Published by
University of Pennsylvania Press
Philadelphia, Pennsylvania 19104-4011

Library of Congress Cataloging-in-Publication Data
Sensible flesh : on touch in early modern culture / edited by Elizabeth D. Harvey.
    p.   cm
    Includes bibliographical references and index.
    ISBN 0-8122-3693-9 (cloth : alk. paper)—ISBN 0-8122-1829-9 (pbk. : paper)
    1. Touch. 2. Senses and sensation. I. Harvey, Elizabeth D.
BF275 .S46 2002
152'.82—dc21   2002074032

Contents

Chapter 1
Introduction: The "Sense of All Senses"
Elizabeth D. Harvey

Everything is given to us by means of touch, a mediation that is continually forgotten.
—*Luce Irigaray* "Divine Women," Sexes and Genealogies

Pain lays not its touch / Upon a corpse.
—*Aeschylus, Frag. 250.*

Touch comes before sight, before speech. It is the first language and the last, and it always tells the truth.
—*Margaret Atwood,* The Blind Assassin

Touch occupies a complex, shifting, and sometimes contradictory position in the representation of the five senses in Western culture. Sometimes depicted as "the king of senses" it was equally likely to be disparaged as the basest sense.[1] Of the five senses, touch is the most diffuse and somatically dispersed, and because the organ associated with it—the skin or flesh—covers the whole body, it is closely associated with corporeality. Neoplatonic thought, for example, relegated touch (along with taste and smell) to the lower, more bodily senses. Indeed, the sense of touch perhaps most frequently evokes the erotic and seductive, and early modern depictions of the Five Senses sometimes portray Touch through lascivious or pornographic scenes. Yet tactility is also associated with authoritative scientific, medical, and even religious knowledge, and it often expresses in synecdochic form creative powers (the artist's "touch"). Tactile contact is central to religious representation; it is evident in depictions that range from the *Noli me tangere* topos to doubting Thomas's touching of Christ's wounds to the figuration of religious healing, all of which signify the dialectic between materiality and resurrection, between physical and spiritual contamination or cure.

In the scientific or medical register, touch is closely tied to pain, to contagion, and to the curative hand of the physician. It is crucial to the history of medicine, anatomy, and science, especially as the instruments of knowing shift from a humoral theory that reads the body through all its senses to an epistemology that grants increasing primacy to the ocular.[2] Although touch is usually associated with the surface of the body, it becomes a metaphor for conveyance into the interior of the subject, particularly the capacity to arouse emotion (registered in the figurative sense of "touching" as kindling affect). Touch evokes at once agency and receptivity, authority and reciprocity, pleasure and pain, sensual indulgence and epistemological certainty. It is precisely the rich ambivalence of tactility's representation that this collection explores.

The impulse of the volume is both analytic and recuperative in that the essays attempt to understand the important history of this sense at a pivotal juncture in its construction and to examine how tactility has organized knowledge and defined human subjectivity. The early modern period is especially significant as a historical moment for this investigation of touch because we can witness then the nascent stages of a consolidation of beliefs about the body's relation to knowledge, sexuality and reproduction, artistic creativity, and "contact" with other worlds, both divine and newly discovered geographical realms. The subsequent relative eclipse of touch as an important sense or topic of interest may be correlated with the increasing predominance of the visual, which, beginning with Plato and then consolidated into a regime of the visual with the advent of modern science, has been privileged as the highest and purest of the senses.[3] While the intricate reciprocity between visuality and tactility that characterizes the representation of the senses from Plato onwards endures,[4] touch as figured within a discursive and iconographical tradition tends to be subsumed into a dominant culture of ocularity. These essays implicitly and explicitly interrogate the preeminence of sight (or hearing, which has its own history), focusing on touch as a more diffuse sense, a world of sensation that incorporates the body, particularly the feminine body, into its operations. Where hearing, sight, and smell extend the body beyond its own boundaries, touch insists on the corporeal because it relies upon contiguity or proximity for its operations. To engage touch as a category of investigation, as phenomenologists such as Maurice Merleau-Ponty, psychoanalytic theorists such as Didier Anzieu, psychoanalytic and feminist theorists such as Luce Irigaray or Julia Kristeva, and poststructuralist theorists such as Gilles Deleuze or Jean-François Lyotard in his engagement of St. Augustine's sensory world have done,[5] is to reactivate the body's material, and often gendered, relation to the world. The exploration of tactility's representation in this volume has an allegiance on the one hand to these theoretical projects in its wish to question the history of the hierarchical ordering of the senses and the philosophical and cultural consequences that derive from it. At the same time, the essays participate in the materialist impulse in early modern studies, exemplified in such recent works as Margreta de Grazia, Maureen Quilligan, and Peter Stallybrass's collection, *Subject and Object in Renaissance Culture*, Patricia Fumerton and Simon Hunt's *Renaissance Culture and the Everyday*, and Lena Cowen Orlin's *Material London, ca. 1600*, which in their different ways seek to recover the "tactility" of culture, the "tangibility" of diurnal life, whether figured in clothing, images, material texts, maps, textiles, money, or mirrors.[6] This propensity to focus on material objects is, of course, already well established in early modern work on the body, whether exemplified, to cite only a few of the many examples, in Gail Kern Paster's analysis of the social meanings of bodily fluids in *The Body Embarrassed*, Louise Fradenburg and Carla Freccero's volume on gender and eroticism, *Premodern Sexualities*, or Jonathan Sawday's treatment of anatomical discourse in *The Body Emblazoned*.[7] What both these theoretical and materialist tendencies share is a recuperative propensity, a wish not just to reconstruct history's "lost" objects, but also to examine what dominant discourses have willfully elided in their reconstruction of the past, whether it is slavery or lesbian sexuality or peasant rituals. Touch has a simultaneously exuberant and deprecated link to materiality, to the body, to eroticism in the early modern period, where it is still central to a set of representational systems that include philosophy, religion, medicine, and art, as the essays gathered here demonstrate in their engagement of numerous discourses and topics (science, eroticism, medicine, disease, temptation, religion, philosophy, first "contact" between European and non-European peoples, visual arts, material artifacts, skin, rhetoric, emotion, pleasure, contagion, and pain). The early modern period might thus be designated as the "pre-history" of our post-Enlightenment construction of touch, a period when it is possible to witness an intensive articulation of the power and danger associated with tactility.

Michael Drayton's sonnet XXIX "To the Senses" in *Idea* captures the privileged positioning of touch in the early modern hierarchy of the senses.[8] The speaker's heart is besieged by "conqu'ering Love," and he thus summons the five senses to his aid, but one by one, each of them is overcome by Love's blandishments. Sight is corrupted by beauty, Hearing is bribed with sweet harmony, Taste is delighted by the sweetness of the beloved's lips, Smell is vanquished by the "Spicerie"of her breath, and finally Touch remains as the solitary guardian of the heart's citadel. Figured as "The King of Senses, greater than the rest," Touch not only yields to Love, handing over the heart's keys, but he also persuasively addresses the other senses, endorsing Love's conquest and telling his companion senses that "they should be blest." The traditional catalogue of the senses that Drayton's sonnet evokes is a topos that has a long tradition extending, at least in its allegorical configuration, from Alain de Lille's late twelfth-century *Anticlaudianis* into an iconographical tradition and into such early modern literary depictions as Marsilio Ficino's commentary on the *Symposium*, Edmund Spenser's *The Faerie Queene*, and Andrew Marvell's "Dialogue Between the Resolved Soul, and Created Pleasure."[9] The judgment about where touch belongs in the sensory echelon has much to do, of course, with definitions of love and lust, the value of eroticism, and the place of the material or the fleshly. The debate also overlaps with and extends into the realms of philosophy, figuring in discussions of perception and epistemology and in debates about the relation between the body and the soul. Aristotle in *De Sensu*, for instance, wavers about whether to give primacy to the visual or the auditory sense, yet he also finds touch essential to life, calling it "the indispensable sense."[10] In *De Anima*, he asserts that "all animals whatsoever are observed to have the sense of touch,"and therefore it must be the "primary form of sense" (413b). For Lucretius, a materialist who believed that all knowledge is derived from sensation, touch forms the basis for the other four senses and, although not explicitly distinguished from them, is implicated in the body's ability to sense pleasure and pain: "it is touch that is the bodily sense, whether when a thing penetrates from without, or when hurt comes from something within the body, or when it gives pleasure in issuing forth by the creative acts of Venus."[11]

Just as there is controversy about the placement of touch in the hierarchy of the senses, so, too is there disagreement about its nature as a sense. Touch is, after all, different from the other senses in that it is not housed in a specific, identifiable organ. Where vision, hearing, taste, and smell are faculties located in and thereafter associated with the eye, the ear, the tongue, and the nose, touch is, as classical and early modern writers were quick to recognize, both everywhere and nowhere. Aristotle distinguished touch from the other senses, both for this reason and because he questioned whether it is multiple, a group of senses rather than a single sense. He considered whether the flesh itself is the organ of touch or whether flesh is the medium, with the "real organ being situated further inward" (*De Anima*, 422b–423a). Phineas Fletcher sums up the paradoxical nature of tactility in this formulation:

"*Tactus* . . . [h]ath his abode in none, yet every place."[12] Touch is ubiquitous, dispersed throughout the body; there is no single place where it is said to be concentrated. Even skin, which as a cutaneous boundary would seem to extend touch's distribution throughout the body, cannot be its somatic harbor, since as Aristotle argues, touch is deeper than skin; the tactile feeling seems, indeed, to be a property of the flesh itself.[13] The inability to locate touch in a specific place in the body seems closely related to the ambivalence about its importance. Fletcher classifies *Tactus* as the youngest but also the oldest of the sensory "brothers," and declares that his function is both the least important and the most necessary (5:55).[14] In John Davies's *Nosce Teipsum*, the essential nature of touch, which Aristotle sees as fundamental to animal life, is caught in the descriptive epithet "life's root," a phrase that signals both the primacy of the tactile and its spatial ability to spread and communicate throughout the body.[15]

Recurrent in the history of Western culture is this sometimes submerged but nevertheless enduring idea that tactility is the "root" of the other senses and, further, that touch is somehow synonymous with life itself. This belief animates the epigraph from Aeschylus; only a corpse cannot feel pain, and conversely, to feel pain is to be alive (or, as Aristotle says, "the loss of this one sense alone must bring about the death of an animal"(*De Anima*, 435b).[16] Given this tradition, how and why should touch have importance as a subject of investigation in what philosophers and theorists have called a resolutely ocularcentric culture? In his sweeping study of ocularity in Western thought, Martin Jay enumerates the sources for this visual hegemony, which include the powerful inheritance of the Hellenic privileging of the visual, what he calls (following Max Weber's use of the term) the "elective affinity" between the emergence of capitalism and the invention of linear perspective (52–62), the complex coupling of the baroque ocular regime and the growth of a dominant scientific method (itself based on a linkage of rationality and the visual) (45), and the enormous influence of Descartes, the "founding father of the modern visualist paradigm"(70). The very predominance of the visual has, not surprisingly, attracted a range of critics who have not only challenged the primacy of the ocular, but also instigated a reconsideration of Western metaphysics and culture. If the narratives that subtend our understanding of our relation to the world, to our bodies, to other human beings, and to knowledge in all its forms are based on an unexamined acceptance of visuality, what would it mean to interrogate these truths in terms of the sensory privileging on which they rely?

This is the question that shapes Didier Anzieu's writing on tactility in

The Skin Ego and related works.[17] He asserts that human subjectivity is generated through touch; early embryonic and infantile tactile experience lays
the foundation of an ego that is rooted in the body and linked to skin as
boundary and receptive organ. Anzieu's theory of the skin ego unsettles the
relationship between inside and outside and situates the tactile organ of the
skin as the dynamic physiological and psychic interface between subject and
world. This question also motivates Irigaray's *Speculum of the Other Woman*, a
text that unrelentingly scrutinizes the persistence of the visual in philosophy
and psychoanalysis. Her book itself replicates in its structure an instrument of
vision, the speculum, [18] providing a temporally reversed reflection of Western
thought that begins with Freud ("The Blind Spot of an Old Dream of Sym-
metry") and ends with a reading of Plato's Parable of the Cave ("Plato's *Hys-
tera*"). At the center of the book there are seven shorter chapters that treat
Plato, Aristotle, Plotinus, Kant, and Hegel, and in the middle of these sections
lies Irigaray's analysis of Cartesian thought, entitled ". . . And If, Taking the Eye
of a Man Recently Dead . . ." In this chapter she examines the Cartesian *cogito*,
interrogating the linkage between rationality and vision and the body's place
in it and concluding with a reference to Descartes's notion of the body as a *res
extensa* (an extended thing as opposed to a thinking thing, *res cogitans*), an
idea that is complicated by her introduction of touch (190).[19] While Irigaray's
resistance to the tyranny of the scopic regime defines *Speculum,* her elaboration of an opposing theory, what we might call a metaphysics of touch, nevertheless undergirds it and achieves a fuller expression a decade later in *An
Ethics of Sexual Difference* and in a lecture printed in *Sexes and Genealogies*:[20]

If we look seriously at this composite and provisional incarnation of man and
woman we are brought back to the sense that underlies all the other four senses, that
exists or insists in them all, our first sense and the one that constitutes all our living
space, all our environment: the sense of *touch*. This is the sense that travels with us
from the time of our material conception to the height of our celestial grace, lightness, or glory. We have to return to touch if we are to comprehend where touch became frozen in its passage from the most elemental to the most sophisticated part of
its evolution. This will mean that we need to stay both firm and mobile in our
cathexes, always faithful, that is, to the dimension of touch. (*Sexes and Genealogies,* 59)

Irigaray's impulse to return to or revisit what has been repudiated in philosophy relies on a psychoanalytic model of temporality that she extends
into a historical register; just as the child abjures the mother in order to enter
the symbolic realm, so does Western culture erase the memory of maternal
origin. As Irigaray says in an aphoristic gloss on *Speculum*: "Surely man fa-

vors the visual because it marks his exit from the life in the womb?"(*Sexes and Genealogies,* 59).[21] She contends that Western philosophy's occultation of the maternal contributes to a metaphysics of visibility (which in turn nourishes the hierarchical ordering of sexual difference), and her reconception of philosophy, which has political, epistemological, psychoanalytic, and ethical implications, involves reincorporating the feminine-maternal body and its "language"of tactility.[22]

Irigaray expands on the topic of touch in *An Ethics of Sexual Difference,* where she engages with Merleau-Ponty's unfinished last work, *The Visible and the Invisible.* Merleau-Ponty claims that both vision and touch are chiasmic or reversible, that is, that each entails a mutual participation of subject and object in the act of perception. The image that he furnishes to illustrate this reversibility is that of two hands touching, a movement that encodes mutuality: each hand feels itself touched even as it touches.[23] But where Merleau-Ponty asserts that seeing and touching are chiasmically interchangeable—the visible is apparent in the tangible, the tangible is apparent in the visible—Irigaray makes manifest the sensory hierarchy upon which this pronouncement depends. As she says, "The visible and the tactile do not obey the same laws or rhythms of the flesh. And if I can no doubt unite their powers, I cannot reduce the one to the other. I cannot situate the tangible and the visible in a chiasmus. . . . [The tangible] remains instead the ground that is available for all the other senses. . . . [It] is the matter and memory for all of the sensible" (*Ethics,* 162–64). She also questions whether the two hands touching can be perfectly reciprocal, for as she notes, one will always be more active or passive, more subject than object. She substitutes instead the figure of two hands held together, palm to palm (cf. Shakespeare's "palm to palm is holy palmers' kiss, " *Romeo and Juliet,* 1.5), a configuration that suggests greeting or prayer. The intimacy of the gesture Irigaray uses replaces Merleau-Ponty's more epistemological touch with a touch that evokes undifferentiated uterine or maternal contact, what she calls the prenatal moment where the subject is "palpated without seeing"(*Ethics,* 154). Irigaray's notion of touch also evokes its properties of contiguity (as Aristotle reminds us, "touch alone perceives by immediate contact"; *De Anima,* 435a), which is consonant with her privileging of metonymy, her figure for maternal genealogy.[24]

Irigaray's idea of a forgotten maternal substratum in which sensory experience dominates can be compared to Julia Kristeva's most recent description of the semiotic chora. In *Time and Sense: Proust and the Experience of Literature,* Kristeva describes what she calls a "sensory cave,"a place where sensation is experienced that cannot be expressed in language and that is at once reminiscent of the fusion with the maternal but that continues to be experienced by the adult.[25] The overwhelming of the subject by sensation that has no articulation or only a troubled articulation is characteristic of autism or hysteria (235), but the impulse to convert deep sensation into language produces "literary style" (234), a dialectic between the linguistic realm and the affective, corporeal, sensory world that lies before and beneath it. Both Kristeva and Irigaray argue that sensation, and especially touch, subtend human experience as a primordial memory and as the residue of what must be repressed or molded in the child's passage into the symbolic. For both, although in very different ways, the recovery of repressed sensation is crucial; for Irigaray it is necessary in the formulation of a new ethics of sexual difference, and for Kristeva the dialectic between the semiotic (or, what she calls in *Powers of Horror* the abjected maternal) and the symbolic is constitutive of art and literature and of a fully embodied humanity.[26] In *Powers of Horror*, Kristeva's exploration of abjection offers often startling insights into the para-Nazi and anti-Semitic writings of Paul Céline—the simultaneous attraction for and repulsion of an other that is characteristic of abjection—and she thus demonstrates the political implications of the psycho-analytic and linguistic analyses she performs.

These psychoanalytic, philosophical, and linguistic accounts of the "discourses of touch" are consonant with (and historicized by) Norbert Elias's description of the "civilizing process."[27] Elias argues that the transitions from warrior to courtly societies (the medieval and early modern periods in Europe) entailed a progressive controlling of the "animalistic instincts"(455), the "raw material of the drives" (487), a rationalizing and curbing process that was enacted both within the individual (the ego or super-ego controlling libidinal impulses [455]) and also as a social molding. Although Elias does not specifically address the senses in his description, the instilling of this social and bodily decorum, whether it refers to sexual behavior, nose-blowing, or the use of eating utensils, implicitly or explicitly orders the senses. Touch and smell in particular, which imply bodily proximity, become subordinated to the senses that support a greater distance between bodies (vision and hearing). In *De civilitate morum puerilium* (1530), for instance, Erasmus provides a list of admonitions and recommendations about table manners, many of which have to do with touch: do not put your hands in the dish as soon as you sit down ("Wolves do that"); "Do not be the first to touch the dish that has been brought in"; "To dip the fingers in the sauce is rustic"; "To lick greasy fingers or wipe them on your coat is impolite"(quoted in Elias, 73). Elias traces the progressive integration of eating utensils—especially the fork and spoon, which replace and/or extend the hands and thus distance touch—into civilized society. The codes that govern the use of utensils and manners distinguish human from animal behavior (this is a constant refrain in early modern books of etiquette), and they also tend to separate people from each other, accentuating individually segregated eating as opposed to the sharing of food from a communal receptacle.

Elias's analysis of the early modern period as a crucial point of transition for the civilizing process offers a critique and a trenchant explanation of psychoanalysis, for, as he claims, the distinctions between what Freud called the conscious and unconscious or the ego and the id are the result of a historical operation; the rift between the conscious mind, what he calls "rationalization" and the drive impulses and affective fantasies becomes wider until the "wall of forgetfulness" separating the two becomes increasingly impermeable (487–88). If the mechanisms of restraint and control that we tend to think of as "natural" are historically instantiated, as Elias argues, then to investigate the historical and material construction of touch is to recover as well what for Kristeva and Irigaray is not only the prehistory of the subject but also the ways in which touch is occluded, repressed, and rendered subordinate as part of the social and individual civilizing process. Rather than setting historicism against psychoanalysis as contradictory and mutually exclusive discourses, then, we might then consider them, as Elias does, as complementary. This is especially important for an investigation of touch, since it could be hypothesized that as the physical properties of tactility— which evoke in the early modern period eroticism, pain, and the appetitive in general—are subordinated during the process of instilling social restraint, they migrate into an affective realm. Elias argues that the civilizing process is one that interiorizes emotion. He cites La Bruyère's description of a man of the court, for instance, as someone who "is a master of his gestures, of his eyes and his expression; he is deep, impenetrable" (476). Emotion does not vanish, of course, but is directed internally, producing a split in the subject between drive and affect impulses and their expression; the result is that the subject "conceals his passion," "disavows his heart," and "acts against his feeling" (477). We might speculate that one of touch's discursive transpositions mimics this civilizing trend: in the same way that physical impulses are curbed and directed inward, so does tactility become, in addition to the more obvious physiological responses, "feeling"—the emotional desires and urges that are presented in explicitly physical terms in the early modern iconography of touch. Perhaps the most powerful of these physical desires that is transposed inward and made progressively emotional and "secret" is the erotic or libidinal, the arena recurrently associated with touch for early modern culture and the urge arguably most obsessively charted by psychoanalysis. The discourse most suited to analyzing the affective, "feeling," is of course, psychoanalysis, and it is not accidental, then, that touch and the senses should play pivotal roles in the work of Kristeva and Irigaray. Tactility is, like Kristeva's semiotic, linked to a forgotten world—of childhood, of a less completely "civilized" time, of a more completely realized embodiment. As Lynn Enterline astutely notes, however, the construction of a maternal abject or a semiotic chora is always a "retroactive, recursive cultural fantasy" that is "necessary to establishing a symbolic order."[28] Thus, bodies and sensory "feelings"are always mediated by a symbolic system; we have access to them only through the elaborate patterns of the symbolic—language, cultural habits, and material practices.

Merleau-Ponty makes tactility a property of the flesh or the body as a whole, but he also uses the synecdoche of the hand to represent touch. While the identifying feature of tactility in the early modern period is precisely its resistance to being identified with a single organ, the hand nevertheless appears with some regularity as a signifier of touch. George Chapman's apostrophe to "Feeling's organ," the "King of the king of senses" in *Ovid's Banquet of Sense*, where tactility is synechodized by the fortunate hand that touches Corinna's breast, sums up this strand of tactility's history.[29] When the five senses are portrayed through the sensory organs, touch sometimes appears as hands held over a flame (a conjunction of pain and tactility), as a clenched fist, or as hands clasped or being rubbed together.[30] Yet the identification between the hand and touch is neither perfect nor symmetrical: the hand is an instrument of mastery, control, creativity, and gesture as well as tactility, and the sense of touch is not confined to the hand but is distributed throughout the body.[31] The relatively unstable identification between the hand and tactility is accentuated in the divergence of allegorical and anatomical representations. That is, whereas touch in the allegorical tradition is linked to specific animals (parrot, falcon, tortoise, spider) or to scenes of seduction or erotic exchange, the figuration of touch as a property of physiology (often depicted in conjunction with the corresponding ventricles of the brain), which takes the hand as chief signifier, tends to pass into anatomical illustrations. Chapman's memorable phrase describing the hand's royal power to touch is an erotic apostrophe, but in Helkiah Crooke's *Microcosmographia*, touch, "the onely Sense of all Senses," is localized in the hand as the "Judge and discerner of touch."[32] The hand in the medical and anatomical context does not just serve as an emblem of touch, then, but also controls its dangerous, seductive, and potentially delusive aspects.

For the physician and the anatomist, the hand signals agency rather than receptivity, the power of sensation harnessed to the service of medical epistemology. The images that most haunt early modern anatomical practice are the Vesalian "muscle men," bodies divested of the skin in order better to display the structures of muscles, organs, and veins beneath. Paradoxically, perhaps, given that anatomy involves peeling away this vast sensory covering organ, the figure of the anatomist is synecdochized by the hand, as if the power of tactility lost by the corpse were displaced and concentrated in the touching, probing, dissecting hand. Galen, of course, begins with the hand in *De usu partium*, and early modern anatomies frequently follow his model. As Katherine Rowe puts it, "the hand becomes the prominent vehicle for integrating sacred mystery with corporeal mechanism. . . . The dissection of the hand in particular, from Galen to the seventeenth century, persists as one of the central topoi of anatomy demonstrations: celebrated for its difficulty and beauty, it reveals God's intentions as no other part can."[33] In the portrait of himself in *De humani corporis fabrica* (1543), Andreas Vesalius clasps the hand of the corpse, whose arm and hand are flayed to expose its underlying structures of bone and muscle. This "touch," unlike the reciprocity of Merleau-Ponty's touching hands, unites the living, mastering instrument of anatomical knowledge (the Vesalian hand) with the dissected hand that is the object of investigation.[34] The anatomical gaze thus converts the material and implicitly sexual hand of "Tactus" in the tradition of the Five Senses to an instrument that in medical and scientific contexts becomes progressively the "handmaiden" of the eye.

In contradistinction to this anatomical heritage, the depiction of Touch in the literary and pictorial catalogues of the Five Senses emphasizes the erotic and animalistic. Aristotle asserted that "without touch it is impossible for an animal to be"(*De Anima,* 434b), thus firmly coupling the human and the bestial in their sharing of this fundamental, appetitive, and life-sustaining sense. With respect to touch, he said, "we far excel other species in exactness of discrimination"(*De Anima,* 421a). Pliny echoed this judgment, inaugurating a tradition of using animals to exemplify the senses: he wrote in the *Naturalis Historia* that, whereas eagles surpassed humans in sight, vultures has a more developed sense of smell, and moles had better hearing, touch was most highly developed in humans.[35] Although tactility is supremely achieved in human beings, it nevertheless also accrues animal exemplars. This animal symbolism evolves in the second-century A.D. *Physiologus*, medieval bestiaries, and treatises on nature, and it joins with a specifically erotic tradition in Richard de Fournival's thirteenth-century *Bestiare d'amour*.³⁶ The tortoise appears with some frequency in these images and texts, registering touch in the paradoxical sensitivity of its shell, but the parrot or falcon and the spider furnish the most resonant animal representations of tactility. As Sander Gilman notes, the biting bird connects touch with the simultaneously pleasurable and painful penetration of the flesh associated with the loss of virginity (the breaking of the hymen) and/or the sexual penetration of the body.³⁷ In Crispyn van de Passe the Elder's late sixteenth-century engraving *The Seasons and the Senses*, for instance, the personification of Touch, a woman with bare breasts, holds a falcon, which is poised to bite her. Her other hand rests on a turtle shell, and a scorpion (the zodiacal sign that rules the genitalia) lies at her feet.³⁸

In the fourteenth-century wall painting of the Wheel of the Five Senses in Longthorpe Tower, each of the senses is represented by an animal, with touch located in a privileged position on the wheel and depicted through the figure of the spider.³⁹ Gino Casagrande and Christopher Kleinhenz point to a crucial passage in *De Anima* where Aristotle makes touch the "paradigm and structure of the intellect." If thought and perception are analogous, as Aristotle claims, then "We know the world around us because the mind is able to through touch to *grasp* the form of things."⁴⁰ It is tempting to read the image of the spider and its web in conjunction with epistemological gathering. Just as the spider's web extends its tactility, allowing it to sense the world around it, so does touch spread itself throughout the body in a system of web-like nerves. John Davies sums up this arachnoid faculty in *Nosce Teipsum*: "Much like a subtill spider, which doth sit / In middle of her web, which spreadeth wide; / If ought doe touch the vtmost thred of it, / Shee feeles it instantly on euery side" (1:70).⁴¹ This image of touch as a communicative network may be at work in his phrase describing touch as "life's root," and it is certainly imaged in various physiological depictions (including Descartes's) that demonstrate the link between the hand and the brain.

The figuration of tactility in the spider has other, less exalted connotations as well. Edmund Spenser depicts the spider as one of the odious creatures that besiege the "bulwarke" of Touch in the assault on the Castle of Alma in Book 2 of *The Faerie Queene*:

But the fift troupe most horrible of hew,
And fierce of force, was dreadfull to report:

For some like Snailes, some did like spyders shew,
And some like vgly Vrchins thicke and short:
Cruelly they assayled that fift Fort,
Armed with darts of sensuall delight,
With strings of carnall lust, and strong effort,
Of feeling pleasures, with which day and night
Against that same fift bulwarke they continued fight. (2.11.13)

The associations of touch with sensuality and carnality are intensified by the references to the spider, the hedgehog, and the snail (which secretes a sticky substance that leaves a palpable trail, a kind of visual trace of its touch). While the spider exemplifies tactile sensitivity, it is also entangled through touch with eroticism. The *locus classicus* for this association may be the weaving contest between Athena and Arachne in Ovid's *Metamorphoses*, for Arachne's tapestries portray the sexual crimes of the gods, and it is these scenes of seductive transgression that incite Athena's anger and her punitive transformation of Arachne into a spider.[42] In Spenser's *Muiopotmos*, the web that the "cursed creature" Aragnoll weaves in order to trap Clarion is likened to the net that Vulcan fashioned to capture the adulterous Mars and Venus.[43] Spenser's simile evokes and reverses Ovid's description of the marvelous net made of fine links of bronze that Vulcan devised to ensnare the lovers: "non illud opus tenuissima vincant / stamina, non summo quae pendet aranea tigno; / utque levis tactus momentaque parva sequantur, / efficit et lecto cir-cumdata collocat arte" (4: 178–81) (Not the finest threads of wool would sur-pass that work; no, not the web which the spider lets down from the ceiling beam. He made the web in such a way that it would yield to the slightest touch, the least movement, and then he spread it deftly over the couch.) The spider's web for Ovid and Spenser is thus at once the instrument of capture, the net of rational (or jealous) control, and a figure of the tactile sensitivity that fuels sexual trespass in the first place.

The ambiguity of the web is well exemplified in Bartolomeo Delbene's *Civitas veri, sive morum* (1609), a dream poem that Frances Yates describes as an allegory of the *Nichomachean Ethics*.[44] In the poem, the soul is repre-sented as a city, which can be entered by five portals or gateways. The illus-tration of the Portal of Touch is an elaborately architectural gateway covered with ivy (a plant that touches or clings to a support); on the lintel Mars and Venus lie bound in Vulcan's spidery net, captured in their moment of sexual union by the image that comes to signify tactility (the web).[45] It is hard not to read the allegorical implications of the image as a warning: indulgence in tactility leads to capture, and in order to elude ensnarement (and the derisive laughter of the gods as well as the ensuing humiliation for the lovers that follows in Ovid's narrative), touch needs to be monitored and controlled. Vulcan, the weaver of the net, is in this narrative both the spy who succeeds by means of tethering tactility to the desire for knowledge and also a figure of agency. Similar associations subtend the allusions in Guyon's binding of Verdant and Acrasia in the Bower of Bliss: the veil of silver and silk that covers (or rather dis-covers) Acrasia's lower body is, as Spenser tells us, a web more subtle than even Arachne can weave (2:12:77). The veil, which "hid no whit her alabaster skin" seems almost to be synonymous with the skin itself, a description of the organ, which, like the spider's web, is a network of sensation that spreads feeling through the body. Verdant, asleep with his head in Acrasia's lap, is the very image of tactility's erotic conquering, for he has hung up his "warlike armes" (2:12:80), succumbing completely to concupiscence. As with the illustration to Delbene's poem, the web is associated both with the ensnarements of desire and also with the reassertion of continence and rational control, for Guyon and the Palmer throw over the lovers a "subtile net" (2:12:81), which was "frame[d]" by the Palmer (reason). The confluence of these images and meanings may help to explain the association of touch and weaving in a German Renaissance engraving that depicts the personification of Touch at a loom.[46] The frequently cited etymological derivation of "text" from the Latin *tex-ere* (weaving) evokes not only the sense of the literary work's tactility, its woven, web-like, or indeed, cutaneous properties, but also the incessant dialectic at work in writing between the tactility of language, its sensuous, captivating elements, and the rational, ordering properties of the symbolic. This is the dynamic that Kristeva describes as the irruption of the semiotic into the symbolic in poetry, or that Irigaray sees as the "passionate" foundation of philosophical discourse, the constant interplay of tactility's capture within the net of language.

It is with this background in mind that this book seeks to examine touch in early modern culture. If touch is a sense that mediates between the body of the subject and the world, the chapters that follow make apparent the frequently disregarded lexicons of tactility that lie behind and beneath early modern discursive constructions of eroticism, knowledge, and art. The early modern period is rich territory for investigations of touch and the body partly because the boundaries between discourses now considered separate were not then firmly established. Literature, art, philosophy, religion, science, and medicine overlapped discursively and practically, and the body and its sensorium are thus diversely represented in the cultural imaginary. Developments in human anatomy, particularly the publication of Andreas Vesalius's *De humani corporis fabrica* in 1543 with its groundbreaking anatomical illustrations and descriptions helped to disseminate a radically changing conception and practice of anatomy that was intimately linked to the history of touch. Illustrations of dissected bodies, anatomical demonstrations, controversies about the nature and function of body parts, and new theories of disease reshaped not only knowledge but also the way early modern subjects inhabited their bodies. Where pre-Vesalian anatomies involved both *demonstrator* (the assistant who dissects) and *ostensor* (the professor who indicates the relevant bodily parts with his pointer), the famous title-page of the *Fabrica* unites these roles in the new figure of the anatomist, who stands beside the corpse, his hand pointing into the interior of her dissected torso. This Vesalian anatomist represents a turn away from inherited knowledge of the body that was derived from the books of classical authorities and a turn toward an empirical science, one whose erudition depends upon experience and observation. For the anatomist, of course, knowledge necessarily involves touching the corpse, a contact that was essential but one that also dangerously allied the physician—both actually and symbolically—to the death and disease he studied.[47] The power of touch as epistemological tool was thus joined with the legacy of touch as contagion, just as the history of tactility simultaneously signals the dangers of erotic touch and the possibility of contact with divinity.

To investigate the history of touch in the early modern period is also necessarily to engage the interface of the psychic and the corporeal, a border that becomes apparent in the significatory migration of words like "touching" or "feeling." The intertwined physiological and psychological aspects of the tactile are reflected in the disparate methodological approaches of the individual chapters, which, while predominately historicist, also make frequent reference to psychoanalytic theory. Carla Mazzio and Douglas Trevor have recently argued that where historicism and psychoanalysis have been positioned as incompatible methods, not only has some recent theory explored the links between body and psyche, but the complexly intertwined material and psychic dimensions may be "integral to many early modern discourses."[48] While we may attribute the idea of a bodily ego to Freud and to subsequent elaborations in the writings of Jacques Lacan, Jean Laplanche, Didier Anzieu, and others, the relation it figures of soma and psyche have clear roots in Aristotelian discussions of the body and the senses. As Rebekah Smick asserts, Aristotle believed that sense perception and emotion were closely related, since both partake of the appetitive part of the soul. Helkiah

Crooke's confident assertion in *Microcosmographia*, following Aristotle, that touch is the fundamental sense and that the experience of touch in the womb is foundational for human subjectivity, for example, presents an uncanny precursor to Anzieu's notion of the "skin ego."

Several chapters thus link historical approaches with insights derived from psychoanalysis. Scott Stevens explores the relationship between skin and subjectivity and between otherness and incorporation (cannibalism), for instance, in his analysis of the historical contact between Europeans and "naked" indigenous peoples. He argues that it was not only a physical encounter with material repercussions but that it was also a confrontation with alterity that became crucial to the formation of European subjectivity. Carla Mazzio investigates the highly intricate exchanges between the material, bodily nature of grief, guilt, and revenge in the drama of the period and its conveyance into metaphoric language or its reembodiment on stage. Her attention to tactile and bodily metaphors buried in words illuminates the dislocations between the linguistic, somatic, and psychic registers, demonstrating in the process how touch is transposed to cultural habits of disciplining the body ("tact," "intact") and its unruly emotions. Lynn Enterline insightfully addresses the psychic/somatic nature of touch in her afterword on rhetoric and the body. Her discussion of Ovid's "touching rhetoric" draws attention to Ovid's emphasis on linguistic materiality, to its disruptive potential. Grounding her observations in recent psychoanalytic and theoretical writings on the body (Judith Butler, Julia Kristeva, Jean Laplanche), she suggests that the materialism of Ovid's language and his figuration of maternal form are powerfully imbricated, a linkage that points to the tension between the abjected corporeality of language and its gendered shaping in culture.

Five chapters in the first part of the volume consider the consequences of medical or anatomical touching, an act that was necessary to empirical study but carried a legacy of erotic prohibition on the one hand and the hazards of contagion on the other. Margaret Healy scrutinizes the intersection of the amorous and medical touch in early modern constructions of the pox—syphilis and bubonic plague—an analysis that is extended to consider various kinds of touch and the contagion such contact might confer. The permeability of the early modern humoral body rendered it vulnerable to often indiscernible infectious agents, and Healy explores in both medical and literary texts the anxieties that circulated in the period about the dangers posed by erotic and social contact and thus circumscribed social and bodily relations. Sujata Iyengar's chapter on Spenser, Ariosto, and Shakespeare also examines the boundary between disease or contagion and eroticism. She confronts a tension that subtends medical discourse; the healer must often touch the patient in order to cure, yet tactility was always suspect because of its potential to incite erotic feeling. She explores a theme crucial to romance, the conjunction of the medical and amorous in which physical healing paradoxically inflicts emotional "wounds" of love. Situating her analysis within a cultural medical context that prohibited women from practicing surgery, Iyengar investigates the representation of the curative touch and the ambivalent role of the virgin healer in fictional and dramatic texts.

Two chapters concentrate on female anatomy: Eve Keller scrutinizes the representation of birth in medical discourse, and Bettina Mathes focuses on the organ that was thought to be the locus of female desire, the clitoris. Touch is centrally important in Mathes's analysis of the figure of the early modern anatomist and his dissection of the human body, for she argues that depictions of the so-called monstrously enlarged clitoris are less a reflection of female sexual transgression than a displacement of sexual power from women to the male anatomist. Her canny account of this "phallic" investment allows her to reinterpret Lacan's theory of the phallus/penis dissociation as well as to revise the relationship between the visual and tactile in early modern medicine. Keller examines early modern medical case histories in order to consider the relationship between medical practitioner and childbearing woman. Countering Martin Jay's line of argument, in which science and medicine and their authoritative claims are increasingly linked to the predominance of the visual, Keller asserts that touch in the arena of childbirth is endowed with an almost "magical prowess" and that its power becomes closely allied to emergent obstetrical authority. Where the "handling" of a woman in labor had been the traditional territory of midwives, physicians in the early modern period began to describe how their touching of women's "privities" and their "handling" of the uterus (podalic version, pelvic manipulation) facilitated delivery. Keller's treatment of the intersection of midwifery, early obstetrical practice, and the rhetorical strategies of the case history reveals a shifting patient-physician relationship, one that replaces dialogue with tactility and one that increasingly silences the female patient.

Elizabeth Harvey studies allegorical and anatomical representations of bodily interiority in Spenser's *The Faerie Queene* and Helkiah Crooke's *Microcosmographia*. Her analysis considers how Crooke incorporates Spenser's allegory into his anatomical structure; she argues that we can chart a transition in Spenser and Crooke around tactility that moves from according tactile power to the skin as a sensing organ to consolidating the potency of touch in the rationalizing synecdoche of the hand. She juxtaposes the allegorical and anatomical images of bodily interiority with a series of Italian eighteenth-century wax anatomical models that were used to display the inside of the female body. These models—which like the Vesalian "flayed" corpses, depict bodies without skin—were, she contends, a visual and powerfully tactile way of treating the flesh that normally obscures human interiority from sight.

Whether juxtaposing political and theological prohibitions, discussing the legacy of the sensual in Platonic theories of love and the generative principle in architecture, considering the place of nakedness and tactility in early colonial encounters, or scrutinizing the nature of female desire, the subsequent chapters share a preoccupation with the material substratum inherent in discourses that seek to transcend their own fleshly, tactile origins. Several chapters (Stevens, Sauer and Smith, Smick) address the early modern discourses of tactility that demarcate boundaries at either end of the cultural spectrum: the sacred and secular principles concerning what is touchable and "untouchable." These ideas determine what is holy or polluting (to use terms of religious significance) and what is privileging or disempowering (to use economic and social terms). The essays draw on a variety of cultural texts and ideas that include Christianity and Platonism, politics and architecture, early colonialism and theories of subjectivity. The authors explore the theological, legal, linguistic, and aesthetic discourses that define sexual and material ownership of property in a period that witnesses the emergence of capitalism and individualism (and that in England follows the dissolution of the monasteries). Notions of the "proper" or "property" are constructed by establishing boundaries around, for example, the female body or the land, markers that limit those who might attempt to touch or possess that body or that land.

Scott Stevens's "New World Contacts and the Trope of the 'Naked Savage' " takes the early colonial moment as crucial to the history of tactility. He literalizes the often metaphoric construction of "first contact" by investigating the recurrence of the figure of the 'naked savage' in a variety of writings in the literature of the Encounter. These narratives reveal various representations of indigenous peoples of the Americas, and in them, nakedness is an important signifier of cultural difference—one that simultaneously invited touch and repelled cultural contact. Bound up within the history of this "contact" between peoples is not only the horrific consequence of contagion (whether constructed as the introduction of syphilis into Europe or as the scourge of disease that Europeans inflicted upon indigenous peoples), but also the confrontation of custom (whether constructed as the innocence of Edenic nakedness or as the sexual licentiousness of the "uncivilized").

Elizabeth Sauer and Lisa Smith's chapter also invokes the early colonial context; their analysis takes as its informing moment the episode in John 20: 17 in which the newly risen Christ forbids Mary Magdalene to touch him with the famous command that is rendered in the Vulgate as "Noli me tangere." This is a distinctive and uncharacteristic moment in the gospels because Christ is repeatedly depicted performing healing miracles through touching the afflicted person's body, and more generally allowing contact between with those deemed "untouchable" (lepers, Samaritans, prostitutes, or the poor). The very first law in the Old Testament prohibits Adam and Eve from eating, or even touching, the tree of the knowledge of good and evil. And almost every reference to touch in the Pentateuch, especially the Levitical codes, involves restrictions about touching something or someone that is holy (e.g., Mount Sinai in Exodus 19: 12–13) or something that is unclean (e.g., a menstruating woman in Leviticus 15: 24).

That these prohibitions—Christ's admonition to Mary Magdalene and God's interdiction against Adam and Eve's touching the Tree of Knowledge—take place within a garden setting, defined by its enclosing wall or fence, inspires Sauer and Smith to consider analogous political and economic regulations against touching and transgressing, notably the English Enclosure Acts. They transpose their analysis to early colonial discourses, noting astutely that the quintessential act of imperial domination was to erect a fence and cultivate the land. Their analysis takes within its purview a consideration of property rights and women's reproductive rights. They return to Milton's *Paradise Lost* in order to examine the gendered politics of labor in the poem, the expulsion from the garden, and the establishment of a private enclosure within the individual subject. Both this essay and Rebekah Smick's analysis of the erotics of architecture consider the points of contact between religious or universal abstractions and the erotic, mortal, fleshly body. Where the impulse of some theological or philosophical discourses is to prohibit or exile tactility and to circumscribe touch, both of their essays demonstrate the way the sense of touch nevertheless animates connections between the human and the divine and structures social relations.

The last group of essays ponder the place of touch in language, art, and architecture. Misty Anderson's chapter provides a compelling reading of Margaret Cavendish's closet drama, *The Convent of Pleasure,* focusing in particular on the sensuality of objects and the potential for eroticism within this community of women. The sensuality of tactility plays a central role

in Cavendish's opposition to the implications of Cartesian rationalism and
Locke's theories of knowledge, for both tend to exile materiality in ways that
have gendered repercussions. Like Lucretius, Cavendish considered the body
and the senses, tactile sensation in particular, as instruments of knowledge.
The drama provides a critique of property relations in patriarchal society,
and represents the convent, by contrast, as offering material goods not for
exchange but for sensory pleasure. Among the objects that furnish the convent are textiles, which not only represent the tactile feminine world of the
convent but also figure cloth as a woven web of texture sensible to the touch.

The conviction that knowledge and sensation are linked, which informs
Cavendish's utopian fiction, is also evident in Rebekah Smick's reading of the
Hypnerotomachia Poliphili, a Renaissance work remarkable for its encyclopedic character. Smick interprets the work as an erotic text that offers particular insight into the history of tactility. Focusing on Poliphilo's encounter
with the personifications of the five senses and his descriptions of buildings,
she argues that the book offers a powerful allegory of the importance of the
material to Renaissance architecture. Smick asserts that the allegory provides
a counter-discourse to Renaissance Platonism in its recuperation of a
Scholastic approval of sensation. She examines the place of eroticism and
fertility in architectural creation, suggesting that imagination and sensation
are linked within the creative act, and that knowledge is not independent of
human physiology but closely tied to it.

The eliciting of emotional response in spectators is the subject of Carla
Mazzio's study of "tact" in relation to English Renaissance theater. She simultaneously resurrects the touching body that is linguistically (and metaphorically) submerged in "tactfulness" and investigates the role of tactility in the
production and the reception of early modern drama. Considering such
works as *Hamlet* and Thomas Tomkis's 1607 *Lingua, or the Combat of the
Tongue and the Five Senses for Superiority*, she argues that the very dispersal
of the sense of touch throughout the body, its lack of location within a particular sensory organ specific to it, means that its polymorphous character is
often represented in this ironic "failure of synecdoche." Early modern touch
is both everywhere and nowhere; it disrupts a sensory anatomy that would
house each sense firmly within a corresponding organ, just as it also complicates the relation between an inside and an outside, between body and affect,
between drama and audience.

Jodi Cranston's essay examines the vital relationship between the creative process and the spectator from a different perspective. She focuses on
the Renaissance notion of *energia*, that quality of vividness that makes the

work of art seem alive to the viewer or reader. Discussions of *energia* are often formulated in terms of vision, but Cranston's "revisionary" approach integrates the importance of the sense of touch. Her resulting analysis allows her to examine the rivalries between painting and sculpture as well as to understand how touch figures in theories of mimesis. If the senses are the body's gateways, as St. Augustine and many others have suggested, then tactility is, as we have seen, especially problematic. For where the corporeal "bulwarks" of the mouth, eyes, ears, and nose are relatively easily fortified or guarded, touch is located wherever skin is—indeed throughout the body, and localized with special intensity in particular areas (the hands, the genitals). Not only is touch asserted to be earliest and most fundamental sense, not only does it seem recurrently to be the sense most resolutely yoked to corporeality or materiality, but touch as the "feeling" sense calls up a generalized world of sensation, both as physical sensation and as that sense perception is transposed into the register of passion or affect. Touch, perhaps more than any other sense, is a mediator—between the body and what transcends it, whether in St. Augustine's yearning for divine contact or in the search for the objectivity of rational knowledge. Tactility, often despised, repudiated, forgotten, or subsumed into the other senses, is an insistent reminder of corporeality as the necessary condition of our humanity.

Chapter 2

Anxious and Fatal Contacts: Taming the Contagious Touch

Margaret Healy

Contagion, is an evil qualitie in a bodie, communicated unto an other by touch, engendring one and the same disposition in him to whom it is communicated. . . . For very properly is he reputed infectious, that hath in himselfe an evil, malignant, venemous, or vitious disposition, which may be imparted and bestowed on an other by touch, producing the same and as daungerous effect in him to whom it is communicated.

—Lodge, A Treatise of the Plague, 1603

Intimately implicated in the transmission from body to body of material, supernatural and moral "evil qualitie(s)" circa 1600, "touch" was undoubtedly experienced as the most hazardous of the senses and was the source of considerable individual and collective anxiety. Indeed, intense fear about harmful contagious bodies and their effects was rife in the early modern period, producing its own epidemic of discursive speculation about where harmful "venoms" originated, how they were "caught," and how best to avoid them.[1] The signs and symptoms of the two preeminent contagions associated with touch in the sixteenth and seventeenth centuries—the new venereal disease of the Renaissance, the French or great pox, and the more mysterious and deadly plague or pestilence (bubonic plague)—together encouraged lurid, colorful, and fanciful depictions of the agents of pollution that circulated in print raising questions about the types of contact that were most hazardous and about the nature of "touch" itself. By the late sixteenth century, with the upsurge in Neoplatonic, Paracelsan, and alchemical medical ideas, the body's fleshy envelope was imagined to be so fragile and permeable that it seemed to provide very little protection against incursion by a panoply of "evil" enemy agents ranging from airy spirits and bad angels to corrupting "miasmas" and "seeds." Furthermore, the transmission of "evil qualitie(s)" across the protective corporeal carapace could occur by "fascina-tion" and without tactile contact: some Puritan clerics and physicians be-lieved that fear alone was sufficient to attract evil contagion into a poorly fortified body and soul.[2] Indeed, in this heavily speculative and mystical context, in which medical schemata of bodily functioning were very differ-ent from today, "touch" was clearly construed and experienced in radically "other" ways. In fact, as the following examination will reveal, you could be "touched" in this period without being touched—without the mediation of the senses.

Keeping these problematics to the fore, this chapter will probe the inter-face between medical, religious, and belletristic discourses of contagion in the Renaissance, scrutinizing the aesthetic responses to the anxiety generated by the diseases themselves and by new theories of contagion. It will explore discursive attempts to "project" and "tame" fear associated with anxious and potentially deadly contacts, examining the ancient, durable, and little cri-tiqued thesis that the "healing words" of poetry function mysteriously in an Apollonian manner positively to "transform" the pain, fear, and grief associ-ated with morbidity.[3] In this connection I shall particularly consider Fracas-toro of Verona's poem in the manner of Virgil, *Syphilis*, which mythologized the pox (giving syphilis its modern name),[4] and Shakespeare's epyllion, *Venus and Adonis*, written during the plague epidemic of 1592–93, which is poignantly (and wittily) preoccupied with the erotic touch and its repulsion, with sickness, corporeal decay, explanations of bodily misfortune, and pre-mature death.[5]

Throughout the ancient, medieval, and early modern world outbreaks of deadly "plagues" were associated with a special type of touch—with blows, strokes and wounds (see *OED2*, Touch I, 4)—inflicted by an archer god, a sword, a serpent, angels or spirits, as punishment for human trans-gressions: "*Plaga* signifies a stripe, and this Sicknesse, comes from a blow, or stripe, given by the hand of Gods Angell, when (as he did to *David*) he sends him to strike a people for their sins."[6] As Thomas Dekker's plague pamphlet foregrounds, the word "plague" is derived from the Latin word "plaga," which actually means "a blow, a stroke, a wound" (*OED2* [1]). "Touch" and "plague," then, are etymologically related in an extremely close way, and once had overlapping signifieds. Within this imaginative framework the "blow" might reveal itself on the victim's body as a mark or "token"; hence any disease that produced skin lesions had a pronounced tendency to be attributed to sin and to punishment meted out by an angry deity. In the biblical plague of Ashod, for example, sufferers significantly "had emerods [swellings] in their secret parts" (1 Sam. 5: 9). Throughout medieval and early modern Europe the lurid purple swellings or buboes produced by bubonic plague were popularly understood in this way, as Thomas Lodge's medical treatise describes: "[The Plague] is a popular and contagious sicknesse for the most part mortall, wherein usually appeare certaine Tumors, Carbuncles, or spottes, which the common people call Gods tokens."[7] While some religious extremists insisted that supernatural agents like God's smiting angel spread the plague around London throughout the early decades of the seventeenth century, others—following the official government line on plague contagion—implicated more material, secular mechanisms in the transmission of this devastating sickness.

Corrupted, "miasmic" air arising from dirty stinking environments was probably the most commonly cited cause of plague, but increasingly through the course of the sixteenth century infected people (especially poor people living in close, overcrowded environments) were singled out as plague transmitters. *A Moche Profitable Treatise against the Pestilence* (1534) explains: "For from suche infected bodies commethe infectious and venemous fumes and vapours, the whiche do infecte and corrupte the aire"; consequently "greate multitude and congregation of people" should be avoided as "the breth of one infected person may infect a hole."[8] "Conversation" (both verbal and sexual) was considered especially hazardous in plague time ("the venemous ayre it selfe, is not halfe so vehement to enfecte, as is the conversacion or breath of them that are infected already") and attention became focused on the dangers of any close bodily contact.[9] In 1543 the Privy Council stated unequivocally that plague increased "rather by the negligence, disorder and want of charity in such as have been infected . . . than by corruption of the air": from that point onward, segregating the sick from the healthy through a policy of "shutting up" the infected in their homes was the favored containment strategy.[10] The famous Italian physician and poet Fracastoro of Verona published his influential theories of contagion (which lent weight to segregation policies) in 1546, describing "semina" or "seminaria": seed-like entities capable of generation that could infect bodies by direct contact or through fomites—intermediaries—such as a piece of material, or at a distance borne by air.[11] This theory of seeds of disease chimed to a certain extent with the Paracelsan doctrine (which gained ground in England from the mid-sixteenth century) that after the Fall "impure seedes" were one of the causes of sickness and that "the fruites of the seedes being knowne, the seedes or rootes of diseases are knowne . . . because the fruites, viz. The panges, fits, passions, and maner of the diseases, are brought forth like to the rootes."[12]

These strange live infective agents with individual constitutions (the precursors of modern "germs") helped to explain why contact with bedding, clothing and other fabrics that had belonged to plague victims could mysteriously pass on the disease. Lodge, for example, warned that plague was "a certaine hidden content communicated by touch," which could remain concealed a long time, especially in fur gowns. Citing Fracastoro's treatise on contagion, he described how in 1511 numerous people died in Verona, one following hot on the heels of another, after wearing the same fur garment.[13] Thomas Cogan's *The Haven of Health* (1584) warned its readers against receiving bedding and clothes from infected places and against lodging with strangers because "the poyson" remained in people for "the space of two monethes," while "the houses and the householde stuffe . . . keepe their venom for the space of a yeare or more."[14] Simon Kellwaye (1593) agreed that "things that have bene used about some infected body" were most dangerous,[15] while William Vaughan (1600) advised his sister that the preferable materials to have next to the skin were silk and buckskin, "for it resisteth venome and contagious aire."[16] Cotton, wool, and fur garments were considered particularly "venemous": presumably the real vectors of bubonic plague—rat fleas—were particularly partial to these fabrics.[17]

Such rampant hypothesizing in print about how plague was transmitted encouraged an analogous form of speculation about "fascination": "the power and act of imagination, intensive upon other bodies than the body of the imaginant . . . wherin," according to Sir Francis Bacon, "the school of Paracelsus and the disciples of pretended Natural Magic have been so intemperate."[18] If "evil qualities" of a material or airy nature could pass from body to body by touch without the senses registering them, why not less tangible moral, spiritual, and psychological "qualities"? The *Advancement of Learning* articulates this trend of reasoning:

Others that draw nearer to probability, calling to their view the secret passages of things, and especially of the contagion that passeth from body to body, do conceive it should likewise be agreeable to nature that there should be some transmissions and operations from spirit to spirit, without the mediation of the senses. . . . Incident unto this is the inquiry how to raise and fortify the imagination."[19]

Ideas—indeed beliefs—about psychic transmission were certainly not limited to a few dubious eccentrics dabbling with the occult. The eminent Dutch physician Levinus Lemnius, who had a considerable English following, saw fit to warn his readers about "bad angels" and spirits that could infect the body in the manner of plague contagion: "Now, for so much as

Spirits be withoute bodies, they slyly and secretly glyde into the body of man, even muche like as fulsome stenche, or as a noysome and ill ayre is inwardly drawn into the body."[20] Happily in Lemnius's system there were "good angels," too, who could infuse more positive qualities into their unsuspecting but grateful hosts.[21] Henry Holland's *Spiritual Preservatives Against the Pestilence* was far more pessimistic, describing how evil spirits could be "caught"; this time by "piercing" the bodies of men and "mingling" themselves "by meanes of some imaginations conceived." Thus, Holland declares, "we are all become the subjects, vassals and uncleane cages of wicked spirits."[22] Meanwhile, Dr. John Cotta's *A Short Discoverie* of 1612 dwelt at length on the power of the imagination to both induce and cure diseases.[23] It seems that Paracelsan medicine had done much to encourage such mystical trains of thought, as Bacon (above) regrets and Robert Burton confirms:

The air is not so full of flies in summer as it is at all times of invisible devils: this Paracelsus stiffly maintains, and that they have every one their several chaos; others will have infinite worlds, and each world his peculiar spirits, gods, angels and devils to govern and punish it.[24]

Burton is not, however, dismissive of this airy malevolent context for understanding "disease" but regards it, rather, as "a serious question, and worthy to be considered," proceeding to a lengthy "digression" on "the Nature of Spirits."[25]

Indeed, as these now obsolete definitions reveal, psychic and moral "touching" was a particular preoccupation of the late sixteenth century and the first half of the seventeenth century:

*OED*2 III, fig. 1. The act of touching or fact of being touched 1586. B. spec., An impression upon the mind or soul; a feeling, sense (of some emotion, etc.) 1586. 2. A faculty or capacity of the mind analogous or likened to the sense of touch; mental or moral perception or feeling 1656.

Far from constituting a mere figurative device, psychic transmission was construed by many as a real phenomenon; one that was rendered plausible, and was even empirically sanctioned, through the observation of the passage from soma to soma, "without the mediation of the senses," of plague contagion.[26] It is no coincidence, of course, that witch beliefs were also at their zenith in this period.[27]

It was incumbent upon every person to fortify his/ her self against incursion by this host of malevolent forces recoursing constantly around the

soma. Yet, somewhat paradoxically, "fear" of the evil "touch" was most hazardous to health as this minister of religion explained in 1603:

From the heart proceed . . . vitall spirits, whereby man is made active and couragious.
If they by feare be inforced to retire inward, the outward parts be left infirme . . . so
that as enemies easily scale the walles of a towne abandonned by souldiers; so the
Plague . . . doth find readie passage into the outward parts of a man . . . feare (adversarie to faith) pulleth to the wicked the evill which he feareth."[28]

Fear—"adversarie to faith"—carries a considerable negative moral and spiritual charge here, yet profound anxiety about contagion was an inevitable and
intolerable consequence of plague epidemics. As the following poignant
words reveal, neighbors, friends and loved ones could become deadly enemies in plague time:

Our houses are left desolate, and men abborre their owne inheritance. Wee are one
afraid of another, men hardly trust themselves, yea, scarcely the clothes of their
backes.[29]

Love was a fault, and Charitie a sin;
When Bad did fear infection from the Good,
And men did hate their cruell Neighbourhood.[30]

So, towns fear'd townes, and men ech other fear'd;
All were (at least) attainted with suspect,
And, sooth to say, so was their envy stirr'd,
That one would seeke another to infect.[31]

Now Friends, and Neighbours keep at distance, fear
T'approach their nearest kindred, for life's dear:
The Father dreads to see his only Son,
The Son to see his Father too doth shun,
The Husband dreads his Wife, whom he with dear
Embraces us'd to hold, durst not draw near,
The Wife's afraid her Husband to behold,
Whom on kind Arms she used to infold.[32]

Whom most they love, must most of all avoyde.[33]

These moving eyewitness, confessional-style accounts of the uncharitable,
sinful emotions generated by intense fear of the contaminated touch, suggest that articulating, recording and sharing this experience with others
might have served a positive function—perhaps analogous to the Catholic

confessional, or to the counseling experience of today. Externalizing and objectifying terrifying events and intolerable feelings by verbalizing them and committing them to print might distance and help "domesticate" them, as Sander Gilman's seminal work on disease and its representation suggests:

> It is the fear of collapse, the sense of dissolution, which contaminates the Western image of all disease. . . . But the fear we have of our own collapse does not remain internalized. Rather, we project this fear into the world in order to localize it, and indeed, to domesticate it.[34]

But can we probe the power of words a little further? Might imaginative, creative responses to disease-generated anxiety have operated in other more elusive, health-promoting ways in a pre-scientific world? Did poetry in particular provide a form of comfort that medicine—in the absence of "cures"—was powerless to supply? Certainly, from the Pythagoreans of ancient times through to the Renaissance philosophers of nature (this includes physicians), music and harmonious words were held to exert a restorative effect on the imbalanced (sick) body and soul. Francis Bacon's *Advancement of Learning* comments on the long-standing and appropriate union of medicine and music in the figure of Apollo:

> This variable composition of man's body hath made it as an instrument easy to distemper; and therefore the poets did well to conjoin Music and Medicine in Apollo: because the office of medicine is but to tune this curious harp of man's body and reduce it to harmony.[35]

Like a musical instrument producing discordant sounds, the distempered humoral body had to be "tuned" into harmony. "Poesie," according to the ancients, was divinely inspired and, in a not dissimilar manner, Renaissance humanist scholars, namely here Sir Philip Sidney, maintained that "with the force of a divine breath" poets could deliver a "golden" world to a "brazen" one corrupted by sin.[36] Within this imaginative framework "words set in delightful proportions" and "the enchanting skill of music" could be construed as going some way toward repairing the ravages of the Fall, prime among which were disease and pain (608, 609–10). The Italian physician-poet, Fracastoro, certainly believed in the mysterious healing powers of poetry, and I shall return to this later, but, while we are in lapsarian territory, I intend to dwell rather more fully on corruption and its alluring early modern embodiments.

Sin and suffering, we should remind ourselves in this context, were initially introduced into Paradise through Eve's imprudent "touch." This is how the Geneva Bible (1599 ed.) described the divine taboo:

> But of the fruite of the tree which is in the midst of the garden,
> God hath said, Ye shall not eat of it, neither
> Shall ye touch it, least ye die. (Gen. 3: 3)

Indeed, in the moralizing emblem books of the seventeenth century, touch became synonymous with transgression and disaster. These, for example, are the words of Francis Quarles's coquettish Eve responding to the serpent's temptations:

> Wisest of Beasts, our great Creator did,
> Reserve this Tree, and this alone forbid;
> The rest are freely ours, which, doubtlesse, are
> As pleasing to the Tast; to th'eye, as faire;
> But touching this, his strict commands are such,
> Tis death to tast, no less than death to touch.[37]

In the end, of course, Eve did "pull" and then "taste," and proceeded to tempt Adam "To know the secrets of this dainty."[38]

Pandora, Eve, and Venus—the three notorious mythological embodiments of beautiful but dubious womankind—have all, in their time, been associated with dangerous touching proclivities that have inflicted a Pandora's box of disease and suffering on mankind. Shakespeare's hugely successful erotic epyllion *Venus and Adonis* rewards study from this perspective. This is a poem that is centrally preoccupied with touch and its multiple binaries: with attraction and repulsion, with infection and healing, with mercy and punishment, with lust and chastity, and with love and death. The poem's structure and devices—its numerous antitheses, paradoxes, and balanced lines—skillfully articulate its subliminal concerns and convey the uneasy conjunction of these polarities in this period's most hazardous sense personified in the ambivalent "honey secrets" (16) of Venus. At its most extreme, the troubled world of *Venus and Adonis* is one in which Cupid's arrows of love are horribly confounded, and—to Venus's horror—eventually substituted by Death's grisly equivalents:

> Love's golden arrow at him should have fled,
> And not Death's ebon dart, to strike him dead. (947–98)

In a similar way affectionate caresses and kisses of desire become daubed with the contaminating and disfiguring brush of lust, infection, and the kiss of death. Ultimately Adonis's very touchability proves his nemesis: "He [the boar] thought to kiss him, and hath kill'd him so" (1110).

As in the poignant accounts of plague survivors cited above, kissing and killing, caresses, love, hate, and death become intimately intermingled— inverting and subverting usual relations and emotions. In fact, Shakespeare's epyllion seems to harness just the kinds of paradoxical, equivocal and prob- lematic emotions generated by fear in plague-infested London, translating them into a tissue of witty and erotic allegories and myths. It is no coinci- dence, then, that the poem's "sick-thoughted Venus" (5) appears preoccupied with touch ("Though neither eyes nor ears, to hear nor see / Yet should I be in love by touching thee" 437–38), sickness and the need for "cures," as well as love-sick for Adonis. Thus the kisses that she has inveigled from Adonis through pretending she is collapsed and unwell provide the opportunity to proclaim a wistful cure for plague (Petrarchan style) residing in her lover's "verdurous" lips and healing "breath":

Long may they [his lips] kiss each other for this cure!
O never let their crimson liveries wear!
And as they last, their verdure still endure,
To drive infection from the dangerous year!
That the star-gazers, having writ on death,
May say the plague is banish'd by thy breath. (505–10)

At this point the real world about 1592–93, with its "star-gazers," converges on that of the poem in a deeply poignant and disturbing way, as it does in the later evocation of "poor" doomed "Wat" (697), whose grief resembles "one sore sick that hears the passing-bell" (701–2). Similarly, Adonis's demise becomes the occasion for Venus to rail against the prime evocation of Plague-Death of the 1590s: that "Hard-favour'd tyrant, ugly, meagre, lean, / Hateful divorce of love" (931–32) clutching his "ebon darts" (948), who had pitched his tent (according to Thomas Dekker's plague pamphlets) in the suburbs of early modern London.[39] The personified adversary—Death— who struts around the pages of this poem and the plague pamphlets causing pain and havoc, looms as a considerable threat. However, unlike the situation in real life, the threat is controlled and contained by the pages of the book, which serve to put a comforting barrier between Death and the writer/ reader, at the same time providing a vivid target for the healthful release of anger and rage. Death personified can even—as in Dekker's tracts—be productive of regenerating mirth and laughter.[40] It is fair to speculate, therefore, that this poem might have had a certain, albeit limited, medicinal remit.

In another witty and inventive mythological aside, Venus construes Adonis's extreme beauty not as a healing force, but, contradictorily, as the source and fountain of all misfortunes and maladies. Cynthia, angered that Nature has stolen "moulds from heav'n" and simply made Adonis too fair, has bribed the "destinies" to mingle beauty with "infirmities," unleashing a Pandora's box of calamities, including:

Burning fevers, agues pale and faint,
Life-poisoning pestilence, and frenzies wood,
The marrow-eating sickness whose attaint
Disorder breeds by healing of the blood. (739–42)

Yet, true to the style of this poem, Adonis eventually retaliates, rebutting Venus's unsought advances with the priggish and malicious accusation that she is motivated not by "love" but by "sweating lust" that "lends embracements unto every stranger," feeding "Upon fresh beauty" (794, 790, 796). Adonis claims to have rejected her strangling "embracements" and kisses because—as he insinuates—her sinful sickness will destroy his beauty, "blotting it with blame" (796). The flip side of the Venus love-lust woman construct thus becomes synonymous with honeyed deceit and with "the marrow-eating sickness" alluded to above—with early modern syphilis.

Polluting Venus (Eve-Pandora)—the embodiment of the erotic contaminated touch—was happily not the Bard's invention; indeed, she was a well-worn motif of European belles lettres, music, and painting by the 1540s. Jean Cousin's *Eva Prima Pandora* (c. 1550), is a conflation of these deadly female types symbolized by the skull on which its alluring naked beauty languidly rests her arm. Figuring a splendidly erotic Venus, as well as a personification of honeyed deceit and an image of a syphilitic victim, Agnolo Bronzino's *Allegory of Love* (c. 1546), now in the National Gallery, London, is another spectacular evocation of this type.[41] There were even art-songs (consisting of lyric and visual tableau) to celebrate her pains and pleasures. Hubert Naich's madrigal, "Per Dio Tu Sei Cortese," probably written and composed for Cosimo I's Florentine court, was typical:

Good Lord, what kindliness, O Love,
To reward my excellent service
With a dose of the French pox!
Does my goddess have those lovely eyes,

A sweet expression redolent with virtue,
An iv'ry throat and the canker (may it strike her!)?
These sores and aches
Lurked within my lady's downy breast,
As did the secret venom
That you concealed, which now becomes apparent.
So, since it is thus, may you be full of it,
And may your wings be riddled with the French pox![42]

Shakespeare's anacreontic sonnets, 153 and 154, also preoccupied with the erotic union of beauty and destructive disease in an alluring "mistress," seem to inhabit very similar emotional and mythological territory to this art song. They dwell playfully, too, on one of the posited healthful remedies for venereal infection in the late sixteenth centuries: the "seething bath." But how did this extraordinarily vivid and ambivalent personification of "secret venom . . . concealed" come about, and why did the belletristic motif of polluting Venus become so pervasive?

The story must inevitably begin with the mysterious introduction into Europe in the 1490s of a "new" contagious venom that was linked (from its earliest manifestations as a painful and deadly skin disease that gradually consumed the sexual organs) with the most intimate touching of all—copulation and kissing. This is how the physician Peter Lowe described the horrific progress of the affliction:

Thys part [the penis] being infected with that venim, it entereth into the little vaines, and afterwarde into the great, and lastly into the liver. . . . They ingender abounance of externall ulcers and pustls, falling of haire, both of head, browes, and beard: griefe in the joynts, head, leggs, and armes, with divers evill accidents . . . yet chiefly in the night.[43]

While theologians railed against the sin of "whoredom" as the origin of God's scourge, medical men like Lowe tended to concentrate on more material sources:

The most probable of all, is the opinion of the Spanish Historiographers who doe report, that it was brought among the Christians . . . 1492 by a Spaniard called Christophorus Columbus, with many other Spanyards, accompanied with some women, who came from the new found Iles occidentalls.[44]

Infected women in the New World had transmitted the "pernitious seed" to Columbus's sailors, who later participated in Charles VIII's invasion of

Italy in 1494, effectively spreading the disease throughout Europe: "When K. Charles . . . of Fraunce besieged Naples . . . some of the Spanyards came to him, . . . and spred this pernitious seed, and termed it the Indian Sicknes."[45] Other writers suggested more lurid and fanciful tactile origins: a particularly tenacious belief was that it resulted from the intercourse of a leprous knight and a courtesan, another was that it emerged from the unnatural coupling of men with monkeys.[46]

The much disputed origin of the disease remains unresolved today, but wherever it came from it had infiltrated Britain by the late 1490s and early measures to control it confirm that "the fowle scabbe and horryble sychness called the freanche pocks" was understood to be transmitted by intimate sexual contact.[47] On April 21, 1497, for example, the council of Aberdeen ordered brothels to be closed down and prostitutes ("licht women") to be branded on the cheek:

The said day, it was statut and ordanit be the alderman and consale for the eschevin [eschewing] of the infirmitey cumm out of Franche and strang partis, that all licht wemen be chargit and ordaint to decist fra thar vicis and syne of venerie, and all thair buthis and houssis skalit, and thai to pas and wirk for thar sustentacioun, under the payne of ane key of het yrne one thar chekis, and banysene of the towne.[48]

In a desperate move a few months later James IV decided to banish all persons infected with the "Grandgore" to the island of Inch Keith in the Firth of Forth; an order that proved impossible to enforce for fairly obvious reasons.[49] The popular Scottish name for the new venereal disease—"Grandgore"—has been linked with the French, "a la grande gorre," and thus with "a la grande mode," which points to it having been understood as a fashionable disease, closely linked to a leisured class of men as well as to their partners in "venerie."[50]

Nevertheless, the medical accounts of venereal disease—directed at the literate males who purchased them—concentrated unremittingly on the ingenious ways malicious alluring harlots spread their "burnynge" venom:

This impedyment dothe come whan a harlot doth holde in her breth and clapse her hands hard togyther and toes in lyke maner. And some harlotte doth stand over a chafynge dyshe of coles into the which she doth put brymstone and there she doth parfume herselfe.[51]

That venereal disease was often hidden in "secret places" constituted a particular problem for anxious libertines:

This thing as touching women resteth in their secret places, having in those places litle prety sores ful of venom poison, being very dangerous, for those that unknowingly medle with them, the which sicknes gotten by such infected women, is so moch the more vehement and grevous, how moch they be inwardly poluted and corrupted.[52]

However, by the late sixteenth century some physicians were of the opinion that "common women" (prostitutes) were actually less harmful than those who loved their partners because female pleasure during copulation was implicated in the greater likelihood of male infection.[53]

Although the Queen's surgeon, William Clowes, designated "Morbus Gallicus" "the pestilent infection of filthy lust," other forms of contact were implicated in its transmission "to the better sort":

Some tyme also the childe receiveth the infection of the parentes: And manye tymes nourses be infected by geving such to such infected children. This sicknes is many times bred in the mouth by eating, and drinking with infected persons. . . . Some tymes by lying in the bed with them, or by lying in the same sheets after them: sometymes it is sayd to come by sitting on the same stoole or casement which some infected person frequenteth.[54]

Nevertheless, he concedes, "accompaning with uncleane women" was the main reason why the Pox "overfloweth . . . the whole world" by 1579.[55] It seems that women simply could not win: in the face of fear generated by the rampant progress of the "new" venereal contagion, and tarred with the stigmatizing legacy of Eve's corruption, all sexually active women ("common" and non-common) were increasingly construed in print as the potential agents of male harm.

According to all these medical tracts, the pox (Spanish, French, Indian disease, Grandgore, Morbus Gallicus) was primarily the disease of venery and hence of the act of Venus (as sexual intercourse was euphemistically termed) and—because it was a fashionable disease liberally afflicting gentle and noble men—the bitter pill of sin had somehow to be sweetened and rendered more palatable. A variety of playful taming mythologies readily grew up around the new disease, key among them being polluting Venus. In 1525 Jean Lemaire de Belges published an extended poem called, *Trois Contes de Cupido et d'Atropos,* which proved extremely popular.[56] Briefly, it tells how Cupid and Death meet, drink, boast of their conquests and exchange their bows and arrows. The consequence is that the young die and the aged fall in love. Venus's young Volupté is wounded by an arrow of Death, and subsequently, in an angry fit, Venus throws the bow and arrow into the stream flowing about the Castle of Love. Fearful of what she has done, Venus tries to sweeten the waters with flowers and honey, but pollution remains and the spring is poisoned. Lovers drink the waters and with them the terrible infection. Mercury hears the pleas of Death and Love for new, appropriate weapons but decides that the tainted stream must remain, a warning to the ardent lover not to "nager en suspecte riviere." The "suspect stream" is, of course, all dubious womankind and the basic motifs of this poem about the fatal paradoxes that cohere in Venus, clearly inform many later belletristic forays, including—as we have seen—Shakespeare's.

Before probing the therapeutic boundaries of these lurid and fanciful poetic representations of contaminating womanhood, I should like briefly to consider the rather different "healing" strategies of the most famous sixteenth-century poem entirely about the "new" venereal affliction—Fracastoro of Verona's *Syphilis* (1530). In its fulsome dedication to the nobleman-scholar (and later cardinal) Pietro Bembo, this Virgilian-style Latin epic (in three books) makes much of its Apollonian credentials and medical propensities:

Bembo, Italy's fame and glory. . . . Do not disdain my undertaking, this labour of medicine, such as it is. The god Apollo once dignified these matters: small things, also, often have within them their own particular delights. Be certain that beneath the slender appearance of this topic there lies concealed a vast work of Nature and of fate and a grand origin. (31)

Simultaneously mathematician, geographer, scientist, botanist, physician and poet, Fracastoro was a distinguished Renaissance scholar who, as we have already heard, can be partly credited with having put modern exopathic and ontological theories of contagion on the medical map. Although a respected early scientist in the Baconian mold, who among other things rejected number mysticism, he seems to have believed that the harmonizing pursuits of medicine and poetry were linked in mysterious ways that largely defy rational explication. He shared Sir Philip Sidney's conviction that the poet was the best teacher and guide, because he could make things more memorable and present them how they should be (rather than how they were in a corrupt world), through the beauty and harmony of word pictures. The poet's capacity to delight and instruct was greater than that of the philosopher, because only the poet had the license to create fictions. Furthermore, the music of the poet's verse was itself mysteriously inspirational: Fracastoro claimed to have become possessed and frenzied while writing about the "wonders" of Syphilis.[57]

The result of this "possession" is a strange poem that graphically explores the terrors and tragic injustice of this creeping affliction "whose habit
is to snake inside the body" of men (71): "someone sighing over the spring-
time of his life and his beautiful youth, and gazing with wild eyes down at his
disfigured members, his hideous limbs and swollen face, often in his misery
railed against the gods' cruelty" (57). However, this physician's poem notably
and steadfastly draws a veil over the new disease's known primary route of
transmission—sexual intercourse. The activities of airborne seeds and the
wayward heavens are blamed for the disease's eruption and rapid spread, and
transmission by touch is even refuted: "seeing that in the first place we can
show many who without touching anyone, with no intermediary, yet felt the
effect of this same plague and have been the first to suffer" (41). Two intrigu-
ing allegories provide mythical explanations for the origins of the disease
and inventively convey the major posited "cures" for the disease in the Renaissance: mercury and leaves from the guaiacum tree. Syphilis takes its
name from the second of these myths: Syphilus is a shepherd who, in the face
of climatic adversity, blasphemes against the gods and sets up altars to the
earthly king Alcithous. The enraged sun god punishes the shepherd by in-
flicting him with "disfiguring sores . . . sleepless nights and tortured limbs"
(103), and the disease—whose symptoms can mercifully be alleviated by
leaves from a "Holy Tree" (guaiacum)—is born. The comforting message is
that through supplication and sacrifice the terrible affliction can be overcome, the disfigured body *can* be restored to health.

But what are we to make of this medical poem's obdurate denial of
syphilis's transmission through intimate touching? It is hard to reconcile this
both with Fracastoro's later work on contagion and with demands from
other noted humanist writers like Erasmus and Montaigne that, in order to
avoid this disease, young men—indeed boys—should receive sound and
early instruction about the need to "safeguard their chastity."[58] Pietro Bembo's response to *Syphilis* does, I feel, provide us with a clue to its wilful obfus-
cation: Bembo commended the poem "as a charming dignified account of
the disease."[59] What Fracastoro's patron desired then, was a "charming . . .
dignified" interpretation of the affliction; presumably one that tamed the
sinful implications of the disease and mitigated some of the fear engendered
by it: an account that was "healing" and pleasurable for its noble and gentle
reader-victims—not necessarily honest. Poetic license, and Fracastoro's frenzied inspiration, arguably produced harmony from a tissue of myths and the
music of verse (mingled with some medical facts and advice), dignifying and

taming the gruesome, terrifying affliction and perhaps, thereby, providing some comfort for sufferers. By comparison, all that practical medicine could offer syphilis victims were excruciatingly painful and ineffective treatments: there were no "cures" for syphilis. The base-line requirement of medicine in any culture is that it should attempt to order bodily disorder and to make patients feel they have some control over their wayward bodies:[60] consoling, explanatory myths such as Fracastoro's *Syphilis's* are the obvious medical recourse when science has no answers.[61]

Poetry might function in medicinal ways then; but—I would argue—some mythical representations, particularly those associated with the contaminating touch, have darker implications that may seriously compromise any positive "healing" function. It is time to revisit the spectacular early modern representations of polluting Venus-Eve-Pandora described earlier, and to probe their "taming" remit. Sander Gilman's *Disease and Representation* suggests that by projecting a serious fear about well-being onto an "other," we locate and "distance" it, rendering the threat less terrifying. Furthermore, art forms—the pages of a book, the frame of a painting—serve to put comforting boundaries between "us" and the diseased, contaminating "other."[62] But, as Gilman's work also foregrounds, what we are talking about here are stereotyping mechanisms, and, as such, they are hardly innocuous: "comforting" psychological strategies may have a high price tag attached to them and contain their own inherent dangers. They are inevitably associated with locating blame for a disease within a certain social group and with harmful scapegoating mechanisms. From the early modern female perspective, there was surely little that could qualify as "domesticating," "healing," and "consoling" about depictions of contaminating womanhood such as this:

There be devilish women desirous to be handled and dealt withall, who will beautifie themselves, to inflame mens hearts to lust towards them; abandon these your company, and thrust them out of the doors and house: let none of that hue be seen in your diet.[63]

Through the course of the sixteenth and seventeenth centuries such misogynist expressions of corrupting womanhood—the natural progression of stigmatizing stereotypes of female vectors of the pox—became commonplace in belletristic writings:

Take from them their periwigges, their paintings, their jewells, their rolles, their boulsteringes, and thou shalt perceive that a woman is the least part of her selfe. When they be once robbed of their roabes, then will they apeare so odious, so uglie, so monstrous, that thou wilt rather think them Serpents than Saintes, and so like hagges.[64]

Woman! The fatal Authress of our Fall:
Woman! The sure Destroyer of us all,
Like Sodom's apples pleasant to the Eye,
Within pale rottenness, and ashes lye.[65]

    Shakespeare's *Venus and Adonis*, as we have seen, contains a milder, wittier version of this stigmatizing male fantasy of the contaminating female touch, while Fracastoro's *Syphilis* completely evaded, indeed denied the realities of the disease's transmission through male libertine behavior. From the female perspective, again, surely there was nothing "medicinal" about this deliberate obfuscation. Which brings me to the vexed question of poetry's mysterious ability—or not—to transcend and transform the disease experience. Humanist beliefs in such a phenomenon have proven remarkably durable as this recent assertion attests: "Poetry attempts to accept the pain, fear, and grief of sickness and death with healing words, artfully distancing and transforming physical suffering."[66] While, as I have illustrated throughout this essay, it is quite possible that words and myths functioned in limited healing ways in this pre-scientific world, I do wish to inject a note of caution and skepticism into such rhapsodic claims for Renaissance verse. We should perhaps begin to ask for whom such poetry as I've described above was "healing," and at whose expense? Wide social implications of a harmful nature were surely contained in male poets' "artful" evasions of their sex's involvement and culpability in the transmission of a disease that was devastating to both genders. However successful, artistically, such poetry might be, we should seriously qualify, therefore, any account of its ability generally to "accept" and "heal" the disease experience, and to "tame" the anxieties associated with the contaminating touch. Furthermore, it seems to me that all the words studied in this chapter—poetic and prosaic—were rather too tenaciously rooted in the fleshy, "artful," material domain ever to achieve any mystical "transformation."

Chapter 3

"Handling Soft the Hurts": Sexual Healing and Manual Contact in Orlando Furioso, The Faerie Queene, and All's Well That Ends Well

Sujata Iyengar

Richard Braithwait's treatise *The Good Wife, or, A Rare One Amongst Women* (1618) urges the male reader "to loath" and never to marry "formalists, *She-doctors*, who have sought / To teach far more then ever they were taught." Having listed the physical and social characteristics of bad wives (prohibiting "faire" and "foule" women, "gay nor sluttish" ones, "niggard[s]" and "gadder[s]"), the speaker castigates a series of professional women: the "liquorish Gossip" (the midwife), the "coy precisian" (the scholarly woman), the "*She-doctor*" (the healer or teacher), and the "wanton that will prostitute / Her soule for sensuall pleasure" (the sex-worker). These women are all dangerous, claims the speaker, because they are "selfe-singular" and their "owne instructresse"; possessing their own learning, their own knowledge, and even their own professional income, these women threaten to "orethrow" their husbands, supplanting "through presumption" the natural order in which men rule, teach and subjugate their wives.[1]

Braithwait's train of association, from midwives to learned women to "she-doctors" and finally to "wanton[s]," surveys the ambivalent status of female healers in early modern England. Such women ranged from Margaret Roper, the daughter of Sir Thomas More, who treated her household with nonsurgical simples, fomentations, or vigorous massage, and Lady Hoby, who recounted the radical surgery she performed on a village child,[2] to lower-class women whose attempts to heal the sick (whether by medicines or by surgery) led to their denunciation as whores or witches, like Geillis Duncane, the Scottish maidservant whose execution for witchcraft is recounted in *Newes from Scotland* (1591).[3]

Early modern anxieties about female healing, I will argue, coalesced around fears of the dangerous, tactile, female supplement. In three literary episodes of early modern sexual healing, the cure of men by she-doctors be-comes a kind of supplementary sexual act, through a tactile process that allows the female physician to penetrate the male patient's body. Ariosto's "proud" Angelica squeezes the "juyse of . . . flowers" into Medore's wound (19.16); Spenser's chaste Belphoebe "scruze[s]" medicine into Timias's thigh (3.5.33). This healing supplement not only endangers the conventional sex-roles of active/passive, healer/healed, but also threatens to supplant het-erosexual penetrative intercourse and class boundaries. The wounding, unresponsive female mistress whose eyes shoot darts, flames, or other weap-ons that weaken or emasculate the male poet is a ubiquitous Petrarchan trope; in the cases I discuss, the wounds of love, literalized, contain the threat of sexual reversal by offering a kind of painful equality as penetrating, hith-erto untouchable women and penetrated men become mutually wounded and open to each other. Angelica falls in love with Medore, and virginal Belphoebe is nonetheless wounded herself by Timias's apparent faithlessness when he strives to become a healer in his own right by "handling soft the hurts" that Amoret has received. In contrast, I suggest, the scene of healing between Shakespeare's Helena (2.1.78), and the suffering King of France must take place off-stage—precisely to defuse the threat posed to virginity by manual intervention (historically the only known cure for the fistula that ails the King) and to rank by the "poor physician's daughter," just as the famous "bed-trick" simultaneously destroys and preserves virginity by distinguish-ing between *pucelage* and virginal innocence.[4]

Jacques Derrida suggests that "the supplement supplements. It adds only to replace. It intervenes or insinuates itself *in-the-place-of.*" Indeed, "the supplement will always be the . . . acting through the hands of others." Der-rida finds the fear of the supplement in Rousseau's account of autoeroticism, when the young Jean-Jacques discovers the difference between virginity and *pucelage* (literally, "hymen"), or, how to retain a technical virginity while en-joying sexual satisfaction. Masturbation allows the young man to remain technically pure even though he has lost his sexual innocence, shed his spiri-tual virginity. Rousseau argues that the delicious pleasure of onanism "cheats Nature" because the imagined sexual partner "out-distances" the real, just as, writes Derrida, the absent sign supplants the present object, writing sup-plants speech, frustration supplants pleasure, which supplants death.[5]

Having identified lower-class she-doctors as faulty supplements who fail to acknowledge their own subordination, King James's *Daemonologie* (1597) cleverly avoids denying witches' healing powers, instead affirming that the female healer is effective only as "Gods Ape," God's mimic or agent. Just as Braithwait worries that learned or professional women will refuse to allow their husbands to act on their behalf, so James accuses witches of refusing to acknowledge that they are merely vessels for divine power, of believing that they "them selves" can heal the sick. The accusations against Geillis Duncane, who "took in hand to help all such as were troubled or greeued with any kinde of sicknes or infirmitie," imply that her agency or personal will (she "took in hand") contradicts the "most miraculous" nature of her successes. Duncane subsequently named eight other "witches," including one woman accused of "bewitching to death" the last earl of Angus, "who died of so strange a disease, as the Phisition knew not how to cure or remedy the same."[6] Occasionally an impoverished healing woman might escape the charge of witchcraft; Margaret Kennix, a "poore woman," convinced Francis Walsingham to defend her right "quietly to practise and mynister to the curing of diseases and woundes, by the means of certain Simples," but such instances are rare.[7] Women were not permitted to become members of the Royal College of Physicians, founded in 1518, and the lower-ranked Guild of Barber-Surgeons likewise stipulated on its creation (1540) that "No carpenter, blacksmith, weaver or woman shall practise surgery"—although one scholar argues that women were already acting as surgeons: "Prohibitions are not imposed unless there is something to prohibit."[8] Walsingham's eloquent defense of Kennix indicates a gray area within the law. The regulations of the College and of the Guild forbade women to compound elaborate physic, or to wield instruments or tools to probe wounds, but since Kennix healed her patients with "Simples," single-source herbal remedies, not with complicated elixirs or surgical intervention, her work was arguably legitimate.

The ban on instruments seems to suggest a cultural fantasy about surrogacy or supplementarity, an anxiety that, given mechanical means or agents, women would supplant men in professional and sexual life. The prohibition against she-doctors using tools not only pushed women out of surgery but, ultimately, excluded them from what had previously been their unique province in sixteenth-century medicine—midwifery. Midwives traditionally used their hands to detect pregnancies, predict delivery dates, monitor fetal health and even turn around "breech" babies in the womb, but "with the introduction of the 'mysterious' forceps by the Chamberlain family,"[9] appliance-wielding men-midwives gradually muscled out their female competitors.[10]

Similar anxieties about women's use of instruments emerge in accounts of women who employed rubbing as a means to sexual pleasure (frottage) rather than solely as a healing device (massage). Katherine Park identifies fears of supplementarity or heterosexual obsolescence in early modern French accounts of "tribades" or lesbians who supposedly pleasured themselves through frottage or by using instruments, namely dildos.[11] Women were thought to be especially susceptible to tactile arousal by frottage; as Thomas Laqueur observes, female pleasure in heterosexual intercourse was considered to be the result of "rubbing," while the early modern French word for a homosexual woman is *fricatrice,* "one who illicitly assumed the active role, who did the rubbing when she ought to have been primarily the one rubbed against."[12] Ambroise Paré (1579) particularly recommends that men encourage their wives to experience sexual pleasure (thought to be necessary for conception) through friction: "if [the husband] perceive [the wife] to be slow, and more cold, he must . . . tickle her."[13] Anxieties that midwives, who used their hands to examine women's bodies, were engaged in illicit activities, both social (concealing the illegitimacy of children, or committing infanticide) and sexual (touching women inappropriately during examinations) would seem to sustain Laqueur's emphasis on rubbing.

Park criticizes Laqueur, however, for failing to take into account that early modern descriptions of tribadism find women who not only rub one another with their bare hands but who also use dildos, instruments, or their own enlarged clitorises to penetrate other women to be more menacing than *fricatrices.* The former engaged in acts that "qualified unambiguously as sodomy, . . . generally defined as the insertion of an inappropriate organ into an inappropriate orifice";[14] early modern male medical writers worried that these handy women would eventually decide that men were superfluous, that supplementary sex, or same-sex sodomy, would replace heterosexual penetrative intercourse altogether. Helkiah Crooke's *Microcosmographia* (1615) treats frottage as merely the prelude to female sodomy, claiming that, after rubbing, the clitoris or "womans yard" can grow "to such a length . . . and . . . rigiditie" as a "mans member"; this hard yard, he continues, is "this part . . . which those wicked women doe abuse called Tribades."[15] The history of midwifery likewise supports Park's thesis: while early modern husbands may have regarded female midwives and their touch with suspicion, the prospect of female midwives managing instruments, engaging in penetrative acts, seems to have been intolerable (hence the prohibition against female surgeons). Pamphleteers suspected male midwives, too, of illicit sexual activities,[16] but the homoerotic threat posed by she-doctors seems to have outweighed heteroerotic concerns about medical men.

Orlando Furioso (1591) neutralizes the threat of female penetration when the hitherto impossible, capricious, and heart-whole princess Angelica is finally wounded by love as she treats Medore's injury. Angelica "infuse[s]" the herbs into Medore's wound, aiding him with skill inherited from her father:

She having learnd of Surgerie the art,
(An art which still the Indians greatly prise)
Which fathers to their children do impart,
Whose knowledge in tradition chiefly lies,
Which without books the children learne by hart:
I say Angelica doth then devise
By skill she had in juyse of herbs and flowers
For to renew Medoros lively powres. (19.16)

Angelica, variously called the "Indian Queene" (19.15) and the princess of "Cataya" or Cathay (19.12), possesses a royal, healing touch, which the poem also explains in practical, prescriptive terms as the "skill she had in juyse of herbs and flowers." She may be skilled in "Surgerie," but on this occasion she uses a simple, the herb "Dittamy," which she crushes between two tiles or rocks "to stanch the blood" (19.17). Harington hastens—and chastens—Ariosto's cure: in a twentieth-century translation, the healing process involves smearing the lotion on Medore's "chest and belly, down to his hips,"[17] squeezing the flowery juice into Medore's open body in a supplemental act of heteroeroticism.

This act of sexual healing is not, however, a true supplement, but a perverse foreshadowing; Angelica's flowery cure stanches Medore's flowing blood in a strange, predictive parody of her own defloration and blood-loss. At the very beginning of the *Furioso*, the narrator mocks Sacripant's belief that Angelica "Had still preserv'd the floure of her virginitie," calling the suggestion "incredible" while conceding doubtfully, "it might be true" (1.55–56). In contrast, Angelica's defloration, a direct result of Medore's own injury, provokes the most direct assertion of Angelica's prior virginity; the narrator confirms her physical maidenhead most assuredly only as she bestows it on Medore:

She suffers poore *Medoro* take the flowre
Which many sought, but none had yet obtained,
That fragrant rose that to the present houre
Ungatherd was, behold *Medoro* gained. (19.25)

"Roses" or "flowers" are early modern terms for menses and, perhaps, for the blood resulting from breaking a hymen; having stanched Medore's blood with flowers, the newly deflowered Angelica finds herself bleeding as if in sympathy with Medore's newly closed wound. Although "Angelica, as a woman, is marked by her anatomy as . . . 'cut,' " writes Deanna Shemek, "Medoro's wound . . . becomes the mark of Angelica's desire," in a mutual wounding that allows the lovers to sacrifice integrity for "exchange with the world."[18]

John Harington reads the "allegorie" here as service conquering assertiveness: "*Angelica* is taken for honor, which brave men hunt after by blood and bettells and many hardie feats and misse it, but a good servant with faith and gratefulnesse to his Lord gets it" (19, Gloss). "Honor" for Renaissance women is a synonym for chastity; Angelica signifies honor and glory for Medore only when her own honor can be first stated outright, then given up, pronounced when renounced. Indeed, says the narrator, the logical outcome of Angelica and Medore's therapeutic encounter is the loss of Angelica's own technical and emotional virginity, as she learns her cure "by hart" in both senses: "while she heald his wound, another dart / Did wound her thoughts and hye conceits so deep / As now therewith was ravisht her proud hart" (19.22). Medore's wound lies in his bosom, and as his hurt heart heals, Angelica receives a wound in her own, as if to neutralize or attempt to undo the seeming sexual reversal taking place during Medore's cure.

This humbling involves Angelica in a loss of class status as well as a return to the conventions of femininity and intercourse. The reference to Angelica's *proud* heart reminds us that Medore is Cloridano's squire, while Angelica is a queen or princess, of Cathay or of India (in fact, the narrator confides, her medicinal skills depend on her status, and Cupid is punishing her for "great . . . folly" and "vaine . . . pride" by matching her with a social inferior [19.14]), as if there is an interchange of status, physical and mental health, and sexual integrity between she-doctor and patient.

Angelica and Medore are sexually and textually entangled; prescription and inscription surround their affair:

Their manner was on ev'rie wall within,
Without on ev'rie stone or shadie tree,
To grave their names with bodkin, knife or pin:
. . .
Angelica and Medore in ev'rie place
With sundrie knots and wreaths they enterlace. (19.28)

The writing on the wall provides the link between inside and out, "without" and "within"; their writing instruments—"bodkin, knife and pin"—become metonymic substitutes for the worlds of warfare, medicine, and domesticity. These worlds are entwined in a gendered or "sexual chiasmus" (Linda Woodbridge's term for "the crossing over of qualities between the sexes"[19]): Angelica-and-Medore now functions as a single, hermaphroditic unit, each half erotically wounded or penetrated by the other.

Later, when the lovelorn Orlando reads these engraved erotic texts, the wounding writing functions as the "sign [that] is always the supplement to the thing itself";[20] Orlando "knew the hand" (23.79), Angelica's "pretie hand" (23.80), which acts as a surrogate for her body, through a series of supplementary synecdoches: "the hand" is her *hand-writing*, her *hand in marriage*, the point of contact between her body and those of others; her fingertips become the instruments that evoke her ghostly, absent presence for Orlando. By being engraved, the writing moves from the merely graphic or textual to the realm of the tactile: the *hand* that Orlando knows can be traced and fingered by his own. Crazed with grief, Orlando engages in further fantasies of substitution or supplementarity, imagining that both he and Angelica have split personalities: "There may be more *Angelicas* than she" (23.79); or he himself might really be called Medore, and Angelica "might understand / His name and love by that same new inditing" (23.80).

Orlando Furioso breaks down the barriers of class and chastity, but when Spenser rewrites this episode of loving healing in *The Faerie Queene* (1590–96), erotic love between a virgin queen and a humble squire proves impossible. After three foresters wound Timias and leave him for dead, chaste and skillful Belphoebe rescues him, but even as his body heals, his soul throbs with a wound of impossible love—impossible because Belphoebe, as the adopted daughter of the goddess Diana, is committed to perpetual virginity. Belphoebe's cure seems to involve many early modern medical therapies, including rubbing, simples, fomentation, and surgical investigation:

Meekeley she bowed downe, to weete if life
Yet in his frosen members did remaine,
And feeling by his pulses beating rife,
That the weake soule her seat did yet retaine,
She cast to comfort him with busie paine:
His double folded necke she reard vpright,
And rubd his temples and each trembling vaine;
His mayled haberieon she did undight,
And from his head his heauy burganet did light.

Into the woods thenceforth in hast she went,
To seeke for hearbes, that mote him remedy;

For she of hearbes had great intendiment,
Taught of the Nymphe, which from her infancy
Her nourced had in trew Nobility:
There, whether it diuine *Tobacco* were,
Or *Panachea*, or *Polygony*,
She found, and brought it to her patient deare
Who al this while lay bleeding out his hart-bloud neare.

The soueraigne weede betwixt two marbles plaine
She pownded small, and did in peeces bruze,
And then atweene her lilly handes twaine,
Into his wounde the iuyce thereof did scruze,
And round about, as she could well it vze,
The flesh therewith she suppled and did steepe,
T'abate all spasme, and soke the swelling bruze,
And after hauing searcht the intuse deepe,
She with her scarfe did bind the wound from cold to keepe. (3.5.31–33)

The first course of treatment is external examination (checking that the patient's "pulse [is] beating") and chafing ("rubd his temples"); the second stage is diagnosing the ailment and treating it with the correct herb. Spenser coyly refuses to tell us which particular herb Belphoebe uses, but it is tempting to imagine her using "Panachea," which, according to the herbalist Thomas Thomas (1587), "of some . . . is taken for Angelica."[21] Next, Belphoebe "scruzes" the juice into the wound and probes it before bandaging it. Just as Timias's thigh was pierced by the lance, so Belphoebe's heart is "pierced" with pity and so Timias is pierced once more by the healing process:

O foolish Physick, and unfruitfull paine,
That heales up one and makes another wound:
She his hurt thigh to him recur'd againe,
But hurt his hart, the which before was sound,
Through an unwary dart, which did rebound
From her fair eyes and gracious countenance. (3.5.42)

In the process of healing, the she-doctor initiates a thematic and sexual chiasmus similar to that we encountered with Angelica and Medore. While Medore's breast is injured, in a physical manifestation of his wounded heart, Angelica's juices enter Medore's open wound in an upwardly displaced parody of penetrative heterosexual intercourse. Timias' wound lies in his thigh, and seems to render him penetrable, feminized (like Shakespeare's Adonis, gored in the thigh by a phallic boar). Having entered and bound up Timias's feminizing wound, having restored his thwarted masculinity, Belphoebe replaces the mortal wound in the thigh with the painful but ultimately curable wound of love.

What I am arguing is that in these texts femininity is not just absence, castration, either a psychoanalytic "lack" or an Elizabethan "nothing," but presence—the presence not of a phallus but of a "wound." A ribald sonnet in *The Passionate Pilgrim* (1599) imagines a wound in the thigh as female genitals, in a development of the standard early modern conceit of female sexual parts as "nothing":

"See, in my thigh," quoth [Venus], "here was the sore."
She showed hers, he saw more wounds than one,
And blushing fled, and left her all alone.[22]

Sexual chiasmus occurs at moments of supplementary sex: moments when healer and healed, man and woman, active and passive, instrument and hand, interpenetrate—or, to borrow Donne's "Extasie," *inter-inanimate*— each other: the exchange of sex (in both its senses: of gender difference and of erotic acts) between healer and healed restores each lover to life.[23]

Love inspired by healing and by wounding becomes a process of sexual chiasmus reflected in formal terms in Timias's lament, with the rippling repetition of the refrain, "Dye, rather dy, then love disloyally":

Unthankfull wretch (said [Timias]) is this the meed,
With which her soveraigne mercy thou does quight?
. . .
Dye rather, dye then so disloyally
Deeme of her high desert, or seeme so light:
Faire death it is to shonne more shame, to dy
Dye rather, dy, then ever love disloyally.

But if to love disloyalty it bee,
Shall I then hate her, that from deathes dore
Me brought?
. . .
Dye rather, dye, and dying do her serve,
Dying her serve, and living her adore;
Thy life she gave, thy life she doth deserve:
Dye rather, dye, then ever from her service swerve. (3.5.45–46)

"Dye"—in the Shakespearean sense—is of course exactly what Timias cannot do, barred from the death-throes of sexual release and the agony of consummation. Structurally, the stanzas move from death to disloyalty and then back to death; there is an inevitability about the turn which assumes that the nature of both "love" and the "cure" is in itself "disloyal." Timias's desire is illicit because it is aroused through Belphoebe's healing powers, which are in turn a manifestation of her virginal power; paradoxically, it is this virginal piercing that both heals and destroys the patient, as Mary Villeponteaux observes.[24]

Timias suffers again from the ambivalence of tactile healing when he unsuccessfully battles the rapacious wild man of the forest, who has kidnapped Amoret. Having vanquished the lustful giant, Belphoebe finds Timias alone with the wounded nymph, as Timias, overcome with sympathy for Amoret's bruises, tries to soothe her:

There [Belphoebe] him found by that new louely mate,
Who lay the whiles in swoune, full sadly set,
From her faire eyes wiping the deawy wet,
Which softly stild, and kissing them atweene,
And handling soft the hurts, which she did get.
For of that Carle she sorely bruz'd had beene,
Als of his owne rash hand one wound was to be seene. (4.7.35)

While Belphoebe first appears to Timias as a "goodly Mayd full of diuinities," like Diana herself with her "bow and gilden quiuer" (3.5.34), Amoret exists as a "new louely mate," only as a life-partner or lover. "Louely" means both *beautiful* and *loving*, and "mate" is both innocent (as if she is Timias's playmate or schoolmate, a fellow-victim of the lustful giant) and tawdry (as if she provides Timias with the chance to consummate or *mate* his balked desire). "New louely mate" is filtered through multiple narrative consciousnesses. Is the phrase Belphoebe's description of what she thinks she is seeing (Timias abandoning her and Amoret, sexually wounded by Timias's "rash hand," abandoning Scudamour)? Or is Amoret chaste, but viewed by a sinning Timias as a surrogate "mate" for him?

In contrast to Belphoebe's progressively, clinically-worded cure, Timias's actions confuse sexual and therapeutic contact. Compare the description of Belphoebe's cure, filled with preterites and completed actions ("cast to comfort," "rubd," "reard upright," "found, and brought," "pownded" "did bruze," "did scruze," "did steepe," "hauing searcht" and "did bind") to Timias' attempt, full of gerunds ("wiping," "kissing," "handling"). While Belphoebe's verbs themselves seem sexually equivocal (especially the progression from "cast to comfort" to "rubd" and then "reard upright"), the simple past tenses insist that Belphoebe's actions are exceptional, speedy, and purposeful, even clinical. The narrator carefully places the most intimate and penetrative part of the cure, probing the wound, as a participially completed past action ("hauing searcht") rather than presenting it to us even as a preterite. Timias's present participles and the grammatically confusing "atweene" instead imply a protracted process of simultaneous fondling. If "atweene" refers (as A. C. Hamilton's note suggests) to Timias's alternating actions of kissing, wiping, and handling, then it is an adverb, qualifying his movements; there is equally, however, a strong sense of "atweene" as a preposition, locating Timias's kisses in a bodily way, so that the reader imagines Timias kissing Amoret between ("atweene") her weeping eyes, and grasping Amoret's whole body "atweene" his arms. As readers, we see Timias's fondling through the narrator's eyes, filtered through Belphoebe's consciousness. Spenser's carefully displaced epithets confirm this confusion; "soft" works adverbially to modify Timias's "handling," but echoes erotically as an adjectival description of Amoret's skin.

Belphoebe, convinced of Timias's faithlessness, responds with magnificent brevity: "Is this the faith, she said, and said no more, / But turnd her face, and fled away for evermore" (4.7.36). Belphoebe's technical purity or *pucelage* never comes into question, but the scene before her calls up her emotional innocence and her awareness of sexual pleasure. Her words echo Timias's lament, "is this the meed," and her anger with Timias makes clear the relationship between sexual and curative touch, complicating her own avowal of chastity: even necessary, healing physical contact sullies the healer by association (or by "touch" [*OED* sb. 2c]). Abandoned by Belphoebe, Timias runs mad, like Orlando in the *Furioso* after he discovers Angelica's engraven love for Medore. In his madness, Timias himself carves Belphoebe's name "on euery tree" (4.7.46) and a stunned Prince Arthur later witnesses his etchings.

The very next canto sees the squire "receiv'd againe to former fauours state" when he convinces Belphoebe that her anger is the result of "misdeeming," or misinterpretation, and urges her to "deeme aright" and forgive him (4.8.17); even now, however, Timias is not cured, but only in remission. The hapless squire is bitten by the Blatant Beast and filled with "poysnous humour" (6.6.2) before being healed by the words of the Hermit. The Blatant Beast attacks those who, like Arthegall, lay themselves open to slander or scandal. Timias's recovery depends upon the retention of chastity, both as *pucelage* and as sexual innocence. The Hermit can only heal Timias's wound if the latter agrees to

avoide the occasion of the ill:
. . .
Abstaine from pleasure, and restraine your will,
Subdue desire, and bridle loose delight,
Use scanted diet, and forbeare your fill,
Shun secresie, and talke in open sight. (6.6.14)

The Hermit implies that, since Timias cannot control his emotions, the only permanent cure is to avoid temptation altogether, to maintain technical and emotional chastity. From a therapeutic point of view, the Hermit puts Timias on the equivalent of stress management, low cholesterol, and the talking-cure, adding prophylaxis and psychotherapy to Belphoebe's acute medical intervention.

Belphoebe's maidenly touch embodies only a limited aspect of chaste sexual healing. Busirane's wounding of Amoret moves the Petrarchan trope of the maiming mistress across gender and genre, transforming a cruel sonnet-mistress into the cruel master-enchanter of Spenserian romance. Britomart's remarkable cure of Amoret in effect restores Amoret's hymen, like the slow rewinding of a silent film:

The cruell steele, which thrild her dying hart
Fell softly forth, as of his owne accord,
And the wyde wound, which lately did dispart
Her bleeding brest, and riven bowels gor'd,
Was closed up, as it had not bene bor'd,
And every part to safety full sound,
As she were never hurt, was soone restor'd:
Tho when she felt her selfe to be unbound,
And perfect hole, prostrate she fell unto the ground. (3.12.38)

"Perfect hole" means—drastically, reductively—the perfect female, who is *only* perfect whole; Amoret is returned to the state of chaste and holy virginity, a state that in its integrity draws a resemblance between the un-wounded, male body and the body of the chaste female virgin. But "Even closed, this wound remains open, as the pun on 'hole' tells us," suggests Jonathan Goldberg, with the revelation that Amoret is already married to Scudamour.[25]

Amoret's magical healing provides the only solution to the conundrum of married chastity, the only reconciliation between the torn and intact hymen: Amoret both is and is not penetrated, both is and is not a virgin. Elizabeth J. Bellamy argues that Amoret (who, alone of Book Three's heroines, is married) experiences "sexual terror" of Busirane and of submission to Scudamour, before the emergence of the companionate marriage; "the concept of married chastity is itself a kind of 'perfect hole.' . . . [B]efore the married couple can accede to a monogamous state, the chaste virgin must allow her hymen to be penetrated."[26] Spenser's narrative response to the problem of married chastity is to create in Amoret (for whom, as Bellamy observes, there is no direct literary source) a chaste virgin who is both sexually penetrated and a hermaphrodite unable either to penetrate like a man or to be penetrated like a woman.

Indeed, narrative perfection at the end of the 1590 edition resides not in female integrity but in hermaphroditic heterosexual doubling, as Amoret and Scudamour "melt" into one another "like two senceles stocks in long embracement" (3.12.45). The original hermaphroditic embrace of Amoret and her faithful lover Scudamour closes the narrative so thoroughly that Spenser must untwine them, must rewrite the end of the book, before he can continue his epic six years later. "Had you them seene, ye would haue surely thought, / That they had beene that faire *Hermaphrodite*" (3.12.46), comments the narrator; as "stocks," they provide the "stock" or breeding for future generations, but, perversely enough, through cloning or grafting, like the plants they seem to be, rather than through sexual reproduction. This Spenserian hermaphrodite becomes a gender-neutral entity comprising two individuals, male and female, who become an asexual object through their sexual union. Many critics find the image itself distancing, ironic, even perverse,[27] but "stocks" includes a sense of origin, of antiquity, and while the lovers "melt" in sexual bliss, their union equally returns them to a presexual age, that of Plato's *Symposium*, the playful account of human origins that asserts that creatures now-divided by sex used to be "perfect whole," permanently united with another half (of the same or of the opposite sex).[28] Out of time and out of gender, the lovers also recall the classical Baucis and Philemon, who in Ovid's *Metamorphoses* plead to die simultaneously and are rewarded by turning at the same time to "two trees growing from one double trunk."[29]

I suggested earlier that femininity might in Ariosto's and Spenser's texts become not an absence or lack but the presence of a wound, a process that allows healing and touch to effect a sexual chiasmus or exchange, even a kind of equality. Supplemental sex, in other words, is simultaneously onanism or other non-reproductive sexual activities, sexual healing and sexual substitution, all of which leave hymen or *pucelage* intact but threaten emotional and sexual innocence. Shakespeare's *All's Well That Ends Well* (1603–4) features a wounded king, but the wound's location, cure, and significance are shrouded in secrecy, and while, as we shall see, Helena does engage in sexual crossing, the play ends without any assurance of the mutual wounding and pleasure experienced by Spenser's or Ariosto's lovers. There are two curious dramatic ellipses in the play: Helena's mysterious cure of the king's fistula and the bed-trick, in which the abandoned, unbedded wife, Helena, tricks her unwilling spouse, Bertram, into impregnating her by convincing him that she herself has died and that he is deflowering another chaste virgin, Diana, whom he has wooed by stealth. The King attempts at the end of the play to arrange the marriage of Diana, doubling her with Helena and emphasizing her ambiguous status as virgin and not-virgin: "If thou beest yet a fresh uncropped flower / Choose thou thy husband and I'll pay thy dower" (5.3.321–22).

The play draws attention to Diana's ambiguously virginal name and status by Bertram's otherwise inexplicable but florid mistake:

Enter Bertram and the maid called Diana.
Bertram: They told me that your name was Fontybell.
Diana: No, my good lord, Diana. (4.2.1–2)

"Fontybell" is the secret spring of desire; Bertram thinks that Diana is the replenishing waters of Lourdes when she is more "like Diana in the fountain" in *As You Like It* (4.1.154), more like the goddess Diana faced with the trespassing Actaeon, an avenging force ready to chastise illicit desires.[30] Shakespeare's Diana does indeed resurrect the dead, but it is Helena, not Bertram, whom she revives, just as Helena herself can "araise King Pippen" (2.1.75) but not awaken Bertram's love. The audience sees the results of both these events (the happy King, the paradoxically pregnant Helena) but not the actions themselves; they remain narrativized, like supplements to the action on stage.

Mystery surrounds the King's malady:

Bertram: What is it, my good lord, the King languishes of?
Lafew: A fistula, my lord.
Bertram: I heard not of it before.
Lafew: I would it were not notorious. Was this gentlewoman the daughter of
                 Gerard de Narbon? (1.1.30–34)

But the fistula is, indeed, "notorious"—notoriously difficult to heal and notoriously unpleasant. The *OED* defines it as "a long, narrow, suppurating canal of morbid origin in some part of the body; a long, sinuous pipe-like ulcer with a narrow orifice." The medieval physician John Arderne confirms that "a fistule is a depe aposteme, hauyng oonly oon hole somtyme, and . . . oftymes mo, and bredyng in eche membre of the body of aposteme or of a wounde yuel y-cured."[31] While Shakespeare's Boccaccian source describes a wound in the bosom, *All's Well That Ends Well* remains ambiguous concerning the location of the King's ailment, and its bawdy jokes about the wound suggest a potentially embarrassing area.

Where would a Shakespearean audience presume the King's fistula was concealed and how did they assume Helena would cure it? Andrew Boorde's *Breuiary* (1542) locates it "most commonlye . . . in a man's foundament,"[32] and "An Eminent Practitioner in Physick, Surgery and Chymistry" confirms five years later that "the anus, or Fundament, is more subject to Fistulas than any other part in the whole body."[33] *Fistula in ano* was primarily a traditional soldiers' wound, familiar during Arderne's time in the aftermath of the Hundred Years War when men spent many hours on horseback and in conditions of poor sanitation. "[M]ost use of . . . lichery" and, in women, parturition aggravate it. Shakespeare's king suffers, then, from a wound sustained in that most masculine of activities, armed combat, but a wound that is also, perversely, a sign of uxoriousness or effeminacy, too much "lichery."

The Countess voices all the objections toward Helena's attempting this cure:

> How shall they credit
> A poor unlearned virgin, when the schools,
> Embowel'd of their doctrine, have left off
> The danger to itself? (1.3.234–37)

The schools are discharging and disemboweled, gutted by the tenacious disease; their learning has proven to be hollow, like the fistula itself. The Countess has acknowledged the impossibility of a "natural" remedy, just as Helena has denied that the course of "fate" or "nature" or, more dangerously, the divine, can alter the future: "Our remedies oft in ourselves do lie / Which we ascribe to heaven" (1.1.212–13). Helena's "credit" is untrustworthy because she is "poor"; she needs knowledge from books, because she is unlearned; finally, she may need sexual knowledge to cure the King, which she lacks because she is a "virgin." Helena has referred earlier to her father's "prescriptions / Of rare and prov'd effects"; here, however, she seems to take up the Countess's implication that mere book-learning and written notes or recipes are inadequate:

> There's something in't
> *More* than my father's skill, which was the great'st
> Of his profession, that his good receipt
> Shall for my legacy be sanctified
> By th'luckiest stars in heaven. (1.3.238–42; emphasis mine)

"Legacy" takes up the traditional emphasis of the Countess's earlier speech, as does "receipt" (literally, a recipe, but also something received); there is also a continuing emphasis on medicine as theatrical enterprise, picked up in the double sense of "profession." Was the skill of Helena's father only as great as he "professed" it to be and was he *only* "famous in his profession," as the Countess first describes him, famous in his own words? Helena is convinced that there is something "more," some element of showmanship that cannot be written and handed down as a "prescription" a "receipt," or a script, some stage-business that the written playbook cannot show and which, in fact, is never shown on stage. This mysterious supplement to Gerard de Narbon's "receipts" or "skill" is at once the surgical intervention that the manuals insist is necessary, and the "sanctification" of Helena's cherished virginity.[34]

The evocation of Helena's virginity deliberately reminds the audience of her earlier bawdy badinage with Parolles, which centers around the value to be placed on virginity, and on whether, like cheese, it ripens with age:

Helena: How might one do, sir, to lose [her virginity] to her own liking?
Parolles: Let me see. Marry, ill, to like him that ne'er it likes. 'Tis a commodity will lose the gloss with lying; the longer kept, the less worth. Off with't while 'tis vendible; answer the time of request . . . your virginity, your old virginity, is like one of our French wither'd pears: it looks ill, it eats drily; marry, 'tis a withered pear; it was formerly better; marry, yet 'tis a withered pear. Will you anything with it? (1.1.147–60)

From the first scene of the play, then, virginity is "vendible," a token to be bartered for gain, like the medical "receipts" that Gerard de Narbon has handed down to Helena, while the "wither'd pear" of Helena's moldering virginity anticipates the French king's decaying health.

The text during the encounter with Parolles presents both a textual and a figurative crux. Parolles inquires: "Will you anything with it [your virginity]?" The Folio reads then:

Not my virginity yet:
There shall your master have a thousand loves,
A mother, a mistress, and a friend
A phoenix, captain and an enemy,
A guide, a goddess, and a sovereign,
A counsellor, a traitress, and a dear,
His humble ambition, proud humility,
His jarring-concord, and his discord-dulcet,
His faith, his sweet disaster; with a world
Of pretty, proud, adoptious Christendoms
That blinking Cupid gossips. Now shall he—
I know not what he shall. (1.1.165–76)

G. K. Hunter argues in his introduction to the play that there is no reason to suppose that Helena's first line is incomplete, suggesting that the pause is deliberately elliptical, and points to a connection suppressed, for reasons of "delicacy," in front of Parolles. On the other hand, there is a break in the meter. As Gary Taylor observes, Helena's "yet" is both adverb and conjunction. He conjectures that three syllables have dropped out and that those are, simply, "at the court"; Helena is therefore saying both "Bertram cannot have *my* virginity; yet at the court he may have a thousand lovers;" and "Bertram may not have my virginity *yet*, at the court."[35]

But "there" might simply to refer back to the subject of the previous sentence, Helena's virginity, so that the construction is set up in opposition to her clause later in the speech beginning, "*Now* shall he—/ I know not what he shall." "There" is an adverb of time rather than of place. We could gloss "Not my virginity yet . . ." as "I will not barter my virginity at this time, but when I do Bertram shall find my love to be everything he could possibly imagine." The first pause is pregnant, virginity's antithesis, breeding names, just as virginity, according to Parolles, breeds mites like a cheese. The break in the meter ushers in the catalogue of the "thousand loves" that Bertram will enjoy.

These "thousand loves" are a thousand avatars of Helena, and the speech itself predicts the impossible solution, the bed-trick, that she will ultimately use to maintain a status as simultaneously virgin, wife and mistress. "A mother, a mistress and a friend" speaks to Bertram's worst fears and deepest fantasies; Janet Adelman argues that it is precisely the fear that his "mistress" may also be his "mother" that drives Bertram to flee his mother's choice in the first place,[36] a problem that Helena herself articulates when she hurriedly corrects the countess's chatty, "I am a mother to you" (1.3.133) with "Mine honourable mistress" (1.3.134), as if she "saw a serpent" (1.3.136). The only solution is incest:

Helena: You are my mother, madam; would you were—
           So that my lord your son were not my brother—
           Indeed my mother! Or were you both our mothers
           I care no more for than I do for heaven,
           So I were not his sister. Can't no other
           But I, your daughter, he must be my brother?
Countess: Yes, Helen, you might be my daughter-in-law. (1.3.156–62)

Bertram marries, as he fears, a mistress chosen by his mother, a mistress who "had [her] breeding at [his] father's charge" (2.3.114).

   "Friend" is a similarly loaded term. The Clown convinces the Countess that he "hope[s] to have friends for [his] wife's sake" (1.3.37–38), responding to her contemptuous response, "Such friends are thine enemies, knave" (39) with the following syllogism: "He that comforts my wife is the cherisher of my flesh and blood; he that cherishes my flesh and blood loves my flesh and blood; he that loves my flesh and blood is my friend; ergo, he that kisses my wife is my friend" (1.3.44–48). Adultery is the prelude not to divorce but to domestic happiness, as indeed the bed-trick, in which Bertram may imagine a "thousand loves" (may, indeed, enjoy the full benefits of a Derridean, onanistic, imaginary love) but impregnate only his legal one, will prove to be.

   "A phoenix, captain and an enemy" glance forward to Helena's phoenix-like resurrection from the dead in the final scene, her smart captaining of the bed-trick and Bertram's hate-filled flight. Helena herself is the "jarring-concord" and "discord-dulcet"; she is also "humble ambition" (she observes earlier, "Th'ambition in my love . . . plagues itself") and the "traitress" who arranges the bed-trick. Bertram himself is blinded like "blinking Cupid," or like Parolles in what Ann Lecercle calls the "hood-winking" scene where his boastful lies are exposed.[37]

   With her "thousand loves" and her thousand healing powers, "Doctor She" (2.1.78) puts ink in Charlemagne's pencil, erects King Pepin, and makes the King of France frolic like a young goat:

Lafew: . . . I have seen a medicine
          That's able to breathe life into a stone,

> Quicken a rock, and make you dance canary
> With sprightly fire and motion; whose simple touch
> Is powerful to araise King Pippen, nay,
> To give great Charlemain a pen in's hand
> And write to her a love-line. (2.1.71–77)

The "love-line" is not merely "great Charlemain['s]" restored inscriptive potential but also the love- or heart-line on the palm. The revitalized King can "dance a coranto," turn physician and prescribe (to continue the pun) not only whom Helena must marry but the manner of their union, in a series of "love-lines" that lead Helena after Bertram.

But despite Lafew's, Parolles's and even the Countess's sustained sexual innuendo about the invigorating powers of virginal lady doctors upon elderly male patients, a function of Helena's backstage cure is to *de*-naturalize both female healing and heterosexual intercourse. Why indeed might Shakespeare's King of France have a fistula whose location is the subject of such indirection and sexual innuendo, when Boccaccio states clearly that "the French King had a swelling upon his breast"?[38] From 1574 to 1589 the king of France was Henri de Valois or Henri III, assassinated at the age of thirty-eight after establishing a court notorious for the presence of his "mignons," or male favorites. (The court of King James in 1604 was, of course, well known for similar reasons.) Henri was also widely satirized in both France and England as a transvestite and an alleged hermaphrodite (a word used loosely at this time to implicate any kind of cross-dresser, male to female or vice versa). Contemporary commentators believed that Henri's love of masquerades contributed to the allegations of cross-dressing (the French word for "transvestism," one notes, is *travestissement* as well as *transvestisme* and "to cross-dress" is *se travestir*). Lorraine Daston and Katherine Park have pointed out the association of the hermaphrodite with "the sodomite" and transvestism in early modern France, and more recently Park has discussed the charges leveled against both Henri and his mother.[39] An account of Henri's behavior from 1589 illuminates the connections pamphleteers drew between cross-dressing, anal intercourse, and femininity:

He was always so effeminate, that he used to make himself up as women do . . . he would mimic their gestures and expressions, and he used to cherish among his dearest wishes one to be transformed into a woman, in order to experience the delights of the female sex . . . he imagined that he could by artificial means be transformed in his body, and so that he could achieve his devilish desire all the better, he had all the most excellent Surgeons, Physicians and Philosophers of his time meet, and allowed them to cauterize his body, and to make all the openings and wounds they wished, so that they could make him able to conjoin with a man: in the pursuit of which they cut him in several places, and burned him. But he remained in the end with God's sufferance, useless to both sexes.[40]

The title of this anecdote reads: "Le songe creux envoyé à Henry de Valoys par un Parisien." A *songe-creux* is a visionary, one whose dreams are hollow or insubstantial, or an empty fantasy. The ribald rhyme and the slanderous story are literally *creux*, hollow, because the King allows his body to be hollowed out by the master-surgeons and his gendered identity to be eroded through acts of mutilation.[41] The pervasive cultural myth here is the notion of the impenetrable male; this fantasy imagines that the only way two men can make love is, first, only through penetrative intercourse and, second, only if one of them becomes a woman, a process seen as the inevitable result of cutting or hollowing, of adding wounds.[42]

The fistula in Shakespeare might then represent (like Timias's wounded thigh in *The Faerie Queene* or Venus's thigh in *The Passionate Pilgrim*) not merely castration or loss, but a growth or addition: the King's feminization is achieved not through the loss of the phallus but through the opening of another passage, through supplementation or even multiplication, rather than subtraction. Patricia Parker analyzes early modern accounts of male impotence or softening in order to put the well-known tales of female-to-male metamorphosis in a context of gender fluidity and to argue that such accounts reveal that early modern masculinity is tentatively acquired, tenuously held, and tenaciously debated.[43] The fistula marks the King's impotence on a number of levels, political, social, and sexual: the first marriage the King arranges is severed by Helena's supposed death, just as his legal attempts to unite Bertram and Diana come to confusion; his final promise to marry off Diana to the suitor of her choice is followed by an Epilogue that asserts "the King's a beggar" and cannot heal himself. Boorde says that the King's Evil (scrofula) is "much like to a fystle," but that the King cannot always cure it, because

as muche as some men dothe judge divers tyme a Fystle or a French pocke to be the kynges evyll, in suche matters it behoveth nat a Kynge to medle withall, escept it be thorowe and of his bountifull goodnes to geve his pytyfull and gracious counsel. For kynges, and kynges sones and other noble men, hath been eximious Phisicions.[44]

Thus the King cannot heal himself, nor can he heal others; the very nature of sovereign power is called into question.

The staged identities of Helena as penetrative virgin and the King as penetrable male are neither androgynous (of indeterminate sex) nor neuter (possessing the characteristics of neither sex) as much as hermaphroditic—enjoying the attributes of *both* sexes. The King's debility and his association with the domestic world of the court rather than the martial world of Bertram render him impotent or effeminized. Helena herself, who performs a man's surgical role but refuses, in contrast to the professional performances of Portia and Viola, to dress as a man, already participates in the transvestism of the early modern theater. Anti-theatrical writers worried that the presence of beautiful boys in women's clothing on stage would inspire a corresponding lust in both men and women audience members—lust for the body of the boy-actor as well as for his female character.[45] Shakespeare's chaste married heroine defuses the threat of illicit audience arousal just as she relieves the King's symptom, detaching sexuality from healing, and even from conception. She reproduces as if by herself, like the "phoenix" to which she earlier compares herself and which, according to legend, immolates itself after laying an egg from which it will be reborn (1.1.168). Like the figure of Venus Genetrix, the self-reproducing goddess in Spenser's Garden of Adonis in Book Three of *The Faerie Queene*, and *unlike* the asexual Spenserian hermaphrodite who closes that book, the phoenix in *All's Well* is, strangely enough, feminine by default (where femininity is equivalent to and defined by reproductive capability). Shakespeare enshrines the phoenix as an emblem of "married chastity" in "The Phoenix and Turtle"; like the fertile but asexual phoenix, Helena "riddle-like lives sweetly where she dies" (1.3.212).

Adelman aptly observes that "Helena can . . . simultaneously cure through her sexuality and remain absolutely pure. This simultaneity should seem familiar to us: it in fact rules the presentation of Helena's cure of the king."[46] This presentation is ambiguously sexual (remember Lafew's description of skipping King Pippen) and ambiguously chaste. Helena's pregnant body belies the threat of male heterosexual obsolescence, and it also neutralizes the threat that tactile healing poses to distinctions of rank. If the healing process involves a mutual surrender or sacrifice and the opening of love's wound, then the King ought to fall in love with Helena, or she to seek *his* hand in return for effecting the cure. In contrast to Ariosto's and even Spenser's examples of tactile healing (Angelica loses her rank altogether, and Timias's unrequited love for Belphoebe threatens, although it does not diminish, distinctions of rank), Helena's fixing on Bertram as the object of her choice stabilizes the more frightening option of royal corruption by "a poor physician's daughter."

The ending of the play reflects these ambiguities. Nowhere is the adverb "well" made to work harder than in the play that punningly employs it in at least three different ways. "All yet *seems* well," concludes the king, where "all" is at once the King's mysterious malady, the relationship of Helena and Bertram, the putative future marriage of Diana to a suitor—as yet unnamed—of the King's choice and the health of the body politic. The King's condition (in both a physical and a grammatical sense) obviously marks doubt and irresolution within the world of the play. Bertram himself ends lamely and half-heartedly: "If she can make me know this clearly / I'll love her dearly, ever, ever dearly" (5.3.309–10). The weak end rhyme and the repetition of "ever" and "dearly" to make up the meter emphasize the impossibility of Bertram's request to know "clearly" what has happened, who is and who is not a virgin. Bertram's reluctant acceptance of his new bride suggests that Helena usurps the ban on instruments and dares to use the dangerous supplement, but that what is supplanted is not patriarchal power but female sexual pleasure. Maternity supplements and eventually supplants erotic joy. Sexual enjoyment is furthest from Helena's motives: "[her] Dian / [is] both herself and love" (1.3.207–8); deifying Diana, rather than Venus, as love's goddess, Helena redefines the meaning of married love, establishing herself as its chaste yet fertile priestess.

In *Orlando Furioso* and *The Faerie Queene*, the dialogue between *pucelage* or hymen and sexual innocence emphasizes the importance of the latter, suggesting female erotic joy and the possibility of mutual wounding and regard (what I have called a painful equality) as a legitimate reason and justification for married sexual love. Angelica may or may not have lost her hymen, according to the narrator, but with Medore she loses another kind of virginity, her sexual innocence, when she becomes aware of pleasure through touch, and falls in love. Medore suffers likewise from his wounding and healing, both at her hands, creating the hermaphroditically united figure who carves their names on every tree. Belphoebe always retains her technical purity, but her sexual innocence is briefly threatened when she is wounded by pity for Timias and angered at the sight of him "handling" Amoret's hurts, an awakening that seems to compromise her fierce purity but also enriches her understanding. Because Timias must always "avoid the ill," avoid both physical and emotional vulnerability, mutuality between the huntress and the humble squire is impossible. Amoret loses her hymen to Busirane, but is then revirginized in order to enjoy the simultaneous loss of technical and emotional virginity with Scudamour. Finally, Helena sacrifices *pucelage* or hymen during the bed-trick, but retains her emotional virginity, her ignorance of sexual pleasure. In Shakespeare's play, virginity is *only* hymen, only technical, and the justification for marriage is maternal, not sexual, desire. In this sense, Helena's situation resembles that of Timias: the potential for mutual regard disappears under royal or aristocratic diktat, and the barriers of both class and sex remain, like the other Diana's hymen in the play, intact until the end.

Chapter 4
The Subject of Touch: Medical Authority in Early Modern Midwifery
Eve Keller

In his 1733 *Essay on the Improvement of Midwifery*, the London surgeon Edmund Chapman tells the story of a "poor unhappy woman" who had been plagued by violent, periodic pains in her belly and back for seven days. She was attended by "several persons of an inferior Class in the Practice of Physick," as well as by a number of midwives, but everyone, including the woman herself, was, Chapman says, "confounded, and at a loss," unable to make sense of her condition.[1] When "at last" he was called, Chapman sent out all but a few of the "numerous company" that had gathered about the patient and then proceeded to establish the following information through a remarkable physical exam:

Where the Rima Magna should have been there was only the Appearance of a small Slit or Aperture ... Nor was there the least Sign of the Clitoris or Nymphae to be seen or felt. This imperfect vagina, or rather slit, before mentioned, was just big enough to receive one Finger, with which I endeavoured to find out the Mouth of the Womb, but in vain; for on the Hinder-part, or towards the Os Sacrum, there was no passage at all, whilst Forwards, and under the Os Pubis, it admitted my Finger, without much Resistance. At this Part, (which was also very dry,) there was not the least Force, Pain, or Swelling; whilst wholly Backwards, at the Anus, there were all. The Anus was dilated to a great degree, (even enough to receive my Hand,) tho' very thick and much swelled quite round. In that Part too there was a large Tumour which bore hard down, and even out of the Body at every Pain. (89)

By performing his manual maneuvers, Chapman realized that the woman's distended intestine harbored a child pressing to be born. After allowing the midwives to "see and feel how things were," Chapman made an aperture with his lancet, dilated the orifice with his fingers and delivered the woman "of a child at the anus." The "unfortunate woman," subject of this "strange and unnatural" case, he tells his readers, was "quite spent, before I was called in"; she lived two or three days, and then she died. In closing, however, Chapman suggests knowingly that "she might have been saved, had the Operation been performed sooner, and in time" (90).

Chapman clearly has some lessons to teach with this "strange and unnatural" case, the most obvious among them the need to call for appropriate help in a timely manner and the importance of surgical intervention in certain medical contexts. But surely more is going on here. Told as a first person narrative, the case allows Chapman to construct himself as the solitary authority in an otherwise communal endeavor. Where others display dangerous ignorance, Chapman achieves unequivocal certainty. By touching the woman inside and out, Chapman establishes precise and exclusive knowledge both of her strange anatomy and of what's going on inside it. Eliding any illicit or unnatural associations of his manual penetrations—his finger in her slit, his hand up her anus—Chapman presents himself as a paradigm of decorous rationality: by touching what the others gathered have not, he acquires privileged knowledge and acts with unchallenged efficiency; any irrationality is displaced onto the others in the room and onto the "strange and unnatural" body of the woman herself.

Chapman's case history—and particularly its reliance on touch to construct Chapman's exclusive authority in the doomed birthing room— suggests the need to complicate somewhat the often-rehearsed story of the emergence of male-midwifery in the late seventeenth and early eighteenth centuries. Typically told as something of a morality tale, the story appears in one of two opposing forms: in the early histories of obstetrics starting in the late nineteenth century, the medical men are educated and compassionate and their eventual triumph over ignorant, intrusive midwives is understood as an aspect of the medical Enlightenment.[2] After the 1960s, when women began to write about the topic, the men become self-serving and avaricious, wielding instruments as if as weapons, and their forcible ejection of capable women from the only profession in which they historically held a monopoly is understood as an instance of women's social oppression.[3] Assessing the history of the debate, Lisa Cody has neatly encapsulated its opposing evaluative terms: the emergence of male midwives is an example of either "medical glory" or "gory misogyny."[4]

If in recent years the debate has become somewhat less of an exercise in polemic, its assumption that gender drives the story of early-modern midwifery and should therefore drive its analysis has not dramatically changed. Adrian Wilson, for example, has argued that male-midwifery could have succeeded only if women wanted it to, since it was typically women who determined whom to call to their deliveries and when.[5] Wilson's claim that childbirth was "still a collective female affair" even as men overtook the profession adds nuance to the story, but the story is still primarily a gendered one.[6] Even as careful a scholar as Doreen Evenden is willing to caricature the efforts of the eighteenth-century man-midwife: "By the 1750s," she says, "midwives' traditional, practical skill proved no match for the claims of the male midwife, waiting in the wings with his shiny instruments and promises of 'scientific expertise.' "[7] Modern scholarship seems to replicate the gender conflict that underlies the history it studies: male scholars analyze with varying degrees of approval the emergence of male-midwifery, while women scholars analyze the same set of circumstances with varying levels of disdain.

To be sure, there is ample reason to read the story of the shifts in early modern midwifery practice in terms of the gender divide between male and female practitioners. Jane Sharp, who in 1671 was the first woman to publish a midwifery manual in English, explicitly addressed her guide to her "sisters," the "midwives of England," and, while she "cannot deny, that men in some things may come to a greater perfection of knowledge than women ordinarily can," she nonetheless claims women's authority in the birthing room: it is, she says, "the natural propriety of women to be much seeing into that Art."[8] Sarah Stone, writing over sixty years later and the first Englishwoman to write an original midwifery text, similarly speaks to her "sisters in the profession" and rails against the "boyish pretenders" who, she complains, typically enter the birthing room "when the work is near finish'd; and then the Midwife, who has taken all the pains, is accounted of little value, and the young men command all the praise."[9] The works of these midwives attest both to women's articulate awareness of a gender-based shift in their profession and to their ability to combat it with gender-based arguments.

But even if some of the midwifery texts of the period were written as explicit endorsements or rejections of the entrance of men into a traditionally female profession, the gender-based conflict between practitioners is not the only—or even the predominant—ground of conflict in them. Despite the increasingly vociferous complaints about men in the profession, even in the 1730s the majority of midwives were women, and midwifery books written by both men and women were addressed to women (both female midwives and childbearing women generally) rather than to men (who arguably needed the most instruction, given that they could not have had much experience in attending normal deliveries).[10] And if many of the texts detail the horrors committed by ignorant female midwives, so do many detail the butchery of unskilled men, both midwives and surgeons. Although he has much to say against meddlesome midwives, the seventeenth-century physician and man-midwife Percival Willughby includes in his *Observations in Midwifery* the story of a gentlewoman who "rotted in the womb" and subsequently died after a "man midwife" inadvertently wounded her with his crochet during a delivery. Willughby complains that "his work was carried on with much unhandsomenes, and accompanied with great ignorance."[11] Similarly, half a century later, Edmund Chapman recounts the story of a man-midwife who used the hook to extract a child he had mistakenly taken for dead; when the child emerged from the womb alive, says Chapman, "the wounded infant by its cries and agonies gave much greater pain to the lamenting mother than she had felt before" (Preface). Stories such as these— written by men about the horrifying errors of men in the birthing room— suggest that to think of the tensions of these texts exclusively in terms of the gender of the practitioners (the men want to oust the women; the women want to ward off the men) is, if clearly not wrong, then at least somewhat limiting.

One way to expand the analysis of the manifold tensions of the midwifery texts of the period is to consider the ways in which they negotiate the tenuous borders dividing medical fields. Traditionally, midwives were called upon to handle all normal deliveries; if a problem arose—say, because of prolonged obstruction or uncontrolled bleeding—so that the mother's life was perceived to be in danger and the child was assumed to be dead, a surgeon would be called in to extract the child forcibly (and in pieces, if necessary) with obstetrical instruments such as the hook and crochet.[12] At least in theory, the roles of midwives and surgeons were fairly discrete, and physicians generally were not involved in process of childbirth. One of the innovations of late seventeenth- to early eighteenth-century midwifery was a gradual diluting of this divide among differing types of practitioners. As the position of the so-called man-midwife began to form—as, that is, physicians began to attend deliveries and as surgeons began to attend normal deliveries—the boundaries that distinguished among and therefore defined the different occupations began to loosen. If this process promised an expanded arena of medical practice for physicians and surgeons, it also jeopardized the integrity of midwifery as a discrete endeavor. Regarded in this way, the threat posed by the emergence of man-midwifery was understood to be a threat to the preserve of midwifery as a distinct field, at least as much as it was perceived to be an attack on the expertise of women as practitioners.

Jane Sharp's response to this threat is therefore twofold: she is interested in asserting the privileged authority of women *as women* in the birthing room; but, reacting to a perceived effort to break down the boundaries of midwifery from competing practitioners outside her field, Sharp asserts, at least implicitly, the right of midwives to perform the obstetrical functions of surgeons, thereby endeavoring to expand the boundaries of her field from within. Most of Sharp's chapter on "rules for Women that are come to their Labour," for example, is filled with general instructions on how to use "Chirurgeons Instruments" to extract presumably dead fetuses. Yet, oddly for someone presumably seeking to educate, Sharp provides very little actual instruction. Here she describes how to remove a dead fetus that presents feet first:

If the feet come first fasten the hook upon the bone above the privy parts, called os pubis, or by some rib or back bones, or breast bones; then draw it not forth, but hold the Instrument in your left hand, and then fasten another hook upon some other part of the Child right against the first, and draw gently both together that the Child might come equally, moving it from one side to another until you have drawn it forth altogether; but often guide it with your fore-finger well anointed; if it stick or stop any where, take higher hold still with your hooks upon the dead child. (148–49)

Surely there's not enough information here actually to teach anyone wielding an instrument. But by its very insufficiency as instruction the passage asserts its unspoken claim that midwives have both the right and the ability to use the instruments of a surgeon. Sharp similarly tells her "sisters" that in certain cases they "must divide the skull and take it out by pieces with instruments for that purpose"(149): if no midwife could learn by that sentence how to perform a craniotomy, she would at least learn that it is within her province to do so. In devoting the majority of her chapter on "rules for Women when near their Labour" to the midwife's use of surgical instruments—and yet in not providing any really useable information about their employment—Sharp implicitly claims that midwives, regardless whether they are men or women, can assume the obstetrical work of surgeons.

That such paucity of practical information in early modern midwifery books is not unique to Sharp suggests that, if we want to get a fuller sense of the cultural work they actually performed, we need to look beyond their authors' routine claims that they wrote the books strictly for educative purposes. Doreen Evenden has demonstrated the existence of an elaborate apprenticeship system in London that would have obviated the need for instructional books altogether; considering published material nearly irrelevant for her purposes, Evenden relies exclusively on archival records to re-construct her picture of seventeenth-century London midwifery. Contemporary writers—even those who published—would probably have agreed with Evenden's conclusions: Sharp introduces herself on the title page of her midwifery manual as a "Practitioner in the Art of Midwifery above thirty years," resting her authority exclusively on her years of practice rather than on any knowledge she gleaned from books; Stone admits that it's not "improper" to read anatomy, but, she claims, had she not been instructed by her mother and been her apprentice for six years, "it would have signified little."[13] Both these writers are here pitting their practical experience against book learning in order to establish their authority over the pretensions of Latined men; but for authors of published books to discount the usefulness of books to their practice suggests as well that the work accomplished by those books was not purely instructional. Helen King sums up her sense of the midwifery manuals as a group: "Midwives books' could . . . be described as a combination of antiquarianism, irrelevance, salaciousness and the blindingly obvious. There is very little on midwifery itself."[14] Though perhaps somewhat of an overstatement, King is surely right to note that these books cannot logically be taken simply as textbooks, revealing what practitioners really did.

The work of social and medical historians has thus begun to suggest the need to assess these texts in other ways, pointing us toward the value of reading them not as straightforward records of history but as primarily rhetorical constructs, as public performances put on for commercial consumption, intended not so much to offer instruction as to promulgate certain images and identities of the practitioners. That they were essentially commercial ventures—more than altruistic efforts in education—is repeatedly evident. The enormously prolific Nicolas Culpeper characteristically presents himself as a medical reformer struggling against the presumed monopoly on knowledge and care possessed by university-trained physicians, but this image must be qualified by his manifest interest in selling lots of books: he routinely refers his readers to the many other books he's written or translated, stressing the importance of his works as a group.[15] Similarly, eighty years later, Chapman announces his wondrous ability to extract obstructed infants alive with the use of the fillet, but, being an instrument of his own invention, he refuses to divulge the details of its construction or the manner of its use (30). Presumably the strategy would encourage women to seek his expertise in their time of labor. These vernacular texts, in other words, were chiefly commercial ventures, so that, whatever actual medical information they conveyed, they functioned to construct and commodify a public image of the practitioner of childbirth.

The rhetorical construction of early modern midwives is of course only one factor in the gradual emergence of medical authority in the early modern period. Aside from making claims about the empirical success of treatments, practitioners sought legitimacy through a range of cultural means—by affiliating with prestigious or charitable institutions, for example, or by adhering to accepted codes of gentlemanly conduct.[16] But a rhetorical analysis of vernacular midwifery texts affords a relatively unexplored opportunity to examine with some specificity the manner and minutia of a practitioner's self-production.[17] Attention to the rhetorical details of the narratives that comprise them turns books about the delivering of babies into efforts at erecting the public personae of early modern medical culture.

My interest here is in a particular subsection of these books, namely a group of early case histories written between the 1670s and the 1730s. Until the late seventeenth century, English midwifery texts were largely unoriginal, being mostly translations and compilations of Latin and continental sources. They were furthermore written didactically, giving putative instruction on what one was to do in any given circumstance, rather than recounting what the practitioner did him- or herself. But by the end of the seventeenth century a new kind of midwifery text began to appear, both in manuscript and in printed form, which focused on the particular experiences of individual practitioners. These are among the first collections of medical case histories in English, and they differed from their predecessors both in being largely original and in their focus on the character and accomplishments of the practitioners who wrote them. Considered with an eye to questions of character, the productive dynamics of these texts shifts from the relation between competing male and female practitioners to the relations among practitioners—whether male or female—and between the primary practitioner and the childbearing woman. This is still a gendered story, but it is perhaps a more subtle one than those that have been told about the tensions between traditional midwives and male practitioners. For the gender issues here have less to do with the sex of the practitioners and more to do with the relative subject status of the practitioner and his or her patient, and, most particularly, with the medical techniques that establish these positions. As I will argue, the rhetorical representation of the techniques of touch, through a gradual accretion of associations, produces an unprecedented authority for the medical practitioner of childbirth. As it is rhetorically constructed in these texts, touch, traditionally a mark of mere manual labor, becomes over time a sign of almost magical prowess, so that midwifery, historically among the least prestigious of medical practices, becomes the place where the modern image of the medical miracle-worker is born.

· · ·

In order to get a sense of the rhetorical effect of a practitioner's touch in the context of childbirth, we need first to get a sense of the nearly complete absence of physical contact in contemporary medicine generally. As physicians typically performed it in the seventeenth and eighteenth centuries, medical diagnosis made almost no use of physical examination of the patient. Roy Porter describes the typical medical encounter, in which the patient's telling of his own history was paramount:

[The patient] would tell the doctor what was wrong: when and how the complaint had started, what events had precipitated it, the characteristic pains and symptoms, its periodicity. The patient would also describe to his physician key lifestyle features—his eating and sleeping habits, his bowel motions, recent emotional traumas and so forth, not to mention the perhaps slightly indelicate matter of his indulgence in home-made, quack, or patent medicines.[18]

A physician might make some limited physical contact—for example, feeling the pulse to determine its character—and he would make a gross visual assessment of a patient's condition, perhaps noting skin color or the evidence of lesions—but any physical examination was entirely secondary to a patient's verbal reporting of his condition. Porter even notes that William Cullen, the top medical practitioner in eighteenth-century Edinburgh, routinely diagnosed his patients by post.[19]

This absence of physical contact between practitioner and patient had less to do with norms of modesty than it did with an interest in maintaining distinctions among types of practitioners: licensed physicians were university men, trained in the rigors of intellectual labor; it was not within their province to perform manual labor, which was carried out by surgeons.[20] In the highly diversified marketplace of early modern medical practice—a marketplace that included not only physicians, surgeons, and apothecaries, but also midwives, uroscopists, herbalists, empirics, astrologers, lithotomists, and others—a housewife or wisewoman of a village might provide care as readily as a licensed physician, and self-diagnosis and self-treatment were not at all uncommon.[21] But given this diversity—or maybe precisely because of it—there was some effort to enforce a divide between those who thought and spoke and those who acted and touched. A physician's physical examination and diagnosis did not become an integral aspect of the medical encounter until the nineteenth century; before that, speech was more important than touch, and it was primarily the speech of the patient that mattered.[22] As W. F. Bynum argues, "the patient's own description of his illness was the pivotal point in the diagnostic process."[23]

To some extent, the practice of midwifery differed significantly from the practice of other kinds of medicine, for midwifery was always "a work of the Hands," as one man-midwife put it.[24] Midwifery's associations with manual labor are in part what kept physicians out of the field for so many years: surgeons, who already worked with their hands, might be called in to take care of obstructed births with their instruments, but physicians, being thinkers and not touchers, did not belong. Yet even within the context of a profession that required physical contact, it was still a patient's telling of her condition that was paramount: she determined when her child quickened in the womb, and she was considered able to inform others whether it had died. So important was the childbearing woman's telling of her body that Wilson wants to call her a "participant" rather than a "patient" in the process of birth.[25]

The technical innovations and rediscoveries of seventeenth- and eighteenth-century midwifery that involved the use of touch—such as podalic version, pelvic manipulation, and the use of the forceps and fillet—changed more than the norms of handling difficult deliveries and the rules for who got to handle them.[26] These shifts in medical practice, as they are recorded in the case histories and treatises of those who promoted them, also produced shifts in the self-presentation of the practitioners and in their constructed connection to others engaged in the birthing process. Whatever the historical "reality" of the relative authority and engagement of the people involved in the birthing process, the childbearing woman is decreasingly present as a subject in these texts; her verbal participation becomes either irrelevant or obviated altogether; gossips and competing practitioners, be they other midwives or physicians called in before the author's arrival, are similarly constructed as a backdrop to the author's self-construction. Advocating the advantages of touch and yet seeking to establish their authority, practitioners had to counter the cultural norms that aligned touch at best with manual labor and at worst—given what they were touching—with outright lechery.[27] In these texts, touch gets reconceptualized, to become newly aligned with the masculine attributes of reason and decorous action; the generating woman gets positioned as the generally silent object of a practitioner's magisterial performance, and a refashioned image of the midwife emerges: one who is self-sufficient, possessed of native authority, and power-fully effective in the world of action by a unique ability to merge mind and body, knowledge and practice.

Percival Willughby was a practicing physician and man-midwife in both London and Derby during the mid- to late seventeenth century. Toward the end of his career and over a period of about a decade, he wrote up his *Observations in Midwifery*, which offers practical advice in the art of midwifery based on and demonstrated by one hundred and fifty case histories.[28] The text as a whole makes two basic points: first, that in normal deliveries, midwives are not to interfere in the process of birth, that they are "but nature's servants in all their performances, and that they must attend her time and motion" (5); and second, that when difficulty does arise, because of obstruction or malpresentation, midwives should perform what Willughby calls "the handy operation"(1)—or podalic version—a method of manually turning an infant to a foot presentation, which allows a practitioner to grab hold of a leg and, by exerting traction, to effect delivery.

Throughout the text, Willughby seeks to distinguish himself from the general cast of midwives by relying on the superior status of intellectual over manual labor and by evoking the mutually exclusive associations of each: Willughby, who works with his head, is rational and effective; midwives, who work with their hands, are dangerously intrusive and aggressive. Touch is thus marked as both female and vulgar. Yet Willughby himself advocates "the handy operation," and he wants midwives to learn it as well. So he must somehow endorse his engagement in manual labor and still distinguish it from the normative labor of midwives. Over the course of the 150 cases he describes, Willughby accomplishes this paradoxical conceptual design by performing two contradictory rhetorical maneuvers: he contrasts himself against other midwives first by setting his compassionate rational labor against their aggressive manual labor and then by ascribing to his manual labor the attributes of reason: he too works with his hands, but his hands, un-like those of meddlesome midwives, are ever guided by his head.

Willughby claims he has learned from experience that in most cases midwives do best when they do least, forbearing any interference in a delivery. That midwives have not themselves sufficiently learned this lesson he demonstrates in his characterization of their intrusive handiwork. Early on in his treatise, for example, he recounts the story of Dorothy North, who, "being great with child, was afflicted with some disquiets in her belly":

Severall midwives were called to assist her; one of them thrust up her hand, and made great struggling in her body; at the taking of it forth, her hand was all over bloody, and this midwife made great vaunts of her skil, and doings, and said, That the Child did stick to the woman's back, but that shee had removed it.

At my coming, I found that the waters had not flowed, and that the womb was closed; I gave her a milky clyster that much abated her paines. I instructed one of the milder sort, that was left alone with her, what to do, and what to observe, and in-treated her to bee gentle and patient with the woman, and to stay the appointed time, assuring her, That the fruit would fall off it-self, when that it was full ripe.

Some two or three dayes after my departure, shee was well delivered by this midwife, but her child was dead. (7)

The midwife who precedes him at the labor acts with both unthinking aggression and unjust self-promotion: she "thrust up her hand," "struggl[ed]" within the woman's body, removed her hand "all over bloody," yet nonetheless "made great vaunts of her skil." Willughby by contrast uses his head: all the verbs that describe his actions indicate the considered rationality of his behavior: where the midwife thrust and made vaunts, Willughby "found," "instructed," and "intreated" the midwife "to be gentle and patient." And though he presumably did perform a manual examination to determine that "the womb was closed," he entirely occludes his touch from the case. The rhetorical effect of the absence of Willughby's hand underscores the contrast he constructs between himself and the midwife already present: she, who thrusts her hand, is associated with violence, haste, and self-promotion; he, who seemingly uses only his head, is associated with compassion, patience, and modesty.

Having thus affiliated his efforts with the head—with the rational intellect—Willughby must shift his self-presentation when he comes to re-count his own manual interventions in delivery. In contrast to the typi-cal midwife who, having quickly "daubed" her hands with oil, is given to "haling . . . pulling, and stretching" women's bodies, Willughby seems quite the gentleman, instructing midwives instead to "slide" their hands "anointed with oil" into a woman's womb (6). In recounting his delivery of a woman who had been in labor for three days before his arrival, Willughby describes how "between the child's head, and her body, I put my two fingers, and lifted up the skin toward the fundament over the child's head. Then it pleased God to suffer the child's head to slide into the world" (61). Compared to the mid-wives who stretch the parts and thrust up their hands, Willughby's manual maneuvers seem as gentle as they are efficient. His actions are both deliberate and moderated, and, presumably because of this, his manual intervention becomes the medium for achieving God's ends: lifting up the skin as if it were a veil, Willughby reveals the child beneath and thus makes it possible for God to suffer its birth.

Willughby's instructions on how to perform "the handy operation" similarly attempt to refashion the hand's associations with unthinking aggression. A midwife is told, in reducing an arm presentation, "leasurely to slide up her anointed hand over the child's arme, and gently to force it upward" (92); elsewhere, he advises that if "you have a desire to turn the child, when that it hath too great a head," you should

Slide up your hand anointed into the woman's body, and, afterward, spread it flat upon the child's head, and gently force the child back . . . until you have roome enough to search for the feet, and having found a foot, draw it leasurely forth, holding the foot in your hand griped [sic] between your fingers. The infant's body will turn easily round, and so bee drawn forth. (75)

Willughby's recourse here and elsewhere to the oxymoron "to gently force" suggests the rhetorical struggle he's engaged in—to make the obstetrical hand an instrument of gentility and leisure. In striving to do so, Willughby strives as well to make of himself an expert practitioner whose manual skills are not opposed to, but are rather manifestations of, a reasoned and deliberate mind.

Willughby advocates manual techniques that were intended to reduce the need for the destructive instruments of obstetrical surgeons. By urging the use of podalic version, Willughby seeks means to deliver living children in birthing situations that might otherwise have resulted in the death of the infant, the mother, or both. The identity he constructs is based precisely on his reliance on the power he assigns to the combined effects of head and hand, intellect and experience: he is rational, prescient, kind, patient, effective, and pre-eminently in control. Even his occasional admissions of failure add to his constructed subjectivity—he is a reasonable man, man enough to admit his mistakes.

Willughby was a physician as well as a man-midwife, so, theoretically at least, his aim in writing his text was not so much to replace the office of the midwife as to change some of its standard techniques. In the 1730s, however, two books on midwifery were published that were more explicitly intended to limit the midwife's role. Edmund Chapman and William Giffard were the first two to announce in print the uses of the forceps, an instrument that had been used secretly by the Chamberlen family for several generations and that was reputed to be able to aid in the delivery of obstructed head presentations. As obstetrical surgeons, their practices would have been generally limited to emergency situations, when the life of the mother was thought to be in imminent danger. But the forceps made it at least theoretically possible for an obstetrical surgeon to deliver an obstructed infant alive, if, among other things, the surgeon was called in early enough to save it. Thus, although both men claim to be writing to educate midwives, they seem to want most to urge midwives, as Chapman says, to "send early for Advice upon the Appearance of Danger and Difficulty" (Preface). Seeking therefore to delimit the role of midwives to "normal" deliveries and to expand the role of surgeons, both authors are boldly self-promoting, and both construct themselves as exclusive authorities against a diminished or degraded female presence.

Chapman announces at the beginning of his text that midwives should make themselves masters of the forceps or the fillet, a related instrument of his own invention. Such knowledge is crucial, he claims, because when difficult births cannot be effected by the hand alone, they can be accomplished with the aid of these instruments, which, he says, are perfectly safe and innocent (Preface). Yet rather than teaching midwives how to use the instruments or perform manual version, Chapman trains his attention on his own exquisite achievements in childbirth. Although, like Willughby, he occasionally admits committing some mistakes (as when he accidentally "snapped" a child's arm in an effort to extract it [58]), he generally comes off less as a conscientious practitioner advocating a particular point of view about medical practice than as the self-proclaimed hero of numerous medical dramas.

Chapman's astonishing talents are most obviously manifest in his repeated assertions of the "great ease" with which he routinely effects difficult deliveries. When a woman is unable to deliver after several hours of effort, Chapman determines that it is "necessary to have recourse to Art, and so with great ease as well to my patient as to my self, [I] passed my hand, and in one minute delivered her of the child" (55). Entirely avoiding any information about what precisely he did when he "passed [his] hand" into the woman's body, Chapman's focus is on his own accomplishment: a one-minute delivery of a child the woman couldn't herself produce after hours of exertion. In another case, Chapman describes the history of a woman who had two or three times been delivered of obstructed head presentations by a man who used the hook to extract them. At her next labor, Chapman was called in early; finding that, although the child lay in the right posture, it "made no advance," Chapman receives permission to use art: "I now had leave to act as I should think fit; upon which I put the woman in a proper posture . . . then gently passing my hand into the womb, I took the child by the feet, and so delivered her in two or three minutes, with great ease and safety" (53–54). This time we hear in general terms what he does with his hand in the woman's womb—he takes the child by the feet. But how does he do this? How does he find the feet? How does he turn the child in the womb? The lack of instructional detail only highlights Chapman's unparalleled accomplishment: his delivery "with great ease" in "two or three minutes" of a woman who previously had to suffer the surgeon's hook.

Touch, it seems, is being stylized in these cases as a mechanism of medical efficiency. A practitioner passes his hand into a woman's womb, but we, as readers, are made to imagine not the actual, material mess of that touch—the waters and blood of birth—but rather the remarkable efficacy of a medical man's prowess. In the process of being purified of its associations with labor and matter, the practitioner's touch bequeaths a power that is meant to mark incontestable efficiency and authority.

That Chapman's touch confers—or should confer—unique authority in the birthing room is evident from his descriptions of what ensues when authority is not granted to him. In the case of a clergyman's wife, for example, who "had a sudden discharge of some ounces of blood from the womb" in the seventh month of her pregnancy, Chapman's warnings "both to her and her Husband" that she was in mortal danger went unheeded. He was therefore not permitted "to have the liberty to do as [he] judged proper," which was to extract the infant "by art." By the time he was called back to the woman's house, therefore, it was "too late": the woman was seized with violent flooding, and, though he was able to deliver her "in less than a minute," the "unhappy willful Lady was lost" (59–61). The woman dies, in other words, because of what Chapman presents as the obvious stupidity of the balance of power in the birthing room. Clearly, he knows both first and best: he knows that a detached placenta is causing her "flooding" and that it threatens her life. But though he implies that his superior knowledge should grant him authority, he must attend upon the wishes of the family; they must grant him the "liberty to do as [he] judge[s] proper." The suggestion is that it is both unjust and dangerous to subject Chapman's inherent "liberty" and earned authority to the uninformed wishes of others.

The fact that Chapman narrates his cases in a way that consistently maximizes the legitimacy of his implicit claim to authority and mastery does not mean that he occludes entirely the experience of the expectant mother. Indeed, the sufferings of the mother are everywhere apparent in Chapman's record, from the "poor tender-hearted mother" forced to see her child "brought in the world a cripple" when a man-midwife "lopped off" its presenting arm because he mistakenly believed the child to be dead, to the "young healthy mother cut off in the bloom of life and cast into the cold arms of death, just as she was about to clasp her first-born in her own": she died because the midwife tore out her "matrix" having mistaken it for an afterbirth "stuck" inside her (31, 83–84). But his recourse to melodrama ("tender-hearted mother," "bloom of life," "cold arms of death") only underscores his own heroics: tales of woeful mothers are depicted at least in part to advance his polemic against competing practitioners—both men and women, surgeons and midwives—who, it seems, needlessly torture women already in distress. Thus his sympathetic portrayal of childbearing women works to advance his own self-construction as an obstetrical hero: he comes, with hand and tool, to relieve "in a minute or two" the dire sufferings of women.

If Chapman constructs the mother as a suffering subject in order to advance the lessons of his own heroics, Giffard nearly effaces the mother altogether or simply reduces her to an extrapolation of her parts. Although most of the 225 cases he recounts in his posthumously published *Cases in Midwifery* do not involve the use of what are called "Mr. Giffard's extractors," the first case in which he describes using them successfully neatly demonstrates the rhetorical relation between the practitioner's touch and the mother's disappearance as a subject:

June the 28th, 1728. I was called upon to go to see a poor Woman in Labour: the Midwife told me the Pains were short, with long intervals. I felt her pulse, which was regular and strong, and upon Touching her, found the Child to present its Head, but high: . . . the next morning I . . . found the Child but little advanced, her pulse very quick and labouring, and the Womb very much spread, so that I could entirely pass my Fingers round the Head to the Ears, for it was no ways engaged, but loose; the Vagina was large, she having had seven or eight Children before; wherefore considering that her pulse grew languid, and that her strength decreased, I thought it advisable to attempt her Delivery. I endeavoured to press the child back, that I might be able to turn it and get the Feet; but it was so locked at the shoulders, I was not able to move it; whereupon I passed my Extractor and drew it with much difficulty forwards without the Labia, and then taking hold of the Head on each side with my Hand (which cannot be done whilst it lies in the Vagina) I drew the shoulders out; the other parts readily followed. . . . The Child was born alive.[29]

In the scene Giffard conjures, the childbearing woman is simply a "poor Woman in Labour" who, after her initial introduction, fades from the case as a subject. Other than conferring with the midwife, Giffard's interactions are entirely with body parts rather than with people. The mother's absence from the story even registers grammatically: after saying that "the midwife told

[him] that the pains were short," Giffard says, "I felt her pulse . . . and upon Touching her, found the Child to present its Head." Although the context demands that the repeated "her" refer to the woman in labor, she's been excised from the rhetorical reconstruction of the scene, so the grammatical antecedent of the pronouns is, illogically, the midwife. This grammatical glitch recurs in the next sentence as well, in which the only and absurd antecedent of the "her" in "her pulse" is the Child. By the time we hear something of the woman's history—that she has had seven or eight children before—she seems at best an extrapolation of body parts and functions: vagina large, womb spread, pulse strong or languid. The woman simply does not exist in the case history as a complete presence—he never speaks to her, gleaning nearly all his information by touching her parts—and, unlike the child whose fate we learn, the woman's outcome is unrevealed. Although it's not always the case that the childbearing woman is entirely absent from Giffard's text—we might learn, for example, that a woman died from flooding because the midwives didn't know to call him early enough or that a woman "recovered very fast" after he revived her with "the use of proper Cordials"— she is rarely presented as volitional (62, 72). Agency is transferred to Giffard, whose cases record his efforts with wombs, infants, and extractors, but not per se with mothers.

I am trying to point to a pattern in the midwifery case histories of the late seventeenth and early eighteenth centuries in which the construction of medical authority emerges as the effect of a new reliance on touch and a newly imagined network of associations for touch. In the common rhetorical maneuvers of these texts, touch creates an image of the medical practitioner that contrasts sharply with what we know about the practice of medicine at the time: whereas medicine generally and childbirth particularly were essentially communal endeavors, these case histories typically construct an individualized and exclusive expertise for their authors. The claim to this authority is based on the superior knowledge that touch generates, which allows the practitioner to offer diagnoses that the others collected in the birthing room generally either don't know, deny, or cannot even fathom. The effect is moreover compounded by the rhetorical manipulation of arguably the most important subject in the birthing room, namely the childbearing woman, who is made either into a victim in need of heroic rescue or, more dramatically, into a mangle of body parts confidently prodded by the practitioner.

Considered collectively, the medical practitioners that emerge from these rhetorical patterns form a fairly familiar identity: one possessed of individual sovereignty, rational prowess, and discrete manual dexterity; one who can handle, with patience and efficiency, crucial moments in life and death. This, paradigmatically, is the Enlightenment hero, who, having sought knowledge from books, values equally the knowledge of experience, who is endowed with a native liberty that only the ignorant would deny, and who, because of that knowledge and the exercise of that liberty, is able to be generous and compassionate to those who suffer.

This is of course a masculine model more than a generically human one, and the construction of this model in the texts of male practitioners who were making their way into a workplace that had previously been exclusively female suggests the importance of gender in the process of its construction. But the gender issue here is not simply tied to the sex of the competing practitioners, because the rhetorical effect of this model is to generate medical authority even as it evokes a mode of masculine identity. I am arguing, in other words, that medical authority gets established in the birthing room as the agents who practice there represent themselves—regardless of their sex—in accordance with contemporary ideals of masculine identity. And that the subtle rhetorical manipulations of the new techniques of touch, precisely because they collectively permit the alignment of the practitioner with both mental and manual power, are instrumental in the generation of this unprecedented authority.

That touch is a key mechanism for making medical authority is neatly demonstrated by the work of Sarah Stone, the first woman to write an original midwifery text in English, whose collection of forty case histories, published in 1737, contains what is perhaps the most exaggerated version of this constructed identity. Keenly aware of the gender politics of her profession, Stone addresses her treatise to her "sisters," warning against the embarrassment and danger of exposing oneself to the "boyish Pretenders" in the field who, at best, derive their knowledge of women's bodies from "dissecting the Dead" and necessarily lack the "natural Sympathy" that exists among women who "have gone thro the Pangs of Childbearing" (vii, xiv–xv). Stone considers men inadequate for the job of midwifery and believes that, with the proper education, female midwives will be able to "deliver in difficult labours, as well as those that are not so, which in turn will keep women from being "forced to send for a Man" (ix, vi). The elaborate title of her book gives a sense of what she thinks of its contents:

A complete practice of midwifery, [which includes, in addition to] forty cases . . . selected from many others, in the course of a very extensive practice, many necessary cautions and useful instructions, proper to be observed in the most dangerous and critical exigencies, as well when the delivery is difficult in its own nature, as when it becomes so by the rashness or ignorance of unexperienc'd pretenders.

Stone, it seems, intends her book to provide precisely the education midwives need to keep them from being "forced" to call on men; her forty cases will serve as exempla: this is what I did in this difficult instance; do the same and you won't need men. But rather than provide the advertised education, the text works hardest to create an authoritative image of Stone herself.

Her very first "observation" sets the pattern:

At Bridgewater, Somersetshire, 1703. I was sent for the Huntspill, to a Farmer's wife, who had been in Labour three days: her pains were declining, and she reduced to the utmost degree of weakness; not having been in Bed all that time, (which is the common, but very bad, practice of the country midwives.) When I came, I found her spirits quite exhausted; and her midwife, being also fatigued, was in a sound sleep. I laid the Woman on the Bed, and by Touching her, found the Child lay on the Os Pubis (or share-bone). The Waters being gone, made the remaining part of her Labour the more difficult: however, relieving her Child from the Os Pubis, which strengthen'd her pains, I deliver'd her of a Daughter alive, and that in the space of three hours; to the grand surprise of her Midwife, when awake, who seem'd glad the Child was born alive, she believing it dead the day before." (1–2)

We have here all the by now familiar elements: a woman exhausted and in danger and a typically incompetent country midwife who here sleeps through her patient's decline. In the context of this exhaustion—the others have, it seems, given up, the midwife believing the child to be dead—Stone is all action and determination; she is the subject of all the active verbs in the story: I came, I found, I laid, I deliver'd. Stone's success is due to her "Touching"—since it's that touch that shows her that the child lies on the share-bone—but Stone provides no information at all either on how to touch to determine the child's position or on how to remove the child from the share-bone. So what lesson is taught here? What about midwifery is a reader to learn from this "observation"? When others sleep, Stone moves to action.

Again, Stone is called to a shoemaker's wife. She finds her in so "deplorable" a condition that all her friends have given her over to death. Says Stone: "I touched her, and assur'd them all, that, with God's assistance, I did not doubt of delivering her in two hours; which I accordingly did: both Mother and Child did well" (12). Here Stone seems nearly divine: merely by touching the woman, Stone is somehow able to know the future (that she will deliver the woman in two hours) and to perform an apparent miracle: the delivery of child from mother and mother from death. Without any information about how or where to touch a laboring woman, Stone's educative project is belied: her rhetorical use of touch is purely in the service of her own self-construction: only she touches, only she knows, only she does, so only she succeeds. Touch in these cases seems less like a specific medical maneuver than like a mode of medical magic, and the practitioner who performs that magic seems not simply the rational hero of a medical enlightenment, but more nearly the wonder-working hero of medical myth.

After the 1730s, men increasingly entered the profession of midwifery, but their rise to medical prominence was neither easy nor swift. Resistance came from female midwives who derided the men's reliance on instruments and denounced them as patent dangers, but it came also and increasingly from men, deeply suspicious of the art of touching, who condemned male-midwifery as an only barely disguised indulgence in sexual license.[30] That male-midwifery gradually overcame these obstacles, evolving eventually into the field of obstetrics, was due to a combination of social forces. Especially in well-to-do areas of cities like London, male midwives were thought to be superior to their female counterparts both because of their access to formal education and because of their advertised skills in using costly instruments that enabled them to handle successfully difficult as well as normal deliveries. But these early collections of case histories add another aspect to this already gendered story: when read not as tracts intended to provide an education in the practice of midwifery, but rather as rhetorical performances that construct newly fashioned identities for their authorial subjects, these case histories collectively demonstrate an important avenue for asserting medical authority. Touching the silenced body of a childbearing woman, a practitioner is newly made, self-born as the singular subject of the birthing room.

Chapter 5

The Touching Organ: Allegory, Anatomy, and the Renaissance Skin Envelope

Elizabeth D. Harvey

Helkiah Crooke, physician to James I and author of the influential English anatomical treatise *Microcosmographia* (1615), is one of the most eloquent defenders and articulate explicators of the complex early modern sense of tactility. A writer who mediates between the body's physical architecture and the soul that inheres invisibly in every part, Crooke moves as fluidly between the anatomist's external view of the dissected cadaver and the internal spaces of the lived body as he does between allegorical and anatomical discourse. In the first book of *Microcosmographia*, for instance, which is an extended defense of anatomy, he addresses the reader with an invitation to enter the "Sacred Tower of *Pallas*, I meane the braine of Man" (15).[1] He guides us through the marvelous interior structure of the skull, the "arched Cloysters of that princely pallace," "the Porches & goodly frontispiece," the "Labyrinthæan Mazes and web of the small arteries" (15). He calls attention to the "glittering Crisstall" of the eyes, the exquisite workmanship in the bones and tunnels of the ears, and the membranes, sinews, and bridle of the tongue before turning to the miraculous structure of the heart, with its ventricles and vessels "whereby the whole body is watered and refreshed" (15). The goal of this display of the body's inside is to show how divine workmanship manifests itself in every aspect of the human frame; as we are told, the body is like a "dumbe Schoolmaister" and a book of "vulgar Divinity" (15) in its capacity to reveal God's creativity. Crooke's tour of these hidden somatic spaces poses a series of questions about the epistemological and discursive consequences of entering the human body. How was this inward space imagined, conceived, and produced? How does the anatomist or guide position himself in relation to the cadaver he dissects, given that he, too, possesses a (live) body similar to the (dead) one being anatomized?[2] How are the senses, touch in particular, implicated in a post-Vesalian anatomy in which the anatomist dissects and handles the corpse in order to partition it and demonstrate its structures?[3] Finally, how is allegory materialized in anatomical discourse, and what does allegory and its gendering give to the anatomist?

The body's interior was turned inside out in a variety of ways in the early modern period, and I will be examining here two overlapping discourses that explored this inside: anatomical and allegorical depictions of the body. The traffic between these discourses is apparent not only in early modern visual anatomical representation but also in the linguistic depictions of bodily innerness that I will examine, the dialogue between the Spenserian intertexts that structure *Microcosmographia* and Crooke's anatomical reworkings of Edmund Spenser's allegory, on the one hand, and Phineas Fletcher's allegorical and anatomical rewritings of Spenser in *The Purple Island*, on the other.[4] What unites these seemingly distinct corporeal representations is that both, although in different ways, confront the relation between a body and the animating principle it harbors. Rather than formulating the encounter in these rather starkly dichotomous terms, however, I want to consider the relation as one of shifting boundary or threshold, a border that is presided over in early modern allegories of the body by the senses, which stand as sentinels, what Helkiah Crooke called the "intelligencers between the body and the soul" (6). One sense, tactility, is especially pertinent to this notion of boundary. Touch, which Crooke, following Aristotle, considered to be the foundation of all the senses (6), is unique because, unlike sight, hearing, taste, and smell, it is not located in and thereafter identified with a single organ.[5] Instead, it is frequently depicted as a property of the skin, and tactility is thus dispersed throughout the body.[6] Because the skin or flesh bounds the body, defining its margins and marking the division between inside and outside (as Crooke says, skin is "the limit and border as it were of all the parts" [84]), I will claim that an investigation of the history of tactility that considers skin, that sheath of sensation that both clothes the body and renders its inner spaces secret, will allow us better to understand how interiority is ideologically constituted for the early modern subject.[7]

In his essay "Visceral Knowledge," David Hillman concisely summarizes the effect the burgeoning of anatomy that followed the 1543 publication of Vesalius's *De humani corporis fabrica* had on the body: he reminds us that it made the corporeal inside into a "visible spectacle," both within the anatomy theater and in the period's effusion of anatomical texts and accompanying illustrations (83–84).[8] This exposure of somatic interiority to the emergent scientific gaze was part of a process that he calls the "technologizing" of the body's inside, which contributed to the ultimate triumph of the Cartesian or mechanistic view of the body's relation to its corporeal and psychic inner-ness (84). Yet this narrative of changing conceptions of interiority, persuasive as it is, relies upon a privileging of ocularity, which was increasingly impor-tant to anatomists.[9] The well-known portrait of Vesalius in *De fabrica* (and in the contemporaneous editions of the *Epitome*) seems to insist, however, that we also consider the essential role of touch in the practice of anatomy, for while Vesalius fixes the reader with his penetrating gaze, and while he ex-hibits the arm of the corpse to the spectator's vision, the center of the image features the prominently displayed hands of the anatomist, one clasping the cadaver's elbow, the other extending its fingers.[10] The skin—the organ of tactility—of the hand and arm is flayed so as to expose the muscles beneath. The portrait illustrates what I will argue is an ideological intersection signifi-cant to the history of tactility, a confrontation between the hand as a touch-ing instrument and the tactile, obscuring flesh. In other words, as I will claim, early modern anatomy involves not only peeling away the body's out-ward sensory covering in order to discover visually the body's inside but also subduing and harnessing tactility and displacing its distracting sensuality into the mastering agency of the hand.

Interiority and the Body's "Skin Envelope"

The role the senses play figures prominently among the controversies raised by Helkiah Crooke's description of the vessels and muscles of the face in Book 8. Crooke provides a compilation of continental anatomical sources in the thirteen books of his treatise, but in the "Controversies," the eight sections that lie between these anatomical partitions, he engages the philo-sophical, medical, and spiritual questions that surround the early modern practice of dissection. In the "Controversies belonging to the senses," Crooke cites poets (Ovid, Horace, Virgil), philosophers (Plato, Aristotle, Lucretius, St. Thomas Aquinas), and physicians (Galen) to debate the nature of the senses: whether the senses are actions, whether they are passions, the number and proper ordering of the senses, whether the senses require a medium or a mean, and many questions that pertain to each individual sense. Crooke be-gins with Touch, which he calls "the onely Sense of all Senses" (648). He sug-gests that all the other sensory faculties derive their seemingly distinct abilities from touch, and whereas the other senses are "restrained" within small organs within the brain, touch is "diffused through the whole body" (648). He asserts that touch fundamentally shapes human experience:

For first, it is by the benefit of Touching that we are conceived and formed in the fertile Garden of our Mothers wombe. For our wise and provident Nature ayming at Eternity, hath endued the partes of generation with a most exquisite sense of Touching, for the conservation of the Species or kindred creatures, so that the creatures beeing ravished with an incredible kind of pleasure, doe more readily apply themselves to venereall embracements, (otherwise a thing filthy and abhominable) and endeavor the procreation of their owne kindes. When the Infant in the wombe yet liveth onely a vegetative life, hee is first of all endued with the sense of Touching; whereby hee is cherished, nourished, and encreased, and is at length perfected; for so long as he is in the prison of the wombe, he neither seeth, nor heareth, nor smelleth, nor tasteth any thing, but yet hath absolute necessity of the sense of Touching, that he may be able to avoyde imminent dangers. (648)

Crooke depicts tactility's primacy as possessing both an originary and generative power. Touch is the "root" sense because it informs sexual pleasure, which in turn engenders life. The organs of generation are imbued with a "most exquisite sense of Touching," a ravishing pleasure that overcomes the disgust supposedly ordinarily evinced for the "filthy" procreative act. The ubiquitous linkage between sexuality and tactility that informs early modern representations of touch is here subsumed into (and celebrated as) a reproductive impulse, an urge for eternity.

The passage begins and ends with a sense of enclosure. Crooke's syntax implicitly removes human agency and resituates the generative principle in the personification of Touch, and the child that is so conceived and formed in the "garden" of the maternal womb is thus appropriately entirely governed and furthermore rendered secure by its sense of tactility. Crooke imaginatively enters this chora, this prison-house of embryonic unfolding, asserting that the developing fetus is effectively blind and deaf, incapable of tasting and smelling, and thus entirely dependent on its sense of touch. The growing child is doubly contained: within the flesh of the mother's body and within the envelope of its own skin. As Crooke tells us in Book 2, which treats the "parts Investing and Conteyning the whole Bodie," the skin "is the Organ of externall touching, and sole judge of all tactile qualities" (85). That the fetus should be defined by its casing of tactility acknowledges skin and touch as foundational in a way that strikingly anticipates the particular sense of subjectivity elaborated by the late twentieth-century French psychoanalyst Didier Anzieu. In *The Skin Ego*, Anzieu says that from "before birth, cutaneous sensations introduce the young of the human species into a world of great richness and complexity, a world as yet diffuse, but which awakens the perception-consciousness system, forms the basis for a general and episodical sense of existence and opens up the possibility of an originary psychical space"[11] Both Crooke and Anzieu make the skin a container and both judge the tactile properties of the cutaneous membrane to be the earliest, fundamental, and most definitive aspect of human development. Expanding on an idea that Aristotle articulates in *De Anima* and that recurs in subsequent discussions of the senses, that touch is analogous to thought, Anzieu uses cerebral neurophysiological research to explore the notion that skin belongs simultaneously to the organic and imaginary orders.[12] He posits two mutually dependent ideas: that the psyche is intimately bound both to the biological and the social body and that the skin thus contains individuality or subjectivity (the skin ego or *le moi-peau*) (3–4). Anzieu suggests that the importance of touch and skin to our sense of self is registered in the lexical richness of the English language: the entry for "touch" is, he asserts, the longest in the *OED* (13). If the skin and tactility are foundational to the instantiation of the subject, and if the physiological and imaginary extension of this cutaneous envelope forms a corporeal and psychic boundary for the self, yet that margin nevertheless provides only an illusory distinction between inside and outside.

From the Renaissance on, Anzieu alleges, Western thought has recurrently employed an epistemological paradigm that sees knowledge as spatially situated on the inside (in a core or nucleus) and protected by an exterior rind or outer shell. Yet neurophysiological research suggests that the skin and the brain of the human embryo are both formed from the ectoderm; the difference between the brain and the skin is neither originary nor definitive. In other words, Anzieu asserts. what we are used to thinking of as a relation of inside to outside is actually a relation of surfaces (10). As he puts it, the paradox of rethinking the spatial properties of knowing is that "the centre is situated at the periphery" (9). I want to extend the implications of this reterritorialization to consider the anatomical and allegorical entry into the early modern body, especially as that body is bounded and covered by flesh or skin. What would it mean to breach the skin envelope, to cross the border into the body's "inside"? Although early modern anatomy would seem to open the body's interior cavities to scrutiny and thus set up a clearly demarcated distinction between inside and outside, I will suggest that skin provides a more complex border between inside and outside, one that emphasizes the shifting, dynamic relation between the two. The figure of the *écorché*, the Vesalian body flayed of its skin in order better to display the underlying structures of muscle and vein, offers, like Anzieu's theorization of the ectoderm, a body that is both all surface and all inside. While it could be argued that psychological allegory gives external form—a body—to otherwise invisible concepts and that anatomy peels away the external coverings in order to reveal a hidden inside, in fact, as I will contend, early modern allegories of the body and anatomical writings are discursively intertwined. There is perhaps no better place to see the allusive intertextuality of these discourses than in the representations of skin.

Spenser's Castle of Alma is bounded by a high wall, too high to climb, and "all so faire, and sensible withall, / Not built of bricke, ne yet of stone and lime, / But of thing like to that *AEgyptian* slime, / Whereof king *Nine* whilome built *Babell* towre" (2.9.21). Most obviously, slime refers to the clay or earth of which the body is made and to which it eventually returns, but it is also the word used in Genesis 11: 3 for the mortar that binds the bricks in the Tower of Babel together.[13] This biblical chapter memorably describes the construction of an edifice and the multiplication of languages, but it also enumerates the propagation and scattering of a people (Shem's descendants). The definition of slime as a "viscous substance or fluid of animal or vegetable origin; mucus, *semen,* etc." (*OED*, 2a; my emphasis) thus shuttles between the architectural and corporeal dimensions of Genesis and Spenser's allegory, alluding both to building and procreation. Spenser evokes the simile of Egyptian mud in the Cave of Error episode (1.1.21) (where he speaks of "fertile slime") and in the description of Chrysogone's conception (3.6.8), and in each case, slime is the elemental building block of life, slightly distasteful in its relentlessly viscous materiality but miraculous in its autogenetic vitality nonetheless.[14] As a boundary, this fleshly wall is "sensible," capable of feeling, and metamorphic, for although of "goodly workmanship," it is destined to "turne to earth" (2.9.21).

The "sensible" properties of this bodily covering are most easily glimpsed when under siege. For Spenser, the five senses are the interfaces between the incarnated subject and the world, and they gather knowledge: sight, hearing, taste, smell, and touch provide data to the subject, information that may be false or delusive. Touch, as the sense most closely linked to sensuality and the skin, is especially vulnerable to this charge, as Spenser suggests in his portrayal of the "tactile"assailants that besiege the "Bulwarke" of touch; this allegorical "troupe" is armed with "darts of sensuall delight, / with stings of carnall lust, and strong effort / Of feeling pleasures" (2.11.13).[15] The attackers replicate the qualities of the sense they assault, and it is fitting that the "Bulwarke" of touch should be assailed by the "Vurchins" (the hedgehog's spines suggest the pain associated with touch and the extension of the skin in protective and sensitive bristles), spiders (the most frequent emblem of tactility because of their capacity to sense their environment through the webs they weave, which become a metaphorical designation for the network of nerves in the skin),[16] and snails (which extrude a trail of slime, a tactile record of their passage). Spenser's description of the body's material as "slime," as we will see, suggests that skin or flesh and its "sensible" characteristics are not peripheral to corporeality or to human nature but constitutive of it. The skin or flesh is at once a figure of covering and protection and a sign of the body's vulnerability to erotic or painful sensation. Joined together, these properties of skin emblemize human life and encapsulate the goal of temperance. The allegorical skin that bounds the Castle of Alma is put into narrative in the Bower of Bliss, where Acrasia's display of "alabaster skin" is the "subtile web" (2.12.77) that ensnares Verdant. Pliny suggested that the filament of the spider's web originates in the womb, and the representation of Verdant, with his "sleepie head " in Acrasia's "lap" (2.12.77) thus accentuates the linkages among skin, web, and female sexuality.[17]

Acrasia is a kind of figure of touch: her display of skin, which seems to be contiguous with the veil that partly covers and partly reveals, and her association with spiders, especially her "sucking" Verdant's masculine vitality, make her almost an allegorical representation of tactility. That Guyon and the Palmer must subdue the enchantress by means of a "subtile net" (2.12.81)[18] suggests through its replication of instrument that the inherent sensuality of skin and flesh cannot be extirpated but only controlled, a kind of allegorical homeopathy. As Michael Schoenfeldt asserts when he describes the workings of temperance, "Self-control is for Spenser a means of legitimating, not negating, desire."[19] The remedy for sensual indulgence, for the kind of erotic paralysis exemplified by Verdant, is not to destroy it, for to do so would be to attack the very skin or flesh that harbors the possibility of erotic surrender as well as life itself, but to control it. The regulating principle, rational control, instead must subdue the flesh's sensuality, transforming the skin's receptive sensory capacities into an active, protective net of restraint. This movement from the representation of skin as an instrument of delusive pleasure to tactility as agency is a transition that we can also see enacted in Crooke's anatomical writings.

Crooke quotes from the Castle of Alma at the beginning of Book 2 of *Microcosmographia*, where he speaks of the "tender skinne" that helps make the body's castle "perill-proof," for as the physician in him knows all too well, "to death and diseases we lie open on every side" (60). As anatomist, Crooke proposes to "draw the Curtaine" and show the "case, rather the Coffin or winding sheete," in which the "living body of death" is wrapped. While this coupling of life and death is, of course, an early modern commonplace, there is also a literal, anatomical sense to his oxymoronic formulation. The rhetoric of the anatomist paradoxically reinstills life in the corpse he dissects in his descriptions of the working organs, their temperature, the flow of blood within the veins. As anatomist, Crooke simultaneously draws the curtain to reveal the spectacle of the mortal body and also peels back the skin to show its animated workings. The body's "case" is, he tells us, made up of four parts: the cuticle or "Scarfe-skin," the skin itself, the fat, and the fleshy Membrane (61).[20] The outer layer, the epidermis or cuticle, is insensible because it must protect the body, but paradoxically it is also the *medium tactus,* the "*meane of touching*" (70–71). It functions as an intermediary, condensing raw sensation into interpretable signals. Flayed of this cuticle layer, even the gentlest touch would breed pain and confuse sensation, and the scarfe-skin thus confers coherence on tactility. Crooke clarifies the seeming contradiction of its sensible and insensible qualities in the Controversies, Question II, "Whether the Skin be the Organ or instrument of touching": against Aristotle, he maintains that the skin, not the flesh beneath it, is the instrument of touching (85). Where other senses (seeing, hearing, smelling) are useful but not essential, touch is "necessary" to life; the medium of tactility is both "internall" and "so joyned with the instrument that it cannot be separated" (85). Skin and tactility are thus bound together in an indivisible union, although touch is distributed inequitably throughout the body: Galen characterized the stomach as the organ of touching, and Crooke notes the "exquisite" sensibility in the mouth and the "partes of generation," but, as he says in conclusion, "the skin is the Organ of externall touching, and sole judge of all tactile qualities" (85).

The coupling of touch with the faculty of judgment is, however, reserved for a body part that Crooke mentions in other contexts—the hand.[21] For Crooke, the hand is a signifier of domination and reason: to compensate for their nakedness, human beings were given "the Hand, the great Organ before all Organes, the instrument of all instruments. By the power of Reason and of the Hand, albeit men be borne weake and naked, yet he is secured from all dumbe creatures" (10). The hand distinguishes human from animal, and its instrumentality is coextensive with that other differentiating characteristic, upright posture ("man onely had an upright frame of bodie, because hee alone amongst all Creatures had the Hand given him by God, an Organ or Instrument before all organs, and indeede in stead of all" [5]).[22] The hand is an organ of touch, but in Crooke's anatomy, its relationship to tactility is different from, though imbricated with, the sensing skin. Whereas, he says, "this touching vertue or tactility be diffused through the whole body both within and without, as being the foundation of the Animall *Being*, which may be called *Animality*, yet we do more curiouslie and exquisitely feele and discerne both the first and second qualities which strike the Senses in the Hand than in the other parts" (730). In other words, tactility, the fundamental sense, the sense contiguous with and essential to all animal life, which is especially pronounced in the vulnerable skin of human nakedness, is paradoxically differentiated from other animals through the concentration of touch in the apprehending and discerning hand. The hand stands for dominion not only over the other animals, but also over the potential for animality within human beings (what Crooke sees as the capacity of human beings to transform through indulgence in the "naked pleasure of the body" into "*Epicurean* Hogges" [646–47], a phrase that evokes the Circean allusions in the Bower of Bliss). The hand is repeatedly coupled with reason in *Microcosmographia*; the hand is "the judge and discerner of the Touch" (730), "by the aid of reason and of our Hands, wee have subdued and brought under the yoke" other, "more puissant creatures" (10), and, in an enigmatical rhetorical flourish that attempts to metaphorize the rational instrumentality of the hand, Crooke tells us that "Reason, is the hand of the understanding, Speech the hand of Reason, and the Hand it selfe, is the hand of Speech" (10). It is as if through this circular logic Crooke were resisting the physicality of the hand, as if calling attention to its gestural, signifiying properties could translate the physicality of the organ into the rational principle it exemplified.

Crooke's celebration of the hand both continues the classical commonplace that joins human erect stature with manual instrumentality and participates in a specifically medical and anatomical privileging of that organ. As he notes, Galen called it the "Instrument of Instruments" and treated it first in *De usu partium* (Crooke, 785). Realdus Columbus, by contrast, left the "wonderful and miraculous" frame of the hand until last in his 1559 *De re anatomica* so that it might "remaine infixed in our memories" (785).[23] Crooke delineates an anatomical pattern that starts with Galen and culminates with Crooke's near contemporary, Columbus; this tradition privileges the hand as the quintessential organ of touch, which as an aid to physicians and anatomists is indispensable (Crooke calls it in this exultant apostrophe: "O healthfull and saving Touch, O searching Sense" [649]). He suggests that without touch the art of "Physicke" would be defective, indeed, medicine without tactility would so "darken the eyes of Physicians" that they would "of necessity grope uncertainlie in darke and palpable ignorance" (649). Crooke's synaesthetic description evokes the necessity of touch by means of sight; without touch, the physician is effectively blind. Worse, he must function in a world that is overwhelmed with touch (groping in "palpable darkness") but never "enlightened" by it. The role of the physician and anatomist is to harness the discerning, judging qualities of tactility to epistemological service. Rather than having the skin as a web of sensory information, a sensual and often erotic net of feeling, the power of the anatomist is concentrated in the hand, as if tactile sensation were transposed from the cadaver's flayed skin into the anatomist's probing hand. That this rational instrument of epistemological palpation is, in Crooke's words, the "hand of speech" has a particular historical valence, of course, because before Vesalius, a dissection was performed by the *sector*, typically a barber or a surgeon, while the *ostensor* or *demonstrator* pointed and the *lector* read. For Vesalius and his followers, the anatomist's dissecting hand became for the first time literally a speaking hand; the anatomist explained and described as he partitioned the cadaver in front of him. Crooke, like Spenser, although in somewhat different ways, considers the dispersal of tactility throughout the body as something to be controlled, subdued under the governing principle of reason, which is synecdochized by the epistemologically searching and newly articulate anatomist's hand.

The Allegorical Body

Crooke's anatomy incorporates Spenser's allegorical representation of the human body as a structuring principle.[24] On the threshold of Crooke's dissection, the Preface to the Second Book, "Of the parts Investing and Containing the whole body: and also the lower belly in particular," as he is about to begin partitioning the cadaver, he says, "Beeing now to dissolve this goodly frame of Nature, and take in pieces this Maister-piece, it shall not bee amisse to take a light survey of all the parts as they lye in order" (60). In the perilous circumstances of the world, he says, only our "tender skinne" stands "betwixt us and our dissolution" (60). The repeated word "dissolve" suggests the integrity the skin bestows upon the body; flayed, the body is in danger of losing its coherence. Indeed, Crooke suggests that it is not "matter" that renders a human being "perill-proofe," since the body's origin is dust and its consummation clay, but rather its "excellent proportion and structure" (60). As he is about to "draw the Curtaine" and show what lies beneath the skin,

Crooke quotes Spenser's description of the allegorical body's architecture in the Castle of Alma:

The frame thereof seemd partly circulare,
And part triangulare, ô worke divine;
Those two the first and last proportions are,
The one imperfect, mortall, fœminine;
Th'other immortall, perfect, masculine. (2.9.22)

Whereas some subsequent critics, such as Spenser's seventeenth-century commentator Kenelm Digby, have interpreted this stanza as an allegory of the body's ligature with the soul, Crooke rather seems to be speaking about the architecture of the physiological body, affiliating the material (and the skin, Spenser's "*AEgyptian* slime") with the feminine, and aligning a more enduring principle—its structural elements, its balance of proportion—with the masculine.[25] The mathematical union provides an implicit defense of anatomy, whose search for the structural laws of bodily organization would seem to justify the flaying of the cadaver and subsequent violation of corporeal integrity in dissection. The organizational principle of anatomy as a material and discursive practice is evident in the formal partitioning of body and text, the arrangement of the always threatened chaos of the decomposing body into carefully schematized sections. This marriage of mortal and immortal, imperfect and perfect echoes the still current account of Aristotelian generation (which is represented in *The Faerie Queene* in Chrysogone's impregnation), and, as I will suggest, it also replicates the impulses of allegory.

Allegory is a mode that is bifurcated by its contradictory imperatives simultaneously to materialize and to make its meaning transcendent of the material signifier. As Gordon Teskey has argued, a gap or rift exists at the heart of allegory, the problem of "*methexis* or 'participation'," the strategy by which "abstractions are predicated of individual things only after being predicated of themselves through the trope of personification, as when Justice is said to be just."[26] Teskey goes on to suggest that the logical concepts that underpin Platonic idealism engage a "metaphorics of *insemination* and *parturition* by which a form like justice can multiply itself through a featureless, alien, invisible mother—even as it continues, in the empyrean, to father itself" (299). In this interpretation, allegory is not just a demonstration of this animated idealism, but a way of perpetuating social hierarchy, a hierarchy in which allegory seeks to capture the (female) material and elevate it to the level of the (male) concepts (300). The very nature of allegory is thus imaged as a violent sexual congress, a version of Aristotelian conception in which the male is the active partner who contributes form to the female's passive matter (297–98). The material in allegory, which Teskey aligns with the feminine, is both the site of the rift at the heart of the allegorical project and also the "other" that remains heterogeneous "to the abstract forms that are imprinted on it." This structure, which Teskey terms the "poetics of capture" (307), has a particular relevance for our readings of Renaissance allegories of the body and also for our understanding of the early modern anatomical figurations of flesh.

Spenser refers to the mode in his "Letter to Ralegh," where he speaks of *The Faerie Queene* as a "continued Allegory, or darke conceit" (15). His meaning is, he asserts, "clowdily enwrapped in Allegoricall deuises," a kind of veil that interposes itself between readers and their direct apprehension of the poem's sense, a veil that tantalizes with its partial vision and frustrates in its refusal to reveal completely. The word conceit derives from the Latin *concipere* ("to take in"), and it thus conveys the physiological sense of generation, of conception, as well as the imaginative and mental faculty (to take into the mind) to which Spenser more obviously alludes. The darkness of the conceit suggests that the mode is itself conceived in the obscure interior of the subject, where the womb and the mind become versions of each other. Indeed, the allegory of the body that we are offered in the Castle of Alma, presents just such an allegorical vision, which leads the knights (and the reader) through the mouth, into the hall of the belly, the parlor of the heart, and, in a movement that replicates the transcendent impulse of allegory, to the turret of the head, where they encounter personifications of mental faculties. If, as Teskey argues, allegory engages a tropology of insemination and parturition that renders the process of conception invisible and effaces the metaphor of female reproduction even as it relies upon it, it is not surprising that Spenser's allegorical representation of physiology would omit a display of the genitals. Michael Schoenfeldt suggests that our recognition of this lack may be historically conditioned; psychoanalysis privileges the genitals, and we may thus be inclined to map the primacy of the sexual onto an early modern culture for which other somatic sites had equal importance. Although Schoenfeldt's remedial interpretation provides an illuminating reading of the alimentary tract, I would agree with David Lee Miller that sexual reproduction, both implicitly expressed and overtly effaced, pervades the castle of Alma.[27] Miller argues that sexuality is displaced through a process of sublimation into an allegorical coupling within the heart.[28] He suggests that the sublimation is both an allegorical movement, a purification or transmutation of fleshly contamination, and also a psychoanalytic refinement of libidinal energy, a channeling of instinct into social interaction. These displacements are also somatically signaled, for the various encounters in this chamber, especially Guyon's meeting with Shamefastness, is marked by multiple occasions of blushing, the visible coloring of the skin by uncontainable "feeling." Thus, in the very center of the body, where the mysteries of the organs of generation should be revealed, we find instead an allegory about the revelation of secrets, whose presence is announced through the sign of a blush, which returns us from interiority to the body's external covering. The movement from centre to periphery recalls not only Anzieu's analysis of the skin ego and the crucial role tactility plays in human social and sexual interaction but also the Castle's "slimy" covering, the implication of skin in early modern representations of sensuality and generation. The enigmatically blank "arras" that hangs in the Parlor ("In which was nothing pourtrahed, nor wrought, / Not wrought, nor pourtrahed, but easie to be thought"[2.9.3]) functions as a figure for skin or Crooke's "curtain," since, although it is without image, it is impressionable and receptive to the inscriptions of thought or passion. In a chamber in which the secrets of thought are continually revealed through blushing, the imageless tapestry registers the skin's receptive displays.[29]

Miller suggests that the union of circle and triangle in stanza 22 "may be Spenser's most explicit reinscription of the human genitals: the privileged signifier of masculinity is a divine circle and that of femininity an earthly delta—geometrical analogue to the Nile river delta, source of Egyptian slime and recurrent image in *The Faerie Queene* of natural fecundity" (182). It is significant that this representation is not sexual in the psychoanalytic sense Schoenfeldt invokes, a sexuality involved in the formation of individual, social subjectivity. The mathematical union partakes of a discourse of cosmic reproduction, a body of natural philosophical speculation on the mysteries of nature and the secrets of human generation.[30] Crooke's intertextual importation of Spenser's stanza on the body-castle's structure functions to stabilize and render the preceding stanza, which describes the material elements of the castle (skin as Egyptian slime, the earth to which all human beings must eventually revert) mathematically transcendent. The geometrical allegory performs the "poetics of capture" at the body's threshold for both Crooke and Spenser: the material or skin is the site of the rift (for the anatomist, the rift is always enacted and deflected during dissection) and the heterogeneous "other" that resists translation into a higher meaning.

The elision of the genitals that is subsequently enacted inside the castle

("Alma's nought," in Miller's memorable phrase) is also found in some anatomical texts: John Banister in his anatomy, *The Historie of Man* (1578), for instance, declines to describe the female reproductive organs (although he provides an extended anatomical discussion of the male reproductive system) because he is "persuaded, that by lifting up the vayle of Natures secretes, in womens shapes" he will "commit most indecencie the office of *Decorum*."[31] He does, however, supply a remarkable description of male and female reproductive organs housed in the ventricles of the brain:

> Behynd this vaulted part in the extreme part of the brayne towardes *Cerebellum*, and in the upper part of the thyrd ventricle, Nature hath feyned certaine eminent partes, which in their upper partes, represent the likenes or Image of Testicles, and so called therfore of Anathomistes *Testes*: neare unto which the which, two other particles . . . called . . . the haunches or buttockes. Betweene which lyeth that hole, which . . . seemeth like unto the fundament. Furthermore in the forepart of these Testicles . . . an other part appeareth, which not unaptly, but very elegantly expresseth the shape or privye part of a woman. (fol. 100v)

That the "privye part of a woman" can be depicted only as an intellectual copy, a "feyned" image lodged in the ventricle of the brain, suggests that the censoring of female sexual anatomy under the "generative partes" reflects both a conventional attention to modesty and also a pervasive anxiety about the materiality of human origin.

As we have seen, female reproduction is bound up with mortality. Skin, touch, slime, fecundity—all connote a vulnerable human condition that allegory and anatomy seek to displace into a higher, more enduring principle. When Helkiah Crooke anatomizes the reproductive organs in *Microcosmographia*, he makes an anatomical rejoinder to Spenser's treatment of the allegorical displacement of the genitals: "the History of these parts of generation it is our task in this Book to describe, over which also we could wish we were able to cast a veil, which it should be impiety for any man to remove, who came not with as chaste a heart to read as we did write" (199). If in Spenser's account, allegory continually inserts itself as a transcendentalizing impulse between the material nature of the body and its representation, Crooke's rewriting of Spenser removes the body's veiling skin. To do so effectively, he incorporates Spenser's own vision of chastity from Book 3 of *The Faerie Queene* (in which Britomart's chastity includes a promised sexual consummation) as a principle of inner restraint that would render this anatomical display "chaste." His use of veil as signifier of modesty suggests, however, that although he represents the sexual organs in word and image, he recognizes that the secrets of generation hidden within the female body are not simply material but are rather infused, as all parts of the body are, by an animating principle, "something Metaphysicall, transcendent above Nature" (4). He distinguishes between what he cannot do as an anatomist, which is to see the invisible, divine aspect of human beings, to "open that shrine which *Nature* her selfe hath veyled and sealed up from our sences" (4), and what he can do, which is "to content our selves to handle that that may be handled," what is "at least subject unto some of our senses" (4). In other words, he can lift the veil of the skin from the body, he can use the sense of tactility to "handle" its organs, but he cannot peer behind the veil that Nature has placed over the essence of the soul.

In his body allegory, *The Purple Island* (pub. 1633), Phineas Fletcher makes the interplay between allegory and anatomy integral to the structure of his poem, thus enacting the rift between matter and meaning that characterizes allegory. The temporal structure of the poem's corporeal allegory, its first three days being devoted to an exploration of the body, replicates the early modern anatomy lesson.[32] The disjuncture between allegory and anatomy is spatialized in the poem's bipartite structure, which consists of seven-line stanzas that occupy the centre of the page and a corresponding anatomical gloss that runs along the side of it. The allegorical description of the flesh, Spenser's skin or slime, is this:

Upon this base a curious work is rais'd,
Like undivided brick, entire and one;
Though soft, yet lasting, with just balance pais'd;
Distributed with due proportion:
   And that the rougher frame might lurk unseen,
   All fair is hung with coverings slight and thinne;
Which partly hide it all, yet all is partly seen:

As when a virgin her snow-circled breast
Displaying hides, and hiding sweet displaies;
The greater segments cover'd, and the rest
The veil transparent willingly betraies;
   Thus takes and gives, thus lends and borrows light;
   Lest eyes should surfet with too greedy sight,
Transparent lawns withold, more to increase delight. (2.7–8)

The gloss, which itself functions to remove allegory's veil, presents the flesh in the following terms: "Upon the bones as the foundation is built the flesh. Flesh is a similar part of the body, soft and ruddy, made of blood indifferently dried and covered with the common membrane or skinne" (27). As we are reminded later in the poem, the flesh is also the medium of touch, since "Tactus" "Hath his abode in none, yet every place: / Through all the Isle distended is his dwelling" (3:55). The image of the veil, both as a figure for allegory and as a trope for the flesh itself, is never seen as static, then, but always dynamic, whether in the splitting of the gloss from poetic description in Fletcher's account or in the interplay of the veil of flesh itself, which always covers even as it reveals. The tantalizing sexuality of Fletcher's simile suggests the feminizing of corporeality, its fundamental secrecy, and its active resistance to, but simultaneous solicitation of, epistemological scrutiny. Fletcher's double depiction incorporates a dynamism akin to Judith Butler's theorization of the matter of bodies not as a surface, "but [as] a process of materialization that stabilizes over time to produce the effect of boundary, fixity, and surface we call matter" (9). Matter, the flesh, and the body are recurrently coded as feminine in a way that accentuates the interiority of the body as the site of the unknowable and the secret. Fletcher's structure records a tension that is also historical, an early modern dialectic between modes of representing the body and its interior that has not yet divided into either a Cartesian or a disciplinary dualism.

The Eloquence of Wax

I want to turn now from the anatomist's hand to the bodies he dissected, to the physical and, more importantly, the palpable representations of the body's inside and exposed surfaces: a series of works that also mediate between inside and outside and between anatomy and allegory, a collection of eighteenth-century Italian wax models of dissected cadavers from the Museo La Specola in Florence. The art of making these wax anatomical models is older than these particular examples, and there are in fact several specimens and written records that document the work of a seventeenth-century ceroplastic artist from Syracuse, Gaetano Giulio Zumbo. His work is significant partly because it was created in an earlier historical period than the other wax figures I will consider and partly because it includes four allegorical dioramas or "teatrini," depicting plague, death, syphilis, and the triumph of time, as well as anatomical models (he apparently made several life-sized models, which included a woman giving birth and a woman who had died in childbirth, but these are no longer extant).[33] His surviving work, both individual pieces and the larger corpus, negotiates between the body's materiality and the metaphysical significance of the corporeal condition; the dramatic scenes, in particular, portray the inexorable encroachments of death and disease. His diorama of a tomb, *Il Sepolcro,* for instance, presents a dramatic scene of architectural and corporeal decay. The crypt is in ruins, its crumbling walls infiltrated by vines and weeds, its ornamental carvings cracked, its funerary urn precariously positioned. The tomb itself is open to view, and the skeletal figure within appears from the scraps of clothing or flesh that still cling to the bones to be actively decomposing,. The foreground is strewn with dead bodies and skulls in various states of disintegration and putrefaction. Presiding over this scene of death's destruction is the perfectly intact figure of a contemplative woman who sits above the tomb, a figure reminiscent in pose and drapery of the central sculpture in Giorgio Vasari's monument to Michelangelo in Santa Croce in Florence (1570).[34] Zumbo worked for Cosimo III de' Medici in Florence from 1691 to 1694, and it was during this time that he created *Il Sepolcro*; we might thus consider the diorama not only as an allusion or homage to Vasari and Michelangelo as artists, but also as a complex commentary on wax as an artistic material. Vasari wrote about wax in his treatise on artistic technique, how wax was used as the "skin" over an armature of a sculptural model, how small "sketch-models" were constructed in wax and then transferred to a full-size model, and how artists created polychrome wax effigies, which were so detailed in their reproduction of hair and clothing that Vasari said these figures lacked nothing "but the spirit and the power of speech" (149).[35] There is, nevertheless, a clear sense of hierarchy in artistic material, and wax (as well as the verisimilitude achieved in these portraits) is for Vasari subservient to the higher forms of bronze and marble. This is apparent from Vasari's comments about the sixteenth-century art of wax portraiture; he says that it would take him too long "to enumerate all the artists who model wax portraits, for now-a-days there is scarcely a jeweller who does not occupy himself with such work" (189). Zumbo's waxen contemplative figure gestures in its visual quotation of Michelangelo's tomb toward the immutability and putative superiority of marble, an inclination toward the transcendence of the corruptible flesh that echoes the impulses of Spenser's body allegory. While the medium of wax did not encode the prestige that marble did, nor could it signal marble's material endurance, Zumbo's mimicking of Michelangelo's tomb sculpture nevertheless suggests an important role for wax. The contrast between the unblemished female figure and the decayed bodies in the diorama seems to argue for the relative permanence of wax, for if human flesh is subject to relentless change and corruption (Zumbo explores the ravages of time and disease in his other *teatrini*), its likeness can nevertheless be captured through his sculptural and scientific ceroplastic art.[36]

The tension between the inevitability of human death and decomposition and the relative immortality wax sculpture could confer is evident in one of Zumbo's surviving scientific works, a partially dissected human head, which, unlike the eighteenth-century wax corpses, incorporates an actual human skull (Figure 1). This head exemplifies the verisimilitude characteristic of the sixteenth-century tradition of wax portraiture that Vasari mentions: the finely worked detail of the head includes a moustache and beard. Half of the head is intact, and the other half is dissected enough to reveal the underlying anatomical structures, the muscles, arteries, and bones. Not only does the piece mediate between a real human body and its uncannily accurate representation, but it also embodies a sense of life, of personality, of emotion. The eyes are partly open, the lips slightly parted, and there is a trickle of blood at the nose and mouth, as if the figure were only recently dead or as if it might waken from what was only a temporary unconsciousness. That Zumbo's head is bifurcated, one half a sculpture and the other an anatomical model, suggests wax's material legacy, its links to artistic tradition on the one hand and its increasing importance in the scientific arena. Both the artistic and scientific associations also call up wax's mnemonic dimension. Georges Didi-Huberman writes that wax is a "magical material, almost alive," and that "from Aristotle to Freud" it "has provided the privileged metaphor of the work of memory, and even of sensorial operations in general."[37] It might be said that these ceroplastic anatomical models, which include Zumbo's works and the eighteenth-century figures in La Specola, incorporate the memory of the dead in a literal way; Ercole Lelli (1702–66), who was a renowned wax modeler as well as a painter, sculptor, and architect, achieved the anatomical accuracy that he did because he studied the organs and muscles of corpses. The archives record that it took approximately two hundred cadavers or parts of corpses to produce a wax model,[38] and the memory of these bodily parts that would have begun to decompose and putrefy immediately after death was thus preserved in the more enduring medium of wax.

Zumbo's head also participates in the cultural habits of memory, the practice of creating replicas of people or their organs in wax. In churches such as Orsanmichele and Santissima Annunziata in Florence, for instance, Poggesi indicates, statues, portraits, organs, and limbs fashioned from wax commemorated the dead throughout the early modern period (10–11). Am-

Figure 1. Gaetano Zumbo (1656–1701), *Anatomy of a Man's Head.* Courtesy of Museo La Specola, Florence. Photo: Marcus Schubert, 1983.

ple testimony survived in the writings of classical authors (Cicero, Sallust, Seneca, and especially Polybius and Pliny the Elder) about the Roman custom of creating wax masks (*imagines,* also called in poetry *cerae,* "wax things"). These wax ancestor portraits were, as Polybius tells us, fashioned from wax and designed to replicate the appearance of the deceased; the masks were kept in cupboards in the atrium of the house, and at funerals, the masks would be removed and worn by actors who resembled the dead man in height and build, an impersonation that was compounded by having actors dress in the dead man's clothes. In this way, Pliny says, the whole family, alive and dead, was present at funerals, commemorated, indeed enacted, by the wax masks.[39] This custom of animating the dead through the use of wax masks continued until the Renaissance and was exemplified in Lorenzo Il Magnifico's funeral.[40] Wax could be said to retain the deep cultural traces of the Roman funerary *imagines* and to provide an ideal material for commemorative portraits and the reproduction of body parts, those synecdoches of memory, because as a medium it is remarkably malleable and capable of retaining the imprint of resemblance. It is perhaps for this reason that it is not only frequently used in commemorative ways but it is also associated with the operations of memory. Freud famously likened a wax tablet, the "mystic writing-pad," to the functioning of memory in the conscious and the unconscious. He argues that all forms of auxiliary apparatus designed to modify or enhance sensory operations are based on the sense organs themselves.[41] The mystic writing-pad thus mimics memory in its engagement of sensory perception, the conscious mind, and the unconscious. The apparatus consists of a wax tablet that is covered by a transparent sheet made up of two layers, a piece of celluloid and a layer of wax paper. (Freud's mystic writing-pad is remarkably similar to Crooke's anatomy of the skin; the "scarfe-skin" corresponds to the protective celluloid, and the skin proper responds to sensation. They function in complex conjunction, just as the layers covering the wax tablet do.) Freud compares the sheets to the mind's perceptual system, for the celluloid protects the mind from excessive stimulation, while the waxed paper receives the impression of sensory stimuli. The pad can be wiped clean by lifting both sheets, but the deep imprint of the impressions or writing may nevertheless be glimpsed in certain lights on the surface of the wax. For Freud, then, wax is closely allied both to the senses and to the foundations of memory; its receptive nature gathers impressions, just as the senses do, and these imprintings stamp themselves into the mnemonic medium as a permanent, though perhaps not always reliable, trace.

Unlike illustrations in anatomy books, however, these three-dimensional models, which record the stamp of the impermanent flesh in wax, are meant to be handled. They are, in a sense, the embodiment of Vesalian anatomical illustrations, for like the *écorchés*, these mostly male bodies are flayed in order to exhibit the architecture of muscle, bone, or veins that lie beneath the surface of the skin (Figure 2). They expose not only the interior organs but also the body's hidden subcutaneous structures, and in-

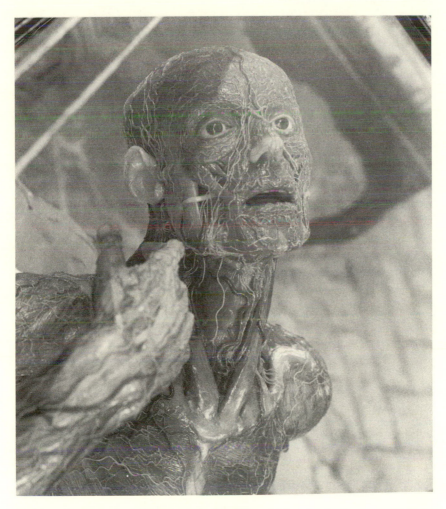

Figure 2. Clemente Susini (1754–1805), *The Skinned Man*, detail. Courtesy of Museo La Specola, Florence. Photo: Marcus Schubert, 1983.

nerness, like the skin, is in this way dispersed over the entire body. Not only does the plasticity of wax, its capacity to respond to heat and become malleable, and its vulnerability to change render it uncannily like flesh, but it is also, of course, an organic material. Extruded from a bee's body, a digested substance, wax issues from the interior, formless and yet quintessentially able to take on the imprint of form. Wax is like flesh in its responsiveness to touch: it warms and changes shape, it seems almost to respond to touch as if it were flesh. It is, then, an ideal medium in which to fashion bodies made to be touched. These scientific models served to illustrate anatomical structure when the numbers of cadavers available for dissection was severely limited and when the practical considerations for preserving a corpse dictated haste in dissection. As pedagogical tools, they were made not only to be seen but also to be touched.[42] Most of the bodies are male and flayed, exhibiting, according to the Galenic isomorphic principle, the anatomical features of the generalized human body. Even without skin, even eviscerated, these bodies retain a haunting life. Their glass eyes are open, seeming to evince an impossible range of emotion through their expressive gaze, and their languid, even rapturous poses paradoxically suggest a lingering responsiveness in corpses from whom all traces of consciousness must necessarily be extinguished. Like Ovid's Marsyas, who continues to speak even as his skin is torn from his body, who questions in his anguish why he is being divided from himself ("quid me mihi detrahis?" "Why do you tear me from myself?"),[43] these wax cadavers seem to transpose the tactile sensation that inheres in the cutaneous membrane into a register of emotive "feeling." The female figures, unlike the male bodies, are not flayed, which makes the juxtaposition between the undisturbed ivory surface, beautifully coifed hair, and jewelry and the dissected torso all the more disturbing. Some of these models contained removable parts, so that the outer layers of the body could be successively peeled away, revealing the human organs and female reproductive system.[44] Interiority, as these models demonstrate, is not only seen but also actively handled, thus clearly announcing the complicated, shifting ways in which skin and tactility are implicated in the body's volatile boundary between surface and innerness. This border simultaneously demarcates the edges and limits of the corpse and is the dynamic interface between the cadaver and the anatomist's touching hand.

As Long as a Swan's Neck? The Significance of the "Enlarged" Clitoris for Early Modern Anatomy

Bettina Mathes

Tangible. *Syn.: material, touchable, physical, corporeal, graspable, visible.*
—Webster's New World Thesaurus

In 1660 the French anatomist and author of the much acclaimed *Anatomia Reformata* Thomas Bartholin wrote in his chapter "On the Clitoris": "It is absolutely true and it is not natural and it is monstrous that it grows to the length of a goose's neck."[1] Bartholin's remark refers to a case described by the Swiss anatomist Felix Platter in his 1583 *De corporis humani structura* whose observation soon became a popular topos in the anatomical writing about the clitoris. In 1691 Tobias Peucer, editor and translator of Stephen Blancaert's *Reformirte Anatomie* (*Reformed Anatomy*), even claims "Platter testifies to having seen one as long as a swan's neck."[2] Bartholin, Platter, and Peucer are no exceptions among early modern anatomists. In general, seventeenth-century physicians, surgeons, and midwives seem very much preoccupied with the size of the clitoris. While the references to a swan's neck underline the extraordinary size of the clitoris, anatomically this organ was considered a "female penis." As Bartholin observes in the first sentence of his chapter on the clitoris, this organ is "similar to the penis as concerns its position, substance, composition, the production of semen as well as erection."[3] Adrian Spieghel, author of *Fabrica corporis humani libri decem*, published in 1627 reports that an enlarged clitoris "often deceives those inexperienced in anatomy to believe that women have been transformed into men, because what hangs out of their privities looks like a male member."[4]

The "monstrosity" of an enlarged clitoris troubled anatomists for several reasons. Women might pass as men or they might hurt their male lovers during intercourse. Moreover, it was regarded as the cause and embodiment of female homoeroticism. Spieghel illustrates the homoerotic implications of an enlarged clitoris: "And even those women are brought to such insane lust that they sinfully lie with other women."[5] In fact, as Valerie Traub has noted, the way early modern anatomy fashioned female sexuality and desire reflects an anatomical essentialism that transmutes "a paradigm of desire into a paradigm of bodily structure."[6] It is because of this homoerotic disposition that Bartholin and many of his colleagues refer to the clitoris as "contempt of men."[7] This "contempt of men" was made visible and intelligible in the figure of the so called "Tribade"—a woman who because of her enlarged clitoris desired and had sex with other women. Bartholin states "sometimes they [women with an enlarged clitoris] abuse the clitoris as if it were a penis and they lie with each other."[8] As Traub notes: "It is not the 'tribade's' inconstant mind or sinful soul but her uniquely female yet masculinized morphology that propels her to engage in illicit behavior."[9]

Feminist critics have argued that anatomy's preoccupation with the clitoris expresses male anxieties about female sexuality and negotiates social and political gender conflicts.[10] In its analogy to the penis as well as in its homoerotic disposition the clitoris figures as a threat to male heterosexual as well as homosocial hegemony. Just how threatening the enlarged clitoris was may be judged from its medical and legal treatment. As Park observes, physicians began considering clitoridectomy, and they recommended this measure not only in cases of clitoral hypertrophy but also as a more general treatment to discipline any kind of transgressive female sexuality.[11] And yet this interpretation is not entirely satisfying because it does not account for the reasons why the early modern Tribade is so prominent in the realm of anatomy and why, despite the anatomist's extraordinary appetite for the Tribade, her anatomy is denied visual representation.

Considering the frequency with which the medical and anatomical literature described the enlarged clitoris it seems significant indeed that those books do not contain illustrations of Tribades or their enlarged clitorises. Rather, anatomical illustrations of the clitoris included in those books are usually small featuring the "normal,"—not enlarged—clitoris, which often enough is barely visible in these small-size images. However, if we leave the realm of anatomia we find numerous visual examples of what the clitoris as long as a swan's neck might look like. Renaissance paintings rendering the mythological story of how Jupiter in the disguise of a swan raped Leda

Figure 1. Correggio, *Leda and the Swan*, ca. 1530. Reproduced by permission of the Staatliche Museen zu Berlin, Stiftung Preußischer Kulturbesitz, Gemäldegalerie. Photo: Jörg P. Anders.

convey a visual impression of the enlarged clitoris's erotic and sexual possibilities. This motif, which abounded in the sixteenth and seventeenth centuries, was rendered by artists like Giorgione, Michelangelo, and Tintoretto.[12] Correggio's version of *Leda and the Swan*, for instance, albeit painted about 1530, before the anatomical rediscovery of the clitoris, might from an anatomical point of view very well be read as an illustration of tribadic sexuality (Figure 1). Early modern anatomy thus associates the clitoris with Jupiter's legendary sexual potency and fertility.[13] But what does it mean that both penis and clitoris are imagined as swan's necks? And why are there no *anatomical* illustrations of the enlarged clitoris? In what follows I argue that this invisibility allows insight into the relation between touch, vision and the tangibility of the phallus.

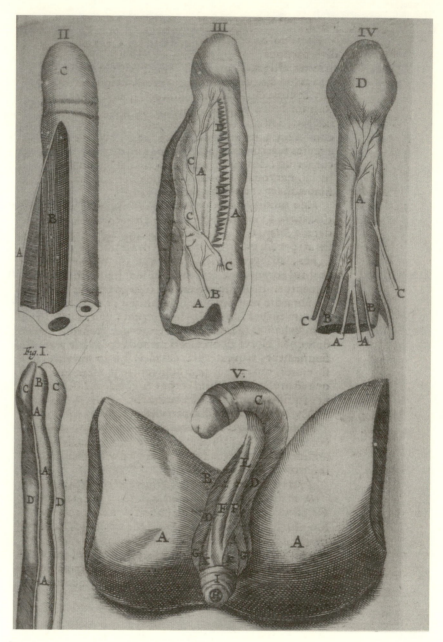

Figure 2. "Anatomy of the Penis," in Thomas Bartholin, *Anatomia Reformata* (Haga-Comitis: Vlacq, 1660), 149. Reproduced by permission of the Staatsbibliothek zu Berlin, Stiftung Preußischer Kulturbesitz, Abt. Historische Drucke.

Typography, Tangibility, and the Phallus

As a starting point for the problematization of this context I turn to some well-known but rarely discussed anatomical illustrations of the penis. The first one is included in Bartholin's *Anatomia Reformata* (Figure 2). It shows the male genital from different perspectives and in different states of dissection. View V features "the penis and its muscles in situ."[14] Perhaps the most unusual feature about this illustration is the shape of the penis, which looks like a question mark. In fact, it almost perfectly matches the question mark of the Antiqua type. In this context, it is interesting to note that the German edition of the *Anatomia*, which uses the image the wrong way round, draws attention to the relation between body part and typography. From this inversed perspective the shape of the penis is said to "represent the shape of the letter S," which of course is the mirror image of the question mark.[15] Notably it is the typographical sign that governs the shape of the penis.

An even more spectacular and clearly sexualized representation of the penis as question mark is featured in Giulio Casserio's *Tabulae anatomicae*, published posthumously by Daniel Bucretius in 1627 together with Spieghel's *Fabrica* (Figure 3).[16] The volume contains 78 large size anatomical plates, "all of them," the subtitle notes, "new and never seen before."[17] The plate displays, according to Casserio's explanation, "the penis in its natural situation without the skin in order to make visible all of its parts." This "natural situation" is a young man in a semirecumbent position with his legs wide open, surrendering his circumcised penis and anus to the gaze of the beholder. Obviously, the carefully designed engraving shows much more than seems necessary for the anatomical visualization of the penis.

This complex image with its multiple layers of meaning profoundly questions the relation between sex and gender. While the penis suggests the maleness of this figure, the excised testes as well as the circumcised penis point to his lack of masculinity. Furthermore, the image suggests that the male is about to give birth: as Sander Gilman notes, the youth's "position of parturition" as well as the protruding anus propose the male's motherhood.[18] Gender ambivalence is furthermore expressed through an iconography that makes use of binarisms. The left foot resting firmly on the ground contrasts with the instability of the right foot's position. The strong left arm clutching the tree and stabilizing the body contrasts with the awkwardly distorted right arm. The stretched upper half of the body contrasts with the twisted lower half. And, finally, the quiet pastoral setting in which the man rests is opposed to the presence of a castle in the background. This

Tab. XV. ❖ Lib. VIII.

Figure 3. "Anatomy of the Penis," in Giulio Casserio, *Tabulae Anatomicae* (Venice: E. Deuchine, 1627), 78. Reproduced by permission of the Staatsbibliothek zu Berlin, Stiftung Preußischer Kulturbesitz, Abt. Historische Drucke.

"incongruence" between sex and gender as well as the combination of masculinity and femininity seem to suggest that the figure represents a hermaphrodite—although he does not possess two sets of genitals.[19] Or does he?

Most interesting in this context is the shape of the penis as a question mark. The relation between penis and question mark not only refers to questions of shape; penis and question mark are also connected by the phenomenon of erection. Remarkably, the question mark, which had been introduced in the early middle ages, becomes erect only during the late middle ages. Before that time it rests horizontally covering the full stop. With regard to the representation of the penis in Bartholin and Casserio, one is tempted to say that the erection of the question mark reflects the questionableness of the erection of the penis. But what exactly is so questionable about an erection? Let me briefly turn to a modern expert regarding the relation between masculinity, sexuality, and typography. In *The Signification of the Phallus*, Jacques Lacan provides the following reason why the phallus "naturally" materializes in the penis: "It can be said that this signifier is chosen because it is the most tangible element in the real of sexual copulation and also the most symbolic in the *literal* (*typographical*) sense of the term" (emphasis mine).[20] Lacan proposes a connection between the penis and writing governed by the phallus. In this view, the erect penis is the incarnation of the symbolic order—the letter turned into flesh, if you will—and the phallus its primary signifier.[21] But what of the question mark? Although Lacan remains significantly silent on this point, I want to argue that the penis as question mark draws attention to both the "costs" and "rewards" that the signification of the phallus entails for the male body. By saying this I do not propose that Lacan's theory contains a historical argument; rather I am concerned with historicizing Lacan. His theory of the phallus has often been discarded by historians precisely because of its ahistorical scope. But although Lacan himself regarded the signification of the phallus as a kind of transhistorical truth, there can be no doubt that his theory is the result of historical processes. Thus even if Lacan's theory tells us nothing about the historicity of early modern bodies, these bodies tell us a lot about the history of the phallus—a history that is concerned with the relation between the body and systems of representation. In this sense, early modern anatomy as a practice that was concerned with providing a visible body for the symbolic order (a body that was fashioned according to the rules of rationality and visuality) must be regarded as an important "step" toward the theory of the signification of the phallus.[22] And from this perspective anatomy allows insight into what the *Signification of the Phallus* remains silent on, namely, that the materialization of the phallus as penis inflicts a "wound" onto the male body.

Of course, the question then is: what kind of penis is this penis as question mark? And in what way is it "wounded"? Again Lacan may lead the way. In the aforementioned quote he characterizes the penis/phallus as "the most *tangible* element in the real of sexual copulation" (emphasis mine). Here he seems to suggest that the penis is the phallus incarnate, because it is "material," "touchable," "physical," even "graspable"—to invoke some synonyms for "tangible."

This is indeed an awkward notion for Lacan considering that the phallus is characterized as actively touching but not as being touched. What does Lacan mean when he talks about tangibility in connection with the penis/phallus? To answer this question I must return to the relation between symbolic order—writing, typography—and the male body. Lacan has argued that the signification of the phallus depends on the threat of castration embodied by woman. This castration, however, also symbolically affects the penis, for the "signifier [the phallus] has an active function in determining the effects in which the signifiable appears as submitting to its mark, *becoming through that passion the signified*" (emphasis mine).[23] In other words, the penis becomes the phallus on the basis of its symbolic castration or circumcision, and this "castration" implies that signification and symbolic castration are inseparable. In her recent *Versuch über den Schwindel* Christina von Braun has elaborated on this context. Drawing on the connection between the ancient Mithras cult, which stages the transformation of biological into symbolical fertility through the castration and killing of a bull, and the history of the letter alpha, which represents the bull's head, she argues that

the Greek alphabet [and the symbolic order it created] must be read as a "circumcision": a "circumcision," that is, which affects the whole body. There is no other sign system which so clearly implies the fantasy of controlling the body and corporeality through the mastery of spoken language as does the Greek alphabet (precisely because as opposed to the semitic alphabet it also writes the vowels). This mastery is experienced as an "act of castration" recurring in every individual. . . . This interpretation implies that the "symbolic castration" does not represent an external threat. Rather, just like the alphabet itself it must be regarded as one of the great inventions of western civilisation—as a self-made "threat" which . . . has become the driving force behind the western search for invention and innovation."[24]

Of course, the Greek and later the Latin alphabet with their dissociation between body and language inflict a "wound" onto the female body as well. But unlike the male's hers is "not chosen"—to borrow Lacan's choice of words—to incarnate the symbolic order but rather its "Other."[25]

While von Braun describes the *symbolic* "cuts" the male body is subject to, early modern anatomists used *real* knives, cut into *real* flesh, and produced *real* castrates in order to create an ideal and rational body. In this sense, the practice of anatomical dissection is itself—literally—an *incarn-ation* of the symbolic order's castrating power. It is exactly this reality of the symbolic castration that Casserio's image makes visible. The male body has been circumcised and castrated by the dissector's knife, his penis and testes have indeed been tangible. But this castrated penis has also become the ideal penis, the visible embodiment of the phallus.

At this point I could have ended my consideration by concluding that early modern anatomy translated symbolic violence into carnal violence in order to provide a body designed according to the laws of the symbolic (phallic) order. It was the question mark that urged me to further explore this context. For the image poses two questions: how do we deal with this wound and what are its rewards? The answers early modern surgeons provided are evasive, because the surgeons went at length to distance themselves from the tangibility of th(eir) penises. Curiously, it is the clitoris and the swan's neck that came in handy when the anatomist struggled to cope with the threat of castration. And from this perspective it will also become clear why "visible" may serve as a synonym for "tangible."

Therefore, I want to suggest that we take a fresh look at anatomical illustrations of the genitals, a look that is not guided by the verbal explanations fixing the putative meaning of these illustrations. In what follows I want to suggest that it is precisely the penis as question mark that provides a "disguise" for the *visual* representation of the tribadic clitoris in early modern anatomy books. The reason why the clitoris as long as swan's neck is imag(in)ed as the penis as question mark has to do with the specific tactility and tangibility of anatomical illustrations that produced and requested a *visual* touch that proved different from the dissector's *manual* touch. And, second, I argue that the wound inflicted by the symbolic might be "closed" by the fantasy that man and woman become "one flesh"—a fantasy that is dear to Christianity and also structures anatomical images in Christian Europe during the early modern period. To develop this context I shall now turn to the dissector's hands and the reader's eyes—before I come back to penis and clitoris.

Touch and Vision

In 1543 Andreas Vesalius published the *Epitome*, a "less expensive companion book to the *Fabrica*."[26] It contains a very brief summary of the structure of the human body along with nine larger than folio-size anatomical illustrations, which "may be compared to fugitive sheets."[27] In the preface the author writes about the purpose of this book: "Here, we have dismembered the human body's history on a few pages, so that now the most important part of Nature's course may stand clear before the readers eyes just like a mirror."[28] Vesalius furthermore places particular emphasis on the fact that this knowledge about the body's anatomy can only be gained by opening up the body with one's own hands: "No-one will be able to gain knowledge about the human body unless he dissected bodies with his own hands."[29] Thus those large size plates that the *Epitome* as well as the *Fabrica* became famous for are based on the dissector's handiwork. Although Vesalius strives to make visible the body's interior, it is important to note that he does not mention his own gaze into the corpse, but seems more concerned with his touch. What in the *Epitome* appear to be two distinct activities—touching and looking—are really a complex negotiation between tactility and visuality.

Vesalius's emphasis on the importance of manual investigation for anatomy was in part a reaction to medieval teaching traditions, where university-trained physicians used to lecture about anatomy while leaving the actual dissection to low-ranking barber-surgeons. In the preface to the *Fabrica* he sharply condemns anatomists who shied away from using their hands: "we see learned physicians abstain from the use of the hands as from a plague lest the rabbins of medicine decry them before the ignorant mass as barbers and they acquire less wealth and honor than those scarcely half physicians."[30] He also deplored that "everything is wrongly taught in the schools," because the physician "has never applied his hand to the dissection of the body" and thus "haughtily governs the ship from a manual."[31] Vesalius did not stand alone in his plea for the physician's hands-on investigation. Frequently, as Katherine Rowe has observed, early modern anatomists reflected on the function of the hands for their work. Helkiah Crooke, for instance, warned his colleagues that without the sense of touch physicians "must of necessity grope uncertainlie in dark and palpable ignorance."[32] Consequently, for Crooke "the sense of Touching . . . so without doubt deserves the first place: For this is the ground of all the rest," even the "only Sense of all senses" (293). While Crooke acknowledged that the "tactive quality be diffused through the whole body both within and without," he nevertheless claimed that "we do more curiouslie and exquisitely feele and discerne [those] qualities which strike the Sense in the Hand than in other parts" (296). What makes the hand so very meaningful for anatomical dissection are not only its tactile qualities but also its connection to reason. Crooke fashioned the hand into an instrument of the surgeon's will when he noted that the "proper action of the Hand is Apprehension, and Apprehension a Motion depending on our will" (299). For the surgeon to perform a perfect dissection, it is essential, Crooke says, to combine cutting, "the action which is done with the hand," with the rational "habite of the minde" (291). The anatomist's hands are thus so "curious" and "exquisite" precisely because they execute his will: "The hand executeth those things which are commanded, our comandments are subject and obedient to Reason, and Reason it selfe is the power, force and efficacie of understanding" (285). Crooke thus does not simply praise the mechanical skill of the hand; he also celebrates it as an instrument without which the surgeon would not be able to control and master the bodies he dissects: "Reason, is the hand of understanding, Speech the hand of Reason, and the Hand it selfe, is the hand of Speech" (285).[33] Speech in this rational context must, of course, be understood as written speech. And within this framework, the hand, acting as the agent of writing, inscribes the symbolic into the body. The dissector's touch is celebrated for its rational and distancing qualities advancing a notion of dissection that is predicated upon a clear split between subject and object, or rather: between the passivity of the corpse on the dissection table and the anatomist's touch.

Two things become obscured in this praise of the anatomist's handiwork. The first, of course, is the violence with which his hands cut into the flesh and tear apart tissue. Crooke's rhetoric betrays his anxious attempt to obscure this violence when he writes that "the first requisite [is] that the parts bee so separated from another that they may all be preserved whole, not rent and torne asunder. Next, that those which grow not togither, be gently divided. Thirdly, that those which do grow together, be carefully separated" (293). As Rowe has observed, "In other contexts, this activity would produce pain and physical outrage," for the manual investigation of the body's interior involves "placing the hands inside it, lifting successive layers of tissue to reveal their point of origin and arrival" (293). Moreover, the dissector's touch seems to be a touch whereby the hand that touches remains itself untouched. This kind of touch is, of course, deeply gendered. As Sander Gilman notes, by the seventeenth century touch and the tactile were regarded as feminine while the act of touching (without being touched) was construed as masculine.[34] By penetrating the corpse with his hands the surgeon both provides new knowledge about the body's interior and constitutes his masculinity. This split between touching and being touched is a version of either having or being the phallus. The dissector's rational and controlling hand "has" the touch (and the phallus) while the dissected corpse "is" the touch (and the phallus). It is this phallic potential of the hand that charged its dissection with special meaning for anatomy. In the anatomical literature the dissection of the hand is usually treated with special attention and dealt with either at the very beginning or at the very end.[35] Vesalius's famous portrait on the front page of his *Fabrica* represents the hand's outstanding position for the anatomist as well as for anatomy (Figure 4).

The anatomist is fashioned as someone whose work is characterized by manual penetration and who best proves his anatomical skills by dissecting the hand, which, notably, is represented in such a fashion that obscures its state of decay and powerlessness. As if to underscore the priority of touch over vision, Vesalius himself does not look at the anatomized hand he puts up for display. And yet these efforts to honor the primacy of the hand are, albeit unintentionally and perhaps unnoticed, subverted by the practice of anatomical illustration, which since the times of Vesalius had gained increasing importance in anatomy. Starting with the *Fabrica*, "illustrated texts in anatomy became the predominant format and by 1650 anatomical knowledge was conveyed as much by illustrations as by texts."[36] As opposed to their medieval predecessors, early modern anatomists were very much concerned with the visual representation of the knowledge they had gained by their manual investigations. Vesalius's *Fabrica* contains 17 page-size plates and more than 250 smaller woodcuts; Casserio's *Tabulae* contains 78 very sophisticated copper plates larger than folio format. Both Vesalius and Casserio had been concerned with finding new ways to visualize the human body, and they may be considered pioneers in this field. Vesalius's books were most famous not for their written text, which did not substantially differ from older works, but for their illustrations, which were widely copied.[37] The illustrations in the *Fabrica* and the *Tabulae* display great artistic skill, and they are believed to stem from the workshops of famous artists like Titian and Tintoretto.[38] Early modern anatomists, artists, and readers of anatomy books alike were so enthusiastic about anatomical illustrations because they regarded the information conveyed by visual images as more reliable than that conveyed by verbal descriptions.[39] Leonardo da Vinci, who was himself very much interested in anatomy and who also performed dissections, wrote about the inadequacy of language in his *Notebooks*: "And you who think to

Figure 4. "Portrait of Andreas Vesalius," in Andreas Vesalius, *Fabrica corpore humanis libri septem* (Basel: Johannes Oporimus, 1543), n.p. Reproduced by permission of the Staatlsbibliothek zu Berlin, Stuftung Preußischer Kulturbesitz, Abt. Historische Drucke.

reveal the figure of man in words, with his limbs arranged in all their different attitudes, banish the idea from you, for the more minute your descriptions the more you will confuse the mind of the reader and the more you will lead him away from the knowledge of the thing described."[40] Da Vinci's preference for images is based on a critique of writing, that is, on the experience of a distance between body and the language representing it that could not be bridged. Images, however questionable this may seem today, seemed to promise unmediated representation of the body. Anatomical illustrations were regarded as truthful substitutes for the body's structure, shape, and functions. They were even regarded as superior to actual dissections since they were not subject to decay, spared the viewer feelings of "natural repugnance," and brought together the information of several dissections, since it was not possible, as Leonardo da Vinci notes, "to observe all the details shown in these drawings in a single figure, in which, with all your ability, you will not see nor acquire a knowledge of more than some few veins; while in order to obtain an exact and complete knowledge of these, I have dissected more than ten human bodies."[41]

The confidence in as well as the success of the visual representations of the body's interior were very much enhanced by the reintroduction and technical innovation of linear perspective into European culture during the fifteenth and sixteenth centuries. Technically linear perspective was considered a technique for representing three-dimensional space on the two dimensions of the flat canvas. But since it involved the construction of a vanishing point, the artificial partition of the visible world into geometrical space as well as the fiction of a fixed, one-eyed, distant, and sovereign spectator, it possessed broad social and cultural consequences.[42] As John Berger has noted, linear perspective "makes the single eye the centre of the visible world. . . . The visible world is arranged for the spectator as the universe was once thought to be arranged for God."[43] This controlling, distant, separating, voyeuristic, and uncorporeal gaze, which allows no visual reciprocity, displays the same phallic features as does the anatomist's touch. And although contemporaries regarded linear perspective as opposed to the abstraction and fragmentation caused by writing, it adheres to the same logic. In fact, perspective succeeds in making abstraction seem natural by making it visible. Considering that anatomical dissections, which had been performed on a regular basis since the end of the thirteenth century, gained new meaning during the Renaissance and also considering that anatomical illustrations played an important role in this process, it seems that both are indeed a result of linear perspective.[44] Linear perspective thus appears as the medium in which the "culture of dissection" comes to be communicated.[45] Envisaged in this way, the anatomist's phallic touch seems to be an effect of linear perspective as well as an integral element of visuality. This formative function of perspective seems to modify Foucault's theory of the "speaking eye," on which Sergei Lobanow-Rostovsky bases his argument when he notes that "what is created by this process of dissecting the body is not knowledge but a gaze that affirms the anatomist's subjectivity. Anatomy solicits the gaze, constitutes it as a form of language."[46] This argument, however, tends to underestimate the way linear perspective structures early modern anatomy. The perspectival gaze charged anatomy with this specific logic of partition, separation, detachment, and visibility that distinguishes it from its medieval tradition.

Just how far-reaching perspective was for anatomy may be judged from the fact that it not only revolutionized the visual representation of the body's interior but also created a new dimension of touching. The anatomical illustrations translate the dissector's manual touch into a visual touch for the viewers and readers of anatomy books. Instead of just putting the anatomist's handiwork before the reader's eyes—as Vesalius would have it—the images developed a tactile dynamic of their own. It is precisely because theses images stand in for the mortal and decaying body that they translate not only the body's structure and shape but also its tactility and tangibility into the realm of visuality. Indeed, anatomical illustrations request this kind of touch and tangibility, for the spectators are supposed to reiterate the surgeon's handiwork with their eyes. Far from denying the corpse's tangibility or the anatomist's handiwork, anatomical illustrations create their own kind of tactility and tangibility. Anatomical illustrations "work" because and only if the spectator has accepted, or rather learned to accept, that visuality implies the substitution of visual for manual touching. It is the gaze that assumes (part of) the function of the hand, and seeing thus becomes a form of touching.

The science of anatomy is, of course, by no means the only discourse negotiating the relationship between touch and vision. Oil painting, which just like anatomical illustration is connected to the use of linear perspective in the early modern period, also engaged in translating touch into vision. As Berger observes, "What distinguishes oil painting from any other form of painting is its special ability to render the tangibility, the texture, the lustre, the solidity of what it depicts."[47] The painter's rendering of different materials appeals to the spectator's sense of touch and "what the eye perceives is already translated, within the painting itself, into the language of tactile sensation."[48] As a cultural practice relying on both touching *and* looking, early modern anatomy thus seems a particularly interesting example if one wants to find out more about the relation between manual and visual touches.

Quite a number of frontispieces represent precisely this translation of touch into vision and are therefore conclusive for a discussion of this process. Although these images certainly function as a visual introduction to the complex practices of anatomy, they also tell us about the displacements that occur when the surgeon's handiwork is turned into an anatomical illustration. What critics so far have tended to overlook is the fact that in most of the frontispieces in which the anatomist invites the reader to take a look into the body's interior the anatomist himself does not look at the body he presents. The *Fabrica*'s well-known frontispiece is a very good case in point. The image shows an anatomist proudly presenting the opened-up body of a woman to a curious crowd. The pointing gesture of his right hand leads the spectator's gaze into the body's interior, promising deeper and more detailed insight on the pages that follow. The image suggests that the anatomist's mastery of the female corpse is based on his manual investigation, for he does not even look at the body whereas the readers'/spectators' mastery of the body's interior depends upon their reiteration of this touch through their gaze. In other words, whereas the dissector's potency is constituted by the touch the viewer's potency is constituted by the gaze. In this view, the anatomist's authoritative gesture at the women's body with his left hand might be read as a reminder not to forget that seeing is touching. Notably, it is the surgeon himself who is implicated in the production of this visual touch, not only because of his emphasis on the visual aspects of touch but also because of his interest in visibilizing what his hands had touched. Just like Vesalius's portrait in the same volume, the frontispiece suggests that what the reader/spectator sees is what the anatomist had touched. However, manual and visual touches are not identical. First of all, they belong to different "worlds," since the touch of the anatomist's hands is connected with decay, while the touch of the viewer's gaze connects to immortality. And second, the translation of touch into vision is much more complicated than the mere substitution of one sense for another. As Christina von Braun has argued, since the early modern period "visuality has created its own sense of touching," which in turn has affected notions of corporeality, sexuality, and gender.[49]

Genitals: Same and Different

In 1536 Andreas Vesalius claimed to have had a professional, albeit gruesome encounter with a female corpse.

While out walking, looking for bones in the place where on the country highways eventually, to the great convenience of students, all those who have been executed are customarily placed, I happened upon a dried cadaver. . . . I climbed the stake and pulled off the femur from the hip bone. While tugging at the specimen, the scapulae together with the arms and hands also followed, although the fingers of one hand, both patellae and one foot were missing. After I had brought the legs and arms home in secret . . . [I] allowed myself to be shut out of the city in the evening in order to obtain the thorax which was firmly held by a chain. I was burning with so great a desire . . . that I was not afraid to snatch in the middle of the night what I so longed for. . . . The next day I transported the bones home piecemeal through another gate of the city . . . and constructed that skeleton which is preserved at Louvain.[50]

Vesalius's rhetoric combines his anatomical interest to obtain corpses for dissection with his desire for the possession of a female body. The dismemberment of the corpse is staged at once as a passionate and illegal endeavor compelled by "so great a desire . . . that I was not afraid to snatch in the middle of the night what I so longed for." As Jonathan Sawday has noticed, "the language with which Vesalius arranged the nocturnal rendezvous with the object of his desire is the language of courtly love: illicit, secretive. . . . All that is missing is the balcony—an office supplied, however, by the gibbet upon which Vesalius clambered."[51] For Sawday this translation of courtly love and erotic poetry into the realm of anatomy is an example of the exchanges and circulations constituting the culture of dissection: "Both sought to gaze upon the body which they dismantled, piece by piece" (197). However, Vesalius's desire was directed not at gazing on but at "snatching" the body he "so longed for." Observing the importance of touch in this eroticized professional endeavor is crucial for an understanding of the way sexuality and desire are constituted and figured within anatomy. The manual possession and dismemberment of the female corpse allows the male dissector the fulfillment of his barely disguised sexual desire, indeed his sexual and erotic desires depend upon manual investigation and penetration. What the episode clearly shows is that the practice of anatomical dissection fashions sexual potency in terms of tactile potency. The female corpse and the male anatomist indeed show what strange "bedfellows"—to invoke Sawday's term—the culture of dissection could encourage (196).

Anatomical illustrations, by contrast, encouraged a very different kind of sexual and erotic satisfaction. The eroticized illustrations of female corpses in anatomy books, which very often "echo representations of female sexuality in Renaissance art," draw on the voyeuristic gaze.[52] The penetration these images requests is, however, performed not by the surgeon's touch but by the viewer's gaze. Sexual potency and pleasure are thus represented in terms of visual potency and pleasure, and sexual penetration equals visual penetration. Considering that during this same period syphilis spread all over Europe, the visual penetration the image invites might be regarded as "a form of safer sex," as von Braun has pointed out.[53] In this sense, tangibility indeed means visibility. Of course, this kind of "safer sex" not only promises protection against infection but also, as von Braun notes "serves as a protection against losing control" (82). In this context, Casserio's illustration invites an unusual sexual gaze. The image represents the early modern heteronormative stereotype of the "passive," "feminized" sodomite whose passivity is characterized by his desire to be penetrated like a woman by other men. This desire is represented not only by the inviting gesture of the right hand but also by the protruding anus (which can also be found on Bartholin's plate, Figure 2). Casserio's illustration might thus be read as an early (modern) instance of gay male pornography produced under the auspices of anatomical illustration, because the voyeuristic gaze is supposed to be the anatomical gaze as well. But there is more than sexuality at stake here. As the male's parturient position suggests, this gaze is a fertile one. Obviously, the fertility of the gaze contrasts with the dismemberment the surgeon's handiwork performs, just like the male's castration and hence infertility is a contrast to his potential motherhood. Furthermore, Vesalius's nocturnal rendezvous as well as Casserio's pornographic encounter create nonphallic Others and rely on phallic binarisms for the representation of desire and sexuality. But the Others they create are not the same. It is precisely in this context that the construction of the enlarged clitoris gains significance. The fashioning of the clitoris into a monstrous and yet invisible imitation of the penis yields insight into the way manual and visual touches created different bodies. Let me first look at the way the dissector touches the clitoris.

Early modern anatomists anxiously point out that the clitoris immediately responds to (their) touch and that this tactile response is always a sexual response. Colombo states, "not only if you *rub* it vigorously with a penis, but *touch* it even with a little finger, semen swifter than air flows this way" (emphasis mine).[54] Bartholin also connects the anatomist's touch to female sexual pleasure: "if [the clitoris] be gently touched in such as have long abstained from carnal Embracements, and are desirous thereof, Seed easily comes away."[55] Considering that the release of semen was believed to be accompanied by orgasm, the anatomist's touch suggests a pleasurable, even desirable experience for the woman. Moreover, considering that the easily excitable clitoris belongs to a female corpse, its "awakening" might be read as an example for the "resurrection of the flesh" which at least in the early modern period was tied to the erection of another penis: namely that of the resurrected Christ. As Leo Steinberg has demonstrated in *The Sexuality of Christ* the representation of the resurrected Christ's erection—what the author calls the "erection-resurrection equation"—in Renaissance paintings (albeit hidden under prominent loincloths and thus all the more conspicuous) symbolizes victory over death and mortality by a sheer act of the will.[56] Because this erection does not so much refer to the sexuality of Christ, as the book's title suggests, as to his ability to master the flesh, that is, to fertilize dead matter, through the power of his will.[57] In this sense, the erection (and ejaculation) of a dead woman's clitoris assumes the quality of resurrection—albeit with a crucial difference: the clitoridal erection does not prove volitional and autonomous female power over the flesh, since it is the anatomist's finger that causes the erection and awakens the female corpse to life. However, the penis *is* involved in this resurgence of female flesh.

Apart from the strange morbidity of this scene (how did the anatomist turn on a female corpse?), two things are important here. First, the touch of the surgeon's fingers repeats the touch of his penis, thereby fashioning his "Handy Worke" into a supplement of his sexual potency; second, it is this skillful touch that arouses and satisfies women's sexual desire. But while the women the anatomists "have sex with" cannot help but surrender to their touches, the surgeons themselves remain untouched, rational, and distant, thus denying the way this close physical and sexual contact might affect themselves. The clitoris's tangibility allows the anatomist to fashion the touch of his hands into a manifestation of (his) sexual potency and intellectual fertility. When turning his attention to the clitoris, the anatomist's touch—so dear to the authors of anatomy books—testifies to his skillful victory over mortality.

This tangibility of the female genitals is also reflected in the anatomical terminology. Clitoris referred to the verb form *klitorizein*, which, Spieghel notes, was an "obscene verb meaning to rub this part lasciviously with the fingers," and Crooke explains that clitoris "cometh of an obscoene worde signifying contrectation."[58] The term "Tribade" is derived from the Greek *tribein*, meaning "to rub," which first and foremost seems to refer to the enlarged clitoris's extraordinary tangibility. Crooke mentions that the Tribade's clitoris "groweth to such a length that it hangeth without the cleft like a mans member, *especially* when it is fretted with the touch of the cloaths, and so strutteth and groweth to a rigiditie as doth the yarde of the man" (emphasis mine).[59] Despite the fact that anatomists regarded the enlarged clitoris as an organ with which women could actively rub and penetrate each other, they nevertheless focused on its tangibility. For them the Tribade's sexual pleasure is predicated on the need to be touched. Because of this tangibility even the Tribade supports the primacy of the dissector's phallus. Describing and mapping the clitoris as "the most tangible element," as the Other of the penis, finally, offers a welcome occasion to bring the uniqueness of the penis into play as well as to efface the circumcision/castration of the penis through the anatomist's knife. Again and again anatomical texts invoke the originality and superiority of the penis in relation to the clitoris. Not only do its descriptions in anatomy books usually appear before those of the clitoris, thereby introducing the penis as standard and norm. Even more important are the repeated hints that the penis is an organ of extraordinary singularity whose "own character . . . is special and only referring to itself / nothing similar is to be found in the whole of the human body."[60] Although this is certainly true for the clitoris as well, this organ is never characterized as such. On the contrary, as I have indicated, the texts emphasize its derivative nature, its status as imitation of the original penis. For the anatomist, the construction of the clitoris as female penis clearly functions as a device to strengthen and confirm the singularity of the penis. Thomas Laqueur's widely disputed contention that the rediscovery of the clitoris proved largely insignificant for anatomy because all genitals were construed as male genitals so far represents the latest attempt at propounding the singularity of the male member.[61] By the denial of the visual representation of the anatomy of the erect and enlarged clitoris, it remains in the hands of the anatomist, subject to his exclusive touch. Here the different gendered logics that structure the dissector's handiwork on the one hand and its visual representation on the other become obvious. The tangibility of the clitoris is translated into its invisibility while at the same time the penis's putative untouchability is translated into visibility.

And yet for three reasons it would be wrong to assume that visuality implied the complete suppression of the visual representation of the en-

larged clitoris. First and foremost, visuality is not a *technique* that one inten-
tionally exploits *in order to* represent reality, rather it is a cultural paradigm
that fashions bodies, subjectivities, and realities. Second, visuality does not
"aim" at making bodies invisible, but makes them visible *within* its own
logic. And third, this logic in the Christian tradition implies the appropriation of the feminine by the masculine.

Let me therefore return to Casserio one last time. Ironically, the image
itself brings the enlarged clitoris—or, if you will, Correggio's swan—into
play. Indeed, the lower part of the figure's body looks like a swan, with the
thighs and legs as the wings and the penis as the neck. With a bit more fantasy even Bartholin's illustration of the penis resembles a swan or goose (Figure 2). In Casserio's image the penis/question mark seems to provide a
perfect "disguise" for the visual representation of the enlarged clitoris, and in
so doing the image points to the very specific constraints of visual potency
and tangibility that seem to have thwarted any undisguised display of the
Tribade's anatomy. Envisaged in this way, the image represents an attempt at
bringing the enlarged clitoris to bear on the penis. But does this body really
represent a hermaphrodite, as I suggested at the beginning of this essay? It is
true, he has got both penis and clitoris, but he does not possess two *separate*
sets of genitals. Rather the male genital *contains* the female one. In the
anatomical image penis and clitoris indeed become "one flesh": the penis. It
is this visual "oneness" of penis and clitoris in the name and shape of the
phallus/penis that I consider the "reward" for the circumcision/castration of
the penis. In opposition to Thomas Laqueur's famous description of the
one-sex body fashioned by early modern anatomy I argue that this image
shows a *male* body with *two* sexes.[62] The "femaleness" of the male figure is
furthermore suggested by his "vaginal" anus through which he seems ready
to give birth to a child. Thus the "inconsistencies" or "contradictions" between text and illustrations in anatomy books do not necessarily have to reflect "a lack of comprehension of anatomy" nor "a lack of artistic capability,"
as K. B. Roberts and J. D. W. Tomlinson suggest; they also reflect the different
bodies that manual and visual touches create.[63]

This contradictory function within the phallic economy of early modern anatomy explains why the enlarged clitoris figures so prominently in
anatomy books and yet remains (almost) invisible. These displacements and
conjunctions show that in order to reach an understanding of the cultural
significance of gender and sexuality, it is necessary to take into account the
formative power of the media over the senses. Thus the "broader contemporary

concerns related to male privilege and the status of women," which, as Park argues, are reflected in the construction of the clitoris by early modern anatomists might be described as part of the history of touch and vision.[64] Early modern anatomists' and artists' investments with the clitoris (and the penis) not only indicate that visuality created a new sense of touch, they also suggest that the hand and they eye touched very different bodies indeed.

Chapter 7

New World Contacts and the Trope of the "Naked Savage"

Scott Manning Stevens

> How deep are the purposes and Councells, of God? what should be the rea-
> son of this mighty difference in One mans children that all the Sonnes of
> men on this side the way (in Europe, Asia and Africa) should have such
> plenteous clothing for Body, for Soule! and the rest of Adams sonnes and
> Daughters on the other side, or America (some thinke as big as the other
> three) should neither have nor desire clothing for their naked Soules, or
> Bodies.
>
> —Roger Williams, A Key into the Language of America (1643)

Some three decades ago Walter Ong examined Western culture's predilection for visual metaphors and tropes over those based on aural or tactile experience.[1] In a suggestive schema of the five senses, ranging from touch through taste, smell, hearing and sight, Ong notes that the movement from sight to touch is one that may be understood as movement "toward propinquity of the sense organ to the source of stimulus; toward concreteness; toward matter; toward subjectivity." When characterizing the opposite movement from touch to sight Ong describes this as movement "toward greater distance from the object physically; toward greater abstraction; toward greater formalism; toward objectivity; toward idealism divorced from actual existence."[2] I would like us to apply this conceptualization of the senses to the discourse of the encounter between the inhabitants of the Old World and the New during the early modern period. Traditional Western historiography has tended to privilege the notion of "discovery" over "contact" or "encounter." In so doing the reciprocal aspects of cultural exchange and trauma are obscured by a unidirectional and objectifying rhetoric. The New World ("New" of course only to the Europeans) is thereby transformed into an object to be revealed through European exploration. By focusing on "contact," both as a literal and figurative phenomenon, we reorient that discourse toward a more complete understanding of the experiences that constitute the New World Encounter.

Both the land and the inhabitants of the Americas were affected physically and in turn had an affect on the Europeans. For the indigenous population, contact would very often prove fatal and would inevitably result in cultural disruptions that are difficult for most of us to appreciate today. One of the recurring figures within the many narrative accounts of the New World encounters is that of the "naked savage." Here the native body is more than a sign to be deciphered and read—this body is also there to be experienced. Nakedness in such accounts operates on both the literal and symbolic levels. We should begin by acknowledging the native body as the sign and signifier of its own materiality: a mnemonic of our shared human condition by which we are reminded of our common needs, our common desires and our common vulnerability. The naked body, thus absent of identifying and estranging costumes and customs, becomes a problematic signifier. One means of establishing difference must lie in experiencing the body of the Other—whether through sexual contact or by other means. Ong's notion of the rhetoric of the senses underscores the actuality and concreteness of contact, and it is from this position that I wish to approach the broad category of European writings on this subject.

Clearly it was Europe's encounter with the inhabitants of the New World (and subsequently with non-Europeans worldwide) that offered one of the greatest challenges to the accepted notions of self or the category of person and to notions of culture as they had been formulated in the western humanistic tradition. If humanism and the Reformation had contributed to the refinement of the articulation of what Hans Blumenberg calls "human self-assertion," then the discovery of an alien Other laid new demands on that process of articulation. To a large extent these demands were generic. Debora Shuger has defined "habits of thought" as "a culture's interpretive categories and their internal relations, which underlie specific beliefs, ideas, and values." She adds that "Renaissance habits of thought were by and large religious."[3] I argue that it was the "new world essay" as a genre that provided the reading public with a literary model for assessing the *moral impact* of contact with the New World and its inhabitants on their own cultures and beliefs. What then, we may ask, were the interpretive categories available to essayists as they considered the significance of New World encounters? Religion surely informed the thinking of all the early essayists, but at the same time it is important to recognize the relative absence of specifically Christian habits of thought in their writings. This does not automatically place them in the neat pseudo-category of "secular humanists." Montaigne and even more so Bacon were willing to go beyond the humanistic precepts they had inherited from the ancients whenever those interpretive categories did not conform with their own experiences. The early modern essay is thus a proving ground for new habits of thought–informed, to be sure, by humanism but with experience as its highest arbiter of truth.

Essays were taken to be largely concerned with moral philosophy; hence my primary focus has been on the essay as a discourse of Self. In attempting to trace the development of this particular discourse, I find it useful to examine how Montaigne, one of the earliest essayists, went about assaying the unknown Other recently found to inhabit that New World. I call this the "problem of other bodies," taking as my starting point Ludwig Wittgenstein's discussion of "the problem of other minds." This problem, put forward in several forms in his major opus, the *Philosophical Investigations*, can be summarized as follows: "I can never know what another person is really thinking or feeling (nor, conversely, can he or she ever know what I am really thinking or feeling)."[4] I wish to reformulate that problem and examine the implications of encountering an alien Other as a Body first and then attempting to extrapolate a notion of mind from that contact, specifically, the encounter of the Europeans with the indigenous population of the Americas during the sixteenth and seventeenth centuries. In many of the accounts of early explorers and observers, this was an epistemological problem of category or kind: did different bodies imply different selves? Hayden White has proposed that soon after the discovery of the New World the notion of a race of "wild men" created a crisis of category for the general notion of "humanity" developed in western philosophy. This crisis, he holds, led to the development of two opposing views of the inhabitants of the New World, which he describes as follows:

On the one hand, natives were conceived to be *continuous* with the humanity on which Europeans prided themselves; and it was this mode of relationship that underlay the policy of proselytization and conversion. On the other hand, the natives could be conceived as simply existing *contiguously* to Europeans, as representing either an inferior breed of humanity or a superior breed, but in any case being essentially different from the European breed; and it was this mode of relationship that underlay the policies of war and extermination which the Europeans followed throughout the seventeenth and most of the eighteenth century.[5]

White goes on to say that regardless of what position one took it was the mere *differentness* of the natives that would become fetishized and influence all subsequent native-settler interactions. I wish to examine the native body as such a fetishized object in early modern culture and to plot its tropological progression as part of the discourse of subjectivity.

The native body had presented itself to many of the first Europeans that encountered it as an emblem of human corporal materiality. The trope of the "naked savage," or more specifically the naked body of the native as trope, is central to any attempt to understand how this generic crisis of Self was understood, for the signification of this body did not always imply a person. Eschewing a merely punning relationship between terms for clothing the body and larger cultural concepts, we should scrutinize the interplay between such words as covering and discovering, habit, custom/costume, and person/persona (or mask). How is it that so many of the terms associated with "self-fashioning" should have strong cognates with the terms used for clothing or covering the body? The assumption in most contemporary cultures that a body represents a Self plays into a set of essentialist notions that were largely not in place at the point of contact between early modern Europe and the New World. We should also be aware of the long tradition of encountering Others that predates the Columbian "discovery," in order better to understand the often fantastic, ambivalent, and deeply conflicted accounts of those first Europeans in the New World. The classical tradition provided a wealth of sources that we might rightly consider proto-ethnologies, and these contributed greatly to what I call the anticipated body of the Other. These are the monstrous bodies of giants, Anthropophagi, Amazons, acephalous creatures and the like that inhabited the works of such authorities as Herodotus, Pliny, and Solinus. Their accounts of such beings had leached into European folklore with renewed authority with the recovery, translation, and dissemination of previously unprinted texts during the Renaissance.

The medieval period supplied its own authoritative texts which reinforced these inherited beliefs in a fantastic or monstrous other. "True" accounts could be found in the works of the medieval encyclopedists such as Isidore of Seville and Bartholomeus Anglicus. To these extensive catalogues was added an element not often found in the classical sources, namely the desire to submit this body of information to a master narrative (in this case the Christian Bible and the authority of the Church). The observation of the Other began to lead to moral conclusions about the status of these other beings. Blackness, for example, had long been read by Europeans as a sign of divine disfavor, a token of God's judgment on Cham and his descendants.[6] Such interpretations from the Judeo-Christian tradition were combined with Aristotle's notion that "those, who are as much inferior to others as are the body to the soul and beasts to men, are by nature slaves. . . . He is by nature a slave who shares in reason to the extent of apprehending it without possessing it."[7] This challenges the status of the Other at the most profound level of enfranchisement. Even when one group was not directly oppressing another, a habit of thought existed that severely retarded cross-cultural comprehension. It is this moralizing response to the category of difference that would remain the most difficult snare for later observers to escape. One notable exception can be found in John Mandeville's *Travels*. As Stephen Greenblatt has pointed out, "Mandeville's open and lively interest in the customs of exotic peoples, his refusal to invoke demonic causality for unfamiliar or even repellent practices, and his willingness to impute internal coherence to superficially irrational behavior is not tolerance but rather an early instance of what Hans Blumenberg calls 'theoretical curiosity.'"[8] But if Mandeville was disinclined to demonize the alien Other, there were many others who were not.

The cumulative effect of these accounts of encounter was to condition the European mind as to what to expect from the process of discovery and contact. The literature of the Encounter is, as I have said, vast and heterodox, and no formulation of the condition and meaning of the alien Other is without its rival. The monstrous body that was anticipated was often the monstrous body that was found. The fascination for such accounts comes into play in one of Shakespeare's most notable scenes of the interaction between a European and non-European—when Othello, himself a physical sign of the Other, explains how Desdemona came to love him. He claims it was his account to her "greedy ear" "of the Cannibals that do each other eat / The Anthropophagi, and men whose heads / Do grow beneath their shoulders" (I.iii.143–45). Tales of the fantastic body of the Other, it would seem, had a magnetic effect, and many of the early explorers, invaders, and missionaries had an equally greedy will to experience such things. This stemmed from the desire for tangible proof of the anticipated other. Many such reports came back of actual encounters with Amazons and wild men, though few would claim to have seen the more fantastic physical anomalies they had expected. In Ralegh's account of the discovery of Guiana, the monstrous Other, like El Dorado, is always around the next bend or in the next valley. His native informants assure him they're there.

In the absence of the creatures that had been anticipated, attention turned to the inhabitants at hand. They, however, were neither monstrous nor so clearly Other as the sub-Saharan Africans with whom the Europeans were familiar. The Africans' skin color marked them as other, and for many Europeans this was the proof of their inferiority. (Like most tautologies this is an insidious logic—"How do we know they are inferior?" answer, "They are different.") Yet in the report of that first encounter in the Caribbean, Columbus is struck by the physical attractiveness of the natives: "they were all very well built with fine bodies and handsome faces. They all go about naked as their mothers bore them, including the women."⁹ In the account of the first voyage Columbus remarks on the nakedness of the natives no less than sixteen times: "the king and all his people went naked," "these people are very gentle and fearful; naked as I have said," "they come to us naked," and so on. Here the principal sign for the natives' difference is their exposed bodies. For Columbus it marks them as a people "short of everything." Todorov remarks, "Physically naked, the Indians are also, to Columbus's eyes, deprived of all cultural property: they are characterized, in a sense, by the absence of customs, rites, religion (which has a certain logic, since for a man like Columbus, human beings wear clothes following their expulsion from Paradise, itself at the source of their cultural identity)."¹⁰ This aspect of the natives, their nakedness, becomes, I would argue, the central trope that displaces the monstrous Other and comes to be the primary signifier of their difference in the early phases of the encounter.¹¹

Much is made of the native body in travel accounts throughout the sixteenth century. A series of binarisms begins to develop whenever the trope of the naked savage is interpreted. It is always evidence of either the natives' innocence or their sinful natures, their Edenic state or their wretched bestiality. The opposition of "good Indians" and "bad Indians" has been present since first contact, and its history has been explored by a number of scholars.¹² It is worth pointing out though that even though the natives of the New World have always had their champions (let alone those who have completely romanticized native virtues) the path of empire and conquest has never found the "noble savage" useful to its rhetoric of conversion, submission, and assimilation. Either way it becomes the focus of a considerable amount of fetishizing.¹³ Amerigo Vespucci reports that the native women are "quite beautiful and with well made bodies" but dangerous because they are "insatiably voluptuous." Nor do their bodies show the signs of aging but are "marvels worthy of admiration," for well into their later years their "shameful parts" maintained the appearance of those of virgins. Here we are not very far from the rhetoric of the "virgin land" waiting to be husbanded or from Spenser's "fruitfullest Virginia." While Donne's Elegy XIX with its exclamation:

Oh my America! my new-found-land,
My kingdom, safeliest when with one man man'd,
My Mynne of precious stones, my Emperie,
How blest am I in this discovering of thee!
To enter in these bonds is to be free;
Then where my hand is set, my seal shall be.
Full nakedness! All joys are due to thee

makes explicit the connection between the naked body and travel accounts, his melding of the erotics of imperialism and discovery with the exposure of the body seems not half so surprising in the context of the literature of the Encounter. Here, as elsewhere, the dis/covery of an object tempts invasion at a more than metaphoric level. Witness the character Seagull's claim in Jonson, Marston, and Chapman's play *Eastward Ho!* (1605), "Come, boys, Virginia longs till we share of her maidenhead."[14] But to others like Jean de Léry and André Thévet, whose works Montaigne knew, the naked Native body is a contested signifier. Léry, while generally admiring the natives, says at one point of his fellow Europeans, "I find them to be far behind the humanity of these people, whom nevertheless we call barbarians."[15] Yet he finds their nakedness a disturbing sign and relates that "the women could be constrained to wear clothes only by much whipping . . . and even then did not have the sense to cover those parts that to Christians are indecent."[16] To André Thévet and others the exposed body of the native was not a contested sign; the Brazilians were seen as "living like beasts, just as nature had produced them, eating roots, going naked, a people cruel and inhuman." His compatriot Villeagnon found the natives "so different from us and so distant in all proper behavior and humanity that one would think they had fallen among beasts with human faces."[17]

One incontrovertible aspect of the contact between the Old World and the New was that it had deadly and lasting effects on the original inhabitants.[18] Primary among these devastations was the byproduct of actual contact—the spreading of disease. Europeans unwittingly brought with them a host of pathogens. The profound impact this had on native populations is almost incalculable. Disease would act as what James Axtell has characterized as the "shock troops" of the European invasion that, he goes on to say, "swept unseen through defenseless Indian villages with lethal ruthlessness,

dramatically reducing the natives' numerical superiority and exploding for-
ever their mental equilibrium."[19] Whether seen by the Europeans as provi-
dential or accidental, they could not help but note the massive depopulations
that so often followed their arrival. Not surprisingly, then, does Bacon have
the natives of his New Atlantis place the newly arrived Europeans under
strict quarantine.

Though the means of transmission of infectious diseases was not clearly
understood, the Europeans did recognize their effects. One must also remember that to some early modern Europeans the spread of disease was understood to be a reciprocal process. The primary, if not singular, example of this
was concurrent with the appearance of a particularly virulent form of syphilis
in Italy around 1495. Within several decades the spread of this disease had
reached epidemic proportions.[20] It would not be long before several "authorities" on the New World would claim this dreaded disease had its roots in the
Americas. In 1526 Gonzalo Fernández de Oviedo y Valdes published his *Summary Account of the Natural History of the Indies*, in which he claimed concerning "the great pox": "The first time this sickness was seen in Spain was
after Admiral Don Christopher Columbus had discovered the Indes and returned from those lands. Some Christians amongst those who went with him
and took part in the discovery, and many more who made the second trip,
brought back this scourge, and from them it was passed on to others."[21]

As the passage from Oviedo implies, the pox was seen as a punishment
from God. Given the clear association of the disease with sexual intercourse
(as noted later in the same passage by Oviedo), there was an inevitable attempt to understand it as the "wages of sin." Entwined with the American
roots of this sexual scourge was the notion of physical intimacy between the
"civilized" and the "savage." Here physical contact with the natives becomes
associated with sin and death—contact that resists the salvific touch of the
laying-on of hands or the "royal touch." The naked body seemed both inviting and vulnerable to touch and the effects of this contact would have a
lasting and profound cultural impact.

The literature of the Encounter is rife with contradictory accounts of
native sexual mores. Some held the Indians to be insatiably licentious while
others saw them as wholly devoid of this sin. Their nakedness was usually at
the center of both of assumptions. Roger Williams, for instance, marvels at
the paradox of their innocence in comparison with European societies. Writing of what he calls their "two-fold nakedness" (a general lack of clothing in
daily life and stark nakedness in private), Williams concludes, "Custome hath
used their minds and bodies to it, and in such a freedom from any wanton-

nesse, that I have never seen that wantonnesse amongst them, as, (with griefe) I have heard of it in Europe."[22] This distinction between the valences of meaning associated with the word "naked" was a common one in the period.[23] What is remarkable here is the notion that the customary exposure of the body seems to nullify "wantonnesse" rather than encourage it.

That custom could affect the body's physiology was a common enough assumption held by the likes of Montaigne. In his essay "On the Custom of Wearing Clothes," he notes that those who were accustomed to "nakedness" because of their poverty—such as many French peasants were—often seemed able to endure the severest extremes of weather. Roger Williams's observation above, which is typical of European reports on the lack of lasciviousness among the "naked savages," is an argument that custom affects not merely physiology but the also the libidinal urges of humans. The native body exposed for all to see and accessible to touch inspired lust most often in those clothed and most alienated from their own sensual identities. Renaissance commentaries proposed a variety of theories about the physiology of the inhabitants of the New World to explain these differences. Since believing the "savages" to be free of original sin would be heretical, they required other answers. Often theories were proposed using the notion of the domesticated animal versus the wild animal as their starting points.

In his sixteenth-century medical treatise *Erreurs populaires*, Laurent Joubert comments on the physical characteristics of the Brazilian Indians as follows:

I might add here what is written about women from Brazil (a country also called America, discovered and first known by our peers), who never have menstrual flow, like female animals, whose nature and constitution these Brazilians resemble considerably. But since these poor women, living like savages, completely naked and in great hardship, follow the nature of animals, they should not be considered in the present discussion, especially since it is most likely and believable that, if they were to change their climate and living habits, were transported to cooler countries, clothed, nourished, and housed, changing their makeup, they would behave like our women and would accumulate excess blood, which, unless it were used to nourish a child, would flow forth once each month.[24]

The civilizing effects of exposure to European culture are here understood to lead to distinct physiological changes in the natives, which in turn will raise them in status towards a "true humanity."

One can see this concept of physical metamorphosis through acculturation coloring the observations of the seventeenth-century promoter of the

New England colonies, William Wood as well. In a description of the regional flora Wood makes a telling remark: "The cherry trees yield great store of cherries, which grow on clusters like grapes; they be much smaller than our English cherry, nothing near so good if they be not very ripe. . . . English ordering may bring them to be an English cherry, but yet they are as wild as the Indians."[25] Presumably what worked for the cherry would work with the Indians as well.

The same notion of "English ordering" referred to in Wood is most likely the reasoning behind the cultural engineering designed by the English for their Virginia venture. English marriages to the Indians would only follow what Mary Fuller describes as a "careful program of spatial and cultural alienation: removing Algonkian women from Virginia, taking them first to London, then to Bermuda to marry; only once thoroughly socialized in their new culture could they return home to convert and socialize others."[26] Once the native body was domesticated and made fully aware of the implications of "nakedness" and "savagery" it could be incorporated in the fullest sense of the word by English society. But custom was still secondary to environment when attempting to account for cultural difference. Manners and mores evolved, but to the Europeans it was just as often climate that was at the root of savagery. As one scholar put it, "During the development of manual manners for dining the matter of the cannibal's discovered eating hands was blamed on a global theory of touch. . . . Like diverse peoples, the monstrous creatures were determined so by the sense of touch, not in its organic definition as hands but through what hands essentially felt: temperature."[27]

As I noted earlier, Montaigne examines this very phenomenon concerning the effects of our environment in his brief essay "On the Custom of Wearing Clothes." Here he takes a cardinal cultural difference—the clothed versus the naked—and speculates on the root of this difference in the cultures of the New World. "I was devising in this chil-cold season, whether the fashion of these late discovered Nations to go naked, be a custome forced by the hot ayre, . . . or whether it be an originall manner of mankind."[28] Montaigne is often in search of those universal categories that paradoxically can accommodate the maximum amount of individual differences; hence his interest in the variety of manners by which humans approach mortality. When contemplating the effects of climate on the body he takes as axiomatic the assertion drawn from Ecclesiastes that "whatsoever is contained under heaven is subject to the same lawes."[29]

With this axiom in mind Montaigne could be said to posit something akin to Marjorie O'Rourke Boyle's "global theory of touch." It is the sense of touch that primarily governs all human interactions with our environment. Ancient authorities such as Aristotle and Lucretius both recognized touch as dispersed throughout the body and as the foundation of the more localized sensory organs.[30] The naked body of the savage thus maximized the exposure of this sense to the world around it. What Montaigne sought to understand was how a universal condition such as the relationship of touch to climate could produce such a variety of results. Characteristically, in order to do this Montaigne reorients his readers closer to home. He compares French peasants (for Montaigne they are always closer to humanity in its natural state than are the nobility) to the natives and asks how either can endure cold weather scantily clad: "For of those nations that have no knowledge of clothes, some are found situated under the same heaven, and climate, or parallel, that we are in, and more cold and sharper than ours. Moreover, the tenderest parts of us are ever bare and naked, as our eyes, mouth, nose and ears; and our country-swaines (as our forefathers wont) most of them go barebreasted down to the navill."[31] Such a discussion of the naked body (savage or otherwise) exposed to the extremes of heat or cold does not call on us to visualize the body, so much as it requires us to imagine how the body would *feel* in such situations. We are reminded that bodies everywhere are conformable to their climates through touch.

Accounts of the "naked savages" thus abound in the literature of the sixteenth and seventeenth centuries, and Europeans seemed to have a boundless appetite for their description (think of Desdemona's "greedy ear"); they could be said to be enacting a cannibalism of their own on a metaphoric level. But descriptions were not enough: Europeans wanted to experience these exotic people first hand and if they could not go to the New World the natives could be brought to them. This was done on the very first voyage of Columbus, as Columbus's son, Hernando, recounts in his biography of his father. The Indians who were brought back were the only tangible proof that Columbus and his men had of the success of their voyage, and Hernando describes the vast crowds in Lisbon that came to the ships to marvel at the Indians. From that point on, various explorers would attempt to convince, coerce or kidnap natives with the sole purpose of bringing them back to Europe to be exploited for their language skills and knowledge of their homelands.[32] Another general purpose for kidnapping the Indians seems to have been for propaganda and fund-raising. They were brought before kings and merchants, and with the aid of supposed interpreters they told of immense and wondrous riches and the like—but for the most part they function as physical evidence.

In 1509 the first "savages" were brought to Rouen, as merchant investors were sought for France's commercial and colonial enterprise. By 1530 Cartier was able to secure an audience with François I in order to produce his most recent prize, the kidnapped Huron chief Dannoncona. With the success of such displays, a group of entrepreneurs in 1550 staged a "Fête Brésilienne" in Rouen complete with some forty Tupinamba Indians from Brazil. Unsure as to whether forty Indians would suffice, the organizers recruited 250 Norman sailors to go disguised as Indians; this in effect meant that they appeared naked, stained brown, and wearing headdresses. A kind of "Wild West Show" was then staged that included mock battles, dancing, and story-telling. The Fête was a success, drawing the entire court of Henri II and creating a vogue for things Brazilian—most importantly the brazil-wood dye industry.

It was to Rouen that Montaigne traveled in 1562 in order to see and, if possible, to speak with members of the Tupinamba nation. Among the Tupinamba's many reputed exotic practices was the one most taboo, cannibalism. The cannibal had come down to early modern Europeans as the most enduring human monster. From the first encounter in 1492, they had been the spectral "bad Indians" reported by the seemingly prelapsarian Taíno people to Columbus—the people he called the Caribs. As a signifier they are among the most insidious because their outward bodies are not physically monstrous: rather it is their inhuman customs that make them savages. Vespucci's arousing natives were no respecters of kin or kind, and he claims to have seen them "eat up their wives and their children." Peter Martyr, who stresses the Edenic nature of the natives, always opposes them to the monstrous Caribs. When on Columbus's second voyage the sailors manage to capture several Caribs and bring them back to Madrid, Peter Martyr goes to "examine" them and writes, "There is no man able to behold them, but he should feel his bowels grate with a certain horror, so infernal and repugnant an aspect nature and their own cruel characters have lent them."[33] Martyr points out no physical traits in his account; rather it is his knowledge that he is looking at the body of a cannibal that causes his reaction.

The figure of the cannibal is one of the most pervasive and enduring characters in the literature of the Encounter. I would like to suggest here that the cannibal might be understood in part by the Europeans as a monstrous extension of what I will call the "logic of the naked savage." If we consider for a moment how observers in the early modern period could construe customary nudity as removing libidinal urges by habituating the natives to their exposed bodies, we might carry it further and ask if continued access to the naked body might be understood to "desacralize" human corporeality. Consider a process that could be called reverse sublimation. If carnal urges can be sublimated to mental processes in one paradigm, the opposite might be possible in a culture with radically different notions of corporeality and the status of the natural. In this scheme the bare facticity of the human body in such a society might lead to a "super-familiarity" with it and thus be said to change one's notion of its sacred status. What should make the dead body other than flesh? Europeans may have easily and wrongly assumed such a connection between the nakedness of the natives and the supposed fact of cannibalism. The notion of revenge lies at the center of both Léry's and Montaigne's understanding of cannibalism. The eating of one's enemies constitutes a radical incorporation of the other. Cannibalism thus erases the human boundaries formulated and distinguished through touch. Consuming the body, which comprehends its corporeal identity through the primal distinctions made through touch, acts as a revenge beyond blinding or depriving the enemy of their other senses. Murder is not revenge enough in this case, but rather literal incorporation. Whether cannibalism is seen as a dangerous desacralization of human flesh or the ultimate revenge it became a frequent charge against the naked savage.

We know from certain Jesuit writings of the seventeenth century that they sometimes adapted explanations of the Eucharist for the Natives so as to avoid confusing the doctrines of transubstantiation with cannibalism. As Henry Bowden explains missionaries such as Jean de Brébeuf in New France avoided mentioning "eating the body of Christ and drinking his blood," substituting instead "the Huron word for thanksgiving festivals, a purely memorial ceremony." Bowden continues that Brébeuf "must have considered it worthwhile to obviate Tridentine statements about transubstantiation and simultaneously avoid aboriginal connotations of absorbing an enemy's courage by eating him."[34] Elsewhere Stephen Greenblatt has pointed to debates between Protestant Reformers and Catholic theologians over the corporeality of the bread and wine. The sensual and generally tactile experience of communion was still important to Protestants even if the substance did not change. Greenblatt quotes Thomas Cranmer's remarkable statement on the subject of the physical experience of the Eucharist: " 'the eating and drinking of this sacramental bread and wine is, as it were, a showing of Christ before our eyes, a smelling of him with our noses, a feeling and groping of him with our hands, and an eating, chewing, digesting, and feeding upon him to our spiritual strength and perfection.' "[35] If Protestant theologians could discuss the purely symbolic sacraments in such terms, how could the Eucharist in turn be presented to the "savages," let alone the cannibals? Cannibalism represents a crisis of kind.

Unlike the monstrous wild men of the forest or the dog-headed people of folklore, the cannibal's body is the deceiving sign—one that could only be known through contact. Given the cannibal's positioning at the extreme margins of human society, it is not surprising that Montaigne should choose this subject to test his own notions about human nature. "Of Cannibals" is arguably his most famous essay (perhaps the most famous single essay of the early modern period), and readers then as now were often shocked by what seems to be Montaigne's relative indifference to the act of cannibalism—an act he claims we are justified in calling a barbaric horror, even if he then goes on to explain it away as custom. The essayist's relativism is usually seen as Montaigne's primary strategy for recuperating the humanity of the so-called savages. Not long ago however, Tzvetan Todorov challenged this notion of relativism in Montaigne by claiming that what is really at work is a hierarchy of values that valorizes classical authorities while revealing a core indifference to the actual cultural differences found in Tupinamba society.[36] Todorov locates Montaigne's acceptance of and admiration for the cannibals in what he identifies as a misunderstanding or projection onto the Other of an image of the Self—or more precisely an ideal self, embodied for Montaigne in the classical civilizations of Greece and Rome. Insightful as this reading may at first appear, it is important to qualify this observation by pointing out Montaigne's well-known misreadings (or should I say willful misreadings) of the classical past and his willingness to question its authority. What Montaigne values in the Ancients is just as often what he projects onto them. Montaigne's relativism is not as easy to decode as Todorov would have us believe. In fact, Todorov himself ignores Montaigne's biblical references in the same essay in order to claim that Montaigne privileges classical antiquity.

Montaigne's strategy for forming an opinion on the cannibals can be seen, appropriately enough, as a series of tests. In each case the received opinion (that the cannibals are inhuman monsters) is tried against another set of opinions or authorities. Through a series of dislocations we move from the classical and biblical past to the present, and in each case no universal is found. The wisdom of the past provides a variety of opinions that many readers may not have guessed at or been aware of: the classical tradition praised military valor and so do the cannibals; their cannibalism is incorporated into their warfare and their notion of revenge (though it is not the reason for their fighting), also, certain Stoic philosophers, we are reminded, find that "that it was no hurt at all, in times of need, and to what end soever, to make use of our carrion bodies, and to feed upon them."[37] Similarly, the Old Testament provides us with several examples of polygamy (another charge against the cannibals) without condemning it. In each case Montaigne makes no claims to have found a new set of imperatives; instead, he points out the heterodoxy of his own cultural tradition. Moving from the distant past to his own period he looks abroad to the accounts of those who have been to the New World. From their reports he paints a picture of a Golden Age free from the vices common to his own culture.[38] His sources (that we know of) were López de Gomorra, Thévet, and Léry. None of these accounts draw similar conclusions about the nature of the natives or their customs: their value as accounts lies in the documentary witness they bear. The final dislocation in the text is the return of the essayist to his own experience. The self is the ultimate authority in Montaigne's value system and it remains contradictory and mobile. Experience is the final test.

The naked body of the Other in Montaigne's work becomes a trope of an inescapable honesty–one that is blemished, imperfect, beautiful, and present. It becomes in effect the guiding metaphor for the *Essais* as a whole. In the well-known foreword entitled "The Author to the Reader," Montaigne writes: "My imperfections shall therein be read to the life, and my naturall forme discerned, so farre-forth as publike reverence hath permitted me. For if my fortune had beene to have lived among those nations, which yet are said to live under the sweet liberty of Natures first and uncorrupted lawes, I assure thee, I would most willingly portrayed my selfe fully and naked."[39] It is this attitude toward nakedness—read as a trope of honesty and immanence, not unlike More's Utopians appearing to one another naked before settling their marriage contracts—that signals what is at the heart of Montaigne's interest in a culture that he did not, and could not hope truly to understand. The naked body of the native comes to represent humanity before the accretions of culture, or, in Montaigne's view, custom, had covered or effaced our core identity. If he refers to the Golden Age of the Greek poets, he does so in the knowledge that they too could only surmise this state of innocence from a distance. And if we can value this idea in their works we should be willing to recognize its cognate in our own time. We dream our ideals but experience through the body. The cannibals recuperate Montaigne's ideal—that is honesty—by the fact of their bodies and customs, even as they throw into doubt a universal definition of the nature of man. "It is man with whom we have always to doe, whose condition is marvelously corporall."[40] Corporeality foregrounds, both etymologically and figuratively, the centrality of the body in the discourse of human subjectivity and by extension to the sense of touch and its primacy in the body's relationship to the world around it.

Chapter 8

Noli me tangere: *Colonialist Imperatives and Enclosure Acts in Early Modern England*

Elizabeth Sauer and Lisa M. Smith

This chapter situates the *noli me tangere* imperative within theological, early colonial, and feminist contexts by juxtaposing biblical narrative, seventeenth-century English discourses of enclosure, and John Milton's *Paradise Lost.* God's command to Adam and Eve in Eden not to eat of the tree of knowledge, which Eve rewords as "But of the frute of the tre, which is in the middes of the garden, God hathe said, Ye shal not eat of it, nether shal ye touche it, lest ye dye,"[1] initiates a tradition that is echoed in Mary Magdalene's encounter with the risen Christ in John 20. Mary's meeting also takes place within a garden, and she initially mistakes Christ for the gardener. Her misrecognition links the Edenic prohibition to Christ's admonition, suggesting a typological association between the tree of life and Christ, whose body is suspended between its incarnative and risen states ("Touche me not: for I am not yet ascended to my Father" John 20: 17). That these superimposed interdictions against touching take place within gardens activates the etymological root of both garden (Goth *garda*, enclosure) and paradise (Persian *pairidaeza*, park <*pairi*- around + *daeza* wall>) and sets them in relation to the politics of (private) property rights implicit in a biblically sanctioned colonial imperative, as well as English land enclosure acts in the New World and at home (paradigmatic of the passage from feudalism to capitalism) and the early modern history of gender relations, where the colonized female body is the *hortus conclusus*.

In a historical and postcolonial context, our discussion maps the movement from gazing to touching, focusing on the second stage of the colonial experience. If "wonder" is the primary and quintessential human reaction to first encounters, as Stephen Greenblatt has brilliantly demonstrated,[2] then "touch" and the establishment of the conditions for contact and enclosure may constitute the next responses in the process of discovery, conquest, and possession. In the New World, English colonizers, unlike other Europeans, demonstrated their governance through the employment of physical markers, particularly fences. Legal entitlement to the land was reserved not for those who first discovered it but rather for those who "cultivated" and enclosed it. There was, moreover, little criticism of England's adoption of *res nullis*—the Roman "agriculturist" argument that rendered "empty," uncultivated, or unowned lands available for colonization.[3] The decisive acts of colonization in the English Atlantic world were the enclosure of land and planting of gardens, the gardener acting as the supreme colonizer who walled and tamed nature. The English thus appropriated God's command to "increase and multiply" in order to authorize the occupation and domination of the land.

The unique association of Genesis 1: 28 with agricultural practices in English colonialist discourse corresponded with early modern thinking about human reproduction to give rise to a culture in which the female body's potential unruliness was checked and female fertility enclosed and vigilantly guarded. "The bodies of women became analogous to and emblematic of the property whose ownership and government were in dispute in England during this period," Cristina Malcolmson observes.[4] The various applications of the *noli me tangere* topos can in turn best be understood in terms of the investment in personal property rights, which distinguished the English from other Europeans and supported a discourse of exclusivity, purity, and otherness. After all, "colonial domination depends upon who gets to 'frame' colonial space: who is a member and on what terms."[5]

This chapter, then, examines the senses of "touch" and "enclosure" as privilege and entitlement as well as violation and contamination. In particular, we explore the "do not touch" imperative first as it is transplanted from Genesis, Leviticus, and the New Testament into the New World and simultaneously into English soils through the enclosure of the land—a practice more popular in the seventeenth century than at any other time in English history. Early modern legal and cultural discourses on property rights in turn illuminate Milton's use of discourses of enclosure and ownership in *Paradise Lost*, the focus of the second half of our argument. In *Culture and Imperialism*, Edward Said announces that culture has often been the vanguard for empire, preparing the ground, providing the conceptual apparatus and imaginative repertoire, and predisposing the metropolitan pioneers for the tasks and territory they encounter.[6] The epic mode in which Milton chose to recast the biblical story of Genesis—which had itself been repeatedly appropriated to support European imperialism—is invested with an

imperial ideology it also resists. In *Paradise Lost,* Milton simultaneously reinforces and interrogates enclosure acts through his representation of Eden as
an enclosed, unenclosed garden. Also of concern to our discussion are Milton's portrayal of Satan as empire-builder and his characterization of Eve,
whose desire to control the garden by dividing her labor from Adam's results
in the violation of the original interdiction.[7] By the end of book 11 of the
epic, God destroys Eden and banishes Adam and Eve to a "fenceless World."[8]
While the loss of paradise makes room for a "paradise within" (PL 12.587)—a
space of enclosure within the subject—it also sanctions new restrictions on
female roles and behavior.

Biblical Touchstones

The site of our examination of the *noli me tangere* imperative and enclosure
acts is a series of interconnected gardens. We begin with Genesis and the first
interdiction pronounced by God to Adam and Eve in Eden: "Thou shalt eat
frely of everie tre of the garden, But as touching the tre of knowledge of good
and evil, thou shalt not eat of it: for whensoever thou eatest thereof, thou
shalt dye the death" (2: 16–17). Curiously, the yet unnamed and uninitiated
Eve repeats the command to her tempter with some variation: "We eat of the
frute of the trees of the garden, But of the frute of the tre, which is in the
middes of the garden, God hathe said, Ye shal not eat of it, nether shal ye
touche it, lest ye dye" (Genesis 3: 2–3). Eve's recitation of the command,
which included the order not to "touch" the tree, aroused the curiosity of
commentators, though the terms "taste" and "touch" could be used interchangeably, their meanings meeting in the former's etymon—*taxare.* Even
"approaching" the tree, Philo Judaeus maintained in his explication of the
passage, was forbidden since "every sense functions by means of contact." In
his reading of Genesis 3: 3, Jean Calvin concluded: "When she [Eve] says, God
had forbidden them to eat or to touch, some suppose the second word to be
added for the purpose of charging God with too great severity, because he
prohibited them even from the touch. But I rather understand that she hith-
erto remained in obedience, and expressed her pious disposition by anxiously observing the precept of God." Both Johannes Mercerus and Peter
Martyr interpreted Eve's repetition (or addition) of the prohibition against
touching as justifiable since touch is preliminary to eating;[9] and Milton in
Paradise Lost adopts this interpretation when he makes touching and eating
synonymous—an expression as well of his interest in synaesthesia. Thus in

recalling or repeating the interdiction, not only Eve (9.651, 663) but also the poet-narrator (7.46), Adam (9.925), and Michael (11.425) refer to tasting and to touching the tree as the original act of disobedience.

In the New Testament, a garden is the site of another scene of prohibited contact. Mary Magdalene, a fallen Eve in a postlapsarian world, encounters the newly risen Christ in a garden, where she initially mistakes Christ for the gardener. To the approaching Mary, Christ declares *noli me tangere*: "Touche me not: for I am not yet ascended to my Father" (John 20: 17). The marginal gloss on the passage in the Geneva Bible explains that "Because she was to muche addicted to the corporal presence, Christ teacheth her to lift up her mīde by faith into heavē where onely after his ascension he remaineth." The original interdiction has been transferred to the tree of life, a transference enacted by God in *Paradise Lost* (11.93–108), and mentioned in early modern biblical commentaries. The tree of life, moreover, becomes incarnated in Christ, as Pareus and others suggest in characterizing the tree as sacramental. Hesitant about referring to the tree in like terms, Milton describes it as a symbol or a pledge of immortality in *Christian Doctrine*[10] and in *Paradise Lost* (4.200–201, 8.325–26, 11.94–95).

Christ in the New Testament becomes the gardener and cultivator of what Milton identifies as the "paradise within." The seventeenth-century poet Rowland Watkyns develops the analogy by describing Christ as one who "curbs," "cuts," and "weeds" the plant life. In "Chastity," he advises, moreover, "Make not thy self a Common; it is found, / There's better pasture in inclosed ground."[11] Again the condition of the garden reflects the moral state of its inhabitants. When the correspondence between the human and the earthly garden is disrupted, Eden is not only deserted but also destroyed.[12] After the fall, Milton's paradise is transformed into a wasteland, "an Island salt and bare" swept away by the flood (PL 11.834). God breaks the external structure to indicate that he "attributes to place / No sanctity, if none be thither brought / By Men who there frequent, or therein dwell" (PL 11.836–38). Direct contact with God is now prohibited for those judged spiritually unclean.

Scripture is a touchstone for prohibitions against "touching" and for the establishment of the conditions of contact. "Touch" became an integral part of the rhetoric of civility, purity, and entitlement used by the ancient Israelites in outlining social practices and building their exclusive community. The Pentateuch at large is a manifesto and master code for the establishment and policing of boundaries. It is here that the elect first "learn to curse"[13] the violators of the law: " 'Cursed be he that removeth his neighbours marke [land-mark]: And all the people shal say: So be it" (Deut. 27: 17). The Hebrew Bible serves in effect as a narrative of nation-building and of Yahweh's promise of land to the Israelites as a charter of expansion. The acquisition of land depended, however, on the Israelites' observance of the law, which demanded, among other things, the preservation of sexual purity at all costs.

A culture's ideas about purity and pollution are interconnected with the entire culture's structures of thought. In Leviticus, where the organizing principle is a desire for order, all that is deemed unholy, unfit, or incomplete is rejected. Part of the danger is that pollution can spread, potentially infecting the entire community. "Certain moral values are upheld," Mary Douglas explains in her classic study, "and certain social rules defined by beliefs in dangerous contagion, as when the glance or touch of an adulterer is held to bring illness to his neighbours."[14] The discourse of contagion, especially sexual transgression, is used in characterizing social order generally.

Orifices of the body are "margins" and thus are designated as sites of danger and corruption. Sexual transgression is condemned because it involves the collapsing of categories (Lev. 18). The whole of Leviticus is in fact replete with interdictions against touching, including contact with unclean humans, animals, and carcasses (5: 2, 3; 7: 20; 11: 24, 26, 36, 39); contact with creeping animals (11: 31; 22: 5); contact with (or by) the wounded (15: 5–12); contact with a menstruating woman (15: 19–27) or with a woman who has recently given birth (12: 4).

Old Testament senses of touch permeate and sanction social practices and colonial practices, both in the new Israel (early modern England) and in New England. Many colonizing texts used the trope of Israel in Canaan to represent Europeans in the New World, giving rise to a notion not only of defilement but also entitlement. Understanding either concept involves an analysis of the belief in a "godly nationalism,"[15] which is part of what Douglas describes as "a total structure of thought whose key-stones, boundaries, margins, and internal lines are held in relation by rituals of separation" (41). In England, the boundaries were both symbolic and actual, taking the form of fences and hedges, as we discuss in the next section. Furthermore, the site for the demarcation of difference was not only the land but also the body of the other—the native, the uncivilized, the unclean, the woman.

Exclusionary Ideologies

The conditions of obedience and the observance of boundaries established in Old Testament biblical narratives provide a framework for studying early modern social and property rights in England and the New World. Biblical injunctions against intermixing whatever is marked as separate inform England's sense of national identity in the early modern period. As we have noted, the book of Leviticus in particular provides a paradigmatic way of delineating the boundary between the self and the other in the service of both nation-building and a supporting ideology of private property. "Leviticus thinking," Paul Stevens explains, is the "tendency of universalizing Christianity to articulate its own sense of transcendent exceptionalism by reembodying the exclusive, community-building rhetoric of Israel, especially as it is formulated in the Law."[16] This ideology defines the parameters of ordered space thereby dividing the elect (who were defined as the "rightful" wielders of economic power) from those beyond the pale of "civilized" society.

The English "rhetoric of exclusion,"[17] pervasive in articulations of nationhood, was embodied in the definition of private property. Only the English identified ownership by demarcating the "cultivated" from the wild by means of boundary markers.[18] This separation effectively imposes the *noli me tangere* interdiction characteristic of "Leviticus thinking" on both the "uncivilized" English at home and the "barbarous" colonized other abroad. At home, the demarcation of private property transformed the English landscape. Though much of England had already been enclosed before 1600 and enclosure continued until the early twentieth century, the greatest amount of land was fenced in during the seventeenth century.[19]

Whole villages were sometimes depopulated in the seventeenth century as a result of the landlord's decision to enclose land. Enclosures during this period were largely arranged by agreement among wealthier farmers; since the poor lacked a political voice and could be "intimidated" into ceding their common rights, enclosure often went seemingly unopposed.[20] In some cases, those reluctant to enclose were threatened with lawsuits.[21] As a result, peasants, laborers, and cottagers lost rights to resources to which they traditionally had had access and were forced to leave the land. Although common rights varied considerably, they generally included rights of pasture, tillage, and the right to gather wood and peat from uncultivated wasteland, E. C. K. Gonner explains (3–42).

While enclosures were responsible for the social and economic displacement of the rural poor and for the creation of a new class of "masterless men," historians have emphasized that "enclosure was not the uniform and radical process of modernization it was once thought to be."[22] The older perception of the common fields as part of a static feudal system operating in opposition to a radically new privatized system that created a market economy is too reductive. The changes associated with enclosure—the erection of physical markers, the enclosure of common land for private use, and the end of common rights—did not necessarily happen all at once, nor were they enacted in a uniform way, J. A. Yelling maintains (3). In addition, while enclosures did constitute a change toward capitalist notions of private property, enclosure "concerned the emergence of a capitalist form of landowning, rather than of production" (John E. Martin, 103), and thus should not be conflated with an independent though related emergent market economy.

Though Marx's pronouncement that enclosures and the accompanying privatization of property caused the English working class to move directly "from its golden age to its iron age" should be somewhat modified,[23] his statement does reflect the large-scale social upheaval caused by the creation of private property. Seventeenth-century English radicals, like contemporary Marxist historians, regarded enclosure as a decisive act in a fallen world. The Levellers and the Diggers, for example, associated pre-enclosure methods of land use with the Old Testament equivalent of the golden age, the prelapsarian state. In the beginning, the anonymous author of *Light shining in Buckingham-shire* writes, all was held in common until "man following his own sensualitie became a devourer of the creatures, and an incloser" depriving the people from their birthright and enslaving them. As the extended title to this work indicates, enclosure is held to be the "originall cause of all the slavery in the world, but cheifly in England."[24]

The term "enclosure" was used by its critics "as an all-purpose signifier for virtually every negative socioagricultural development."[25] In seventeenth-century England, to enclose was to subscribe to the emerging capitalist ideology legitimizing private property and to erect a barrier that constituted a distinction between the self and the other. When enclosing the commons, landlords redefined already occupied space as unoccupied and those who were expelled as beyond the pale of civilized society.[26] The connection between the eviction of people from land that they had traditionally occupied and the new class of "masterless men" was reinforced by naturalizing the distinctions between those who had a stake in the new economic order and those who were pushed to the periphery. Inside the enclosure, the "reformed" land symbolized the civilized propriety on which an ordered society is based. Outside the enclosure were the vagrants, the masterless men who, if not barred from private property, would unleash violence and disorder, leveling all distinctions of rank and spreading moral disease throughout the commonwealth. The actual and symbolic significance of the ordering of space, then, involved the expulsion of those beyond the borders of newly defined private property.[27] Those violating property rights were portrayed in pro-enclosure literature as transgressing all sorts of boundaries—sexual, political, and social; "to break through bounds in one sense—the bounds of the enclosed private estate—was to destroy all bounds, whether those of marriage or of personal discipline."[28]

The English transplanted this exclusionary ideology into the colonies, where they used markers to divide the colonizers from the colonized. Like the unenclosed commons at home, land occupied by the native American was judged as empty, wild, and in need of "improvement."[29] Defending the British occupation of Virginia, Robert Gray wrote that "some affirme, and it is likely to be true, that these Savages have no particular proprietie in any part or parcell of that Countrey, but only a generall recidencie there, as wild beasts have in the forrest . . . so that if the whole lande should bee taken from them, there is not a man that can complaine of any particular wrong done unto him."[30] John Winthrop also claimed that English possession of foreign territory is legitimate since "the Natives of New England . . . inclose noe Land."[31] The New World is represented as a vast commons in need of the civilizing hand of the gardener, the planter, and the builder of houses.

The expansionist, centrifugal impulse of the English depended upon practices of framing, containing, and literally fencing. That fences were not just intended for utilitarian purposes but buttressed a capitalist and an imperialist ideology is illustrated by the fact that enclosure was regarded as necessary even when impractical. Despite the difficulties of fencing in the vast tracts of land claimed by English settlers, Charles I demanded that every settler "be compelled for every 200 acres Granted unto him to inclose and sufficiently Fence . . . a Quarter of an Acre of Ground."[32] The hedge, fence, and—significantly for our discussion of Milton's representation of Paradise—the garden marked off English territory, separating the wild from the civilized in the minds of the colonizers.

The English garden served as a miniature enclosure signifying the owner's civility and his domination over nature and the "uncivilized" people beyond its periphery. As Francis Bacon writes in his essay "Of Gardens," the ideal seventeenth-century garden "is best to be Square; Incompassed, on all the Foure Sides, with a *Stately Arched Hedge*." This well-ordered garden is even more closely allied with artistic design than are architectural structures: "And a Man shall ever see, that when Ages grow to Civility and Elegancie, Men come to *Build Stately*, sooner then to *Garden Finely*. As if *Gardening* were the Greater Perfection." Without a garden, he claims, "*Buildings* and *Pallaces* are but Grosse Handy-works." Indeed, since "God *Almightie* first Planted a *Garden*," gardening represents an imitation of the divine creation and is "the Purest of Humane pleasures."[33]

Among the texts that also support the nexus of gardening, biblical texts, and enclosure is Ralph Austen's popular treatise on the planting of fruit trees.[34] On the title page is an image of an orchard, arranged as a typical seventeenth-century English geometric garden complete with an intricate knot in the center.[35] The periphery of the garden is encompassed by a high brick wall which is surrounded in turn with a quotation from the Song of Solomon: "A Garden inclosed is my sister my Spouse: Thy Plants are an Orchard of Pomegranats, with pleasant fruits" (4: 12–13). This link between the preservation of chastity and physical enclosure which conflates the female body and the land is repeated in the discussion of the divine "similitudes." The "Virtuous *Susanna*," the "Mirror of Chastity" in the Apocrypha account of Daniel and Susanna, worked in a garden, Austen notes (B3r).

The Bible is in fact replete with examples of gardens, from the Garden of Eden to the Garden of Gethsemane: "a *Garden of Fruit-trees* was the meetest place upon all the Earth, for *Adam* to dwell in, even in his state of perfection" (12); similarly, "for the use of an *Orchard, or Garden,* we have the example of our blessed *Saviour,* whose custome it was to walke in a *Garden*" (14). As an emblem of mystical truths, the fruit tree "beares the figure and resemblance of our *Saviour Christ* in the description of *Spirituall Paradice*" (15). It serves thereby as a reminder of the typological relationship between the tree of life and the body of Christ.

In conjunction with the ideology associated with the pro-enclosure movement, Austen views the planting of fruit trees as a means by which the commons might be reduced to order and by which the deleterious effects of beggary might be remedied. A law is needed "for the *Inclosure and Plantation,* of some of the *Wast, and Common Grounds,* Whereof there are many Thousand Acres in this Nation" (¶ 2r), he pleads. By employing the poor "in Inclosing, and preparing Grounds for Planting, and many other Workes," this law would be the "deliverance of multitudes from *Idlenesse, Beggery,*

Shame, and consequently, *Theft, Murther,* and (at last) *the Gallowes*" (¶ 1v, ¶ 2r). Such a proposal would accord with the Divine Plan, for "Are not these the times of the Gospell prophesied of *Esay* 49. 19, 20. When the *Wast and the desolate places shall be inhabited?*" (¶ 2).

In contrast, radical thinkers of the seventeenth century allied enclosure with privatization; and their outcry against the appropriation of the commons became part of the intellectual ferment surrounding the English revolution. For the Leveller Gerrard Winstanley, the Genesis story indicates that private property does not exist in a state of nature, but is the cause of all social ills stemming from the Fall. "By the Righteous Law of our Creation . . . mankinde in all his branches, is the Lord of the Earth, and ought not to be in subjection to any of his own kinde without him, but to live in the light of the law of righteousness, and peace established in his heart," Winstanley proclaims.[36] All private property is gained and maintained by unlawfully enclosing that which is rightfully common to all. Freedom from tyranny is incompatible with the existence of "Land-Lords" and "the cursed thing, called *Particular Propriety,* which is the cause of all wars, bloud-shed, theft, and enslaving Laws, that hold the people under miserie" (276).

Though Milton does not promote the abolition of private property,[37] he too associates "Particular Propriety" with a fallen state in *Tetrachordon,* claiming that "prime Nature made us all equall, made us equall coheirs by common right and dominion over all creatures" (*CPW* 2: 661). Milton's argument coincides with that of Winstanley, as both allude to the Genesis account in which God grants dominion over the earth to Adam and by extension to Adam's heirs. In contrast to Winstanley, however, who clearly wishes to return to a prelapsarian state, Milton is ambivalent about the creation of private property. At this point, Milton is arguing that divorce, like commerce and hierarchical governments, is an unfortunate necessity in a fallen world. But given Milton's anti-monarchical views, the association between "tyranny" and "propriety" would seem to indicate that private property, at best, is tolerated as a necessary evil. These contending views, we will demonstrate, are exhibited in *Paradise Lost,* which mediates and interrogates early modern discourses of property rights through the representation of Eden and gender relations therein.

Milton's English Garden

Wanton Growth and the "Enclosure Green"

Milton's paradise is much more than a poeticized biblical garden not only because it is teeming with allusions to gardens from antiquity through to the Renaissance but also because it grows out of the seventeenth-century social and political circumstances in which the tragic epic was generated. The description of Eden develops as well in relation to the colonial drama unfolding in England and the New World. The account of the garden corresponds with European reports of the luscious New World whose "incredible abundance" astounded all visitors.[38] This section surveys the parameters of Milton's garden, showing that, while Milton's mindset has "its expansionist, centrifugal sensibility, its enthusiasm for paradisal holiness as overflowing beyond enclosed precincts,"[39] his garden also possesses exclusionary coordinates. The paradoxically unenclosed/enclosed garden is a product of Milton's fervent belief in the free will of God's creation, as well as in national election and the maintenance of established social distinctions and gender roles.

Critics in general concur about the unconventional nature of Milton's paradise; while the concept of the enclosed garden became increasingly important to royalists and the *hortus* was the subject of many meditative poems and emblem books, Eden for Milton does not have the stability accorded to it by earlier poets.[40] Though the garden needs to be defined and circumscribed (PL 4.133), Milton is not simply acknowledging the traditional representation of paradise as a walled garden and in fact discards the *hortus conclusus* as a geopolitical[41] and poetic model. Eden is perfect, not because it is a well-cultivated garden, but because it is overspread and embodies the beneficence of the "sovran Planter" (4.691), while enabling the innocent, carefree existence of its inhabitants that Satan so envies (4.503).

In portraying Eden, Milton negotiates between closure and openness. Like the New Jerusalem,[42] the earthly paradise is circumscribed, but with a hedge of gargantuan proportions—a property line marked by God—which would become in the postlapsarian world the most common type of agricultural fence or boundary. Eden moreover is still "crown[ed]" with an "enclosure green" (4.133), as the poet-narrator reports in charting the voyage of Satan to "the border . . . / Of *Eden*" to which "Access [is] deni'd" (4.131–37). The "verdurous wall of Paradise" (4.143) is of epic proportions and performs the same architectural and ideological work as the less spectacular defense system protecting private property. At the same time, Milton distances his hedge from those emblematic of enclosures by comparing it to a "rural mound . . . grotesque and wild" (4.134–36); Chris Fitter observes that the garden is not really a safe haven since "the defensive tree-walls . . . [are] over-leaped effortlessly within forty-five lines."[43]

Rather than reducing Eden to a static *hortus conclusus*, the poet depicts a fertile, regenerative garden that embodies "In narrow room Nature's whole wealth, yea more" (4.207). In book 4, the poet-narrator develops a loosely structured genesis narrative by detailing the geography and scenery in an Eden created out of and entangled with biblical, mythological, historical, and literary gardens of various kinds; including Ovid's field of Enna, Dante's Eden, Sidney's Arcadia, and Spenser's Garden of Adonis.[44] English writers commonly quoted Roman literature and histories, like Virgil's *Georgics* and Herodian's *Histories*, to justify the planting of gardens as a form of possession and to sanction their occupation of land. In this case, the classical and Renaissance gardens become the intellectual property of an epic poem that installs itself as the heir to ancient Rome and redeems and celebrates English nationhood.

The "wanton growth" in Milton's garden inspires "bliss" beyond the reaches of art and beyond the rules of language. A source of immeasurable delight, nature exudes abundance without restraint. The strict enclosure of nature—with fences or in rhyme[45]—would be antithetical to Milton's declaration that Edenic nature transcends the ordering principles of "nice Art." Instead of distributing flowers "In Beds and curious Knots" (4.241–42), "Nature . . . / Poured forth profuse on Hill and Dale and Plain" (4.243). Milton's Eden, then, is not made in the image of the geometric English garden with its intricate knot in the center, as featured on the title page of Ralph Austen's treatise. To reduce Eden to a *hortus conclusus* would be to transgress Milton's politicized aesthetics of openness and fluidity.

Yet the feminized landscape requires cultivation or, more specifically, husbandry. Samuel Purchas's courtship of Virginia—the first American colony, identified by Michael Drayton as "Earth's onely Paradise"[46]—encapsulates the colonist's relationship to the feminized land: "Whether shall I warble sweete Carols in prayes of thy lovely Face, thou fairest of Virgins, which from our other Britaine World, hath wonne thee Wooers and Suters . . . to make thee of a ruder Virgin, not a wanton Minion; but an honest and Christian wife?" Only the English were suitable husbands, since "savage inhabitants" were "unworthie to embrace with their rustike armes so sweet a bosome," Purchas states categorically.[47] Milton's God uses the same contractual language in discussing real estate with Adam: "This Paradise I give thee, count it thine / To Till and keep, and of the Fruit to eat" (8.319–20).

Entitlement to the land entails the ordering and maintaining of "wanton growth" (4.629), as Adam informs Eve in book 4; he continues: "Those Blossoms also, and those dropping Gums, / That lie bestrown unsightly and unsmooth, / Ask riddance, if we mean to tread with ease" (4.630–32). In an early modern context, figuring disorder as "unsightly" and in need of "reform" accords with pro-enclosure discourse in which containing "waste" was seen as a moral imperative. As James R. Siemon notes, "the language of Tudor-Stuart authority on behalf of enclosure" is ridden with "values of industry, thrift, individual discretion, efficiency, and private property rights."[48]

Within the garden, the mutual love of Adam and Eve is the "sole propriety" (4.751); everything else is shared, thus recalling Milton's pronouncement that "prime Nature" made humanity "equall coheirs by common right" (*CPW* 2: 661). The concept of private property is as alien to Eden's inhabitants as it was believed to be to the native Americans, J. Martin Evans declares.[49] Yet unlike the uncolonized New World, the English garden that constitutes Milton's Eden requires cultivation—a sign of obedience in the prelapsarian world and of rightful ownership in the postlapsarian. The notion of ownership enters paradise at the point when Adam's and Eve's relationship to each other and to the land is articulated. As a requisite of order and colonial power, moreover, a gender hierarchy must be enforced, and thus Adam is cast as the proprietor of the feminized land and of Eve. Eve requires governance because she is prone to err (in the etymological and the current sense of the word).

The genesis stories that Adam and Eve each narrate reinforce this distinction. Both accounts refer to the stimulus of touch long before the interdiction is pronounced; but in each case the act of touching indicates the character's place in the chain of command and establishes the conditions for proprietorship. In his creation narrative, Adam's first sensation is tactile, anticipating his "euphemistic identification of the primal effect of sexual contact or 'touch' on his reason."[50] Touch leads directly to gazing at the "ample Sky" and finally at the "shape Divine" in his dream (PL 8.295), so that Adam ultimately secures his title to the natural world through surveillance. Eve, who is misled from the start by fixing her gaze on herself, must be both verbally redirected and seized by the hand in order to assume her proper place in relation to her husband at the end of her account (PL 488–89). She is excluded from a panoptic vision—except in her book 5 dream, which Satan induces. Otherwise her experience of Eden and its history is mediated by Adam, who tempers his words with "soft imbraces" (4.471) and "conjugal Caresses" (8.56).

In the received tradition of the Genesis account, Eve, who is defined by her bodily, maternal function, is called to obey God's command to "increase and multiply." The Pentateuch transfers the blessing of Adam and Eve to Noah, then to the Hebrew patriarchs, and finally to God's chosen—the Israelite nation.[51] In the Reformation period, this primordial blessing was conventionally interpreted by Protestant leaders as a conferral of dominion and ownership and as a mandate to procreate. In England alone was Genesis 1: 28 invoked in defense of agricultural rather than just human fertility, so that the divinely ordained command to reproduce determines the colonist's relationship to the land.[52] After the fall, the blessing becomes a curse, affecting the land and female body. The sentence that the Son passes on Adam recalls Genesis 3: 16–19: "Curs'd is the ground for thy sake, thou in sorrow / Shalt eat thereof all the days of thy Life" (10.201–2). Eve's labor will also prove painful: "Thy sorrow I will greatly multiply / By thy Conception; Children thou shalt bring / In sorrow forth" (10.194–95), she is told. The second half of her sentence reads: "and to thy Husband's will / Thine shall submit, hee over thee shall rule" (10.195–96), reinforcing Milton's belief, stated in *Christian Doctrine*, that the "husband's authority became still greater after the fall" (6: 355).

In book 9, the fall is anticipated when Eve for the first time initiates the dialogue to convey her anxiety about the great abundance of Eden, which "outgrew / The hands' dispatch of two Gard'ning so wide" (9.202–3). In recommending the division of labor, Eve proposes that the couple separate for the sake of controlling overgrowth in the garden. Because nature requires taming, the couple must increase their efficiency lest "th' hour of Supper come unearn'd" (9.225). Offering her own way of governing the garden, Eve "introduces a mercantile element into the theological equation" to tend Eden.[53] As Maureen Quilligan argues, Eve's "desire for efficiency labels as postlapsarian her proto-capitalist program (whereby she trades labor of the body for 'earnings' and food as a reward for efficient work)."[54] Again enclosure, for those who promoted it, meant reclaiming "waste" land and increasing production. This time the proposal to reform the land, which was made earlier by Adam (PL 4.625–32), is misdirected because it calls for separate work places and is construed as something that must be exacted in return for wages rather than as a duty "assign'd" by God (9.231). Labor, however, as Adam stresses in his response, must be distinguished from "irksome toil" (9.242), for which God's creation was not intended.

Eve insists that being physically circumscribed is incompatible with freedom and contentment. "*Eden* were no Eden" (9.341) if her movements are to be restricted, she maintains. Yet because her gender relegates her to the domestic sphere—"nothing lovelier can be found / In Woman, than to study household good, / And good works in her Husband to promote" (9.232–34)—Eve's desire to wander outside the proscribed bounds precipitates the fall. Peter Stallybrass argues that the affiliation between women and property is paradigmatic in early modern England, where woman is considered "the fenced-in enclosure of the landlord, her father, or husband."[55] Innocence then, is, associated with containment and the preservation of sexual purity, the virgin state. The location of the female body and the extent to which it is controlled serve as indicators of how well the space of the nation or colony or household is managed; "Eve wanders and thus begins the displacement of paradise."[56]

The "Fenceless World"

Satan's incestuous affair with rebellion begins with sexual contact, that is, with the violation of the *noli me tangere* imperative. Sin is born of Satan's self-division, self-contradiction, and self-love, which lead to their incestuous affair. Sin herself is a "Sign / Portentous" (2.760–61), who "signifies the commandment 'noli me tangere!' "[57] After violating this mandate, Satan continues on his imperial mission to the New World, an epic journey that is mediated through various frames of reference, from classical to contemporary.[58] Upon entering Eden, Satan is likened to a "prowling Wolf," that "Leaps o'er the fence with ease into the Fold" (4.183–87) and as "a Thief bent to unhoard the cash / Of some rich Burgher" (4.188–89). The identification of Satan as the "first grand Thief" (4.192), however, naturalizes the distinction between those enclosing their property and the growing class of the "masterless men." He becomes a trespasser who boasts about his entry into the "Ill fenc't" garden, which he reduces to "narrow limits" (4.372, 384).

In book 9, Satan's imperial vision projects a Ptolemaic view of earth (9.99–113) and transforms Eden into a *hortus conclusus*. By adopting various animal guises, the devil perverts their nature for his own intents (395–410). The first "Artificer of fraud" thereby moves down the chain of being until he *encloses* himself in the serpent (9.494–95), the lowest of creatures. In Leviticus, any creature that does not inhabit one sort of element or has an indeterminate mode of locomotion confounds the categories of creation and is branded unclean.[59] If we read *Paradise Lost* more specifically as a poem about politics and empire, then the metamorphosis of Satan throughout books 4 to 10 also represents a series of declines from "a rebel against authoritarianism and an indomitable laborer and builder in the wilderness to an imperialist policy maker and insatiably combative technocrat."[60] In his intersecting roles as buccaneer, pilgrim, and empire-builder, Satan in fact "rehearses virtually all the major roles in the repertoire of English colonial discourse."[61]

Satan's first conquest is prompted by wonder, defined by Greenblatt as "the instinctive recognition of difference."[62] At the center of the colonizer's text "stands the ravished observer, fixed in awe, scanning the New World scene, noting its colors and shapes, recording its plentitude and its sensual richness."[63] We originally view paradise through Satan's eyes in book 4, the poet-narrator reminds us: "with new wonder now he views / To all delight of human sense expos'd / In narrow room Nature's whole wealth, yea more" (4.205–7). The newly created Adam and Eve likewise induce Satan's "wonder" (4.363), which "brings with it all the associations of an Exodus to this Earthly paradise or New Canaan, a voyage with purpose not just to wonder at but also to colonize."[64]

Satan's address to Eve, the first object of his colonial conquest (9.532–48), recalls the enchanter's approach to the Lady in *Comus* (264). Lacking the lady's fastidiousness, Eve is led along a circuitous path to the virgin fruit, the "greater store of Fruit untoucht, / Still hanging incorruptible" (9.621–22). In response to Satan's temptations, Eve twice repeats the interdiction, both times invoking touch and taste (9.651–52; 9.659–63). Insisting that Eve has been misled by the divine command, the tempter offers counter-evidence of the effects of touching the tree: "look on mee, / Mee who have touch'd and tasted, yet both live, / And life more perfet have attain'd than Fate / Meant mee" (687–90). Overcome by curiosity and appetite, Eve grasps the fruit, plucks it, and eats it insatiably.

Disobedience to the law, enacted here through contact with the interdicted tree, results in the contamination of humanity and the pollution of nature. Conversation as both sexual intercourse and dialogue is affected. When Milton earlier explains that Adam and Eve did not refuse "the Rites / Mysterious of connubial Love" (PL 4.742–43), Williams notes, he is "going farther than most of the commentaries [on Genesis] warrant," and Turner likewise reminds us that Milton made "an unprecedented investment in prelapsarian sexuality.[65] Sex after the fall involves a different kind of contact, one motivated by lust and uncontrolled appetite. In tracing the roots of sin back to Adam and Eve, Milton in *Christian Doctrine* conflates sexual excess with the consumption of the forbidden fruit: "It was evil desire that our first parents were originally guilty of. Then they implanted it in all their posterity, since their posterity too was guilty of that original sin, in the shape of a certain predisposition towards, or, to use a metaphor, a sort of tinder to kindle sin" (6: 388).

Verbal exchange is similarly infected; thus the postlapsarian Eve speaks "with touch of blame" (9.1143). The poisoned language of Adam and Eve in *Paradise Lost* and their "learning to curse" separate them from the edenic community and relegate them to the wilderness, the "wild Woods forlorn" (9.910). Milton imports the images of corruption from the feminized East and the New World; reduced to a fallen and primitive state, the fallen couple cover themselves with the leaves of the Indian fig or banyan tree:

> both together went
> Into the thickest Wood, there soon they chose
> The Figtree, not that kind for Fruit renown'd,
> But such as at this day to *Indians* known
> In *Malabar* or *Decan* spreads her Arms
> Branching so broad and long, that in the ground
> The bended Twigs take root, and Daughters grow
> About the Mother Tree . . .
> Those Leaves
> They gather'd, broad as *Amazonian* Targe,
> And with what skill they had, together sew'd,
> To gird thir waist, vain Covering if to hide
> Thir guilt and dreaded shame; O how unlike
> To that first naked Glory. Such of late
> *Columbus* found th'*American* so girt
> With feather'd Cincture, naked else and wild
> Among the Trees on Isles and woody Shores. (9.1099–1118)

Paradise is lost on both sides of the Atlantic (as well as the Pacific), and the postlapsarian condition of Adam and Eve is registered in the entanglement of mythological and historical identities, geographical locations and place names, and diverse historical moments. Like the East and the New World itself, the Indian fig tree is feminized both by the description of the "Daughters [that] grow / About the Mother Tree" (9.1105–6) and by the comparison of its broad leaves to the "*Amazonian* Targe"—the target or "crescent-shaped shields" of the female warriors of Greek legend, identified by Virgil in the *Aeneid* (1.490). The description of the Indians who are "naked else and wild / Among the Trees on Isles and woody Shores" echoes the reference to "wild Woods forlorn"—the place now occupied by the fallen inhabitants of Eden. The conscious and unconscious mixing of names, while intended to reflect and compound the shame of the barbaric transgressors whose identity is now enmeshed with that of "th'*American*,"[66] also exposes the poet's imperial vision.

The first transgression now contaminates the whole human race. When Michael and Adam in book 11 of *Paradise Lost* ascend the highest hill of Paradise in order that Adam may view the history of his descendants, Michael warns him that the contagion has spread (11.423–28). God therefore will abandon the cursed, "vicious Race," leaving his peoples "to thir own polluted ways" (12.104, 110). "One peculiar Nation to select / From all the rest" (12.111–12) will serve as the elect nation; and the story begins again.

The dispossession of the Canaanites becomes the standard biblical precedent for the forcible settlement of America. The ever-expanding English garden encroaches upon and envelops the New World through a series of transplantations of the *noli me tangere* imperative. This chapter has traced the transference of the interdiction from its origin in Genesis, through Leviticus where the conditions for the exclusive Israelite community were established. Then, inherited by the New Israel (early modern England) and imposed upon the New World, the prohibitions against touching materialized as enclosure acts intended to secure property rights over the land and the people marked by the sign (and sins) of otherness or incivility. Milton's garden is the site of this inheritance, and the multiple senses, privileges, and consequences, of "touch." His representation of the concept of private property in *Paradise Lost* ultimately situates him on both sides of the property line and the colonial divide. By explicitly identifying property as a postlapsarian development and by describing Eden as a blissful place of wanton disorder, he counters the depiction of Nature as in need of an artful ordering principle. Though the fecund disorder of the feminized landscape is celebrated as beyond the bounds of human comprehension and control, this very disorder supports, paradoxically, the need for a hierarchical ordering based on gender. By relegating both the garden and Eve to a circumscribed space, Milton's poem buttresses the tradition associating women with land in need of improvement and enclosure. It is at this point that the depiction of an originally natural state in which all things are held in common dissolves and the ideology of property rights takes root in Milton's English Garden.[67]

Chapter 9

Acting with Tact: Touch and Theater in the Renaissance

Carla Mazzio

Toward a History of Tact

> *Of all the creatures, the sense of tact is most exquisite in man.*
> —*Alexander Ross,* Arcana Microcosm *(1651)*

> *A Tactation, or a touching, is that whereby we discern the difference of objects, and the nature of things.*
> —*Randle Holme,* Academy of Armory *(1688)*

To have "tact" is to have just the right touch, a manifest sensitivity to one's linguistic and social surround. But in contemporary parlance, to be "tactful" is not to be full of touch. When the contemporary philosopher Jean-Luc Nancy writes that "one has to understand reading as something other than decipherment. Rather, as touching, as being touched. Writing, reading: matters of tact," he hopes, at least momentarily, to bring dead metaphors back to life.[1] But here, as elsewhere, the language of emotional and social interaction offers less a touch than a trace. This may always be true, that is, if metaphors of touch are in some sense dead the very moment they enter language. But as any reader knows, words can move away from themselves and into something else, such as a pulse, whisper, or kiss, the very moment they touch another. Or in spoken discourse, they can come to life in and as language, capable not only of "moving" the listener, but of physically touching the body of the speaker at the moment of utterance. If the Renaissance divine William Perkins is to be believed, there is no such thing as a dead metaphor in a world where words can come back to haunt, taunt, and even hurt the body of the speaker. According to one 1595 sermon, upon cursing "God's blood," a young man was touched to the quick: "immediately the blood aboundantly from all the joynts of his bodie, as it were in streames, did issue out most fearefully from mouth, nose, wrestes, knees, heeles, and toes, with all other joynts, not one left free, and so died."[2] This is one of a cascade of narratives offered by Perkins on the power of words to touch the speaker back: it's hard to imagine a potential backbiter leaving this sermon without watching his back.

The always potentially undead quality of metaphor was at the very heart of early religious rhetoric, but what other Renaissance discourses of touch might call for a kind of "interpretive literalism" on the part of the critic?[3] Indeed, what do we make of the lexicon of touch, of tactually imagined emotions, behaviors, and interactions (being "touched," having "tact," being "tactless") in a period of history when to have "tact" meant, quite literally, to have the sensation of touch, and when the word touch (like the word "feeling") signified both affective and physiological forms of receptivity? Thomas Cooper's 1578 definition of the term (from "tango") speaks to the complexity of the term: "To touche: to mooue or grieue: to come: to deceyue: to quippe: to taunt: to take up: to write: to speake or mention a thing."[4] This single entry links sensate experience with concepts of affect (to move or grieve), communication (to write or speak), and representational instability (to deceive). With attention to the interrelationship of these three aspects of touch, I will argue throughout this chapter that the referential and epistemological dynamism of this sense complicated attempts to reify touch as a "medium" and category of sensation in classical and Renaissance medical and philosophical writing. As such, it consistently disrupted normative epistemologies and the process of metaphoric deadening itself. After exploring the relationship between touch and categories of knowledge in analytic and quantitative thought, I will ultimately argue that it is the resistance of touch to conceptual models that in many ways enables the "life" of this sense in the drama of the period. But further, by examining attempts to restrict or kill off the life of touch in both revenge drama and antitheatrical discourse, I want to examine the costs of controlling touch in the domain of social interaction and the articulation of affect.

As Cooper's definition might suggest, touch is not only difficult to "pin down" in language but also in thought. As Didier Anzieu notes in *The Skin Ego*, an exploration of the tactile substrate of linguistic and psychological development, not only is the English language rife with tactile forms of expression, but in fact the entry for "touch" is one of "the longest in the *Oxford English Dictionary*."[5] The resistance of touch to definitive linguistic and conceptual categories makes it an elusive subject of history. While the historian of touch might turn to the recent accounts of the hand as an icon of agency and instrumentality in the Renaissance, it is worth noting that the parts of the hand considered most sensitive to touch are parts that *can't* be instrumental to basic forms of social agency. [6] While hands are instruments of touching others, as representatives of this *sense* (as opposed to *act*), they work metonymically, associated with the palm and fingertips. That is, while one "gives one a hand" to collaborate or help in some act of labor, if the hand represents touch, it is to signify the palm and receptive digital tips that were said to enable the most exquisite forms of tactile pleasure. Romeo and Juliet touching each other's palms and lips the moment they meet is imagined as lovers kissing twice at the same moment.[7] In short, to touch with the hand informs metaphors of social and erotic interaction that are quite different from other manually inflected forms of engagement such as "manipulation," "grasping," and "clutching." "Wind and water press against us and move us," writes Susan Stewart in *Poetry and the Fate of the Senses*, "but they cannot be grasped . . . we cannot contain them in our hands for more than a moment."[8] It is the reciprocal, fleeting, and "nonteleological" aspect of touch that Stewart, drawing on Levinas, emphasizes.[9] For when humans touch there is a reciprocity of sensation at once physical and psychological that may be felt but not fully grasped. The cost of a touch that "grasps" is embodied in the myth of Midas, whose touch turns everything to gold, "permitting him to freeze his own emotional life at the high point of desire."[10] For Midas, as for any theorist of touch, to get a "handle" on touch, to reify it, may be to eclipse its power.

This problem of rendering static the conceptual dynamism of touch may be a problem for the historian of the senses. In Renaissance studies of the senses, vision and hearing have been most fully explored as dominant, and historically contingent, structures of cognition. Histories of drama, following Andrew Gurr, regularly explore the sensory dimensions of what it meant to be "audience" and "spectator," and studies ranging from Bruce Smith's *The Acoustical World of Early Modern England* (1999) to Michael O'Connell's *The Idolatrous Eye: Iconoclasm and Theater in Early Modern England* (2000) map out the historical contours of these particular sense perceptions.[11] Since Aristotle, touch has been aligned with both human and animal capacities, and contrasted with vision and hearing as senses integral to the ethical and intellectual contours of what it means to be human.[12] As such, it is no surprise that sensory modes traditionally linked with the work of the mind are frequently privileged in discourses of historical phenomenology and even audience-response. But what of touch as a cultural phenomenon? A word used as often as "spectator" and "audience" to describe playgoers in the Renaissance was the "assembly," a word I will soon examine because it implied not only a coming together of persons, but a physical touching of bodies in space. Given that touch is integral to humoral physiology (as touch detects temperatures and textures), to literary allegories of the senses and to social rhetorics of persuasion, sexuality, affect, disease and public health, it is interesting that touch has not been as fully explored as vision and hearing.[13] So too, with the recent focus on the material object (as textual artifact, stage property, object of exchange, cultural spectacle, sumptuary habit), we might consider what happens to the tangible object in the domain of sensory perception. We might ask with the editors of *Subject and Object in Renaissance Culture*, not only "where is the object?" but where is the object that is touched, caressed, taken in hand?[14] It is the hand that enables production, but it also touches—and is touched by—products. But as we will see, in early modern representations of touch, the question becomes less "where is the object?" than "why *isn't* the object there?" Putting touch into a mix of material cultures seems to gesture toward a kind of materialism without an object, or more precisely, without specific objects. It is the resistance of touch to specificity, conceptual stasis, and rational models that is arguably at the heart of Renaissance representations of touch.

Indeed, the relative marginality of touch as a subject of Renaissance history is arguably rooted in the conceptual history of touch itself. The five senses were classically defined by specific organs, mediums, and objects (for example, eye, air, and celestial objects, respectively). As Helkiah Crooke put it in *Mikrokosmographia: A Description of the Body of Man* (1615),[15] "Sense is a knowledge or discerning of the Object receyued formally in the Organ," and "in euery Sense there be three things especially to be stood vpon, the Object, the Medium and the Organ" (653, 722). Touch, however, consistently eluded the specifics of all three categories, disrupting basic systems of classification that the senses "stood vpon." In terms of organs, for example, from classical to Renaissance treatises on anatomy, the entire body, the nerves, skin, fingertips, tongue, palms, the region about the heart, were alternatively imagined as the locus of touch.[16] "This sense is exquisite in men," writes Robert Burton in *The Anatomy of Melancholy* (1631), "and by his nerves dispersed all over the body."[17] Or, as Crooke put it, "al other Senses are restrayned within some small Organ about the brayne, but the Touching is diffused through the whole body" (648). Whereas eyes, ears, nose, and tongue symbolize the modes of sensory perception they enable, touch is more difficult to represent, localize, and demonstrate. As such, as a facet of bodily, cognitive, and psychological experience, touch tends to resist the very operations of representation so integral to early modern somatic symbolism: synecdoche and metonymy.

This is not simply a theoretical point, but one integral to the representation of touch in the visual and verbal arts of the Renaissance.[18] Although one might think the human hand an easy metonymy for touch, this was not always or even usually the case. One early allegorical drama of the five senses features characters named "Eye" for vision, "Ear" for hearing, and "Tongue" for taste, but simply "Touch" for touch; thus, in terms of basic forms of personification, touch here remains a sense without a synecdoche, a mode without a metonymy.[19] This sense without a metonymy itself becomes metonymic in much Renaissance drama for the psyche's approach to what the psyche cannot precisely locate or measure. The limitations of touch to be clearly represented become a source of comedy in Thomas Tomkis's 1607 *Lingua, or the Combat of the Tongue and the five Senses for Superiority,* an academic drama about the psyche that was performed at Cambridge, was reprinted five times by 1657, and featured a young Oliver Cromwell as Tactus in an early production.[20] In this play, whereas Olfactus is represented by Odor (bearing Tobacco) and Auditus by Comedy and Tragedy (bearing music, poetry, and other acoustical artifacts), Tactus is represented by Mendacio, aligned the first with qualities of elusiveness and representational dispersion. Following Aristotle, touch is positioned here as the one sense most threatening to intellectual and ethical systems. But more precisely, as we will see, touch challenges the logic of synecdoche and metonymy on which analogies between macrocosm and microcosm depend.

Tomkis's play is part of a tradition of academic dramas of the period, where students would inhabit theatrical parts that were *also* systemic parts (for example, the senses in "Microcosmvs," the affections in "Pathopolis," grammar in "Grammarland," or parts of rhetoric and mathematics).[21] Given the frameworks of knowledge these plays staged, it is no surprise that they were particularly attentive to the operations of pars pro toto, of the capacities and limitations of parts to represent anything at all. In the 1602 *Narcissus,*[22] performed at Saint Johns, the status of the theatrical prop becomes a source of comedy: "a buckett" is used to signify the well into which Narcissus looks to find himself: "Suppose you the well had a buckett, / And so the buckett stands for the well; / And 'tis, least you should count mee for a sot O, / A very pretty figure cald *pars pro toto*" (II.508–11).[23] Pars pro toto is, of course, at the core of dramas of persons, props, and personifications on stage. But when the whole is elusive, mythical, or hopelessly fragmented, the representative "part" can become an embarrassment. In *Lingua*, with the five senses at war, each sense vies for superiority by asserting his individual powers: Odor, a quality of Olfactus, claims to command such intoxicating fragrances that "You in your heart would wish as I suppose, / That all your Body were transformed to Nose" (Sig. H3). The idea that man might be represented by such an undignified part sends up strategies of representation and dramatic conflict in allegorical drama. But it is Tactus in this drama who most powerfully represents the failure of pars pro toto. Of course, the body simply couldn't be all "Nose," but it *is* in many ways "all touch," and the question of how to represent that through organs and objects (and indeed, mediums) creates high points of comedy in *Lingua*.

What these plays demonstrate is that disintegration in the epistemological realm means dramatic potential in the literary and theatrical realm. This is particularly pointed in the domain of touch in Tomkis's play, which converts conceptual disintegration into comic tension. At the outset of the play, Lingua (the tongue) and Mendacio (the lie) conspire to undermine the pentarchy by setting the senses at odds. They plant a crown and robe for the senses to discover and fight over. Tactus is the first to discover these items; he covets them and mayhem ensues. In a formal competition for the crown, judged by Common Sense, the senses each put on a show featuring the "objects" they bring into this little world of man. Tactus, when asked to signify his "dignity by relation" (sig. I2), first locates himself in that Galenic "instrument of instruments, the hand," but quickly dislocates himself both rhetorically and conceptually: "I am the roote of life, spreading my virtue / By sinewes that extend from head to foot / To euery liuing part." His narrative disperses as he proceeds to speak about every known medical and scientific commonplace about the necessity of touch, from protecting the body from danger to enabling it to feel a kiss, until Common Sense abruptly says, "*Tactus*, stand aside," and proceeds to judge on behalf of those senses nearer to the brain. While Tactus fails to represent himself "by relation" to a particular organ, perhaps more importantly, his actual "show" highlights his failure to represent himself with specific "objects."

Whereas particular smells, sounds, sights, and tastes in Renaissance iconography quickly signify the power of discrete senses in relationship to the outside world, touch—by virtue of its sheer diversity—is not easily demonstrated by any particular object. Indeed, Tactus's "show" fails miserably because his cast of objects never "shows." " My lord, I had thought as other Senses did, / By sight of obiects to haue proued my worth," staging "a Gentleman enamored, / With his sweete touching of his Mistresse lippes, /

And gentle griping of her tender hands, /And diuers pleasant relishes of touch," but his mistress has such a complex costume that after five hours "shee is scarse drest to the girdle":

Thus 'tis, fiue houres agoe I set a douzen maides to attire a boy like a nize Gentle-woman: but there is such doing with their looking-glasses, pinning, vnpinning, setting, vnsetting, formings and conformings, painting blew vaines, and cheekes, such stirre with Stickes and Combes, Cascanets, Dressings, Purses, Falles, Squares, Buskes, Bodies, Scarffes, Neck-laces ... Borders, Tires, Fannes, Palizadoes, Puffes, Ruffes, Cuffes, Muffes, Pussles, Fussles, Partlets, Frislets, Bandlets, Fillets, Croslets, Pendulets, Amulets, An-nulets, Bracelets, and so many lets, that yet shee is scarse drest to the girdle: and now there's such calling for Fardingales, Kirtlets, Busk-points, shooter &c. that seauen Pedlers shops, nay all Sturbridge Faire will scarce furnish her: a Ship is sooner rigd by farre, then a Gentlewoman made ready. (Sig I2)

The heap of absent objects clearly displaces the representational prob-lems of touch onto the female sex. The character Fantasy responds: "Tis strange, that women being so mutable, / Will neuer change in changing their apparell" and indeed, as Patricia Parker has argued about this play as a whole, what is on stage here are male anxieties about the effeminizing potential of representation.[24] But there is another realm of signification at work, for this lavish insult backfires in a particularly effective way. Like the logic of the ex-cessive insult, where terms of abuse pile up, become detached from specific contexts, and ultimately refer to insulter rather than insultee, so here imag-ined objects accumulate to the point of being detached from both the specifi-cally gendered world and, more importantly, the specifically material world. Although Tactus should be undermined by so many absent objects, in fact this works as a brilliant form of self-reference, a demonstration of the infinite diversity of touch, which subtends (and yet is not limited to) the entire world of drama. Through the absent materialization of a kiss and a couple gently touching, and the infinite world of props and objects that touch the actor's body, Tactus at once suggests his lack of dependence on any specific domain of "objects" and asserts the dependence of the other senses at play in the the-ater on *him*. That is, through their absence, the missing lovers and the missing objects work to evoke conceptions of touch subtending the domain of "show."

It may well be said that it is precisely the failure of a body to "touch" the world, persons, and objects around it that may be its ultimate victory as a symbolic mode. For touch can seem all the more alluring and powerful when objects are held at a distance. Perhaps more interestingly in terms of pars pro toto, the failure of synecdoche is in fact the only way in which the polymorphous diversity of touch can be signified. For locating the many possibilities and powers of touch *simultaneously* is in and of itself a seemingly impossible task. If one dimension of touch is located in one part of the body, the other sensitive parts, functions, and capacities would be necessarily neglected or eclipsed: the touch of a blind man understanding depth and visual space with his hands could not also represent the force of a puncture or the unexpected touch of another; the feel of coins in a hand could not signify the place of touch in detecting temperature in and out of the body; the light sensation of a fingertip (or the fantasy of God *almost* touching Adam's finger) could not signify the rough, soft, or liquid textures of food in the mouth. This is simply to emphasize that Renaissance allegories of the senses, depending as they did on synecdoche and metonymy, worked according to a logic that the diversity of touch could not accommodate.

It is important to note in this respect the recurrence of one motif in many allegories of the senses. It was a particular kind of touch (that which Tactus longs to represent): the erotic pleasures of lovers touching. The realm of the erotic, with desire always in some sense linked to what is not there, is perhaps the most powerful vehicle for representing the infinite potential and the elusiveness of touch. Lovers can touch heatedly, softly, blindly, roughly; they can touch each other's clothes, gloves, and jewels; they can devour each other, wound each other, and break each other's hearts, so perhaps the recurrence of erotic interaction as a "specific" kind of touch implies the very antithesis of specificity and categorical distinction: the real power and danger of this sense in the early modern world.

The representational resistance of touch in terms of specific organs and objects was also operative in the theoretical realm of "media." Indeed, touch is hard to theorize because it is (in the most classical sense) "unmediated," or, to quote Aristotle, "immediate" (*De Anima*, 435a, 16–20). "Immediately," currently a term signifying a lack of distance between coordinates in time (simply meaning *now*), meant at an earlier period a lack of distance between objects in space. Of the five senses, touch was the most "immediate," at once resisting temporal stasis and having no spatial "medium" between the body and the touchable world (be it in the form of objects, bodies, textures, or temperatures). The other senses, writes Aristotle in *De Anima*, "produce sensation by means of something else, that is, through media. But touch occurs by direct contact with its objects and that is why it has its name. The other sense organs perceive by contact too, but through a medium; touch alone seems to perceive immediately" (435a, 16–20).[25] How does one account for a sense without a medium? What happens to this "unmediated" sense in early medical and contemporary theoretical accounts of representation that look to the "medium" as the message?[26] Not surprisingly, the messages become difficult to decipher and even detect. In the context of studies of communications that have focused so heavily on "media" and "sense ratios," technologies of touch often go relatively unnoticed. This is true even in the most practical sense: as Malcolm McCullough writes about contemporary computing: "Touch technology is underdeveloped, and few interaction devices provide force or tactile feedback. Without touch, currently the most common complaint about computers is not about overload but deprivation. It is about the inability to touch one's work. Being *out of touch* is considered an occupational hazard: regular sensory deprivation turns you into a nerd."[27]

Like so many other physiological metaphors now wandering ghostlike through the lexicon of computer interaction, "digital" technology seems to have left those fleshly little digits in the dust. It is precisely to the question of digits (meaning both fingers and numbers) and sensory deprivation that I would now like to turn. For when the body in the Renaissance was imagined in quantitative terms, touch was either neglected or conspicuously disruptive. For "touch" complicated not only categorization in medical thinking (organs, objects, and media), but the possibility of categorization as such. This sense is not only difficult to account for, but difficult to count.

Calculating Minds: From Synesthesia to the Sixth Sense

> *The number of the Senses in this little world, is answerable to the first bodies in the great world: now since there bee but fiue in the Vniuerse, the foure elements and the pure substance of the heauens, therefore there can bee but fiue senses in our Microcosme, correspondent to those, as the sight to the heauens, hearing to the aire, touching the earth, smelling to the fire, and tasting to the water, by which fiue meanes only the vnderstanding is able to apprehend the knowledge of all Corporeall substances.*
>
> —*Thomas Tomkis,* Common Sense, Lingua *(1607)*

Quantitatively speaking, a "touch" is a relatively insubstantial unit: not even a piece or a part, but rather a point so small as to almost resist quantification. How is touch measured? The anthropologist David Howes writes of "the importance of approaching other cultures through their own sensory ratios, instead of analyzing them through the Western order of sensory preferences, with its visual bias and passion for measurement."[28] But Tomkis's play begins by questioning that very order in the west. For in *Lingua* the "passion for measurement" and the "visual bias" of sensory perception are turned inside out and upside down. This allegory is preoccupied with the question of "sense-ratios" (what sense is valued most being the central question of the play) and particularly with the vulnerability of quantitative models.

Tomkis makes light of the quantitative disruptions at once threatening and subtending the "five senses," which were among the many numerically conceptualized systems of the period (" 'the four seasons,' 'the four elements,' 'the four temperaments,' 'the seven arts,' 'the seven deadly sins,' 'the seven ages of man,' 'the twelve months,' etc.") [29] This is made explicit from the first, as Ladie Lingua (the tongue and language) craves to be the "sixth sense," hoping to make just a slight alteration to the order of things (Sig. A3). Despite Auditus's discouragement, "what Sense hast thou to be a Sense / Since from the first foundation of the world, / We neuer were accounted more than fiue" (Sig. A3), this "vp-start" organ forges on, determined to "increase the number" and be reclassified with the best. This urge to recalculate systems of knowledge is mirrored in the subplot by Lingua's culinary counterpart, Appetitus (a representative of Gustus), who hopes to expand the seven liberal arts to eight, including "the honorable art of Cookerie" (Sig. D2). "As for the *Academie* it is beholding to mee, for adding the eight prouince vnto noble *Heptarchie* of the liberall sciences" (Sig. D1). The distance from five to six, or from seven to eight, a single digit out of place and the integrity of the whole is undermined. The link between Lingua and Appetitus recalls Plato's *Gorgias*, where cookery (as opposed to medicine) is established as an art of deception and explicitly aligned with the deceptive powers of rhetoric. As such, Tomkis here emphasizes the moral as well as epistemological stakes of sensory unaccountability. But while it may be easy to discount a wagging organ and an appetitive chef as viable contenders in the "Academie," the numerical unaccountability in *Lingua* expands to the work of the five senses and, beyond, to the status of memory and history. While Mendacio alludes to "Master Register trudging hether, as fast as his three feete will carry vp his foure Ages" (Sig. F1), Memory himself complains about the chaos of contemporary "history": "A dog cannot pisse in a Noblemans shoe, but it must be sprinkled into the Chronicles" (Sig. D3). Memory is so overwhelmed that he loses track of time and things: he forgets himself, but remembers where he left his spectacles: "I left them in the 349 Page of *Halls* Chronicles" (Sig. F3). It is the hopelessly particular realm of number that now preoccupies even the mnemonic function in this body of man. This play is not only about a world of sense perception where measuring itself fails to measure up, but about the relationship between problems of integrity and possibilities of drama.

The concept of a world that is whole or "intact" is itself a world detached from the complexities of touch. The derivation of the word "intact" comes from *in* (not) and *tactus* (touched). The distinctly numerical failure of "integrity" in Tomkis's allegory is part of the elaborate comedy of *Lingua's* "irrationality," but it is also integral to the synesthetic ordering and disordering of experience. Indeed, as the senses become divided against each other, they seem capable not only of "duplicity" but of infinite divisibility,[30] and, importantly, it is Tactus who is the sense most capable of being protean and self-different. As we will see shortly, Tactus is capable of taking many different forms: literally he lies, shape-shifts rhetorically, psychologically, and theatrically, dupes Olfactus, and "schemes" against the others. It is not only Ladie Lingua but Tactus who powerfully challenges the foundation of ethical, social, and cosmic forms of "integrity." In the sensory domain of the play, the concept of a quantitatively challenged "sense" is perfectly embodied in Tactus, whose power extends to "euery particle of the body" (Sig I3). If "allegories generated by the analogy of macrocosm to microcosm," as Marshall Grossman notes, "reach synecdochic closure when the analogy assures that each and every perceived object, if viewed correctly, will produce a cosmic totality," then *Lingua* explores the perils of synecdoche in a microcosm "in touch" with itself.[31]

Importantly, this drama of irrationality is less an inversion of the classical hierarchy of the senses than a logical extention of classical thought, where touch was impossible to accommodate within categorical systems.[32] Ladie Lingua's inaugural challenge to the order of five senses reflects a quantitative disorder already implicit within the "pentarchy." Of course in the allegorical system of the senses the tongue can only signify *one* sense, not two. In the allegory and iconography of the period, the tongue (for example in Fletcher's allegorical poem *The Purple Island*) was a stand-in for all things gustatory.[33] So the very idea that Lingua might signify another sense seems absurd. And yet, if we consider debates in the period about the fact that the tongue itself might represent not one but two senses, and that the sense of taste and touch were difficult to distinguish, the premise becomes a little less absurd. As Aristotle put it in *De Anima*, "The tongue perceives all tangible objects with the same part with which it perceives flavor. If then the rest of the flesh also could perceive flavor, *taste and touch would seem to be one and the same sense*" (423a, 19–21; emphasis mine).

More dramatically, he writes in his *Ethics,* taste "depends entirely upon touch. . . . This is why one gourmet prayed that his throat might become longer than a crane's; which shows that he took pleasure in the actual contact."[34] Renaissance medical texts endlessly cited Aristotle on the debate about whether taste and touch were one and the same. For Crooke this was a matter of serious concern because it threatened the analytical order of anatomy. He argues vigorously for an affinity rather than an equivalence between the two senses, carefully reading Aristotle's statement that "taste must be some kind of touch" (*De Anima,* 434b, 22): "if hee [Aristotle] had meant that the Tast and the Touch did not differ in *Specie,* hee would neuer haue sayd that *Gustus* was *Tactus quidam,* but simply and plainly *Gustus* is *Tactus,* hee would not have sayd that Tast is a kinde of Touch, but that Tast is a Touch" (716). Aristotle's distinction is crucial here for Crooke as a way of maintaining that these two must be "esteemed distinct Senses":[35]

> It may be also objected, that because both the Taste and the Touch are together in one & the same Tongue, that therefore they should be one and the same Sense. But the consequence is not good, for there is no organe of Sense, which beside his proper Facultie of Sensation is not also furnished with the Sense of Touching. But because the Sense of Tasting is not alwaies found where Touching is, and where it is found there is no other Faculty of Sensation: *I conclude that not onely all the other Senses but the Taste also is a distinct and different Sense from the Touch.* (717–18; emphasis mine)

Practically speaking, it does seem somewhat of a shame that the entire body cannot, as Crooke notes, experience taste. Such a conflation of senses for Crooke is "not good" not only because it poses a problem of epistemology, but because the conflation of touch and "all the other Senses" would challenge the hierarchy of the senses that helps distinguish man from animal.[36] But the ideas and the vocabularies of taste and touch were deeply entwined in anatomical theories of this period, and this partnership extended into the domain of metaphor in the realms of music, rhetoric, and theology (where, for example, Eve's palm became as important as her tongue in the representation of original sin).[37] And in the rhetoric of love it is the sweet touch that lingers in the memory, the beloved one devours with kisses, the gentle brush of a hand one might relish or savor or hunger for. But Crooke's preoccupation is less with the possibility than with the problems such a conflation would entail. This is to say that, while Tomkis's Ladie Lingua upsets the sensory system by her gender and linguistic non-sense, what is also at work is a broader question of anatomical categorization, sensory discrimination, and the distinct status of human perception.

It was not simply the potential equivalence between tasting and touching that concerned Crooke and others, but the idea that every sense was a kind of touch. As Crooke puts it, "Aristotle doth oftentimes affirm that all sense is a kinde of Touching; from whence it would as well follow that there is but one Sense, that is, the Touch, then which nothing can be more absurd" (716). This seems a clear misreading of Aristotle, who does argue that "without a sense of touch it is impossible to have any other sensation; for every body possessing a soul has the faculty of touch" (*De Anima*, 434a, 13–15), but still maintains the distinctions between the senses: "Democritus and most of the natural philosophers who treat of sensation," writes Aristotle, "produce a most unreasonable hypothesis: for they make all sensible objects objects of touch" (*De Sensu*, 422a, 30–33). But the implications of this "unreasonable hypothesis" would, for Crooke, lead to a condition of cognitive and synesthetic disorder: if "the faculty of sensation is euery where one and the same, neither is there any difference in the faculty whereby wee heare, nor in the faculty whereby wee smell, or from the faculty whereby wee taste: but all the difference ariseth from the disposition of the organ. The Foote would see, and the Elbow would heare, and the sides would smell, and the crowne would taste, if in these parts there wer[e] a disposition to receiue the objects of these Senses" (725). What is suggestive here is that debates about touch in relation to the other senses provides a kind of physiological basis for synesthesia, the interanimation of sensory modes that surfaces so frequently in literary texts of the period. Indeed, if touch could be thought to inform all modes of apprehension linked to sensate experience, then literary tropes of synesthetic disorder might be illuminated not only by explorations of biblical tropes of sensory mismatch, by historical accounts of disordered physical and political bodies, but also by basic debates and confusions in medical texts about the nature of the senses.

The tactile substrate of sensory perception is integral to a number of early theories of sense. Despite the "distance between organ and object" required by visual apprehension, for example, the debate about whether eyes emanated rays or received particles through the air when visualizing objects speaks to a material process of visualization at the most basic physiological level.[38] So too, despite the privilege given to auditory consciousness in much religious writing of the period, the force of sound and air waves was generally understood to have the power to damage the brain, hence the structure of the auditory canal to protect the brain from direct acoustical contact: as John Davies puts it, "So in th'Eares' labyrinth the voice doth stray / And doth with easie motion touch the braine."[39] Given the proximity to the material world necessary for the functioning of taste and smell, these senses were more explicitly aligned with the touchable world. But the logical conclusion of the necessity of touch for the functioning of all of the other senses is, for Crooke, no less than the decay of all intellectual knowledge: "Furthermore," he writes, here reading Aristotle correctly, "if we will stand to *Aristotles* determination, that there can no other Sense subsist without Touching, then will it follow that this being taken away no sense can remaine. Now if the Senses be taken away, the whole family of Arts (which we said before did depend vpon their credit) must needs decay, nay you shall remooue the Sunne it selfe out of the World. If any Man doubt of this, let him seriously suruey all the Artes both Liberall and Mechanicall" (649).

It is no surprise that Tomkis's Tactus aligns himself with Aristotle: "Tell me what sense is not beholding to mee? / The nose is hot or cold, the eies do weepe / The eares do feele, the tast's a kind of touching, / That when I please, I can command them all, / And make them tremble when I threaten them" (Sig. I3). A bit like Shakespeare's Bottom fearing he might frighten the ladies with a roar, Tactus takes himself just a touch too seriously. Or does he? For without him, as we have seen above, no show could possibly go on. In the synesthetic dimensions of theater, it may be that only touch can really pull things together. For Crooke, if Aristotle is correct that no sense can "subsist without Touching," then the absence of touch would extinguish all possibilities of sense, at once conceptual and cultural, including "all the Artes both Liberall and Mechanicall" (649). This threat materializes in *Lingua*, but in a slightly different way, where the presence of touch potentially *expands* the number of the arts and sciences (as Appetitus would have it, from seven to eight) and the senses themselves.

Indeed, what I now want to consider is the extent to which touch was imagined not only to disable ways of calculating knowledge, but to open up new possibilities for articulating and understanding the sense of things. While direct contact was integral to medical explanations of touch, the idea of touch in literature often stretched the domain of the tactile beyond the bounds of the body itself, implying conditions of hyper-awareness and -sensitivity. The commonplace iconography of the spider as a representative of touch, for example, is worth exploring in this respect because it expands the realm of sensitivity from body to environment. As Davies writes, "Much like a subtill spider, which doth sit / In the middle of her web, which spreadeth wide; / If ought doe touch the vtmost thred of it, / Shee feeles it instantly on euery side." This passage has often been read as alluding to the spread of nerves throughout the body. But the simile also relocates touch from the physically proximate to the relatively distant space of environment, perhaps providing the closest Renaissance analogy to the contemporary notion of the "sixth sense," that eerily inexplicable receptivity to seemingly undetectable environmental stimuli. Francis Bacon would liken excess emotional receptivity to a whole environment of cobwebs, a "Cob-web Lawn . . . so tender as to feel everything." [40] Indeed, one might consider Leontes's famous allusion to having "drunk and seen the spider" in *The Winter's Tale* as much in terms of his inexplicable oversensitivity to the environment *around* him as of his consciousness of feeling a poison *within* him.[41] It is as if only he can detect the erotic touch of the world around him: "Is whispering nothing? / Is leaning cheek to cheek? is meeting noses? / Kissing with inside lip? . . . wishing clocks more swift? Hours, minutes? noon, midnight? and all eyes / Blind with the pin and web, but theirs; theirs only" (I.ii.284–92). This is a touchy king indeed, with a kingdom perhaps as sensitive, as fragile, and ultimately as small as a web of his own making: "If I mistake," he says of his jealous thoughts, "In those foundations which I build upon, / the center is not big enough to bear / a school-boy's top" (II.i.100–103).

While spiders make webs to protect themselves and entrap others, what makes them a powerful paradigm of "sensing" in this period is that they can feel without direct contact. The arachnid, or "extrasensory," powers of touch as an alternative mode of receiving information are in fact highlighted by Tomkis's *Tactus*, where the spider works less as a simile of tactile sensitivity than a condition of knowing. "For as a suttle Spider closely sitting, / In the center of her web that spreddeth round, / If the least Flie but touch the smallest thred, / She feels it instantly; so doth my self" (Sig. I3). The analogy between nerves and the webbed texture of the spider is expanded out in this play from the domain of the physical body and into the untouchable realms of the cosmos. As one character tells us, Tactus stands ready to battle for supremacy in the Microcosm: "Besides a monstrous troupe of vglie spiders, / Within an ambushment he hath commanded, / Of their owne gutts to spinne a cordage fine,/ Whereof t'haue fram'd a net (O wondrous worke) / That fastned by the Concaue of the Moone, / Spreds downe it selfe to th'earths circumference":

The maskes are made so strong,
That I my selfe vpon them scal'd the heauens,

And bouldly walkt about the middle region,
Where in the prouince of the Meteors,
I saw the clowdie shops of Haile and Raine,
Garners of Snow, and Christals full of dew,
Riuers of burning Arrowes, Dens of Dragons,
Huge beames of flames, and Speares like fire-brands.
Where I beheld hotte Mars and Mercurie,
With Rackets made of Spheares, and Balls of Starres,
Playing at Tennis for a Tunne of Nectar. (Sig. E2)[42]

What is stunningly articulated here is a vivid form of "gut" knowledge, or what David Hillman has called "visceral knowledge," at odds with emergent forms of scientific inquiry in the Renaissance.[43] The spiders "Of their owne gutts to spinne a cordage fine, / Whereof t'haue fram'd a net (O wondrous worke) / That fastned by the Concaue of the Moone, /Spreds downe it selfe to th'earths circumference." "Cordage," invoking the Latin for "heart," joins the nerves and sinews in a unaccountable way of perceiving the world. Rather, it is unaccountable in terms of logic based on other sensory modes, such as vision. For the expanded sphere or "web" of perception enabled by touch in this passage foregrounds the centrality of touch in detecting temperature, climate, and the structure and motion of the cosmos. Given the lunar and astral forces at play, it is worth noting that in this period the tactile operated under a very different sphere of influence (to be "touched," for example, as the "lunatic"). Of course the concept of *agency* behind the whirling spheres and stars is rather suspect, reduced to a kind of random physics in an astral game of tennis. These are gods made flesh in deed. The web of associations in the sphere of touch are rendered further suspect given that many of the objects in this ekphrastic whirlwind traditionally belong to Visus (such as the planets, the heavens, the stars, all visible from a distance). This contrasts with Visus's use of Terra in his own performance: for while the earth is visible, it was elementally linked with the properties of touch. Visus only "shows" Terra, noting "t'were an *indecorum Terra* should speak" (Sig. G1). (For if the earth should speak, it might well speak with tact.) The fact that these senses are fighting for world domination produces a series of implicitly or explicitly synesthetic playlets, all hinting at the necessary interanimation of the senses in the theater of perception. Not all senses integrate Olfactus, but they do all depend in some sense on Tactus, muted or no. While touch may be fundamental (linked with the "firmament"), the fact that it may also enable a kind of extrasensory (or suprasensory) mode of knowing is at once asserted and undermined in the passage above: not the least because it is Mendacio who is Tactus's spokesman in this instance.

The inflated and deflated powers of this sense are worked into the plot in psychological as well as physical terms as Tactus first feigns madness and then becomes mad in fact. For to be "touched" in this period involved a psychophysiology of temperament, where one could be physically affected and imbalanced by humoral and environmental forces. This concept was so common that Tactus takes full advantage of it. To deflect attention from the coveted crown and robe he sits upon to hide, Tactus performs his own cultural signification: he pretends that he is "touched," melancholy, and so "out of touch" with his rational faculties that he thinks himself a glass urinal. He says to Olfactus, "when I had ariu'd and set me downe, / Viewing my selfe, my selfe ay me was changed. / And thou now seest [me] to be a perfect vrinall." "I am an vrinal I dare not stirre. / For fear of cracking in the Bottom" (Sig. B3). More telling than this fragile firmament *extraordinaire* are associations that Tactus makes in imagining himself a man of glass: a fantasy with roots in medical and classical lore that is reimagined in scatological terms. Tactus narrates his apparent transformation to glass by alluding to Momus's well-known fantasy that all men should have been made with a glass window, so that one might be able see into the innermost "core."

No sooner had I parted out of doores,
But vp I held my hands before my face:
To sheild mine eyes from th'lights percing beames,
When I protest I saw the Sunne as cleer,
Through these my palms as through a prospectiue.
No marueil, for when I beheld my fingers:
I sawe my fingers neere transform'd to glass,
Opening my breast, my Breast was like a window,
Through which I plainely did perceiue my heart:
In whose two Concaues I discernd my thoughts,
Confus'dly lodged in great multitutes. (Sig. B3)

"[W]hy this is excellent," responds Olfactus, "*Momus* himself can find no fault with thee / Thou'st make a passing liue *Anatomie*. / And decide the Question much disputed: / Betwixt the *Galenists* and *Aristotle*" (Sig. B3). What begins as a vivid account of touch being able to detect his own interior (while still a "liue Anatomie"), accessing that "confus'd" realm of thought within the body, ends in a parodic transformation of the self to a urinal, an object that most would not care to see inside. Hillman convincingly argues that the anatomical fantasy of accessing and seeing one's own and another's insides in the Renaissance always encodes a powerful disavowal of knowledge, a nonrecognition of the quintessential otherness of both others and selves. In *Lingua*, that very fantasy is made as fragile as glass: self-recognition here hinges on a conspicuous disavowal since Tactus deploys a largely *visual* model of self-investigation. But the audience of this learned play well knows that this is a joke. That Tactus *fabricates* this elaborate disavowal as a way *not* to be seen by others (and in fact to assert his agency) is very much to the point.

Given the complexities of touch as a mode of perception in the play, his parody of Momus's fantasy at the very least evokes the nonvisual correlative of what it might actually mean to know things, in a physiological and affective sense, by heart. Much like Mendacio's dream of touching an untouchable universe, Tactus at least gestures toward the possibility of an alternative way of "plainely" perceiving one's "heart": not just seeing it, but understanding the confused multitude of "thoughts" within. Indeed, this Tactus is less dead than the "liue Anatomies" that people so many Renaissance medical texts, who delicately point to their own grotesque insides without apparent concern, who might dangle their skin over a shoulder like a warm coat on a sunny day, flex their skinless muscles like so many classical bodies, or pose for a guide to the anatomy of the brain with a conspicuously halved cranium.[44] Unlike the living corpses of what Jonathan Sawday has called the Renaissance "culture of dissection," where "the body had become subject to the gaze," Tactus is less a numb body pointing at itself than a "liue Anatomie" trying to speak from inside out.[45]

As tradition would have it, however, Tactus is ultimately "found out." Visus gets the Crown, Auditus is next best, and, though Tactus is deemed a mere "necessity," he gets the robe as a door prize. Common Sense attempts to restore proper numerical and conceptual order: "The number of the *Senses* in this little world, is answerable to the first bodies in the great world: now since there bee but fiue in the Vniuerse, the foure elements and the pure substance of the heauens, therefore there can bee but fiue senses in our *Microcosme*, correspondent to those, as the sight to the heauens, hearing to the aire, touching to the earth, smelling to the fire, and tasting to the water, by which fiue meanes only the vnderstanding is able to apprehend the knowledge of all Corporeall substances" (Sig. I3). But even at the end of the play there is a dramatic dispute over the robe that Tactus has but Lingua wants. While much is made at the beginning of the play that "there is but one [robe]" (Sig. BI), Tactus and Lingua (and implicitly Gustus) continue to battle it out for the same sign, recalling the tension implicit in differentiating the senses of taste and touch, and implicitly, all the senses from each other, in the domain of language and theater. But it also implicates Tactus with the tongue as an instrument of speech, what many considered to be the "sixth sense" itself: Burton writes of the five senses, "you may add Scaliger's sixth sense of *titillation*, if you please; or that of speech, which is the sixth external sense according to Lullius."[46] In *Lingua*, "speech" becomes entwined with sensory activity, for it is Lingua who first tempts Tactus into thinking he might rule the pentarchy, working to "Clad my selfe in Silken Eloquence / To allure the nicer touch of Tactus hand" (Sig. A3). While Lingua ultimately fails "to make the senses sixe" (Sig. A3), what is on display here is the potential power of theatrical language not only to "allure" and "move," but to highlight the mobility and instability of the senses.

Interestingly, it is when Tactus loses his power to infiltrate and complicate the world of knowledge that the single "object," the robe, finally comes to signify touch. But more important, this single sumptuary habit has a somatic analogue in the play in the reduction of sensory complexity to a localized and vulnerable bodily object. Tactus's ability to disrupt or alter the order of things fully diminishes as he becomes vulnerable to physical (as opposed to cognitive and linguistic) forces stronger than he: his perceptual sensitivity is realized in the body as he is tickled: "Ha, ha, ha, fie, I pray you leaue, you tickle me so, oh, ah, ha, ha, take away your hands I cannot indure, ah you tickle me, ah, ha, ha, ha, ah" (Sig. M2). "We see no Man can ticke himslelfe," wrote Bacon in *Sylva Sylvarum*, "Tickling is euer Painfull, and not well endured." [47] Indeed, tickles quickly become unbearable and the tactual takes a turn for the worse, as Tactus is touched with a "pinch," "pinne," and a "stab" (Sig. M3), he is wracked with cramps, "O the crampe, the crampe, the crampe, my legge, my legg" (Sig M.2), and his powers are diminished to sheer reactivity to the physical force of the world he now inhabits. He is actually disabled from wearing the robe (once again resisting the object) because he is overwhelmed by a kind of burning heat: "Oh what a wild-fire creepes among my bowells: / Aetna's within my breast, my marrrowe fries, / And runnes about my bones, oh my sides: / My sides, my raines, my head, my raines, my head; / My heart, my heart, my liuer, my liuer, oh / I burne, I burne, I burne, oh how I burne" (Sig. K3). In this heartburn par excellence, Tactus becomes a kind of grotesque version of the self-demonstrating anatomy, reduced to locating his vulnerabilities in a series of individuated and hurt body parts: "heart," "brains," "breast," "marrowe," "bones," "sides," "raines." "My heart, my heart, my liuer, my liuer." Such a quick journey from a richly textured realm of plotting, perception, and knowing to a self defined by a series of single hurt organs, subject to anatomical investigation. What might have been a kind of tremulous public body becomes a spectacle of individually marked symptoms and vulnerabilities of physical touch. In a trajectory that we will see at work in *Hamlet* and a number of antitheatrical texts, the epistemological complexity of touch in *Lingua* is ultimately contained by its materialization in the domain of hurt. The unbearable lightness of touch, the surprise of a tickle, a hint, or an unexpected twist, in rhetoric and logic as on stage, are extremely difficult—in Tactus's words—to "indure."[48]

Antitheatrical Tactics: From Audience to Assembly

> *For what clipping, what culling, what kissing and bussing, what smouching & slabbering on of another, what filthie groping and vncleane handling is not practiced euery wher in these dauncings? . . . some haue broke their legs with skipping, leaping, turning, . . . and some haue come by one hurt, some by another, but neuer any came from thence without some parte of his minde broken and lame; such a wholsome exercise it is!*
> —*Phillip Stubbes,* Anatomy of Abuses in England *(1583)*

The reduction of "touch" as a sensitive and affective form of response to a specifiable bodily act, process, or habit is a dominant feature of early treatises against the stage. For many antitheatricalists of the Renaissance, dramatic tactics are dangerous precisely because they are tactile: poets in theaters, writes Gosson in 1579, produce "consortes of melodie to tickle the eare, costly apparrell to flatter the sight, effeminate gesture to ravish the sence, and wanton speache to whette desire to inordinate lust."[49]Acoustics touch the ear into whispers of sensation; costumes visually "flatter" (a word deriving from touch, " 'to flatten down'; hence 'to stroke with the hand, caress' ")[50] or "touch" the eye; gestures "ravish" the sense; and words induce states of physiological arousal. Here the senses of hearing and vision, as vehicles of perception, become aligned with the sense of touch. Although, as Andrew Gurr has famously noted, we alternately imagine theater-going collectives as "audiences" and "spectators," it is actually the sense of touch that consistently informs both modes of sensory reception in antitheatrical treatises (perhaps calling for more attention to that third term of persons coming together, "assembly"). Words touch skin, blood and bone, and enter the bodily interior as a kind of liquid physiology, altering the substance of heart and mind: "by the privy entries of the eare [words] sappe downe into the heart, and with gun-shotte of affection gaule the mind, where reason and vertue should rule the roste."[51]

What is suggestive here is not simply that touch encodes a logic of contagion, or that touch results in disrupted boundaries between bodies, but that it disrupts the boundaries between the senses themselves. That is, what emerges in early accounts of "audience-response" is the very phenomenon of synesthetic disorder that features elsewhere in the rhetoric and epistemology of touch and its relationship to the other senses.[52] Although Aristotle would single out touch and taste, as distinct from the other senses, as "brutish" pleasures linked with intemperance, antitheatricalists consistently expand the dangers of sensory perception by aligning them with the sense of touch.[53]

In the early modern lexicon of sensory perception, acoustics was commonly imagined in tactile terms: tickling the ear, the touch of sweet harmony, or, as George Chapman puts it in a comment on listening: "Hard it is in such a great concourse (Though hearers ears be ne'er so sharp) to touch at all things spoke."[54] Considering the literal possibility of hearing through touch, Sir Thomas Browne notes that "when our cheek burneth or ear tingleth, we usually say that some body is talking of us. . . . Which is a conceit hardly to be made out without the concession of a signifying Genius, or universall Mercury; conducting sounds unto their distant subjects, and teaching us to hear by touch."[55] The confluence of hearing and touching (and indeed tasting) emerged largely from the domain of music, where the "soft touch" of fingers on a harp produced "sweet sounds," or where music could be ravishing, soothing, the food of love. As Bruce Smith puts it, in this period "the word 'voice' meant, first and foremost, a concatenation of bodily members: muscles, gristly tissues, fluids, and 'soul' . . . 'voice' never loses its physiological grounding."[56] But exactly what that physiological grounding was is anything but clear. Even as late as Blount's *Glossographia*, one might note a kind of synesthetic slippage in the domain of speech. "Oral," according to Blount, is defined by reference to at least three kinds of physiological ground: "(from *os, oris*) pertaining to the mouth, visage, face, look, favour, or voice."[57] Similarly, in the earlier *Thesaurus linguae Romanae et Britannicae* by Thomas Cooper (1578), "Os, oris" is defined similarly as "The mouth: the visage or countenance: The proportion of all the bodie. Presence. Language. Audacitie, boldenesse or hardinesse."[58] The rich textures of orality produce an overflow of sense, not only in the domain of rhetoric and theater, but in the very definition of the word.

But in antitheatrical discourse, the synesthetic pleasures of theater that "move" become "flattened" in a largely specular economy of bodies engaged in physical acts. Richard Brathwait's treatise on the senses draws on the metaphor of theater to emphasize the shaming gaze: touch is the "Theater of shame if abused, but the eminent passage from a pilgrimage to a permanent Citie, if rightly employed."[59] And for Gosson, this conceit is fully articulated when he famously reimagines the "audience" as a spectacle of conspicuously touching bodies:

> In our assemblies at playes in London, you shall see such heaving and shooving, such ytching and shouldering to sytte by women; suche care for their garments that they be trode on; such eyes to their lappes that no chippes light in them; such pillowes to their backes that they take no hurt; such masking in their eares, I know not what; suche geving them pipins to passe the time; suche playing at foote saunt without cardes; such tick[l]ing, such toying, such smiling, such winking, and such manning them home when the sportes are ended, that it is a right comedie to marke their behaviour, to watch their conceates, . . . or follow aloofe by the printe of their feete, and so discover by slotte where the deare taketh soyle.[60]

Again this passage speaks to the relevance of "assemblies" as a third term in the "audience" "spectator" sensory-triad. According to the *Oxford English Dictionary*, "Assembly" in the Renaissance could suggest physical, military, and sexual as well as a spatial joining of persons: "To join together, unite (two things or persons, one thing to or with another)"; "To couple (sexually)"; "To come together into one place or company; to gather together, congregate, meet," and "To meet in fight; to join battle, make an attack or charge." Gosson's assembly fits perfectly with the tactile surround of the term (where no one seems to be hearing or watching the play). So too, all these meanings converge in John Northbrooke's *Treatise* (c. 1577), where the theater is a place where people are "so fleshlye ledde, to see what rewarde there is giuen to such crocodiles, whiche deuoure the pure chastitie bothe of single and maried persons, men and women when as in their playes you shall learne . . . howe to playe the harlottes, to obtayne one's loue, howe to rauishe, howe to beguyle, how to betraye, to flatter, lye, sweare, forswear, howe to allure to whordome, howe to murther, howe to poyson, . . . to mooue lustes," etc.[61] This theater emerges as a veritable guide for one to learn technologies of touch.

This might seem a most excellent advertisement for assembling, but of course, like Gosson's catalogue of tickling, shouldering, itching, and the like, Northbrooke anatomizes specific forms of touch in order to subject the whole domain of "touch" to shaming gaze: "*Vitanda ergo spectacula omnia.*

All such spectacles and shewes . . . [are] to be auoyded; not onelye bicause vices shall not enter our heartes and breastes, but also least the custome of pleasure shoulde touche vs, and conuerte vs thereby both from God and good workes."[62] The affective power of plays to "touche" and "enter our heartes and breastes" is localized and contained in specific scenes of shame in Northbrooke's theologically coded anatomy theater. What Northbrooke is trying to kill off is far more complex than any kind of physical or even moral touch, it is something perhaps at the core of "touch" as a condition of emotional receptivity, of allowing one's self to be "entered" by simply being curious. Following his diatribe, he reasons, "Therefore, great reason it is that women (especially) should absent themselves from such playes. What was the cause why Dina was rauished? Was in not hir curiositie? The mayden woulde go forth, and vnderstande the maners of other folkes. Curiositie, then, do doubt, did hurt hir." This logic typifies the representation of touch in antitheatrical rhetoric, which restricts the powers of affect and the power of words to assemble people and ideas in new ways by foregrounding the body as the site of touch and extreme vulnerability.

The peculiar vulnerability of touch, as distinct from other senses, was a mark of a range of philosophical and medical as well as moral discourses on the senses. Excess sensation can hurt or destroy sense organs: one can be blinded by too much light; deafened by excess sound; and apparently gustatorily and olfactorily challenged by excess tastes and smells. But to lose one's sense of touch, as Aristotle would write, is to lose not just the faculty of touch, but life itself. "Other senses such as colour, sound and smell, do not destroy the animal by excess, but only the sense organs . . . but the excess of tangible qualities, such as heat, cold, and hardness, destroys the animal . . . without touch an animal cannot exist. Hence excess in tangible qualities destroys not only the sense organ, but also the animal, because touch is the one sense which the animal must posess" (*De Anima*, 435b, 7–9). While touch is crucial to the living being for Aristotle, it is also a danger linking man with "low and brutish" pleasures: "it attaches to us not as men but as animals."[63] This is mirrored by Milton's Raphael in *Paradise Lost*, "But if the sense of touch whereby mankind / Is propagated seem such dear delight / Beyond all other, think the same vouchsaf'd / To Cattle and each Beast."[64] Indeed, the peculiar dangers of touch to both spiritual and bodily life become integral to theories of the five senses, which often single out touch as the greatest enemy to virtue. Lactantius speaks of "libidinous touch" (which stands in as the defining mode of this sense) "which is to be kept back most of all, as it damages most of all."[65]

Although the concept of touch is itself, as we have seen, difficult to grasp, locate, or contain, in so much as it is *fatal*, it is relatively easy to banish in symbolic terms—to kill off in a rhetoric of spiritual, psychological, physiological, and cultural self-protection. In a period of plague and disease, death by contact was a very real concern: the symbolic and etymological links between touch and contagion were linked with conditions of physical as well as spiritual and moral vulnerability. But what I want to argue in the final section of this essay is that the fatalistic trajectories of touch in Renaissance revenge drama stage—and often challenge—the social imperative to banish touch from the domain of intimation, from the rich flickers and hints of physical and emotional contact, to a world where touch not only hurts but kills.

The reduction of touch to toxins in Tomkis's *Lingua* parallels much rhetoric of the period about the dangers of touch as infection and contagion in the theater: for fear of the plague was of course entwined with fear of even a single touch. As Thomas Lodge writes in his treatise on the plague: "Contagion, is an euil qualitie in a bodie, communicated vnto an other by touch, engendring one and the same disposition in him to whom it is communicated."[66] Tomkis calls attention to this commonplace early on in the play: Tactus not only feigns madness, but when confronted with Visus and Gustus, tries a stronger approach, invoking the apotropaic power of infection to keep others at bay. He puts on the robe, and when asked about his "faire habiliments," he claims that some stranger in a vacant town mysteriously threw it at him and fled: "No sooner had I put it on my back, / But suddainly mine eyes began to dim, / My ioint waxe sore, and all my body burne / With most intensiue torture, and at length, / It was too euident, I had caught the plague" (Sig. C1). Visus immediately departs, and although Gustus (ever sympathetic to Tactus) offers to "put my selfe in ieparody to pleasure thee," he is pushed away by Tactus, who says he must die alone. Tactus, delighted at his success, imagines his own epitaph: "Here lyes the Sense, that lying guld them all, / With a false plague, and a fained Vrinall" (Sig. C2). The dangers of "touch" as a form of psychological imbalance and physical contagion are asserted as rhetorical constructs from the first, used to deflect attention from a larger complication at hand: the disruption of reason by passion; of rationality by the complex and ever-shifting forces of touch as a physical, emotional, and perceptual mode. With this point in mind, I now want to consider the fatalistic trajectories of touch in *Hamlet* in terms of the relationship between "touch" as affect and physiology, between elusive forms of knowledge and feeling and the somatization of heartbreak on the Renaissance stage.

In much Renaissance drama, touch is integral not only to "audience response" but to the trajectories of dramatic plots, metaphors, and actions. Much like the trajectories explored above, revenge dramas often shift from an exploration of the symbolism of touch as affect or cognition to a restriction of tactile economies in the body subject to harm. In *Hamlet*, to take a case in point, Hamlet goes from being "touched" (or playing it) to being "touched" (and dead). In the language of the play, touching shifts from the domain of rhetorical pointing to a single moment of fatal bodily contact. Hamlet's "I, there's the point" of the 1603 Quarto (uttered after "To be or not to be") returns materially and conceptually in the final act as he is fatally "touched" with Laertes's "point," "the point envenom'd too!" (V.ii.327).[67] The first "there's the point" is drawn from the rhetoric of reading, used in both oral performance, as the rhetorician used his finger to point to visual information (on a chart or an outline on his other hand), and silent reading, with pointing fingers lining the margins of early books to indicate relevant textual moments.[68] "There's the point" either functions as an acoustical sign, a commonplace detached even from its own manual origins, or accompanies a visual gesture: Hamlet pointing to the very book he holds in his hand.[69] Although this may seem a small point, in fact the detachment of a body from itself and its deployment for the operations of metaphor is the dominant concern of the opening acts of *Hamlet*: a theme marked by the phenomenon of the ghost. "Horatio says 'tis but our fantasy, / And will not let belief take hold of him / Touching this dreaded sight twice seen of us," says Marcellus in the opening moments (I.i.27–28). "Touching this vision here," says Hamlet after his encounter with Old Hamlet, "It is an honest ghost, that let me tell you" (I.v.143–44). Touching, meaning "concerning, of or pertaining to," is here a conceptual gesture as detached from the domain of physical touch as the ghost himself.[70] These early moments return in the form of a single bodily reference as Hamlet is touched with a point: Nothing, says Laertes, "Under the moon, can save the thing from death / That is but scratch'd withal. I'll touch my point / With this contagion, that if I gall him slightly, it may be death" (IV.vii.44–46). And later during the duel, upon the first point of contact, the second Quarto reads: "A touch, a touch, I do confesse" or the Folio "I, I grant, a tuch, a tuch." The term "touche," which acknowledges a solid conversational point, in fact originates from physical contact; the English word "touch" derives from the Old French *touche*, "to touch" or the Italian *tocca*, "stroke, blow, touch" and *toccare*, "to hit, strike" (*OED*, sv "touch"). But in *Hamlet*, the trajectory reverses, the conversational become the contactual and, like the ghost itself, dead metaphors come to life in the form of bodies on the verge of death. Hamlet is not only touched to the quick, but the effect of such a touch is located physiologically in Hamlet's own heart: "Now cracks a noble heart" (V.ii.364)

The heart is a particularly resonant locus of touch and vulnerability, not only for the melancholic but for a physical body literally "touched to the quick." For Aristotle in *De Sensu*, although the sense of touch was somatically dispersed and peripherally epidermal, it was ultimately localized in the region of the heart. Although this locus of touch in the body was much debated, it informs many scenes of cardiac arrest on the renaissance stage: a *topos* that amounts to a kind of emotional open heart surgery in John Ford's *Tis Pity She's a Whore*. If Hamlet's immediate response to the ghost's narrative is: "Hold, hold, my heart, / And you, my sinews, grow not instant old, / But bear me stiffly up" (I.v.93–5), the question is not only of the heart's stability, but of what the heart might hold, can hold, or if the heart can be held or beheld. These are questions at the core of revenge drama. Ford's play explores the question of what it might mean to hold someone's heart in one's hands (literally, as Giovanni touches the still steaming or imagistically *breathing* heart of his dead beloved); Kyd's *Spanish Tragedy* comes to a close with Hieronimo's disconcertingly tactile *Solimon and Perseda* and his own sense of psychophysiologic rupture: "And now to express the rupture of my part / First take my tongue and afterward my heart."[71] This character too moves from psychological and metaphoric to physical forms of "touch," the very materials of writing such as pen and paper are transformed into weapons of destruction. "Reading, writing, matters of tact," to remember Jean-Luc Nancy, here becomes a kind of dramatic principle in revenges where tissues of communication become literalized as "matters of tact."

In all these plays, the heart shifts from the domain of signification as emblem, citational cliche, heard (or sonically imagined) pulses, breath, words, and feeling to a material entity subject to the physical properties of touch. The distance of objects and organs afforded by interanimation of tactile, acoustical, and visual metaphors collapses or, rather, becomes subject to a logic of proximity and material "immediacy." Again (to reappropriate McLuhan's phrase) if the medium is the message, touch over the course of these plays loses its power to signify.[72] Or rather, what these plays stage is the profound difficulty of sustaining concepts of touch *as* complex modes of mediation. This trajectory is marked in *King Lear* as well, where Lear's emotional pain is managed by anatomizing it: "Let me have surgeons; I am cut to th'brains" (IV.vi.190–91) or, earlier, "Let them anatomize Regan, see what breeds about her heart" (III.vi.74–75).[73] If the blind Gloucester manages to "see . . . feelingly" (IV.vi.147), this very idea of a tactile-emotional conscious-ness is at odds with Lear's attempt to use physical pain to avoid emotional pain. While still out in the raging storm which "invades us to the skin" (III.vi.6–7), Lear says "This tempest will not give me leave to ponder / On things would hurt me more" (24–25).

If there is any "touchstone" in *Hamlet*, it is perhaps the grief of Hamlet's own heart. Gertrude suggests as much, noting his "very madness" after killing Polonius "like some ore / Among minerals of base, / Shows itself pure–a weeps for what is done" (IV.i.25–27). But this location of Hamlet's woe as touchstone cannot bear a moment's scrutiny: it is quickly picked up in Claudius's anxious response: "O Gertrude, come away. / The *sun* no sooner shall the mountains touch / But we will ship him hence" (IV.i.28–30). The chemical, physiological, and affective dimensions of touch converge here: grammatically and conceptually, no sooner than the son might touch the mountains he will be banished from the scene, "shipped hence." The nonrecognition of interiority here extends into the realm of theology. The sense of being "touched" with guilt emerges three times (very like the ghost) in the play. As Hamlet puts it, "Your Majesty, and we that have free souls, it touches us not. Let the gall'd jade wince, our withers are unwrung," to which Guildenstern later adds, "I know no touch of it, my lord" (III.ii.236–38, 346). And later Claudius says to Laertes: "l hear and judge 'twixt you and me. / If by direct or by collateral hand / They find us touch'd, we will our kingdom give"(IV.vi.202–4). These tactually inflected metaphors amount to a collec-tive denial of self-touch. It is, to adopt the words of one seventeenth-century writer, "As if men had forgone all touches of humanity and were become a kind of walking-ghosts."[74] It is Hamlet, as both character and play, that bat-tles with these ghosts. In contrast to the antitheatrical conflation of touch with moral death, this play in fact calls for a more nuanced recognition of feeling, of being touched in its many senses, so that one can live—rather than only be touched in death.

This question of how one can touch others in a world where they are not recognized or do not recognize themselves is central to *Hamlet*. The ghost is an embodiment of this. The ghost as a symptom of non-recognition actually emerges in the opening scene of Tomkis's *Lingua*, as Auditus re-fuses to hear the words of Lingua, who then wishes the "houling of tortur'd Ghosts / Pursue thee still and fill thy amazed eares / With cold astonishment and horrid feares" (Sig. A3). She, not unlike Hamlet, has language but no power to "touch" the world she inhabits, and out of her frustration emerges this tortured ghost and her subsequent revenge. Ghosts here and in other

Renaissance dramas become the mark of metaphor dead before its time. Lingua's art is an art of arousal, of "titillation," and touching, but one that has become dissociated from her internal counterpart, the heart, and ultimately, all of the perceptive capacities within the sensory realm. She can simulate and stimulate, but has lost the capacity to "touch." She is both a sixth sense and no sense at all, halfway between the living and the dead, and her words—like those of Tactus—lack the kind of "tact" necessary for individual and self-integration.

As Nicholas Ling put it in 1598, "The sense of touching although it is the last, yet it is the ground of all the rest. One may liue without sight, hearing, smelling, but not without feeling."[75] If we consider "touch," like the word "feeling," in the sense current at the time, "to mooue or grieue," [76] Ling's statement might well describe the work of theater itself. For to speak and not to move, or to speak and not to be moved, is like being in conversation with someone (or oneself) who is "as the air, invulnerable" (*Hamlet*, I.i.150). And it is this drama of non-recognition that drives so much revenge drama, with ghosts entering where words are dying off, hearts bleeding where love can't be seen, and in *Titus Andronicus*, hands circulating where touch has been cut off. But as such, what these plays call attention to is the need for a kind of vulnerable air in the space between persons; a reciprocal sensitivity to forms of touch that don't die the moment they are pinned down: in short, a social and cultural development of that sense "which is most excquisite in man": the sense of tact.[77]

To have "tact" is to have just the right touch, a manifest sensitivity to one's linguistic and social surround. And if it is tact, in every sense of the word, at work in the most powerful tragic dramas of the English Renaissance, it may deserve much more of the very recognition it gives.

Chapter 10

Living in a Material World: Margaret Cavendish's The Convent of Pleasure

Misty G. Anderson

The relationship between post-Cartesian categories of rational thought and the critical premises of feminist and, more generally, critical theory have made it difficult, or at least unlikely, to take tactility seriously as a field of inquiry. Tactility as a sensory category posits the immediacy of bodily presence in ways that are disconcerting to Cartesian rational discourse. The experiential immediacy of touch, like the senses of taste and smell, threatens the separation between subject and object on which modern rational thought depends. My investigation into the philosophical and sexual nature of tactility in Cavendish's *The Convent of Pleasure* suggests that we need a clearer understanding of the historical and philosophical terms of tactility in order to assess articulations of female separatism and same-sex desire in early modern writing; in other words, the terms of philosophy are to a great extent also the terms of gender. Margaret Cavendish's utopian *The Convent of Pleasure* (1668) appeared as Cartesian rationalism and its anglophone Lockean relatives were working their way through English thought but before these systems were ideologically dominant. Her representation of the convent breaks with the paternalistic implications of Cartesian rational thought and Lockean epistemology at the level of "*materialist*" content and structure: her all-female world takes shape through philosophical, political, and formal terms that embrace an intimate connection between cognition and sensation, which both Locke and Descartes figured as separate, particularly in the terms laid out by Descartes's theory of property dualism.[1] The utopian terms of her project participate in a pre-Cartesian discursive exchange *within* the world in which matter and consciousness are fundamentally connected. This philosophical position has profound implications for Cavendish's plot, which explores pleasure in general, but dilates on the tactile immediacy of the convent's pleasures that shape the play's narrative alternative to marriage. Cavendish's emphasis on tactility over vision, like Luce Irigaray's theoretical arguments over three hundred years later, reweaves the feminine maternal body into philosophical discourse as it also maps out the territory of same-sex desire.

The Cartesian Divide

Cavendish represents pleasure, which resides within the world of the convent, in terms of an organic materialism, in which knowledge and sensation are inseparable. Her thoughts on the importance of performance and delivery in her preface to *The Worlds Olio* (1655) makes the point that the sensory experiences of her readers are of vital importance to her meaning:

I Desire those that read any of this Book, that every Chapter may be read clearly, without long stops and staies; for it is with Writers as it is with men; for an ill affected Fashion or Garb, takes away the Natural and gracefull Form of the Person; So Writings if they be read lamely, or crookedly, and not evenly, smoothly & thoroughly, insnarle the Sense; Nay the very sound of the Voice will seem to alter the sense of the Theme.

Her caution to her readers, that they must not read crookedly lest they muss her book, places her within a tradition of classical oratory and performance. But her appeal to the need for "smooth" reading takes shape in an analogy to clothing and body shape. The performance of her text is a sensory experience that will impinge on meaning; the words themselves do not exist in some independent and objective space, but instead reach out to the listener in their proper aural form. Her concern about her readers places her words in a living present, where narrative "sense" is dependent upon and intertwined with the senses. The importance of orality (and aurality) to her aesthetic argument is a manifestation of her holistic scientific and intellectual engagement with the world of the senses. As she writes in her *Philosophical Letters*, "it is not onely the Mind that perceives in the kernel of the Brain, that there is a double perception, rational and sensitive, . . . and as there is a double perception, so there is a double knowledge, rational and sensitive."[2] Her relationship to the material world, and in particular to the body's tactile, sensory ways of knowing, allies her thought with Lucretius's *De rerum natura*, the first part of which was freshly translated into verse by John Evelyn in 1656. Lucretius argued for the primacy of touch as the grounding of the other senses. The first book of *De rerum natura* begins with an invocation of Venus as nature, whose bounty he celebrates as he seeks to know "how of their *mat-*

ter nourished they grow" (25). The standard of all perception for Lucretius was tactile; nature is matter that can be tangibly perceived. Evelyn translates this sense of matter as "Bodies," the term Cavendish also favors in her *Philosophical Letters*. Lucretius argues:

> . . . act and *suffer* naught save *Bodies* may,
> Nor anything save *Voyd* give place or way;
> Therefore besides those two no *Third* can rest
> To strike our sense, or sink into our breast . . .
> As Water's *wet*, Earth *heavy*, Fire is *hot*:
> So *Bodies* may be *toucht* and *Vacuum* not. (39)

Sensory perceptions that "penetrate" the body though touch are Lucretius's paradigm for sensation and hence knowledge. Like Cavendish, he vests the tactile encounter between the senses and the material world with a kind of knowledge of its own, as nature's "Bodies . . . sink into our breast."

These same philosophical speculations, however, put her at odds with the rising tide of modern science and its separation of matter and thought after Descartes. Descartes's mind and body dualism gives mind the position of mastery over a faulty material world, which includes nature and the body. In Descartes's sixth meditation, one of his weakest argumentative moments, he presses the logic of his definition of the thinking self in relation to the material body.

> because on the one side, I have a clear and distinct idea of myself inasmuch as I am only a thinking and unextended thing, and as, on the other, I possess a distinct idea of body, inasmuch as it is only an extended and unthinking thing, it is certain that this I (that is to say, my soul by which I am what I am), is entirely and absolutely distinct from my body, and can exist without it.[3]

The Cartesian withdrawal of the soul or the "I" from the body is a condition of knowledge in his philosophical system. Descartes's "I" reflects on the body as an object, like any other "unthinking thing." The body, as a part of the material world, must remain separate from the mastering mind even in the process of perception.

> Bodies themselves are properly perceived not by the senses or by the faculty of imagination, but by the understanding only, and since they are not known from the fact that they are seen or touched, but only because they are understood, I see clearly that there is nothing which is easier for me to know than my mind. (2.58)

Descartes masters the body's contribution of sensory information through the dominance of the intellect, which is credited with true perception and hence understanding. His anxiety about the body and its senses centers on the potentially unreliable knowledge they provide. The realm of the sensuous, in which tactility is the least cognitively mediated sense, is relegated into nonbeing by Descartes's *cogito ergo sum.* The separate, disembodied mind plagued by its dependence on the body and its faulty senses has its heirs in the intellectual self of Locke, the immaterialism of Berkeley, and to a lesser extent the skepticism of Hume, which inform the critical and cultural values of the Enlightenment. These values, particularly rationality and individualism, require protection from the ever-present body, a protection that Descartes constructs by producing the body as other to the self. This philosophical "othering" of the body reproduces a western chain of associations between matter and *mater*, which identify the realm of matter as feminine.[4] In the logic of the post-Cartesian culture of reason, man can be an embodied self pursuing the life of the mind, but woman is contained by the sensuous materiality of the body against which the true self or soul is defined. Hence the terms of her existence vis-à-vis her culturally produced body are also the terms of her nonexistence in the Cartesian model of the self.[5]

It is an instance of comic justice that two women, Princess Elizabeth of Bohemia and Margaret Cavendish, Duchess of Newcastle, should challenge Descartes's disembodied, transcendent "I." In her correspondence with Descartes, Princess Elizabeth mentions the effects of worries, emotions, and "vapors" on clear thought. She argues that Descartes has not accounted for these irrational, bodily circumstances that do affect the thinking being: "It is nonetheless very difficult to understand that a soul such as you have described it, after having had the power and the experience of reasoning well, could lose all this through a few vapors, and could subsist without the body and have nothing in common with it."[6]

Descartes responds by explaining that it is very difficult to understand the concepts of the body, the soul, and their intersection in his work, and he closes with a recommendation that she not concentrate on "metaphysical matters" for more than a few days a year (Correspondance 325). Instead of following his patronizing advice, she suggests in her next letter that his conception of the soul is faulty and untrue to his initial precepts of depending on clear and distinct perceptions.[7] Elizabeth's challenge to Descartes is to incorporate the body within his definition of the self rather than transcend it, but her potential corrective, which might have spared him what Albert Johnstone calls his fate as "ideational scratching post," was met in the end with only his silence (17).

Margaret Cavendish took up the works of notable philosophers and scientists, including Hobbes, Descartes, and Henry More, in *Philosophical Letters* (1664) and *Observations upon Experimental Philosophy* (1666). The imaginative and even dream-like approaches that Cavendish takes to the material world have been dubbed unscientific because of a supposed failure of objectivity on which rationalism depends. Cavendish's resistance to objectivity, however, is a crucial and historically plausible condition of her "radical materialism," through which she represents the material world in its variety of shapes and textures at the atomic level. In her *Poems and Fancies* (1653) she rhapsodizes on round water atoms, pointed fire atoms, flat earth atoms, and long air atoms, which move and interact according to their shapes. Her complex theory of atoms posits an animated struggle between particles that is a constitutive feature of matter. In *The World's Olio*, she likens thoughts to animals, rocks, and even pancakes as a partial response to Descartes's immaterialism, which would become a cornerstone of the later Enlightenment discourse that represented Cavendish as a madwoman and idiot. Cavendish was in the company of many other vitalists, including Spinoza, Ann Conway, and Pierre Gassendi, when she claimed, contra Descartes, that matter has rational and "sensative" powers of its own.[8] Eve Keller has also argued that Cavendish's organic materialism "allows no workable, consistent distinction between rational subject and disparate object," a scientific position that anticipates post-Kuhnian and feminist critiques of "the rational basis of mechanical science."[9]

Her reflections on Descartes in her *Philosophical Letters* are built on a tactile understanding of perception. She rejects the idea that "the sensitive organs should have no knowledge in themselves, but serve only like peeping holes for the mind, or barn-dores to receive bundles of pressures, like sheaves of Corn" (letter 35). Cavendish presents a general model of sensory perception in which the material world of atoms and "bodies" touches the various senses. She argues that sense and perception are "made by a motion or impression from the object upon the sensitive organ, which impression, by means of the nerves, is brought to the brain" (letter 37). She likens the travel of light to a blind man who uses a stick to touch his environment and feel his way; the light similarly touches from sun to earth instantaneously, as the blind man feels through his walking stick. Though this tactile model of sensation, Cavendish argues that "all the sensitive perceptions are alike, and resemble one another." The sense organs, as "parts of the body sentient," are the site of a tactile perception that is relayed to the brain, where it can be differentiated from other sensations. Tactility is then both the sensory encounter par excellence and the boundary of a more radical, threatening permeability. Cavendish expresses some concern about the possibility that "the motions of stone, water, sand, &c. should leave their bodies and enter into the stick, and so into the hand," a concern that springs from her over-whelmingly tactile model of self, which is in such constant contact with the material world. She must, at the end of letter 37, clarify that exterior motions and matter are not the stuff of perception, but rather the occasion for a tac-tile experience that remains within the body.

For Cavendish, the physical sensory organs have a knowledge of their own in their very materiality: "for I believe that the Eye, Ear, Nose, Tongue, and all the Body, have knowledge as well as the Mind" (115–16, letter 36). She asserts that "though Man, or any other animal hath but five exterior sensitive organs, yet there be numerous perceptions made in these sensitive organs, and all in the body; nay, every several Pore of the flesh is a sensitive organ, as well as the Eye, or the Ear," and that "sense and knowledge cannot be bound onely to the head or brain" (35). She is unwilling to centralize intelligence in a mind that leaves the body behind as a secondary consideration, a lower be-ing with peeping holes and "barn-dores." Cavendish's lively "cognative tactil-ity" conflicts directly with the Cartesian division of body and mind, as well as with Descartes's suspicion of the senses. Her materialist account of cognition integrates the functions of thought and knowledge within corporeal experi-ence without denying the category of mind entirely.

Her argument for a sensual plurality of knowledges challenged the ten-dency to abstraction, or what might be called a general method applicable across a range of disciplines. According to Peter A. Schouls, "This universal-ization of method, this single approach to all objects of knowledge, is a cru-cial element in the constitution of the new mentality, and appears as a new element in history. It makes legitimate the application of the phrase 'mod-ern man' as a term quite distinct from 'sixteenth-century man' or 'medieval man.' "[10] But the universalizing terms of modern scientific method position the category "woman" paradoxically, and indeed as *the* paradox of rational-ism, vis-à-vis the difference of their bodies. Women in Cartesian thought were, as in Locke, apparently included in the universal Cartesian category of mind, but in fact took their place outside the circle of full subjectivity and citizenship as objects and goods, a function of their embodied difference. Ironically, this is the very body that Cartesian rationality made "immaterial." The upshot of this Cartesian trap, which severely limited the philosophical or institutional engagement of women with the new science, is that it reifies the terms of sexual difference as a grounding "truth" for the more abstract category of mind. The trap developed methodically over the course of the eighteenth century, effectively marshaling most protofeminist thought into its universalisms and forcing the culture deeper into the looming paradox of the sex/gender split.

Although Cavendish's *Philosophical Letters* were intended to generate intellectual dialogue with members of the Royal Society, her challenges produced no response. Henry More was offended by the idea of replying to Cavendish because of her sex, which would force him to "put on petti-coats."[11] Descartes and Hobbes simply ignored her. Cavendish's position as an open critic of the new science in her utopian writing put her at odds with early scientists who were only too happy to deploy the gendered Cartesian language of separation to critique her "irrationality." Cavendish handed the Royal Society just such an opportunity when she made her famous debut on May 30, 1667. She wore an enormous petticoat carried by six maids, a rather large headdress, and a cavalier-style man's coat, described by John Evelyn in a ballad that commemorated the occasion:

But Jo! Her head gear was so pretty,
I ne'er saw anything so witty
Though I was half afeared,
God bless us! When I first did see her;
She looked to like a Cavalier,
But that she had no beard.[12]

Cavendish's costume, indexed by class as well as gender, was a performative attempt to reconcile the gendered social demands of the Royal Society (writ large in the discourse of an unmarked, masculine objectivity) with the material difference of her female, hence marked, body. Far from allaying anxieties, Cavendish's partial drag act seems to have stirred them up by presuming a masculine prerogative. Speaking of the possibility and the limits of lesbian representation, Valerie Traub has argued that "it is not a woman's desire for other women, but her usurpation of male prerogatives that incites writers to record and thus reveal the anxieties of their (and our) culture," a usurpation that is figured most obviously in drag.[13] Cavendish's drag act continues into the world of gendered concepts, where she challenges the social meanings of masculine and feminine:

I know there are many Scholastical and Pedantical persons that will condemn my writings, because I do not keep strictly to the Masculine and Feminine Genders, as they call them, as for example, a Lock and a Key, the one is the Masculine Gender, the other the Feminine Gender, so Love is the Masculine Gender, Hate the Feminine Gender, and the Furies are shees, and the Graces are shees . . . as for the nicities of Rules, Forms, and Terms, I renounce, and profess, that if I did not understand and know them strictly, as I do not, I would not follow them.[14]

Her explanation of the concepts of gender as pedantic and unnecessary sweeps away the hierarchies of meaning that they establish and makes way instead for a more associative mingling of ideas.

The emerging distinction between sex and gender, which only makes sense in a philosophical framework that distinguishes subjects from objects, reproduces (or, perhaps more to the point, produces) the dilemma of rights that early feminisms try to adjudicate. In order to imagine sex as distinct from gender, some notion of the body as an object of rational and scientific inquiry needs to be distinguished from gender, the social performances through which we know the elusive "subject."[15] While it does not address the problem of selfhood directly, the distinction implies that the mind resides in the realm of gender, the choices and acts that testify to rationality, rather than the realm of sex, the subordinate term on the side of "body." This division, which twentieth-century feminisms have largely maintained, promised to move away from a vision of the self as body, tied to animal impulses and biological phenomena. After such a division of the physical from the "true" self, Mary Astell can ask, "If all Men are born free, how is it that all Women are born slaves?" and Judith Drake can argue that the inequalities between the sexes are a function of education rather than "nature."[16] The rub is that the distinction between "natural" sex and socialized gender actually empowers the category of the natural as the origin of gender identity, as Michael McKeon and others have argued at length.[17] The rise of gender as a social term that promised to save liberal thought from the tyranny of the body still remained tied to some notion of bodily sex, which anchored its meaning. In this capacity, gender could authorize more feminine, passive modes of behavior for women as the social extension of their material bodies, which were at the same time repudiated as "immaterial." Locke's elaboration of this problem, in which he posited women as subjects and objects, as both part of the category "individual" and as a special category of property, is only one among many examples of the trap. The reflections of Johnson on the chastity of women, Astell on slavery and freedom, and Drake on the equality of souls all imply a double status for women as immaterial and material selves. The claim to subjectivity in these arguments is played directly against the claim to a woman's objectivity, which only reifies her position as object or, more specifically, as "not subject." This trap is worth serious consideration because it is the same trap encountered by liberal feminisms, which have yet to come fully to terms with the dissonance between the abstract claims for mental, political, and economic equality and the material realities of sexual differ-ence. Tactility, as a concept that mediates between agency and receptivity, has some philosophical purchase for feminist approaches to the body.

The importance of tactility to Cavendish's organic materialism shapes the philosophical, political, and formal terms of life in the convent, which in-cludes the privileging of female bonds of friendship and eroticism, a feature that has attracted the attention of critics who attend to early modern sexuali-ties.[18] Laura Rosenthal offers an astute analysis of the relationship between homoeroticism and class in Cavendish, and the erotic anxieties of the con-vent have received careful attention in the work of Theodora Jankowski.[19] I argue, however, that the erotic features of these utopias operate within a more holistic and tactile challenge to rationalism. It is the feel of the "Beds of Velvet . . . Quilts, either of Silk, or fine Holland " and the shifts "of the finest and purest Linnen that can be bought or spun" that sustain the erotic appeal of the convent and make it such a pleasing and viable alternative to the less accommodating world outside, particularly after Cavendish's own experience of the English Civil Wars and the loss of much of the Cavendish estate. The recuperation of that loss is here both political and philosophical. The ab-straction and intellectual distance that both Cartesian and Lockean ratio-nalisms demanded are predicated on the thinking self's disregard for the material body, which situates bodily pleasure as well as sexual activity within the lower realm of the corporeal, where it can be effectively marshaled into the service of cultural demands. Modern sexuality, framed in terms of a con-test between the subjective value of sexual pleasure and the objective value of reproductive sex, is produced within the suppositions of mechanistic science and the labor demands of the new economy. This set of connections, inti-mately bound up with Puritan anxieties about sexual pleasure that rational-ism implicitly assuages, remains part of the bone structure of a persistent homophobia that plagues western and particularly U.S. culture. Cavendish's tactile environment offers a glimpse of female same-sex bonds in a world governed by associative logic rather than formal rationality or, to invoke Iri-garay, the mechanics of fluids rather than the mechanics of solids.[20] Amid the political, philosophical, and epistemological crises of the mid-seventeenth century, tactility as both trope and organizing logic presented the possibility of authorizing the experiences of gentle and aristocratic women and articulating an imaginative, though decidedly class-bound, mode of female community and eroticism.

Making a Place Feel like Home

Margaret Cavendish's social situation, as first expatriate then restored but impoverished aristocrat, fostered her sense of imaginative license to question reality. As Cavendish hyperbolizes in *The Description of the New World, Called the Blazing World* (1666), "the Duchess of Newcastle was most earnest and industrious to make her own world, because she had none at present" (98). World-making and self-making were intertwined imaginative activities for Cavendish, anchored in the material realities of reassembling dispersed goods, lost estates, and missing personal property, tasks that awaited many royalists returning from exile. Born Margaret Lucas in 1623 to a royalist family, she retreated to Oxford at the onset of the Civil War and became a maid of honor to Queen Henrietta Maria.[21] She followed the royal family in exile to Paris, where she met William Cavendish, a royalist commander thirty years her senior who fled from England after the serious defeat of his army at York in 1644. They married in 1645 and remained in exile until 1660, when Charles II made William duke of Newcastle and restored some of his property. Although she reveled in the privilege of rank, Margaret did not enjoy the economic and political power her position might have warranted under other circumstances. The ruined fortunes of William and her own relatively small £2,000 portion meant that the couple were often in need of ready cash. She made an unsuccessful trip to England in 1651 to collect money from William's estates, which had been sequestered by Parliament. In 1660 Charles II passed over William for a post at court, a decision that may have been informed by William's retreat after the battle of York.[22] The couple, who had been living beyond their means thanks to William's knack for securing loans, took up residence at Welbeck Abbey, where Margaret wrote her *Playes* as well as *Observations upon Experimental Philosophy* and *The Description of a New World, called the Blazing-World.*

    The Convent of Pleasure, which appeared in the collection of her closet dramas, *Playes, Never Before Printed,*[23] reflects her intense loyalty to the crown in general and to Henrietta Maria in particular. The class politics of the convent relegate women of lesser birth to an internal, all-female labor force in the service of a courtly elect seeking an escape from marriage. The convent is coded in terms of an ideology of a self empowered by aristocratic heritage, with which elite women could identify through the doctrine of absolute monarchy; in Cavendish's case, this ideology allowed her to unite her interests in the physical sciences with overtly gendered questions about social order.[24] But the theatricality and the contemplative seclusion of the convent are tributes to Henrietta Maria. The queen participated in pastorals and plays while at court and while in exile, and expressed a fondness for costume equal to Margaret Cavendish's.[25] At the same time, she also encouraged contemplative study, primarily through Platonic love doctrines, in herself and others. After the execution of Charles I in 1649, Henrietta Maria founded the Convent of the Visitandines at Chaillot, France in 1651. She remained there for much of the 1650s and 1660s, even after the coronation of her son Charles II.[26] These royalist and intensely personal connections between *The Convent of Pleasure* and her time as a maid of honor in exile frame the narrative quest for an alternative to the conventional marriage plot through a same-sex society.

Lady Happy, the founder of the convent, is of the age to marry and anxious for an escape from the constrained, idle life she sees imposed on married women. She gathers together women who share her desire for "a place of freedom, not to vex the Senses but to please them" (220; 1.1) and establishes a geographically separate, fortress-like female space. Lady Happy makes the argument that the senses ought to be delighted rather than denied because it is only natural for people to use the senses that the gods created for them. Her arguments quickly draw fire from her foil, Monsieur Take-Pleasure, who argues that if Lady Happy is "a Votress to Nature, she must be a Mistress to Men" (223; 2.1). Lady Mediator challenges his definitions of women and "Nature," explaining that Lady Happy says men obstruct the pleasures of nature, "for, instead of increasing Pleasure, they produce Pain; and instead of giving Content, they increase Trouble; instead of making the Female Sex Happy, they make them Miserable" (223; 2.2). Lady Happy's radical revision of the 'natural' inspires rage on the part of Adviser, a jealous male critic who calls Lady Happy's opinions heretical and insists she should be "examined by a Masculine Synod, and punish'd with a severe Husband, or tortured with a deboist husband" (225; 2.1). His response allows Cavendish to speak to social and domestic violence against women. The threat from Adviser echoes the specter of torture in witch trials and, more generally, the limited legal recourse that women had in cases of domestic assault.[27]

For Adviser, cultural plurality is not an option; the very possibility of the convent is a threat to hegemonic patriarchal order, which he suggests will maintain its authority through force. The violence that subtends patriarchal attitudes toward marriage echoes the anxieties of Cavendish's *The Contract*, which is plagued, according to Victoria Kahn, by the "feeling of the incompatibility of law and romance, coercion and consent" in its revision of social contract theory.[28] Lady Mediator directs Advisor out of the convent and tells him he should put his complaints in "a Petition to the State, with your desires for a Redress." The invocation of the state in this context is a somewhat snide reference to the expansion of English civil law under Cromwell, which promised equitable, rational solutions to legal conflict in the public sphere. Civil law, however, encroached on the domains of ecclesiastical law, chancery courts, and manorial courts, all of which included space in which women could negotiate marriage contracts and subsequent property claims.[29] Cavendish implies that Lady Happy's rank would support her claims to independence and, by extension, justify the existence of the convent, but the political realities that impinge on women's autonomy introduce the thread of a less idyllic political sphere into her tactile world. The philosophical space of the convent still depends on the political and legal structures that must agree to its existence. In scenes like these, *The Convent of Pleasure* is more philosophically and socially focused than Cavendish's other attempts to render the sexual contract in terms that are palatable to women. It imagines that the sexual contract might be superseded by a sororal compact, a shift with very material consequences. Here, property exists for the immediate tactile and sensual pleasure of women. Material goods become the materials of pleasure for the devotees of the convent rather than the economic terms through which elite women are exchanged on the marriage market. The emphasis on pleasure over ownership suggests that Cavendish's tactile logic (at least in this elite application) might work against alienation in several senses.

Lady Happy and the women of the convent are protected from the specter of institutionalized violence by their fortress-like retreat. Safely within its walls, Lady Happy catalogues at length the textiles and furnishings of the chambers. The description of the rooms is itself a fantasy of sensory pleasure, fueled by an accumulation of detail:

in the Spring, our Chambers are hung with Silk-Damask, and all other things suitable to it. . . . In the Summer I have all our Chambers hung with Taffety, and all other things suitable to it, and a Cup-board of Purseline, and of Plate, and all the Floores strew'd every day with green Rushes or Leaves, and Cisterns placed neer our Bedheads, wherein Water may run out of small Pipes made to that purpose . . . and all the Wood for Firing to be Cypress and Juniper; and all the Lights to be Perfumed Wax. (224; 2.2)

The catalogue moves breathlessly from one season to another, announcing decorative changes that keep the textiles of the chambers central to the description. Lady Happy explains that their bedclothes will be changed every day, that their shifts will be of the finest spun linen, and that, miraculously, the gardens will not need weeding. The monologue, which takes up three pages, serves as a reminder that Cavendish's plays were (by her own admission) not written for the stage. More important, its unapologetically run-on form manifests an indulgence in the tactility of the spa-convent and its pleasures, which are only available to the aristocratic women who have been invited to join Lady Happy.[30] Lady Happy sings:

Wee'l Cloth our selves with softest Silk,
And Linnen fine as white as milk.
We'll please our Sight with Pictures rare.
Our Nostrils with perfumed Air.
Our ears with sweet melodious Sound,
Whose Substance can be nowhere found. (221; 1.2)

Cavendish uses cloth to link the female realm to the tactile pleasures that her textual vision of feminine space has to offer. Following her philosophical claim that "every several Pore of the flesh is a sensitive organ" (letter 35), her creative, world-making descriptions establish an atmosphere of sumptuousness and pleasurable excess brought about by the emphasis on the sensual.

The materials of this description tell us about the terms of the female body within the convent. Cavendish promises "a great Looking-Glass in each Chamber, that we may view ourselves and take pleasure in our own Beauties whilst they are still fresh and young" (224; 2.2). The mirror directs the women to a mildly autoerotic self-relation as source of pleasure; the female body becomes an object of pleasure for their subject-selves, although this pleasure is circumscribed by a conventional aesthetics that does not include older women or laborers employed in the convent. The changing seasons connect women to the temporality of the calendar. Women's time in the convent, as in Julia Kristeva's formulation, is cyclical, and new fabrics punctuate change. These "material" changes, like the flowing water by the beds, reclaim as pleasurable the feminine symbolization that has been used to denigrate women as mere body, unstable fluidity, and vanity. They also acknowledge the importance of the spaces of home and hearth that have long been associated with women and bodily well-being. In contrast to the Lockean interest in furnishing the mind with ideas, Cavendish is very much concerned with furnishing the literal room to accommodate the material body. Cavendish argues implicitly that she needs a separate world with an internal material and sensual logic to claim and to represent the feminine.

Sensory knowledge, pleasure, and sensation all become a part of a utopian alternative that connects philosophy, politics, and form through the troping of tactility. The narrative content of Cavendish's *Convent* builds on this philosophical tactility through its associative logic of form, which lends the latter portion of the play a dreamy immediacy. Grounded in the material space of the convent, the scenes rely on internal associations rather than the logic of a governing plot. Cavendish's montage dramatic style resists narrative unity, causality, and closure by changing scene and topic without regard to a realist standard of objectivity. Other works by Cavendish, including *The Comical Hash, Bell in Campo,* and *The Apocriphal Ladies,* reject the structural demands of dramatic form for the freedom to ramble, explore, and reinvent social paradigms. Indeed, most of her plays would have been impossible to stage in the Restoration, though they are amenable to the contemporary technologically rich media of film and computer animation. The plays favor sequentially numbered scenes and multiple plots over the structure of acts and the architecture of a main plot and organized subplots.[31] Cavendish's creative response to an aesthetic question of structure exposes an ideological aspect of the so-called unities: Why should characters' lives be "presented in a circular line, or [brought] to a triangular point" when the lives of real people in real communities are not? [32] The geometrical terms of her challenge strike at the aesthetic dominance of the Aristotelian discovery plot and, more to the point, the Oedipal plot, which integrates all plots into the story of a central male character. While the realities of plot and closure are decidedly more unstable in the early and mid-seventeenth century than the Restoration and early eighteenth-century neoclassical discussion about aesthetics would suggest, we should note that Cavendish drew heavily on chivalric and pastoral romances, which organized significant portions of their plots around romantic love and marriage. Cavendish also saw the theaters reopen with the dominant modes of heroic romance and comedy, both of which reinforce the formal necessity of heterosexual closure.[33] The convent, as an explicit alternative to marriage, draws from these pastoral and chivalric materials, but, in a more dilatory narrative procedure, Cavendish weaves in the tactile pleasures of furnishings, environment, and clothing as the conditions for (if not the basis of) an alternative social order.

Getting Dressed Up

Once Cavendish has established the sensual environment of the convent, the surreal dreamscape sequence of embedded plays within her play comences in Act 3 with the tableaux of women's lives. The scenes take up the themes of women who are powerless against the law and betrayed by philandering lovers or husbands and present them in graphic tableaux. They show husbands who bring whores home, women beaten by drunken husbands, and women suffering and dying in childbirth. The scenes, which end with the pronouncement, "Marriage is a Curse, we find / Especially to Woman Kind" (233; 3.10), have been aptly called "antimarriage propaganda" by Linda Payne.[34] The shared physical threat of abuse, unwanted penetration, the potential horrors of childbirth, and the unreliability of children's support for aged mothers unite women at the material level of the sexed body through shared anxieties about reproduction. The fact that all the women are performing the "curse" of marriage within the blessed alternative of the convent, however, suggests that the construction of the female body's social function rather than its essence is the curse.[35]

Freedom from childbirth, Cavendish's own experience, is implicitly linked to female autonomy and female pleasure through the fantasy of the Princess and Lady Happy. The Princess's entry into the convent, however, and her interest in Lady Happy motivate the action of the last half of the play. The pastoral masque sequence of Act 4 inaugurates more dreamy visions of amatory partnership founded on gender mutability, nonreproductive pleasure, and the fantasy of women in drag. Gender-transgressive desire and cross-dressing, often in opulent costume, loom large in the development of Lady Happy and the Princess's friendship, at least in part a tribute to her time with the queen. Keller links Cavendish's frequent cross-dressed characters and her personal penchant for elements of male attire to Cavendish's view that "identity and gender are flexible hybrids" in her organicist (as opposed to mechanist) world view.[36] It also reflects the logic of what Laqueur termed the one-sex body, whose sexual variations are produced by differences in development along a hierarchical axis of female to male.[37] This organicism frames her intellectual desire to resist distinctions between rational subjects and separate, implicitly less rational objects that situates the practice of cross-dressing in the convent. But Cavendish's complex erotics of drag deploys the tactile pleasures of clothing itself in the pleasure of dressing up. Like the fine shifts and fashions that Lady Happy promised her companions as they entered the convent, the pleasures of dressing are intimately related to the pleasures of gender crossing.

After the convent's montage on the trials of heterosexuality, the Princess appears dressed as a shepherd to woo Lady Happy, who is dressed as a shepherdess. They express their desire to "mingle souls together" in a kiss, but the scene is transformed into a rocky shore, where Lady Happy becomes a sea goddess and the Princess is Neptune. There is no overarching cause for the progress of the scenes, no discernible plot, only a sort of mythological free-association. Cross-dressing blends into the dramatic performances that follow in the play; the effect is that the masculine position and, more generally, gender, are exposed as largely constructed. The associative, tactile mode of knowledge that has little investment in an objectifying rationalism is also anterior to the terms of modern gender, which are rendered through the analytic taxonomies of objectivity.[38] But Lady Happy finds herself heavily invested in the play of cross-dressing, which materializes her erotic desire for the cross-dressed Princess. She begins Act 4 by musing, "My Name is Happy, and so was my Condition, before I saw this Princess; but now I am like to be the most unhappy Maid alive: But why may not I love a Woman with the same affection I could a Man?" Lady Happy then stops herself with the couplet, "No, no, Nature is Nature, and still will be / The same she was from all Eternity" (234; 4.1), [39] but the content of this "nature" remains contested: is it nature qua heterosexuality, or nature qua sexual desires? The juridical and ecclesiastical prohibitions concerning same-sex desire dealt largely with male same-sex contact and tended to ground legal prohibitions in the term sodomy, which implies penetrative sex.[40] But "Nature" also signifies the philosophical and scientific accounts of matter, which suggest a more organic connection between physical nature, moral nature, and the material body. The tactile philosophical foundation of the convent in the rightness of pleasure and the harmony with the natural world that it creates makes Cavendish's appeal to "Nature" more unclear than the volatile question itself, which can be answered with a "yes" from within the terms of the convent.

The crisis engendered by Lady Happy's question leads Cavendish further into the issue of same-sex desire, which the terms of tactility would support. When the Princess enters the scene, she tries to console Lady Happy, who confesses her fear that she loves the Princess too much:

Prin: Can Lovers love too much?
Lady H: Yes, if they love not well.

Prin: Can any Love be more vertuous, innocent and harmless then ours?
Lady H: I hope not.
Prin: Then let us please our selves, as harmless Lovers use to do.
Lady H: How can harmless Lovers please themselves?
Prin: Why very well, as, to discourse, imbrace and kiss, so mingle souls together.
Lady H: But innocent Lovers do not use to kiss.
Prin: Not any act more frequent amongst us Women-kind; nay, it were a sin in
            friendship, should not we kiss: then let us not prove our selves Reprobates.
They imbrace and kiss, and hold each other in their Arms. (234; 4.1)

The Princess uses the socially acceptable forms of female friendship to ground a more erotic relation to Lady Happy. After the embrace, the Princess exclaims, "These my Imbraces though of a Femal kind, / May be as fervent as a Masculine mind." The philosophical priority of pleasure in the Convent allows Lady Happy to contemplate the leap from a 'harmless' model of female friendship to an expression of erotic desire, though the possibility of this leap provokes much hand-wringing from Lady Happy.

Lady Happy's love for her "most Princely Lover, that's a she" is undeniably sexual. She mopes through the end of the play, convinced that she is in love with a woman *and* convinced that such a love is illicit. She cries out, "O strike me dead here in this place / Rather than fall into disgrace" (239; 4.1). Madame Mediator also makes it clear that she knows something is going on between the women. She warns the Princess, "I am not so old, nor yet so blind, / But that I see you are too kind" (240; 4.1). In her reading of the play, Donoghue archly questions whether Madame Mediator's suspicions are of a cross-dressed man or a lesbian, which can only be articulated after the (inevitable?) switch: the Princess turns out to be a prince in disguise, and Lady Happy and the Prince are married in the final act. But the reader is not privy to Cavendish's little trick until Act 5, a withholding I have reproduced critically. The courtship of Lady Happy and the Princess is, in the end, carried out between two textually identified women. Although their relationship does lead to heterosexual marriage once the Prince is "out," the reversal cannot completely contain the subversive operations of the play, which are grounded in Cavendish's philosophical tactility. Jacqueline Pearson has noted that, at the least, the play posits the androgene as ideal husband in its world of fluid sexual identities;[41] in a more radical reading, it touches on the possibility of a non-objectivist, non-universalizing separate space that makes possible same-sex erotic bonds that are not repudiated by conventional closure. The list of actors names that *follows* the text of the play notably lists

"The Princess," not "The Prince," as a character in the *dramatis personae*. The play, it seems, does not want to give up on its own alternative vision.

Regarded as insane by most of her contemporaries and many twentieth-century critics,[42] Margaret Cavendish parlayed class privilege and scientific curiosity into the basis for a utopian reflection on a tactile, decentered, women-friendly social order. Cavendish's experimental works illustrate that the rational demand to vest subjectivity in a thinking self was not, as I and others have argued, a gender-neutral proposition.[43] Cavendish's proto-feminist insight into rationalism was its disregard for the body, which was culturally constructed as an impediment to pure thought or an unreliable point of access between the mind and the material world. Her investigation of materialism followed the cultural coding of women as more bodily by nature and hence more of a threat to intellectual and moral coherence, which we can trace back to Plato and his predecessors. But the pleasurable, materially cognized worlds of women that Cavendish presents refuse the negative moral and social stigma attached to the body and sensuality. By addressing materialism through the trope of tactility, she mobilizes pre-Cartesian models of knowledge to represent women and women's pleasure as both viable and laudable in opposition to the heteronormative social contexts supported by rationalism and empiricism.

Cavendish's official ending (technically) reasserts heterosexual order, but her anxious gesture toward social and cultural expectations does not negate the systematic force of her utopian vision. Rather, it suggests that what is at stake when we take tactility seriously in philosophical, cultural, and historical terms is no less than a woman's access to full bodily autonomy, a social proposition Cavendish seems to have blunted at the moment it extended into the realm of sexual object choice. In her convent, where the immediacy of touch, taste, and smell define the terms of existence, bodily pleasures organize social experience, rather than the rational reverse in which the mind's apprehension of economic, political, and cultural demands organize and often curtail the body's pleasures. This sense of immediacy drew Cavendish to imagine (albeit anxiously) the extension of her tactile philosophies in sexual terms, which would include a range of nonreproductive erotic pleasures and the stories they might generate. The cloth, architecture, and pleasures of her convent offer a glimpse into an imaginative, unabstracted, tactile experience of the world, which will become increasingly unavailable under the gendered philosophical terms of the age of reason.

Chapter 11

Touch in the Hypnerotomachia Poliphili: *The Sensual Ethics of Architecture*

Rebekah Smick

For reasons grounded in longstanding conceptions of the Renaissance, the *Hypnerotomachia Poliphili* has often, and in a number of academic areas, been considered the archetypal Renaissance text. The most elaborate of the early incunables, it has managed to exemplify for art historians and bibliographers alike both the Renaissance development of printing and the much celebrated Renaissance sense of design both in its remarkable woodcuts and general layout.[1] The content of the book, which spans a plethora of subjects, has not lessened this impression. For historians of thought, the sheer breadth of its learning as well as its provenance in the Venetian press of Aldus Manutius has made the book a virtual sign for Renaissance syncretism at its most expansive moment. It is also highly symbolic of the humanist recuperative spirit of the Quattrocento in its fierce absorption with antiquity and the host of classical texts it cites.[2] Further, it is of great interest to historians of Renaissance architecture because it contains one of the first architectural treatises of the period, a treatise whose discussion of architecture is not only firmly rooted in Vitruvius, but comparable to that of the contemporary Alberti.[3] Clearly, the book accords in many areas with certain of our most fundamental notions of the Renaissance as a period.

While most scholars would accept this point, there is little else about the book that elicits agreement in the scholarly community, the exact subject matter of the text being one of its more perplexing problems. Yet there is one construct that all would agree governs the text: the book's narration of the amorous adventures of its main character, Poliphilo. This feature has generally been viewed as medieval and derivative for reasons that stem largely from its repetition of well-used formulae from the courtly love tradition.[4] The thirty pages of the text actually dedicated to Poliphilo's romance hardly compete, for example, with the two hundred some odd pages of the book specifically devoted to architectural description. Recently, however, it has been suggested that the book's love story is precisely what orients the entire work not so much through the specific details of Poliphilo's quest, but through its general eroticism, an eroticism that pervades, in this particular view, every part of the book and not just the romance of Polia and Poliphilo. For Liane Lefaivre, the defining feature of the *Hypnerotomachia Poliphili* is the way its author manages to eroticize architecture itself through the metaphor of architecture as human body. In her view, nearly all of Poliphilo's encounters with architecture are like his encounters with Polia, informed by an attention to physical sensation that can only really be regarded as erotic in character.[5]

Again, few scholars would argue the point that the book is suffused, like most syncretic efforts of the humanists of the period, with an overt sensualism. But what Lefaivre observes, that is the sensualism that pervades Poliphilo's various encounters with architecture itself, has indeed not been widely discussed.[6] Starting from the *Hypnerotomachia Poliphili*'s own description of the role and function of sensation, specifically the sense of touch, this chapter aims like Lefaivre to account for the conspicuous eroticism of the book as it specifically relates to the art of architecture.

Interestingly, the view of sensation the text reveals came to fruition in the later Middle Ages and not during the Renaissance, most notably in the writings of St. Thomas Aquinas. For a number of respectable reasons, those who have considered the eroticism of the *Hypnerotomachia Poliphili* have rarely looked to Aquinas or the scholastics as potential influences.[7] So many other more obvious sources, such as Lucretius's *De rerum natura*, are cited in the text itself that ignoring the antischolastic sentiments of the period or medieval moralism in general to consider a potential source in the scholastics hardly seems warranted. Further, such works fit better with our understanding of the sensual character of Renaissance "paganism" toward the end of the fifteenth century.[8] But to look solely at these sources can only partially address the issue at hand which is the relation of the book's sensualism to the art of architecture. For this, one must turn to a very specific context that was dominated by scholastic constructs well into the seventeenth century—Christian ethics.[9] The link between the eroticism of the *Hypnerotomachia Poliphili* and the art of architecture is grounded in the scholastic Christianization of specifically Aristotelian moral philosophy, most notably as expressed in the *Nicomachean Ethics*. This is not an unnoted source for late medieval dream visions and makes an immediate kind of sense when one recalls their character as *psychomachie*, intrapersonal battles between our lower and higher natures.[10] But it is also the context for what we have come to call aesthetics because of the role Aristotle gave to the achievement of pleasure in the realization of ethical behavior. At the most fundamental level, that is the level of our bodily senses, our ethical responses, according to Aristotle, are governed by stimuli that give either pleasure or pain. It is architecture's particular status as a tactile art, an art of the body, that renders it not only a possible stimulant to virtue, but a unique mode of having knowledge of the highest good. While it would be wrong to underestimate the potentially sensualizing effect of the Renaissance rediscovery of the *De rerum natura,* for example, on the *Hypnerotomachia Poliphili,* the erotic character of the text also reflects an intellectual system that had for a long time supported a unique heterodoxy in specifically literary accounts of the rudiments of Christian ethics. It is this system, already well established in the later Middle Ages, that I will explore in this chapter for what it is able to tell us about the potentially salvific character of an eroticized architecture.

The Senses in the Ethical Dream Vision

The storyline of the *Hypnerotomachia Poliphili* surprises no one already familiar with the allegorical dream vision. In this particular instance of the genre, the chief protagonist, Poliphilo, recounts the eventual conquest of his idealized beloved, Polia, as the details of that conquest became known to him in a dream. As an account of Poliphilo's specific pursuit of Polia, the plot of the *Hypnerotomachia Poliphili* adheres to an important branch of the dream vision tradition, the secular love vision. However, the book is more substantially informed by the other primary type of dream vision in the western tradition, the philosophical dream vision. The most famous of these visions were written by Cicero, Boethius, and Macrobius in the late classical/early medieval period. In these, the pursuit is not of a woman, but of moral perfection, where moral perfection is defined as the soul's release from the material confines imposed by the body. In accordance with the Neoplatonic philosophy that prompted the writing of these visions, this state of being could only be achieved through the act of contemplation. Thus, a soul's arrival at pure thought was also its arrival at a state of liberation from the demands of sense. The longstanding interpretation of the idealized lady of the courtly love vision as a personification of this kind of pure knowledge is a consequence of the eventual elision of these two traditions during the later Middle Ages.[11] As a late fifteenth-century example of this elision in line with the *Roman de la Rose,* the *Hypnerotomachia Poliphili* is no exception to this general rule.[12] Poliphilo's pursuit of Polia doubles as his personal search for a knowledge capable of releasing his soul from the exigencies of the flesh.

Yet there is one feature of the book that discloses a very significant variation on this theme of knowledge acquisition as the path to virtue—the book's treatment of the senses. According to the view of morality we've been describing, our sensual existence is a negative thing, something from which it is desirable to be released. The ultimate basis for this negative view of our sensual existence was Platonic emanationism, the idea that what we think is of a higher order than our bodily experiences and that the ideas that constitute our knowledge are innate to the human soul having emanated originally from certain fixed universals. For Poliphilo, however, in the *Hypnerotomachia Poliphili*, the senses have a positive role to play in his search for Polia. Not only do they appear to him in the course of his quest in the form of five female voluptuaries, but these women deliver him into the realm where he receives the most direction as to the steps he must take to find his beloved Polia (1: 74ff.). Plato is not behind this more positive approach to our sensual experience. Rather, the idea is a key tenet of the philosophy of Aristotle. Unlike Plato, Aristotle proposed that our ideas are the result of a progressive process of abstraction that must of necessity come from the information provided by our senses. For Aristotle, our sensual existence was, so to speak, a necessary evil, an unavoidable fact of our condition as corporeal humans.[13]

The appearance of this Aristotelian concept in what was initially a Neoplatonic tradition of literature about gnosis was due to the efforts of one figure in particular, the fifth-century Boethius. Unlike the Neoplatonist Macrobius, who offered a fully elaborated emanation theory in his commentary on Cicero's *Dream of Scipio*, Boethius introduced the Aristotelian idea that all knowledge was derived from sense experience. For late antiquity in the west this was a novel addition, one that helped establish Boethius as the most important early conveyor of Aristotelianism to the Latin west. In the area of ethics, his specific adherence to Aristotelian epistemology was to have a profound effect. Because he gave human reasoning and its abstractive processes a place in the ethical ideal of contemplation, he did much to set the stage for Western scholasticism and its acceptance of rational inquiry into what had been the traditional precinct of theology, the nature of the divine as the highest good.[14] Yet, the effects of Boethius's Aristotelianism did not fall on particularly fertile ground. It was not until the eleventh and twelfth centuries, amid growing interest in recovering the Aristotelian corpus, that his dream vision, *The Consolation of Philosophy*, exerted much influence.[15]

Thus, because of the *Hypnerotomachia Poliphili*'s positive approach to

the senses, it was the Boethian strain of the dream vision tradition that ultimately informed the work, a strain handed down via such important late
medieval allegories as Alain de Lille's *De planctu naturae,* Jean de Meun's *Roman de la Rose,* or the *Divina Comedia* of Dante.[16] However, there occur
in the *Hypnerotomachia Poliphili* some significant changes to the Boethian
model. When compared with the example provided by Boethius, the *Hypnerotomachia Poliphili* in fact adopts a much more strictly Aristotelian view
of the knowledge that the senses provide than what had been proposed by
Boethius, who in the end offered a limited application of Aristotelian ab-
stractionism. The *Hypnerotomachia Poliphili* adheres to certain features of
Aristotelian epistemology with a precision that reflects the ongoing assimilation of Aristotle during the later Middle Ages, in particular, the work of
the most rigorous of the late medieval interpreters of Aristotle, Thomas
Aquinas.[17] The matter of the role of sense-perception in human cognition
was, in fact, signature for Aquinas. With more insistence than any of his contemporaries, Aquinas upheld the Aristotelian position by emphasizing the
sensual foundation of all human thinking.[18] With similar conviction, this
is the position taken by the author of the *Hypnerotomachia Poliphili.* The
Senses, themselves, espouse it when Osfressia, the personification of the
sense of smell, exhorts Poliphilo to give himself over to the pleasure provided
by the various senses because of its ability to lead him to his beloved Polia, or
knowledge.[19]

To this view of the epistemological significance of the senses should be
added another, related, issue that helps further distinguish the arguments of
the *Hypnerotomachia Poliphili* as Thomistic. In the course of his journey,
Poliphilo can only attain final knowledge of Polia after death since it is only
with his death that his soul is free to leave his body and unite with the knowledge Polia represents.[20] While it was not uncommon in the Platonic context
for death to be the prerequisite for a soul's release from the body, the issue
became more pointed in the context of having knowledge of the divine. Did
we have to die to have knowledge of a fixed universal like God? For Aquinas
the answer was yes. The reason he believed this to be the case stemmed from
his view of the relationship between body and soul, another important concept that he borrowed from Aristotle. In Aristotle's view, the individual soul
forms a natural unity with the body and cannot exist apart from it.[21] Among
certain of Aquinas's contemporaries, this was not a popular idea because it
questioned the very notion of the soul's immortality. If the soul was not, as it
had been for Plato, an independent complete substance that could exist apart
from the body, how could it ever fit with the Christian idea that the soul was

also immortal? Aquinas dealt with the problem by suggesting that the soul could gain a separate existence from the body, but that that separate existence could only occur at death when there would be a dissolution of the individual composite being.[22]

While this approach solved the problem of the immortality of the soul, it had certain consequences for the problem of the relation between natural and divine knowledge, how we might have knowledge of God if our souls are indissolubly tied to the material conditions of the body. Aquinas was consistent in his response. Since the soul could not exist apart from the body until death, it followed that full knowledge of God could not occur until death when the soul was finally freed to meet God, so to speak, on his own spiritual terms. Thus, in Aquinas's scheme of things, our knowledge of God is limited, as long as we are alive, to what our reason can suppose about him. In sum, Aquinas's adherence to the Aristotelian union of mind and body obviated the possibility of a mystical cognition of God before the advent of an individual's death, a stand that distinguished him both from the mystics and those who held that direct knowledge of separately existing universals was possible in this life.[23] In the *Hypnerotomachia Poliphili*, it is his approach to divine revelation that is upheld. Poliphilo's *gnosis* can only occur with his death when his soul is finally released from its physicality.

The Ethical Role of Touch

Among those who study the allegorical dream vision, the themes we have discussed are not unknown. The Boethian roots of the philosophical dream vision and the refinement of its scholastic arguments is well trodden ground, especially in the study of Dante who often cited his debts to Thomas.[24] However, these specific features of the scholasticism that informs the *Hypnerotomachia Poliphili*, its insistence on the sensual character of all human knowledge and its investigation of the relationship between natural and divine knowledge, are especially significant for an understanding of the role of touch in the *Hypnerotomachia Poliphili*. Of the five Senses that Poliphilo meets along his way to enlightenment, the Sense of Touch turns out to be the most important precisely because of the place it held with regard to the obtainment of divine rather than natural knowledge *in this life*. Again, this point of view reflects the position taken by Aquinas, an understanding of which sheds considerable light on the special role of touch in the *Hypnerotomachia Poliphili*. Because it first of all clarifies the general function of the senses in bringing one closer to the divine, the place to begin in Thomas is with his ethics.

Again Aquinas was deeply indebted to Aristotle in the development of his moral theory, specifically Aristotle's practical philosophy as espoused in his *Nicomachean Ethics.*[25] Like Plato, Aristotle adhered to the notion that the highest moral good was the act of contemplation. However, because certain of Aristotle's physical and metaphysical theories disallowed Platonic conclusions about the human accomplishment of the contemplative state, the *Nicomachean Ethics* was in part an attempt to fit Aristotelian physics and metaphysics to the idea that morality comes with knowledge.[26] Aristotle's commitment to the unity of body and soul was one such theory, which, moreover, had specific consequences for his understanding of the role the senses played in effecting contemplation. Because Aristotle believed that human intellection is not separable from the exigencies posed by the body, he opened himself up to the possibility that contemplation can be impeded if there is something in our physical natures that is capable of hindering the proper formation of thoughts and the activity that those thoughts engender. The idea that our corporeality is likely in some way to corrupt our thought processes was a longstanding opinion of the classical world that stemmed from the view that our physical natures are in essence faulty or bad. For Aristotle, corruption at the bodily level is also the root cause of unethical behavior in humans.[27] However, in his view, it is not because our sensual experience is in and of itself bad. Rather, it is because there exists an imbalance in our emotional selves that can stand in the way of what he called "right reason." Whenever our emotions are excessive enough to disturb the sensual process by which thoughts are formed, there is, in his view, moral failure.

The reason our emotions were thought especially capable of disturbing the sensual process of thought formation was their own close tie to the activity of the senses. For Aristotle, sense experience is not only the basis for all knowledge, it is the impetus behind emotional response because of the way our emotions can be affected by whatever we touch, taste, smell, hear, or see. While this might seem an obvious observation, the physiology of Aristotle's explanation of the relationship between sense experience and emotion is quite specific. In his view, there is a much more immediate relation between sense experience and the emotions than between sense experience and thought because our capacities for sense perception and emotion belong to the same part of the soul, the lower appetitive rather than intellective part. Though sense experience is essential for thought to occur, the most fundamental response we have to sense experience is, in fact, a feeling that we share with all lower creatures, the feeling of either attraction or avoidance. Insofar as our sense experience gives us pleasure, we will be attracted to whatever it is we sense. Insofar as it gives us pain, we will be repulsed. In Aristotle's view, these two essential responses determine the character of all other human emotions, and it is the possibility of excessive pleasure or pain in our emotional responses to sense perception that can finally affect the formation of thought.[28] What is necessary for right reason to occur is some kind of balance between the pleasure and pain caused by physical sensation.

It is the ultimate source for this balance that provides the final key to Aristotle's moral theory. Since, in Aristotle's view, sensations and the feelings they produce are not in and of themselves bad, the balance required for proper reason to happen must come from those who perceive. It is ultimately our task as moral creatures to exert enough control over our sensual experiences of pleasure and pain that thoughtful deliberation can be made. Precisely how one might exert this control is also taken up by Aristotle. In his view, we can accomplish the necessary equilibrium in our emotions by privileging those passions in any given situation that strike the mean between excessive pleasure or excessive pain. Moreover, the more we strike this mean, the more we will be able to respond proportionately to pleasant or painful objects and situations. We will literally form the habit of being virtuous. Virtue comes, then, for Aristotle, from repeated acts of proper emotional response to sensory stimulus that in the end enable our sense power to have the equilibrium necessary for clear deliberative thought.[29]

From the point of view of ethics, no single sentence could probably better describe the nature of Poliphilo's journey in the *Hypnerotomachia Poliphili* than the one given above. At every step of the way in his story, Poliphilo is beset by varying kinds of sensual stimulus, from the architecture he so loves to the individual stimulations offered by the Senses themselves.[30] Moreover, the sensations he feels affect in him two basic ways. He is either overwhelmed by pleasure and the desire it evokes or he is literally terrorized by pain.[31] Further, Poliphilo's personal response to these varying stimuli is one of the abiding themes of the book, whether or not he will succumb to the emotions created by the various stimulations he encounters.[32] Moreover, there is progressive improvement in his ability to exert control over his emotional responses.[33] One of the clearest indications of the *Hypnerotomachia Poliphili*'s adherence to the Aristotelian model, however, comes at the very beginning of the book, when Poliphilo falls asleep and finds himself in a dark wood. This wood symbolizes Poliphilo's own emotions, which have gotten out of control.[34] As becomes clear from the surrounding text, this condition has arisen in Poliphilo because he has experienced too much sensation, so much that he has been without the ability to make deliberative choices.[35] With this introduction of the relationship between our passions, sensation and our reason, the author of the *Hypnerotomachia Poliphili* lets us know that the ultimate subject of his story is the matter of ethical behavior.

The question remains, however, why the sense of touch has a special status for Aquinas when it comes to achieving the proper balance of emotions necessary for contemplation to occur, especially if this balance is the result of our own moral efforts. Again Aquinas follows Aristotle in this regard. For Aristotle touch is the most basic of the senses because it is the most indispensable.[36] But, touch also has a special, if not clearly defined, relation to the emotions because it is the sensation most directly relevant to the physical state necessary for a proper emotional balance between pleasure and pain. For Aristotle, our emotions directly affect our physical bodies, and, vice versa, the state of our physical selves can have an impact on our emotions. Further, just as an equilibrium between the emotions of pleasure and pain is the most desirable condition for our thought processes, a balance between the elements that constitute the body is the bodily state most conducive to contemplation. It is the most basic of these bodily elements that is relevant to the sense of touch. In Aristotle's view, it is the body's heat that is its most vital element. In keeping with his ideas about the unity of body and soul, he regarded the body's *pneuma*, or innate heat, to be the corporeal medium through which the soul activated the body. The body's heat is thus the physical source of all the body's power. Carried through the blood, its point of origin is the heart, literally the physical center of the body as well as of the vascular system. As the sense uniquely sensitive to variations of temperature in the body, ranging from extreme hot to extreme cold, touch has a relation to the body's heat that the other senses have only indirectly. Similarly, touch is allied to the heart as the organ of heat in ways the other senses are not, proximate as they are to the brain.[37]

Most significant for touch, however, was Aristotle's idea that the body's heat is the source of its power. It was on the basis of this idea that he goes on to reason that shifts in the balance of hot and cold in the body are what finally inaugurates the body's movement of pursuit or avoidance caused by the experience of excessive pleasure or pain. In other words, it is the heat-driven motion of blood in the body that is responsible for the expression of the emotions. It is only when hot and cold blend evenly in the heart that there is a cessation of those bodily movements, or emotions, which interfere with the formation of thought. Thus, according to Aristotle, the most significant balance in the body for the achievement of right reason is a balance in physical temperature. In order for deliberative thought to occur, there must exist a bodily equilibrium between the opposite states of hot and cold.[38]

As becomes apparent in the *Hypnerotomachia Poliphili*, this thermal equilibrium can be achieved through whatever it is we touch or what touches us. For example, Poliphilo's encounter with the five Senses in his journey toward knowledge includes a communal bath where Poliphilo and the Senses participate together in various sensual activities—eating, singing, perfuming— but all within the context of a perfectly warm bath, evenly balanced between the extremes of hot and cold (1: 84–85). It is only on the basis of this equilibrium that Poliphilo is able properly to experience the knowledge that the senses have to offer him.[39] Similarly, when Poliphilo and Polia travel together to the island of Cythera, the air of the island is temperate, or the perfect temperature for Poliphilo's progressing knowledge of Polia (1: 292).

There are, however, ways in which the treatment of touch in the *Hypnerotomachia Poliphili* diverges from its Aristotelian roots, most notably when Poliphilo is finally in the position of touching Polia for the first time. "I felt grasped between warm snow and solid milk," he says when he first takes Polia's hand, "as though I were touching something beyond the human condition."[40] Polia's initial effect on Poliphilo is well in keeping with Aristotelian physiology. When he takes Polia's hand, he experiences an equilibrium formed out of the coincidence of opposing temperatures. In her role as knowledge, Polia embodies the thermal mean required for contemplative thought. However, Poliphilo's sense that he is touching something beyond the human condition exceeds the epistemological boundaries of Aristotelian ethics. Polia represents a supernatural knowledge that is not well developed in Aristotle, but is at the center of Christian ethical reflection of the period, knowledge of the divine.[41] More significant for our purposes, it is the sense of touch in the *Hypnerotomachia Poliphili* that specifically gains Poliphilo an understanding of this divine knowledge.

The sense of touch "as a gateway to deeper contact with God" is a long-standing concept in Christianity that was voiced early on in its history by writers such as Origen.[42] It was especially important for the Christian mystical tradition. But, it is only really in Aquinas that the concept is fitted with any rigor to an expressly Aristotelian ethics and its physiological subsystem, at odds as these were to certain of the Neoplatonic foundations of the mystical tradition. In the *Hypnerotomachia Poliphili*, Poliphilo's further reflections on the experience of touching Polia reveal certain of the specific concerns of

Thomas. "I now felt myself touched by a pleasant warmth," he says, "growing little by little and beginning to melt my frigid fear, and adjusting the heat to the proper degree for genuine love."[43] Again, in keeping with Aristotle's physiological theory of the mean, Poliphilo describes how Polia's perfect warmth begins to melt his fear. For Aristotle, the feeling of fear is due to a re-distribution of the body's vital heat in such a way that the blood runs cold. Thus the effect of Polia's warmth is literally to melt Poliphilo's fear by return-ing his blood to its proper temperature.[44] Contrary to what we might expect, however, the hoped for effect in attaining this "proper degree" is not a ther-mal equilibrium conducive to deliberative thought, at least not directly. Rather, Polia's adjustments to Poliphilo's bodily heat are meant to accom-plish a temperature that can result in "genuine love." It is this "genuine love" that reveals the concerns of Thomas.

Again, that love should be the result of Polia's touching is not out of keeping with Aristotle. It is, in fact, a crucial feature of the Aristotelian ethi-cal system. Because of Aristotle's commitment to the essential unity of body and soul, moral behavior can never be the result of a mere act of under-standing. It also requires a somatic enactment of reason's deliberations. Among Aristotelians, love is a critical component in achieving such activity because it is what makes us physically tend toward what is good for us. Love, in Aristotle's view, is an inclination toward the good that was natural to all creatures.[45] However, the author of the *Hypnerotomachia Poliphili* qualifies the love that Polia's touch engenders as being a "genuine love." He thus sug-gests that there is a love that is superior to other types. This higher objective love is, of course, Aquinas's Christian conception of God's love, but now completely fitted to the mechanics of Aristotelian ethics. In Aquinas's view, the pull toward goodness, or love, which Aristotle observed as fundamental to all creaturely behavior, is a pull toward God's intent for goodness in the world. Moreover, through this pull humans are able to become the agents of God's intent for goodness. From the point of view of touch, the important thing to note is that this desire, because it provokes physical movement, op-erates through the heart, the source and center, as we have seen, of move-ment in all "sanguineous" animals.[46] Thus, according to Aquinas, the human heart as a conduit for God's love is a vitally important component in the achievement of ethical behavior, not only because our natural desire for the good gains its momentum there, but because God's love is able to be directly experienced there. As the sense most directly related to the workings of the heart, touch indeed has a unique position among the senses when it comes to the motivating power of God's love. Through its special sensitivity to the body's heat, it is a physical vehicle for the movement of our bodies in the direction of God's goodness.

The importance of the sense of touch for the enactment of God's goodness, however, constitutes only one part of the sense's ethical significance on account of its unique position with regard to love. Touch also has a special cognitive role to play when it comes to knowledge of God's goodness, goodness that may not always be evident to us in this life.[47] More than any of the other senses, touch allows, through a unique feature of its mode of perception, direct knowledge of the good. To fully comprehend the uniqueness of touch in this regard, it is first of all necessary to know more of Aquinas's epistemology. Again following Aristotle, Aquinas regarded the first stage in the acquisition of knowledge as the reception of sense-impressions through the various sense organs.[48] These impressions are then synthesized by the common sense and stored in the human memory for future cognitive use.[49] The form these sense impressions take once they are synthesized is critical to the special status of touch. They take the form of an image. Thus all thinking, in his view, is predicated on the use of mental imagery.

From the point of view of the hierarchy of the senses, this idea that our thoughts are images lends even greater validity to the longstanding notion that the sense of sight is the superior sense.[50] If thought is visual in character, then vision is more like intellection than any of the other senses. There is, however, a negative aspect to this particular status when it comes to knowing God. Because our thoughts, in Aquinas's view, depend on visual likenesses, our knowledge of God can never be a direct knowledge as long as we are alive and subject to the bodily apparatus of our knowing.[51] It can only be a proximate knowledge because it has to rely on some kind of representation. "In knowledge," he says, "we identify with a representation of what we know."[52] Thus, until we die and our spirits have been freed from our bodies, our creaturely mode of having knowledge will of necessity keep us apart from full knowledge of God.[53]

There is, however, in Aquinas's view, one exception to this rule. An intimate knowledge of God can be had in this earthly life if one avails oneself of a means of knowing that is non-intellectual and therefore nonrepresentational in character. This means of knowing is afforded by humankind's capacity for love. While "in knowledge we identify with a representation of what we know . . . in love," according to Aquinas, "we identify with the thing itself that we love: so love effects a greater unity than knowledge."[54] For Aquinas, identification with the "thing itself" is of crucial significance theologically. In his view, individual things have an integrity as indissoluble unions of form and matter that thoughts about things can never have. Thus, in Aquinas's view, nature is a divinely generated order of perfect things.[55] When it comes to knowing God, the integrity found in things is the highest standard. To know God completely is to know him as form knows matter, to be two things indissolubly joined whose common identity would be lost if one were without the other. Because of the limitations attending the human mind in its present condition, human cognition can never allow for such a union in this life, one that is concrete rather than abstract, original rather than representational. Love, as the desire for knowledge, on the other hand, offers something that the inward moving abstractive processes of cognition lack. Love is naturally drawn to the concrete thing behind meaning, so that its movement is a reaching out to the thing rather than a visual taking in. Love wants the substance, not merely the form of something or its idea.[56] Thus, according to Aquinas, our capacity for love provides us with a means to overcome the natural divisiveness of our representational mode of cognition.

Of all the senses, only touch, in Thomas's view, affords humankind this kind of knowing. The reason for this becomes apparent when one finally considers how the various sense organs were thought to function perceptually. For Aquinas, the process by which the sense organs receive sense data, takes one of two possible forms, spiritual or natural.[57] Spiritual immutation occurs, as in the case of sight, when the form of what is received does not physically alter the sense organ that receives it. For example, when one sees color, the pupil of the eye receives a form of the color being seen, but does not itself become that color. Conversely, a natural immutation occurs when the natural existence of what is perceived alters the sense organ that receives it, as in the case of heat. "For the hand that touches something hot," says Aquinas, "becomes hot."[58] The difference between these two kinds of immutation mirrors, for Aquinas, the general difference between the material and immaterial worlds. Spiritual immutation is of a higher moral order than natural immutation because it is closer to the immateriality of pure intellection. At the same time, however, it creates a distance between sensible object and sense organ that disallows any direct experience of that pure world of perfectly integrated substances that constitutes the sensible world. Spiritual immutation limits direct apprehension of what is perceived, whereas natural immutation means that direct contact between the sensible object and sense organ has been made. Of the five external senses, only the sense of touch, in Thomas's view, can be thought to truly involve a natural immutation whereby the sense organ's experience of the sense object is completely direct.[59] Thus, according to Thomas, touch offers a direct mode of understanding that is essential to our ability to know God's goodness in this life, a mode of understanding premised on touch's capacity for an unmediated experience of what it senses.

In the *Hypnerotomachia Poliphili* touch is similarly awarded pride of place as a mode of apprehension in Poliphilo's journey toward knowledge as long as he remains alive. Indeed, touch provides Poliphilo with the fullest and most direct knowledge he can have of Polia in this life, the union of their spirits being reserved for when Poliphilo's soul is finally released from his body at his physical death. If difficult to make fit with medieval moralism in general, the form that Poliphilo's most profound touching of Polia takes in the *Hypnerotomachia Poliphili* nonetheless makes perfect sense. After all his remarkable travails, Poliphilo is finally united with Polia in the sanctuary of the Temple of Venus in a ritualized enactment of *coitus*, the ultimate touch experience.[60] As is evident from the nymphs who aid the lovers, Synesia (Union) and Philedia (Voluptuousness), union of this kind, which heralds the spiritual union to be had in the afterlife, can only be achieved sensually, or through *voluptas*. Polia, as a figure of God's goodness, cannot break the barrier of hymen that obstructs her union with Poliphilo. Only Poliphilo may accomplish this in his human state, not through any act of rationality, but through the aid of Voluptuousness (1: 361). Until we die, then, our knowledge of the divine must inevitably be governed by *voluptas*.

Revealing his own profound debts to the mystical tradition, Aquinas similarly did not shy away from conjugal imagery when describing how we might, through love, know God.[61] Love, for him, leads to a reciprocal abiding of lover and beloved together; a transport out of the self to the other; a melting so that the heart is unfrozen; a longing in absence; a heat in pursuit; and an enjoyment in presence.[62] Love is the *vis unitiva et concretiva* that leads toward a relationship with God that is comparable to the union of lovers in marriage. Thus, even though Thomas was intellectualist in his belief that what constitutes the highest good is the intellective, spiritual character of God, under the conditions of this life, he valued our sensual understanding more highly than our rationality.[63]

When put into the larger context of Poliphilo's journey, this maintenance of the sensual character of his knowledge right up to his physical union with Polia clarifies a great deal about the sensualism of the *Hypnerotomachia Poliphili*, in particular a choice Poliphilo was required to make early in his journey that has been taken as proof of the book's adherence to a new, expressly Renaissance sensualism. After leaving the realm of Nature,

Poliphilo is taken to three doors by personifications of his Reason and Will. The doors represent the realm of Telosia, or the final good toward which all humans tend. As is explained to Poliphilo, the moral end we seek, Telosia, cannot be known to us as long as we are alive. "For it is not allowed for (her) divine beauty to appear to bodily eyes."[64] Rather, Poliphilo must choose the moral path he will pursue on the basis of the possible form Telosia might take behind each of the doors. Recalling a portion of the *Nicomachean Ethics* taken up by Thomas in the *Summa* where Aristotle discusses the possible goods one may pursue, the doors represent respectively the ways of contemplation, sensual love, and worldly fame.[65] Though he has both his reason and his will to guide him, Poliphilo must decide on just one of these paths of his own free will. Poliphilo's final choice is for sensual love, the figure who occupies the middle door, or median way (1: 134–40). Often regarded as evidence for a specifically Renaissance sensualizing of the intellectualist orientation of classical and medieval ethics, Poliphilo's refusal of the contemplative life in favor of the sensual does seem to overturn the chief principle of classical ethics, the superior value of contemplation.[66] But, as we have seen, scholastic ethics had accomplished this long before the possible impact of the work of such so-called Renaissance sensualists as Lorenzo Valla.[67] Aquinas was convinced, like many mystics before him, both that the highest good is intellectual in character and that revelation of that good is possible in this life. However, his commitment to Aristotle's body/soul composite required him to make adjustments to these convictions that few mystics would have so rigorously entertained. As a consequence, the sensual nature of our earthly knowledge of God receives a theological emphasis in his works that it had not received before, one that, as we have seen, did not harmonize well with both the Platonic censure of the physical world basic to much of western mysticism and the idea that a spiritual knowledge of God is possible in this life.[68] More significant, perhaps, for our purposes, however, is the way Thomas's approach to the body/soul composite so substantially increased the importance of the appetitive character of love as a means of knowing God that there developed, long before the eroticism we tend to associate with Renaissance paganism, what E. R. Curtius has called a "heretical Scholasticism of love."[69]

If especially responsible for a new, expressly theological, understanding of *voluptas*, Aquinas did not, of course, because of it, relinquish the final supremacy of intellection. Similarly, in the *Hypnerotomachia Poliphili*, the extraordinary sensuality of Poliphilo's earthly union with Polia gives way to the propriety of the spiritual as soon as Voluptuousness has finished helping

Poliphilo accomplish his task. What immediately happens to Poliphilo after his physical union with Polia is the perfection, or spiritualization, of his sense of sight. When he raises his eyes to look at the form of Venus in the temple fountain ahead of him, he sees her with a clarity he has never experienced before, a clarity that springs in Aquinas from having attained the highest happiness (*beatitudo*) through an intuitive knowledge or vision of God.[70] Moreover, what Poliphilo sees is devoid of the various illusions, long noted in the history of Western thought, that keep human vision from being an entirely reliable source of information.[71] The water Venus stands in reflects her body without "making it seem larger or smaller, doubled or refracted; it was visible simple and whole, as perfect as it was in itself."[72] Poliphilo's sight, now purged of the human conditions that can make sight unreliable, has been restored to its rightful place as the highest of the senses. More significant, perhaps, is the fact that Poliphilo can see Venus at all since her form was "made from a miraculous compound which humans have never conceived of, much less seen."[73] Thus, what Poliphilo's restored vision allows him to see is the highest composite, the divinely generated union of form and matter, that our imaginative mode of thinking can never completely approach without the operation of God's love through our hearts. There is, however, a price to pay for such clarity of vision. Poliphilo finally dies to his old sensual self even though he immediately reawakens to a new spiritual life.[74]

However much, then, late fifteenth-century syncretism may have contributed to the eroticism of the *Hypnerotomachia Poliphili*, it is clear from this discussion that the rationale for this eroticism was not the product of a new Renaissance sensualism. Rather, it was the result of a very specific ethical theory of the later Middle Ages for which the special, appetitive power of love and the concrete character of touch were critical. But the question remains as to the specific eroticization of architecture that occurs in the book. How does one fit Poliphilo's nearly sexual experiences of buildings with scholastic ethical theory and what, if anything, is the relation of this particular approach to architecture to the sense of touch?

Architecture and Touch

The answer to these questions is still in great part provided by Aristotelian ethical theory and its reorientation of the Socratic contemplative ideal. But, in order to understand the pertinence of scholastic moral philosophy to the art of architecture, it is now necessary to examine what were considered the parameters of knowledge, what was classified as knowledge and how that knowledge was organized. In the *Hypnerotomachia Poliphili*, Polia's name already provides a significant clue as to what was considered pursuable as knowledge. In accordance with the meaning of *poly* in Greek, Polia's name means "many things." Poliphilo's pursuit of Polia is the pursuit of knowledge as encyclopedic. The *Hypnerotomachia Poliphili* thus falls within the tradition of the medieval encyclopedia, in particular those that took the form of allegory in order to dramatize our struggle to know the divine through the knowledge available to us in the variety of things in nature.[75]

It does not take long to note, however, that the book favors one kind of knowledge in particular. Poliphilo's true love is architecture. The entire book is punctuated by Poliphilo's various encounters with buildings. While placed among the liberal arts at various times in both classical and medieval categorizations of knowledge, the fact that architecture should be given such prominence in a book devoted to the possibility of theological understanding indicates some very specific changes that occurred in the history of reflection on the nature and placement of the various arts.[76] The most significant of these changes is the very consideration of architecture as a mode of knowledge. Until roughly the twelfth century architecture suffered the general disapprobation aimed at any art that was more mechanical than intellectual in nature. This view was to change considerably during the later Middle Ages, once again because of the late medieval rediscovery of Aristotle. Yet one of the most substantial changes in attitude toward the lesser arts did not come from Aristotle per se, but from late classical commentators on Aristotle who saw fit to place Aristotle's *Rhetoric* and *Poetics* with his works on logic. The consequence of this placement was to regard these language arts, which had always been considered inferior to philosophy because of their sensual appeal, as a kind of dialectical thinking. At the same time that Aristotle's corpus was finding its way to the Latin West, the assumptions of this commentary tradition were also being conveyed, in particular with new Latin translations of Arabic versions of Aristotle's *Poetics*.[77] From the point of view of the history of the various arts, a very important consequence of this transferral was the establishment of the idea among late medieval thinkers that there was a continuum between what had formerly been considered the very distinctive realms of sense and reason, the lower and higher arts. The way was now open for all arts to be understood according to the model supplied by Aristotelian logic.[78]

While suspicion about the sensual nature of the mechanical arts was far from lost, the possibility that the various arts might function theoretically, as logic did, produced some complex classifications in what became, by the time of the Renaissance, standard procedure in every discussion of the arts, that is, where to place a given art, as a mode of knowledge, in relation to philosophy.[79]

If the mechanical arts were still considered inferior, their placement on a continuum with philosophy nonetheless had some very important repercussions. The approach secured for the traditionally lesser arts a place in moral philosophy. In their new capacity as modes of cognition, they had the potential to function as vehicles for the attainment of some kind of higher, more moral, understanding. Further to this, they began to be viewed according to the concerns of contemporary moral philosophy, most especially after the rediscovery of the *Nicomachean Ethics*, whose insistence on the necessity of the sensual in the achievement of ethical behavior provided the lower arts with even greater validation. Because they could literally motivate us to appropriate choice through their special ability to affect that part of our natures responsible for our physical movement, the lower arts, like any sensual stimulation, were now construed to play a significant role in the attainment of virtue. This was Dante's vision of the poet's task in the *Divine Comedy*. It was his job as poet to create verse that could incite his readers to virtue by its sensual appeal.[80] In the *Hypnerotomachia Poliphili* it is architecture that is regarded as especially capable of achieving this end. Indeed, in his first encounter with architecture, Poliphilo congratulates the architect of the book's famous pyramid for having been able to produce so voluptuous an effect (cum quanta voluptate) (1: 57).

The question remains, however, why architecture in particular should have the choicest position over any other art as a mode of knowledge in the *Hypnerotomachia Poliphili*.

For this one can turn to the book itself. On the basis of a very long-standing comparison of the human body to the building in the history of western thought, architecture is given preeminence in the *Hypnerotomachia Poliphili* because preeminence is also given to the sense of touch. In the same way that touch was thought able to accomplish a direct, nonrepresentational knowledge of God *in this life*, buildings in the *Hypnerotomachia Poliphili* were thought able to provide an experience of the divine that was uniquely direct. What made buildings especially capable of such directness was a specific feature of the architecture as body metaphor, the idea that the walls of a building were like the human skin.[81] While for Aristotle the organ of touch was not the skin but a place near the heart, the skin was generally thought among Aristotelians to be the means by which we first perceive what it is we feel in our hearts, mostly, as we have seen, through thermal variations.[82] Thus the idea that the walls of a building are comparable to the human skin explains a great deal about Poliphilo's virtually sexual encounters with the buildings he meets along the way in his journey toward enlightenment.[83] These experiences mirror the immediacy and directness of his sexual union with Polia. They are encounters that allow Poliphilo to feel the love God has for His creatures and which draws His creatures to Him. As a tactile art, then, an art with a literal skin, architecture allows Poliphilo the possibility of a skin-to-skin knowledge of the *pneuma*, the life-giving spirit of God, that lies within.[84] Buildings are the instruments available in this life, most especially in the form of temples or churches, for human congress with the divine. Moreover, as is evident in the *Hypnerotomachia Poliphili*, their voluptuous effect on us, the pleasure they give, can literally move us in the direction of repeatedly choosing God's goodness as long as we exert proper control over our passions.

Thus the prominence given to architecture in the *Hypnerotomachia Poliphili* is based on a specific understanding of the role of touch in moral philosophy, an understanding that was Thomistic in its focus on the role of the senses in ethical behavior and in its particular view of the perceptual mode of the various senses. As we have seen, this view maintained that the experience of God's love through our ability to feel is the primary motor behind ethical choice for those who decide to heed it. While such a suggestion deserves greater scrutiny, it is not unreasonable to propose from these arguments that the intervention of Thomas on these several issues and the expressly Aristotelian character of those interventions supplied the author of the *Hypnerotomachia Poliphili*, in conjunction with the longstanding metaphor of the body as building, with a working rationale for the promotion of architecture. In this regard, the book can be thought to function as a kind of allegorical *paragone*, an apology for architecture, whose primary point of comparison stems from the aesthetic value placed by Thomas Aquinas on the sense of touch, its ability to allow us to feel directly the heat of God's love as we seek to lead ethical lives.[85]

Chapter 12

The Touch of the Blind Man: The Phenomenology of Vividness in Italian Renaissance Art

Jodi Cranston

Now painting is an art which aims at giving an abiding impression of artistic reality with only two dimensions. The painter must, therefore, do consciously what we all do unconsciously—construct his third dimension. And he can accomplish his task only as we accomplish ours, by giving tactile values to retinal impressions. His first business, therefore, is to rouse the tactile sense, for I must have the illusion of being able to touch a figure, I must have the illusion of varying muscular sensations inside my palm and fingers corresponding to the various projections of this figure, before I shall take it for granted as real, and let it affect me lastingly.

It follows that the essential in the art of painting—as distinguished from the art of coloring, I beg the reader to observe—is somehow to stimulate our consciousness of tactile values, so that the picture shall have at least as much power as the object represented, to appeal to our tactile imagination.

—*Bernard Berenson,* The Florentine Painters of the Renaissance *(1896)*

In the introductory pages to his well-known essay *The Florentine Painters*, Bernard Berenson briefly defines a broad theory of aesthetics which he sees as particularly, if not exclusively, relevant to Florentine Renaissance painting. These painters, he declares, achieve the difficult task of defying the limitations of the two-dimensional art by suggesting—primarily through form, line, light, and shadow—that the figure or object represented has a physical, three-dimensional presence and existence; as beholders, we will translate such pictorial relief into the corresponding tactile values, the "real-world" sensory analogues for the depicted forms, and view, if not experience, the painted figures as though they were real. The paintings of Giotto, the artist who begins Berenson's regional overview, "have not only as much power of appealing to the tactile imagination as is possessed by the objects represented—human figures in particular—but actually more . . . to his contemporaries they [the figures] conveyed a *keener* sense of reality, of life-likeness than the objects themselves!"[1] The "tactile imagination" and "tactile values" encompass Berenson's formalist and psychological concerns by suggesting that specific formal elements evoke sensations or feelings in the viewer: "[form] lends a higher coefficient of reality to the object represented, with the consequent enjoyment of accelerated psychical processes, and the exhilarating sense of increased capacity in the observer"[2] The notion of the "tactile imagination," of the role of ideated touch in viewing pictures, reinforces the location of aesthetic pleasure more in the response of the viewer than in the work of art itself.[3]

Deeply rooted in late nineteenth-century thought, the aesthetic theories of Berenson were immediately vulnerable to criticism; however, his notion of tactile values obliquely raises many of the developing concerns and interests held by Renaissance artists and theorists on the arts. These writers address both the importance of suggesting three-dimensional form through the contrast of light and shade (*chiaroscuro*) and the corresponding effect of this fictive relief on the viewer. For them, the standard of such a conjunction is the notion of vividness rather than "tactile values"; and yet, as vividness becomes the desired effect of painting, the sense of touch and the tactile gradually surface in discussions of the properties of the figurative arts and in some cases replace sight as the primary sense in receiving and understanding representation.

The operations of the senses, especially sight, and their role in judgment receive considerable attention in Renaissance discussions on the arts.[4] Leonardo da Vinci in his ruminations on the art of painting elaborates a comprehensive theory, derived in part from late medieval psychology, on the relationship between the five senses, the *imprensiva*—the receptor of sensory impressions—and the *senso comune*—the place in the mind where all senses run together and enables judgment. But not all the senses communicate with equal speed and directness to the common sense. "The eye, which is said to be the window of the soul, is the primary means by which the *sensus communis* of the brain may most fully and magnificently contemplate the infinite works of nature, and the ear is the second, acquiring nobility through the recounting of things which the eye has seen."[5] His ranking of the senses allows him to compare the arts that correspond to sight and hearing: painting and poetry; but it also introduces an elementary phenomenology into a

consideration of the arts that previously had been limited to issues of execution, or oriented from the perspective of the artist. The nobility of each art
depends on the sense required to receive it and on the kinds of perceptual
limitations suffered in their absence:

Certainly, there is no one who would not choose to lose hearing and smell rather
than sight. By consenting to the loss of hearing, a man surrenders all those sciences
which achieve their ends by words and he would only do this in order not to lose the
beauty of the world which consists of the surfaces of bodies, with their visual effects
and actual forms as reflected in the human eye. . . . A deaf man only forgoes the
sound made by the movement of the percussed air, which is the least matter in the
world. . . . He who loses sight loses the spectacle and beauty of the universe, and
comes to resemble someone who has been buried alive in a tomb in which he can
move and survive.[6]

Without the sense of sight, the blind man loses the ability to judge what
is beautiful and, confined to the world of speech—which, according to
Leonardo, limits expression through a fixed set of words and meaning—lives
as though dead.[7]

Touch only enters into Leonardo's writings when the sense assists sight.
In a specific example of the superiority of painting over sculpture, Mathias
Corvinus, king of Hungary, receives for his birthday both a poem that com-
memorates the day he came into the world and a portrait of his beloved lady.
Distracted and unable to keep his eyes on the book, the king, much to the
poet's consternation, finds the depiction of his beloved more satisfying and
appealing for representing her beauty in a single glance rather than in the
succession of words—a commonplace in Renaissance comparisons of the
arts. Incited by the accusations of the poet, that the king has found appealing
the inferior mode of representation, the king replies:

This picture serves a greater sense than yours, which is for the blind. Give me something I can see and touch, and not only hear, and do not criticize my decision to tuck
your work under my arm, while I take up that of the painter in both hands to place it
before my eyes, because my hands acted spontaneously in serving the nobler sense—
and this is not hearing.[8]

Seeing his beloved represented in the portrait, the king responds as if she
were actually present: he sees and touches the image with the affectionate
glances and caresses of an admiring lover, one may infer. But, touch, in this
example, comes to stand less for an enacted sensuality than for the vividness
of painting, the ability of the art to represent an absent person as though she

were present and accessible to the viewer. Hands, the agent of touch, facili-
tate and assist sight and also have the power to disable sight: with the book
tucked under his arm, hidden away from view, he then extends both hands to
bring the portrait "before [his] eyes," suggesting that touching and holding
serve as metaphors for accessibility, clarity, and visibility.

The portrait, employed by Leonardo as a synecdoche for the art of
painting, exemplifies vividness because the image represents the absent person and must stand as a surrogate for her. Leonardo writes: "And if the poet
claims that he can inflame men to love . . . the painter has the power to do the
same, and indeed more so, for he places before the lover the very image of
the beloved object, [and the lover] often engages with it, embracing it and
talking with it; which he would not do were the same beauties placed before
him by the writer." Portraits place the subject "before our eyes" and bring us
as close as possible to the person without offering him or her in the flesh.
Likewise, Baldassare Castiglione, author of *The Book of the Courtier*, com-
poses an elegy that he pretends his wife Ippolita writes to him in which she
describes her and her son's interactions with his portrait during one of his
long absences from the house: "Only your portrait, painted by Raphael's
hand, bringing back your features, comes near to relieving my sorrows. I
make tender approaches to it, I smile, I joke or speak, just as if it could give
me an answer."[9] The viewers of the portrait, much like the one given to King
Mathias, receive the image as a surrogate of the absent and behave as though
the portrait *is* the person. Clearly an intellectual conceit, Castiglione's elegy is
one of many examples of the Renaissance revival of ancient epigrams that
similarly describe attempted conversations and intimate exchanges with the
depicted.[10]

Portrait-images encourage such imagined participation as the portrait-
sitters begin to address the beholder more directly, rotating from the profile
pose common in the fifteenth century to a three-quarter or frontal pose, and
allow the viewer to have greater physical and emotional access to the depicted. Establishing a face-to-face dialogue that is mutual and shared, these
portrait-images influence the further rotation of the sitters until they address
the beholder from behind, as if they have been touched on the shoulder and
are now turning to the viewer to respond (Figure 1). A formal invention with
an intellectual heritage in the work of Leonardo da Vinci, the "ritratto di
spalla" (literally, portrait of the back) composition dramatizes through the
implied physical movement a corresponding change in states of being for
both sitter and beholder.[11] Simultaneously turned away from and toward us,
the sitter situates us as a distraction from the unknown and hidden object of

Figure 1. Raphael, *Portrait of Bindo Altoviti*, ca. 1512. Reproduced by permission of the National Gallery of Art, Samuel H. Kress Collection, Washington, D.C.

the sitter's attention and gaze, and consequently we understand the decision to turn from there to here through dialectical pairs of emotional conditions: secrecy leads to intimacy and familiarity; comfort and ease lead to a menacing challenge and momentary vulnerability; the unknown and absent lead to the known and present. Figuring various emotional developments, the turn—which moves the sitter from there to here and then to now—encompasses within itself the temporal progression and spatial movement of narrative; however, the direct gaze initiates a largely immanent exchange, supplied by the viewer, in which the narrative conditions of before and now, cause and effect, assume an emotional, atemporal force rather than advance a story. Even when the depicted situation seemingly suggests a narrative by including a second figure, as in Titian's *Il Bravo* (Figure 2),[12] the viewer, in receiving the gaze of the sitter, faces the discomforting physical performance of psychological revelation in which the viewer, arresting the rotation, feels as though he/she should know more than he/she does. Furthermore, when the turning sitter appears alone in an uncircumscribed situation, shown against an abstract background, as in Raphael's *Bindo Altoviti* (Figure 1), for example, rather than within a clearly articulated room or knowable space,[13] the sitter is pure pose and functions more as a rhetorical figure for vividness in portraiture than as a portrait of a specific person; that is, the turning pose figures the surrogacy expected of portraiture—to make the absent now present—and visually evokes the uncanny responsiveness of the sitter to the physical presence of the viewer described by Leonardo and Castiglione (in the voice of his wife). The turning sitter figures the process of putting things before our eyes and suggests that the cause and initiation of the process is the touch, in most cases of the viewer, on the shoulder of the sitter.

The notion that touch offers, if not stands for, intimate and immanent access to someone or something deeply affects the treatment of the sense and its appearance in discussions of matters removed from the base and sensual. Instead of characterizing the animal nature of humans, touch appears paired with sight as senses that ascertain presence and existence. In his *Book of the Courtier*, Baldassare Castiglione speaks of the two faculties, somewhat unexpectedly, in a larger discussion on language and "the manner the courtier should observe in speaking."[14] Count Lodovico da Canossa offers the following recommendations to the circle of interlocutors:

I would have him use certain words sometimes in a sense they do not usually have, transferring them aptly, and, so to say, grafting them like the scion of a tree on some better trunk, in order to make them more attractive and beautiful and, as it were, put

Figure 2. Titian, *Il Bravo,* ca. 1520. Reproduced by permission of the Kunsthistorisches Museum, Gemaeldegalerie, Vienna.

things before our very eyes; and as we say, make us feel them with our hands, to the delight of the listener or the reader.[15]

Evidently the count has read his Cicero, and, in particular, the ancient's discussion of the brilliant style in *De Oratore* and, more programmatically, in

De Partitione Oratoria. Cicero advises in the former text that the orator employ verbal witticisms and "terms used metaphorically and placed in a connection not really belonging to them; or new coinages invented by ourselves."[16] Such an oratorical composition, especially the reliance on metaphors, directly affects the senses of the listener. *De Partitione Oratoria* offers a passage that seems to have had the most influence on the Renaissance reader:

The style is brilliant if the words employed are chosen for their dignity and used metaphorically and in exaggeration and adjectivally and in duplication and synonymously and in harmony with the actual action and the representation of the facts. For it is this department of oratory which almost sets the fact before the eyes—for it is the sense of sight that is most appealed to, although it is nevertheless possible for the rest of the senses and also most of all the mind itself to be affected. But the things that were said about the clear style all apply to the brilliant style. For brilliance is worth considerably more than the clearness mentioned above. The one helps us understand what is said, but the other makes us feel that we actually see it before our eyes.[17]

The idea that metaphors create a vividness in composition by bringing things before our eyes reaches back to an even earlier source, Aristotle's *Rhetoric*, in which he examines the cause of vividness created through metaphor: "Homer similarly endows the inanimate with life in his famous similes, as when he speaks of "arched, crested" waves beating on the shore. He makes everything live and move, and vividness implies movement."[18] The extension of the affect of metaphors to senses other than sight, to allow for and acknowledge that possibility, clearly influences the sequence of the Count's words: "to put things before our very eyes; and as we say, make us feel them with our hands." The brilliant style, with its metaphors and resulting vividness, gives relief, if not a sensuality, to words and phrases.

The association between touch and figurative language extends to the figuration of painted narrative scenes when Giorgio Vasari conceives of touch not as a registration and reception of a written composition in the brilliant style, but as a necessary aspect of making a vivid painting. Responding to accusations that he executed too quickly the Sala della Cancelleria frescoes, he writes the following description in his account of his own life:

But that which becomes apparent and displeases even the lesser intellects is the incredible impetuosity with which I have painted my work, more sketched than finished [*piùttosto abbozzati che fatti*]. My paintings seem to await that magic touch of the brush that transforms dead images into living and speaking figures [*tocco magico di pennello che tramuta le smorte immagini in figuri vive e parlanti*].[19]

More sketched than finished would seem to suggest that the frescoes appear indefinite, indistinct, confused, and roughly conceived and executed; however, Vasari, sensitive to the refinements and nuances of pictorial vocabulary, employs a form of the verb "abbozzare," which refers not to a first conception or thought but to an already clear and determined image that has not yet been brought to completion.[20] The seventeenth-century definition by Filippo Baldinucci articulates and resonates with Vasari's conception of the term: "that first effort which painters make on the canvases or panels, beginning to color the figures in a coarse way [*colorire così alla grossa le figure*]."[21] The return with other colors is what Vasari thinks is missing, the "magic touch of the brush" that animates the figures. His self-appraisal, seemingly casual and marginal, offers a translation and application to the stages of painting of Cicero's (and, by later extension, Castiglione's) prescriptions for the differences between the clear and brilliant styles in oratory. The brilliant style, with metaphors and hyperboles—among other rhetorical colors—makes not just an understandable composition, but one that has relief, life, and movement; similarly, a painting that receives the application of other colors beyond the initial stages of the work will have the same properties. The structure and composition of the painting does not change, but the degree of vividness of the finished work does, and, to such a degree, that the touch of the brush on the surface performs miracles evocative of those performed by the healing hand of Christ, who, through his touch, restores sight, health, and, of course, life to the dead, or by the desirous hands of the sculptor Pygmalion, who animates through his touch his own work in stone.

Vasari evidently invokes these biblical and classical episodes of miraculous restoration and vivification and their parallel with the creation of vivid paintings when he describes in similar terms Michelangelo's *Creation of Adam* on the ceiling of the Sistine Chapel, 1508–12. Describing a fresco which represents nearly touching hands, Vasari considers Adam as a particularly stunning example of vividness: "with the other [arm God] extends the right hand towards Adam, figured—of beauty, of attitude (*attitudine*), of outlines (*dintorni*)—of such kind (*qualità*) that it appears newly fashioned by the First and Supreme Creator rather than by the brush and design of a mortal man."[22] The expression of vividness circulates within the clever slippage that Vasari establishes between hands of the artist and the hands of the Creator: the made (*figurato*) form of Adam appears before our eyes as if he were actually present in the flesh. The "magic touch of the brush" far exceeds what is humanly possible and is here transformed into the magic touch of God, bringing to life the first man.

Throughout the *Lives* we find Vasari returning to both the successful and failed efforts of painters and sculptors to transform static, represented forms into moving, living figures, and these two examples suggest the limited range of his descriptions of the technical means to accomplish these rhetorical standards—in both origin and affect—of vividness. His work, in this regard, follows and extends a Renaissance tradition declared most deliberately by Leon Battista Alberti in his *On Painting* (1435) of asserting painting as a liberal art and, correspondingly, of minimizing the role of the hand in making that art—unless, of course, its touch via the paintbrush approaches the healing powers of the touch of Christ or another holy figure or, more generally, metaphorically implies the expression and figuration of the painter's invention. Later writers on the visual arts only elliptically introduce and acknowledge the artist's manual contact with his or her work in their occasional use of the verb "toccare" (to touch) or "ritoccare" (to retouch) to describe, with slightly greater technical specificity than Vasari's "tocco magico," the final additions and changes to the painting. Advising painters on how to reinforce details, Giambattista Armenini recommends that, after the area is cleaned well with oil, the detail should then be "retouched, reglazed, sweetened."[23] And later, Filippo Baldinucci wrote that "the sketch, painters say, is those light touches [*tocchi*] of pen or pencil with which they hint at their ideas without giving perfection to the parts."[24] Touch can also convey the degree of completion of the sketch and the rapidity of its execution.

Although not widely discussed in writings on the arts, touch becomes for late quattrocento and early cinquecento painters a technique for applying and blending oil paint directly on the panel or canvas. Leonardo da Vinci frequently employed this method in his early works, including those executed while an apprentice of Verrocchio (*Baptism of Christ,* Florence, Uffizi) and his later *St. Jerome, Virgin of the Rocks* (London, National Gallery), *Adoration of the Magi* (Florence, Uffizi), and *Ginevra de'Benci* (Figure 3). Painters regularly use their hands to wipe off excess paint; but in these examples Leonardo used his fingers and the butt of his hand as if they were brushes, sometimes dragging them across the tacky surface of nearly dry paint and sometimes punctuating a stroke with a single fingerprint.[25] With his fingers in the *Ginevra de'Benci* Leonardo could soften the transitions from land to water, from the outer branches of the juniper bush to the surrounding sky, and from face to hair. He could minimize his more decorative use of color and

Figure 3. Leonardo da Vinci, *Ginevra de' Benci,* ca. 1480. Reproduced by permission of the National Gallery of Art, Ailsa Mellon Bruce Fund, Washington, D.C.

thereby more organically connect the unnatural foreground light of the face with the relief-giving dark background of the juniper.[26] Leonardo achieves through a literal modeling and shaping of the paint those tonal effects, especially *sfumato,* that suffuse the entire surface in his later paintings. Practiced in his early works, finger-painting serves as a transition from a pictorial sensibility rooted in the contour line and a saturation and contrast of colors to create relief (more often practiced in tempera paint) to one in which shadow and highlight suggest forms through a gradual building up of the surface with an application of glazes (practiced in oil paint).[27]

However transitional as a technique, the use of one's hands and fingers to execute a painting introduces and figures the phenomenological dimensions of the art, for the painter in particular. Most of the late quattrocento and early cinquecento painters employing this working method appear to have manual contact with the panel or canvas only after the paint has been applied to the panel in order to blend and soften contours, to render the complexity of flesh tones, and to give the slightest texture to the surface—in effect, make the paintings more vivid in appearance by concealing the recognizable and arbitrary signs of art, such as contour lines, and by facilitating the rendering of surfaces better created through judgment than the rules of art, such as flesh.[28] The directly manual approach suggests the importance of the improvisational, the approximate, and the temporal as conditions of both the making of the painting and its meaning: the action of touch—of endowing surfaces with a soft focus—results in the suggestion and evocation, rather than delineation, of forms, and the traces of touch—the fingerprints on the surface—function as signs of the permanent presence of the artist and of the seemingly continuously made, never-finished painting.[29] Anticipating in both method and affect the tonal and structural inventions of sixteenth-century painting, finger-painting similarly encourages a subjective engagement with the image from the perspective of the viewer and more clearly declares the intimate and subjective relationship of the painting to the artist. Marco Boschini describes such a relationship when he relates Titian's use of his hands—although significantly different in intention, intensity, and effect from Leonardo's—in painting[30]: "For the final touches he would blend the transitions from highlights to halftones with his fingers, blending one tint with another, or with a dab of red, like a drop of blood, he would enliven some surface [*invigoriva alcun sentimento superficiale*]—in this way bringing his animated figures to completion."[31] Boschini's language emphasizes the collapse between signifier and signified in Titian's method (the dab of red, the drop of blood) through the ambiguity of his description "invigoriva alcun sentimento superficiale," which simultaneously refers to making vivid a painted surface and to awakening feeling and sensation. The substance of paint, having been worked, shaped, and built up, can *be* the thing or condition represented, having the same composition, texture, depth, and fleeting qualities of light;[32] and the painter's method, in being additive, is more substantively creative: it is Vasari's magic touch less rhetorically conceived.

Unlike the art of painting, sculpture—according to writers who compare the two arts—represents that which exists already in nature and lacks the invention and artifice found in painting. Sculpture is, it seems, a case of perfect mimesis: "It appears that the statues are not only similar, but are the same as the living [thing or body represented]; that is, in size, bulk, hardness . . . and similar things, which are more dependent on the nature of the wood or stone than on the artifice of the sculptor," writes Sperone Speroni in his *Discorso in lode della pittura*.³³ Vividness appears to be a natural condition for sculpture and, consequently, one could imply, the sense of touch would affirm the physical properties of the medium rather than function as a conceptual sign of the presence of metaphors, of invention. Not surprisingly, then, Sperone considers the poetic techniques for creating clarity—metaphors especially—as forms of applied, unnecessary sculptural ornament, and not an integral part of the composition.

To help this impotence [lack of artifice], the ancients thought to make colossi, so that with unnatural size the statues would seem to be art; so that colossi are in this art like hyperbole is in poetics. And they thought to make up for the defect of art with nature in two ways: one was to gild statues, or to make them of the finest marble, which is difficult to find, and carve them; the second was to make the feet and hands or face with ivory, which is difficult to find, and the statue was esteemed to be precious and the sculptor was praised for it. They made statues of bronze and . . . iron. All of these things are similar to affectation in writing; [some writers who master] the art of writing in a simple style think that the simplicity is without art . . . [and adopt] epithets, metaphors, [and] hyperbole in order to make it seem as though it is art and to show the effort required by the artifice. Such a display of artifice affects in a different way from art, is not necessary, and, consequently, is affected.³⁴

Sperone considers applied ornament and rich materials in sculpture as material figurations of the tropes recommended to make a phrase vivid or to give words relief and texture. There is, according to him, no art in making a three-dimensional body as it appears in nature: "in painting, the line and surfaces imitate all of the body, even in the third dimension, which is depth; sculpture . . . imitates the body with the body, which is without marvel."³⁵ An admirable display of art consists of applying paint and employing perspective so that bodies appear to be tangible, where the ornament originates from and clarifies the invention rather than appears grafted and foreign in the case of sculpture.

Giorgio Vasari affirms such views in a comparison of the two arts in a letter sent in 1547 to Benedetto Varchi: modern painting "is full of many ornaments [*ornamenti*]—in the figures and in other appurtenances—and of invention [*invenzione*] . . . which, with sweet features [*dolci tratti*] of poetry under various forms, the soul and the eyes are led to stupendous marvel [*maraviglia stupenda*]. Ancient narrative reliefs show the flights of soldiers, but not the sweat and foam, the glint of the horses' coats, the hair of the tails and manes, the brilliance of weapons, the reflections of figures in them. Sculpture can never do this."[36] In a description that rivals those examples of vividness quoted by the ancient rhetoricians, Vasari asserts that painting, employing the sweet ornaments of poetry, can represent the tangible and intangible and, when such artifice is perfectly worked, is like "embroidery in its gilded ornaments."[37]

For advocates of sculpture, however, the texture of sculpture, the working of the rough block, demonstrates not only the art, but also the way in which the art works toward simulating the natural world—that is, the invention and labor involved in the art. Bernardino Daniello elaborates such ideas in his *Della poetica* (1536) by conceiving the art of sculpture as a process parallel to the tripartite composition of poetry and oratory, as many theorists had done already for painting: the selection of a block of stone corresponds to invention, the division of the block into parts corresponds to disposition, and the polish given to the block seems to correspond to ornament.[38]

One may not say that [the sculpture] is perfect form, nor, on the other hand, simple material, until he, with more subtle chisels and other instruments, has given it such perfection that, although it be without any spirit or feeling, it seems nevertheless, to all who see it, that it lives and breathes.[39]

The act of carving and, above all, polishing transforms the idea into the finished statue by giving the rough block a form that actually seems to possess the tangibility of the thing represented. Although clearly trying to evoke the well-established rhetorical models, Daniello conceives of vividness in terms that derive not from rhetoric or poetics, but from philosophy—and, more specifically, from Aristotle. A near-contemporary of Daniello, Benedetto Varchi, who was also deeply involved in the study of poetics and poetic theory, nearly cites (with the exception of the subjects of the sculptures) in his first *Lezzione* the influential passage from Aristotle's *Metaphysics*. The passage appears within a larger exegetical reading of Michelangelo's sonnet, "Non ha l'ottimo artista alcun concetto":

That which is generated by nature, or made by art, is not only in form, nor only in material; but the whole is composed [*tutto composto*] together; such that, if one asks what is that which a sculptor has done when from a mass of bronze he has cast, for example, a Perseus, we ought to reply that as he has not made the material, that is the bronze, so similarly he has not made the form of Perseus, but the whole *composto*, that is, the material and the form together: and, in short, the Perseus, in which is contained both the bronze, that is, the material that which he causes it to be Perseus, or St. George, or Judith, or another statue, that is the form, not otherwise than in natural generations, where the forms are substantial; a man is not in form only, that is, the soul, nor matter only, that is, the body, but the soul and body together, that is, the whole *composto* of form and matter.[40]

These passages mark a critical moment for a new consideration of the phenomenology of sculpture—in particular, the role of touch in making and receiving the sculpture *tutto composto*.

Varchi raises these issues more fully in his second *Lezzione*, in which he compares the arts of painting and sculpture. Engaging the familiar complaint—that sculpture copies the three-dimensional forms of nature into a three-dimensional medium and, therefore, lacks artifice and difficulty—Varchi once again appropriates Aristotle's conception of art as the integration of form and matter as a way to extend and enlarge the properties and signs of art. For such a revision, he turns to a paradigm of reception that does not involve vision.

It is not true that that which one finds of three dimensions is completely from nature, because if all bodies necessarily have three dimensions, they do not have them in the same way; otherwise the sculptor would do nothing, so that he would make a statue with the same dimensions as the rough piece of marble; for not only are the natural three dimensions found, but in such a way that a blind man knows [*conosce*] it to be a statue. It is not true that only the lines that surround the said body are of art, because, although art works only in the surface, one could not say that the artist makes only the form, but the form with the material together, that is all composed [*tutto composto*], as we declared in the exposition of the first part of the sonnet [in the first *Lezzione* on Michelangelo's sonnet that begins "Non ha l'ottimo artista alcun concetto . . ."].[41]

Sculpture, according to Varchi, requires the presence of art to give the shape, dimensions, and polish that distinguish the properties of a statue, to transform the rough block of stone into a form that can be discerned by the touch of the blind man as something made. Varchi cites the conceit from a letter—which he requested from a number of Florentine artists in preparation for writing the *Lezzione*—written by the sculptor Tribolo, in which the artist raises the story in the context of a commonplace assertion that touch as the judge of sculpture affirms its truth, whereas sight as the judge of painting confirms its being. Touching a painting, according to Tribolo, will reveal none of its virtual suggestions of relief and depth, but feeling a sculpture, with its actual projections and recessions, will confirm the verisimilitude of the art. However, Varchi significantly expands Tribolo's reductive association by reconceiving the *topos* as an extension of his Aristotelian approach, which in turn supports his notion that vividness in sculpture results from the merging of artifice *and* the material properties of the block. The blind man, without sight, runs his fingers over the polished surface of the sculpture, feels the artifice, and simultaneously responds to and affirms the substance, the material. The touching hand traces the lines of art and responds to the presence of the form that determines the lines; the touching hand, as it had in discussions of painting and written compositions, registers the artifice that creates the effect of vividness in sculpture.

However, unlike in these earlier sources, the touching hand in Varchi's *Lezzione* is not conceptual or metaphorical, and consequently it introduces into his deliberate metaphysical and aesthetic arguments the enacted desire and sensuality that attends an actual hand moving over the surface of a sculpture, especially when that touch is not anchored or explained by sight. The blind man's hand travels over the passages of different textures and properties—rough, smooth, cold, hard—and follows the shapes and lines without affirming the verisimilitude of the particular piece of sculpture. As the hand assumes different gestures and positions as it moves across the body—a slight cupping and caressing of the hand around a gentle curve, for example—the mind attributes emotional values to those movements that may or may not bear any significant relationship to what those shapes and surfaces represent. Touch at times, then, is pure sensation for Varchi, and, because, in this form, it frustrates and thwarts the translation and representation of the nonvisual in visual terms or analogies, he turns to legendary episodes of viewers and makers of sculpture and their salacious behavior, which does not involve sight—among them the youth who stains the Cnidian Venus and the myth of Pygmalion. Perhaps a more contemporary figuration of his conception of touch in sculpture would be Michelangelo's so-called *Dying Slave* (Figure 4), who, with his eyes closed, touches simultaneously the ineffective bindings wrapped around his chest and his own highly finished, polished, and supple body. Assuming the pose of sleep, the figure further increases the sense of inaccessibility and alienation of the viewer found in sleeping figures, including Michelangelo's own statue of *Night* for the Medici Tombs, with his seemingly conscious self-occupation. The withdrawn figure draws attention to the form and substance of art—the sensuousness of the finished sculpture—and to the a-discursive quality of pure sensation.[42] In effect, the *Dying Slave* fully and completely figures the autonomy and detachment Michelangelo only imagines for his *Night* in the well-known quatrain in which the artist, in the voice of the sculpture, becomes the anti-speaking image: "don't disturb me, please, speak softly."[43]

ESCLAVE.

Figure 4. Michelangelo, *Dying Slave*, 1513–16. Reproduced by permission of the Louvre, Paris.

A later drawing (Figure 5) attributed to the School of Guercino (early seventeenth century) gives visual form to the complex network of concepts at work in Varchi's conceit: a blind man appears to vivify through his searching touch the already responsive female bust.[44] Depicted as a beggar, with his walking stick and cup, the scruffy man extends his right hand to touch the forehead, especially the "blank" eyes, of the female bust and appears to heal her, to endow her with a lifelike response unexpected for a sculpture, but not unexpected for an interaction between a man and a woman. The painting placed beneath the makeshift pedestal, by contrast, depicts a soldier (wearing a sword rather than a walking stick) who looks at two nude women in poses that allow him (and the viewer) to see multiple sides of the figure, seemingly evoking the scopophiliac tradition of the "lost" bath picture attributed to Jan van Eyck.[45] With his hands behind his back and restricted to looking, the soldier figures the message inscribed on the wall above: "Della scoltura si, della pittura no." However, the drawing would seem to imply that touch not only judges sculpture, but, unlike for painting, also allows for an unmediated sensual access to, and desirous interaction with, the depicted.

Nearly a century after the drawing, in 1709, Roger de Piles, clearly aware of the theoretical tradition of touch as a sign of vividness in painting and sculpture, tells "The Story of a Blind Sculptor Who Made Wax Portraits" in a larger discussion about *chiaroscuro*, or the suggestion of relief in painting, in his *Cours de peinture par principes*.

One day, having met him in the Justinian Palace where he was copying a statue of Minerva, I took the opportunity to ask him whether he did not see just a little bit in order to copy exactly as he did. I see nothing, he told me, and my eyes are at the tips of my fingers . . . I feel out my original, he said, I study its dimensions, its protrusions and cavities: I try to retain them in my memory, then I put my hand to the wax, and by the comparison that I make between one and the other, going back and forth between them several times with my hand, I finish my work as best I can. . . . But without going any further, we have in Paris a portrait by his hand, that of the late Monsieur Hesselin, head of the Bureau of Monies, who was so happy with it and found the work so marvelous that he begged the author to have himself painted so that he could take his portrait back to France and thereby conserve his memory. . . . I noticed that the Painter had put an eye at the tip of each of his fingers in order to show that the eyes he had elsewhere were totally useless to him.[46]

His story of the "seeing" hand, with fingers that work like eyes and assume the cognitive functions attributed to vision, stands as a conceptual (and chronological) bridge between Renaissance theoretical writings on touch and the importance of the haptic for a few late nineteenth and early twentieth century art historians who studied artworks from the early modern pe-

Figure 5. Guercino, *Allegory of the Superiority of Sculpture over Painting* (*Della scoltura si, della pittura no*), early seventeenth century. Reproduced by permission of the Louvre, Paris. Photo: Michele Ballot.

riod. The hand that sees as it feels and makes and feels and makes as it sees, indeed, has its origins in the Renaissance hand.

Afterword: Touching Rhetoric

Lynn Enterline

An important impulse behind this collection has been to read a variety of early modern discourses in a way that asks, as rigorously as possible, what it means to be subject at once to language and the body.[1] Whether focusing on the figure of the anatomist, the healer, or the poet, the preceding essays range across religious, literary, rhetorical, legal, and medical texts in order to chart the stubborn refusal of the flesh to be cast aside by discourses that try to transcend it. Taking touch "as a category of investigation," the editor remarks, enables an approach to early modern cultural studies that "reactivate[s] the body's material, and often gendered, relation to the world." It therefore seems appropriate to bring this volume to a close, and to think about the import of its claims, by returning to a classical scene of touching that deeply influenced early modern representations of speaking, embodied subjectivity. The scene I have in mind is Ovid's prolonged description of Pygmalion's passion as expressed in, and augmented by, the loving caresses he gives to the statue of his own making.[2]

When Jodi Cranston discusses Vasari's figure of the painter's "magic touch" that turns pale images into "living, talking figures" ("il tocco magico di pennello che tramuta le smorte immagini in figuri vive e parlanti"), she reminds us that the idea of animation behind the story of Pygmalion's moving statue did more than spawn a lively literary progeny in the early modern period. It also informed an entire theoretical discourse about the excellence of painting—a discourse that took its inspiration from such classical treatises on rhetoric as Cicero's *De Oratore* and *De Partitione Oratoriae* and Aristotle's *Rhetoric*.[3] When Vasari describes the vividness of painting in *Le vite de' più eccellenti pittori*, Pygmalion's touch is implicit. When Petrarch writes about the vividness of painting in the *Rime sparse*, it becomes explicit. Pygmalion appears in a pair of sonnets designed to take up the conventional dispute of the *paragone*; by the end of the pair, Petrarch's allusion casts Pygmalion in the role of a rhetorician who, by contrast to the poem's speaker, was so persuasive that he convinced his statue to reply.[4] "When Simon received the high idea which, for my sake, put his hand to his stylus, if he had given to his noble work voice and intellect along with form, he would have lightened my breast of many sighs that make what others prize most vile to me. In appearance she seems humble, and her expression promises peace; then, when I come to speak to her, she seems to listen most kindly: if she could only reply to my words! Pygmalion, how much you must praise yourself for your image, if you received a thousand times what I yearn to have just once!"[5] And in the *Secretum* Ovid's sculptor does more than suggest Petrarch's failure to move his audience with convincing words. The idea of Pygmalion's touch allows the poet to confess his own personal, as well as rhetorical, failings. Augustinus indignantly censures Franciscus's stubborn, Pygmalion-like, behavior of carrying an actual painting of Laura around on his person: "What could be more senseless (*insanius*) than that, not content with the presence of her living face, the cause of all your woes, you must needs obtain a painted picture by an artist of high repute, that you might carry it everywhere with you, to have an everlasting spring of tears, fearing, I suppose, lest otherwise their fountain might dry up?"[6] In both Vasari and Petrarch, the idea of Pygmalion's touch—his decidedly physical relation to his statue—is central to any discussion about the merits, and effects, of painting. But Ovid's sculptor is so central, I would argue, precisely because each of these authors is deeply concerned with the claims of rhetoric—with a way of thinking about language that is primarily concerned about the power of representations to touch us.

To understand my reasons for revisiting Ovid's version of Pygmalion here, it is important to remember that while the topic of Ovid's *Metamorphoses* is generally appropriate to this volume—"the changing forms of bodies" (1.1)—the poem conveys its central theme less by depicting corporeal change *tout court* than *as experienced* by its many characters. Fascinated with the question of what it means, for any subject, to be situated in a body that changes form despite its owner's desire or will, Ovid offered a series of mythographic reflections on this predicament—reflections that deeply influenced later European representations of, and thinking about, embodied subjectivity. As my comments on Petrarch's allusions to Pygmalion should make clear, the *Metamorphoses* stubborn persistence as a point of reference for representations of embodied desire was partly due to Petrarch's canny way of reading, and revising, many of the figures from Ovid's poem in the mode of autobiography. That Petrarch chose to recast Ovid's rhetoric of embodied subjectivity as autobiography, moreover, suggests how important a point several critics in this volume make by resisting the too-simple distinction between psychoanalytic and historicist critiques of subjectivity. As Elizabeth Harvey notes, we may "attribute the idea of a bodily ego to Freud and to subsequent elaborations in the writings of Lacan, Laplanche, Anzieu, and others," yet "the relation it figures of soma and psyche have clear roots in Aristotelian discussions of the body and the senses." To that list of influential classical texts about the connection between soma and psyche we need to add Ovid's poem and, by that route, the equally influential discourse of desire and the self that constitutes Petrarch's *Rime sparse*.

In addition, the *Metamorphoses'* persistence as a kind of mythographic lexicon of embodied desire was largely due to Ovid's own abiding interest not simply in the body and subjectivity but in the tropes and transactions of rhetoric. Throughout the *Metamorphoses*, Ovid grapples with the issue of the language's power and its limits, drawing our attention to the ensuing crises of subjectivity that plague human beings precisely because they are subject to bodies that speak. His metarhetorical reflections, in turn, held considerable appeal for early modern writers. Let me try to place Ovid's evocative scene of an artist's touch within the frame proposed by the editor of this collection. Elizabeth Harvey observes that among the many meanings that accrue to the sense of touch, one is directed outward, as a power over the world—for instance, "the artist's 'touch.' " And another is directed inward, as the world's power over the mind—that is, touch as registered "in the figurative sense of 'touching' as kindling affect." When Ovid depicts Pygmalion's infatuation by describing the way he caresses his *simulacrum*, the scene moves between both these meanings—between an act of touching and shaping an object and the sudden apprehension of having been touched *by* that object. In Ovid's scene, Pygmalion's hands produce a beautiful form and at the same time turn him into a lover; they mold a stone into an *imago* and at the same time kindle "the fire of passion" in their owner. As the editor suggests of the general ambiguity of touch, Pygmalion's artistic/erotic "touch" is poised between creative work that hands can do in the world and "a metaphor" that uses the surface of the body to suggest a kind of "conveyance into the interior" of the subject. But what interests me here, and why this scene in particular seems appropriate as an epilogue to this volume, is that when Ovid brings these two senses together—that of a subject "touching" the world or being "touched" by it—he does so by making this reciprocal connection between mind and world a question of rhetoric. This story, in Kenneth Gross's wonderful phrase, narrates the compelling "dream of the moving statue."[7] As such, Pygmalion's touch captures the *Metamorphoses'* intensive reflection on motion as both a corporeal attribute and the chief aim of ancient rhetoric—the aim not merely to please, but to "move" *(mouere)* one's audience.[8]

Ovid tells us that Pygmalion's hands "move" longingly across the beautiful statue of his own making, pleading with it to come alive at their touch. When Ovid recasts an old story about a king in love with a statue as an artist capable of moving his own image, he pushes the considerable erotic charge attached to Pygmalion's caress in a direction consonant with Augustan practice—with what Roland Barthes calls the period's trademark habit of converting rhetoric into a "poetic technique."[9] It is necessary to quote at length to recall Ovid's focus on Pygmalion's touch, the fantasies it engenders, and the way the narrator eroticizes the verb, *mouere:*

. . . operisque sui concepit amorem.
uirginis est uerae facies, quam uiuere credas,
et, si non obstet reuerentia, *uelle moueri:*
ars adeo latet arte sua. miratur et haurit
pectore Pygmalion simulati corporis ignes.
saepe manus operi temptantes *admouet,* an sit
corpus an illud ebur, nec adhuc ebur esse fatetur.
oscula dat reddique putat loquiturque tenetque
et credit tactis digitos insidere membris
et metuit, pressos ueniat ne liuor in artus . . .
ut rediit, simulacra suae petit ille puellae
incumbensque toro dedit oscula: uisa tepere est;
admouet os iterum, manibus quoque pectora temptat:
temptatum mollescit ebur positoque rigore
subsidit digitis ceditque, ut Hymettia sole
cera remollescit tractataque pollice multas
flectitur in facies ipsoque fit utilis usu.

and with his own work he fell in love. It is the face of a real young girl, whom you would believe to be alive and, if modesty did not prevent, that *she wanted to move:* so does art conceal its own art. Pygmalion marvels and a fire ignites in his breast for the simulated body. Often *he moves his hand* to the work with hands that ask whether it is flesh or ivory, nor does he admit that it is ivory. He gives kisses and thinks they are returned and talks to her and holds her and thinks his fingers lie heavy on her limbs when they are touched—and he grows fearful that a bruise will appear on limbs touched like that . . . [W]hen he returned, he sought the image of his girl and lying on the bed gave it kisses: she seems to grow warm; *he moves his mouth to her again,* and tests her breast with his hands; and the ivory, once touched, grows soft and, putting its hardness aside, gives in and yields to his fingers, just as Hymettian wax grows soft in the sun and yields many shapes to the thumb that handles it and becomes useful through use itself. (translation mine)[10]

Here as throughout the *Metamorphoses*, Ovid's narrator signals his poem's double focus on the "forms" and "figures" of the body as well as the "forms" and "figures" of speech. The important verb throughout the scene for Pygmalion's touch is *mouere* or *ad-mouere*, suggesting that Pygmalion's touch is an erotic embodiment of the aims of rhetorical performance. At the same time, he satirizes Pygmalion's touching delusion, reminding us that Pygmalion's erotic fantasy is at the same time a dream about rhetorical power. That is, the *simulacrum* shaped by his own hands becomes an audience who "*wants* to be moved" (*uelle moueri* 10.251).

The narrator's prolonged attention to Pygmalion's eager fingers and the intoxicating fantasies generated by touch tellingly condenses the poem's preoccupation with the mysterious relationship between sexuality and rhetoric, matter and language. When Pygmalion lays hands on his statue—called by turns an *imago* and a *simulacrum*, both of which remind us that the narrator is talking about representation as much as he is about desire—his action recalls another of the *Metamorphoses*' deeply influential stories about embodied desire. Apollo's longing for Daphne turns on several puns, among them the two senses of *figura*, corporeal form and poetic trope. But in the end all he gets to touch is the bark that overtakes that figure: "Hanc quoque Phoebus amat positaque in stipite dextra / sentit adhuc trepidare nouo sub cortice pectus" ("Even now Apollo loved her and, having placed his hand on the trunk, felt the heart still quivering under the new bark," 1.553–54; translation modified). I've discussed the gendered ramifications of both these interwoven stories elsewhere. Here I merely want to draw attention to the double meaning of Daphne's *figura*. Like the two meanings of Pygmalion's *imago*—at once "a representation in art" and "a representation in words"[11]—Daphne's double *figura* tells us that Ovid conceives of language as a material entity, a "form" one can reach out and lay hands on much as one can touch a body. Ovid's poem-long interest in language's material aspect then turns, in the description of Pygmalion's touch, into a specific question of the technology of Roman writing: "the ivory, once touched *(temptatum)*, grows soft and, putting its hardness aside, gives in and yields to his fingers, just as Hymettian wax grows soft in the sun and yields many shapes to the thumb that handles it." The simile of melting wax, used here to characterize the effect of Pygmalion's touch, is consonant with Ovidian practice: he is a poet fond of alluding, both overtly and obliquely, to the medium of the written word. The *Ars Amatoria* gives explicit writing lessons to lovers; the narrator warns them to obliterate all traces of previous characters left in wax tablets when counterfeiting another's handwriting (3.495–96). In the *Metamorphoses*, the story of Byblis's desire for her brother stages a lengthy writing scene: picking up tablets, Byblis "writes and erases" what she cuts into the wax until the surface is completely filled with her words ("uacuam tenet . . . ceram / incipit et dubitat, scribit damnatque tabellas, / et notat et delet . . . plena reliquit / cera manum," "she holds the empty wax tablet, begins writing and pauses, writes on the tablets and hates what she writes, both writing and erasing . . . the wax, now full, leaves her hand" 9.522–65). Just as the vocabulary of "moving" derives from the technical vocabulary of rhetoric in which Ovid was so well trained, it is no accident that this simile for the ivory maiden's animation refers to an actual tool for writing in the Roman world.[12]

The "touching rhetoric" of Ovid's poem, in short, reveals a poet's desire to "reactivate" the body's material relation to the world in a way that does not separate words from matter, idea from flesh. But the poem's meta-rhetorical resonance captures another important aspect of touch that many of these essays have brought up in a number of ways. As I've been suggesting, when Pygmalion and Apollo turn desire into the desire to touch, that desire is more than a sexual one; it is also a desire to touch language itself—be it a "figure" *(figura)*, an "image," or a likeness" *(imago* and *simulacrum)*. Both scenes therefore suggest that poetry and rhetoric are material practices, something that an artist can actually handle. But more important from the point of view of classical rhetorical theory and practice, both scenes also tell us that these "figures" and "images" are less a representation *of* the world than a kind of force exercised *upon* it—that the activities of speaking and writing can change the world (make a tree, a woman, or an entirely new race) rather than merely replace or reflect it. Ovid's metarhetorical versions of touch testify to a speaking subject's relation to the world that is less about knowing it—the narrator never fails to remind us how deluded Pygmalion is—than doing something to it. And running the risk, in turn, of being done to. (Pygmalion is touched by the ivory he touched; Byblis's wax tablets "leave" the hand that writes on them.) What these scenes indicate, in other words, is a thinking about language as a kind of force that may, in fact, confound its use as a tool for representation and understanding. As Carla Mazzio observes, touch "disrupt[s] normative epistemologies."[13] It also exceeds the claims of will or intention, since, as Ovid's poem tells us over and over again, one can be "touched" by language in unexpected and even unwanted ways. Remember, in this regard, the unintended and lethal effect of words in Cephalus's poem to the breeze, in Semele's ill-fated request to Jupiter, or in Apollo's rash oath to grant whatever his son might request.

Pygmalion's story, one might object, briefly imagines that the world can indeed "move" according to a speaker's desire. But remember—as Ovid's poem certainly asks us to remember when it draws attention to Pygmalion's misogyny—that no one asks his statue if she wants to be "touched" this way. And Apollo's attempt at persuasion remains "inperfecta," incapable of bringing about what he says he desires. But Daphne's words—"perde figuram" (1.547)—do in fact do something, though what they do (change her human "figure" altogether) can hardly be said to be precisely what she intended to bring about. In Ovid's poem, language is represented throughout as material, at once palpable and capable of exercising palpable force. But at the same time, that force remains extremely unpredictable. Thus the one who narrates the dream of the moving statue, Orpheus, embodies rhetoric's most seductive fantasy—that one might give life to death by means of the voice—and also falls victim to it. Unable to effect the one change he actually says he wants his words to bring about, Orpheus is eventually killed by a spear aimed at his singing mouth because his once persuasive voice goes "unheard," drowned out by the superior linguistic and material force of Bacchic noise (11.1–19).

Consonant with what the editor describes as this volume's "preoccupation with the material substratum inherent in discourses that seek to transcend their own fleshly, tactile origins," Ovidian rhetoric insists on turning our attention to those origins. And by doing so, Ovid's "touching rhetoric" keeps reminding readers of language's materiality as well as its ability to disrupt reason, will, and intention. Such attention to the tactility of discourse, whether in the essays in this volume or in Ovid's poem, reminds me of a dissatisfaction I've felt for a long time about a certain way of describing the shift that characterized a "Renaissance" way of seeing the world. This shift has been tellingly described as the end of the "age of resemblance" and the beginning of a modern "analytico-referential discourse."[14] Certainly I see the persuasiveness of such a description—as far as it goes. But as a taxonomy that leans on a view of language as an already constituted semiotic system, it leaves something important out of our account of the period's discursive practices—particularly when it comes to understanding how those practices involve the body or the speaking subject's relation to it. While a shift from the order of resemblance (or of metaphor or allegory) to one of reference allows us to think about significant differences in ways of re-presenting or referring *to* the body, such a view is simply not supple enough to address what Shoshana Felman aptly calls "the scandal of the speaking body."[15] And it also leaves out of account the Renaissance preoccupation with rhetoric—or better yet, the preoccupation Renaissance writers drew from classical rhetorical theory, that language can be a kind of action, or transaction, with the power to do something, to touch or "move" its audience.

More important still, such a view makes little room for contemporary theoretical approaches to embodied subjectivity that renew the classical tradition of rhetorical thinking by focusing on language's shaping, disruptive force in the world. Aptly designated by the pun in Judith Butler's title, *Bodies That Matter,* this current branch of feminist inquiry mobilizes its own kind of touching rhetoric, suggesting that the very setting up of a sign system hierarchically organizes, and assigns value to, various bodies in culturally specific and interested ways—and that the bodies thus organized are retrospectively (mis)recognized as having been merely represented or designated by the sign system that they are claimed to precede. What is at stake in this new turn, as Elizabeth Grosz puts it, "is the consequence of a culture effectively intervening into the constitution of the value of a body."[16] Expanding and refining Lacan's debt to Maurice Merleau-Ponty's phenomenological view of the embodied subject's "constitutive presence," both Julia Kristeva and Jean Laplanche elaborated Freud's notion of a "bodily ego" in terms of language's shaping force on the bodies in which we live. In both Kristeva's theory of the abject and Laplanche's account of the genesis of sexuality and of bodily significance, the figure of the maternal body is deeply involved in the initial setting up of any sign system. But it is important to notice that in both cases, such "originary" "maternal" involvement is the phantasmatic after-effect of discursive and material practice. Neither Kristeva nor Laplanche is writing an account of origin or biological destiny. Rather, they are attempting to theorize the pressure of retroactive, recursive cultural fantasy on the various bodies implicated in the practices—at once material and semiotic—necessary to establishing a symbolic order. True to Freud's consistent swerve away from biologism in *Three Essays on a Theory of Sexuality,* Kristeva's notion of the "maternal abject" involves the mother in the initial setting up of a sign system, but only as the *effect* of a patriarchal symbolic that recursively projects the meaning of such an "original" moment.[17] Laplanche, similarly, draws attention to the retrospective distortions of a paternally ordered symbolic system on the "re-finding" of the maternal breast—the prized object of phantasy. In his theory of "zoning" Laplanche argues that "the marks of maternal care" on the infant's as yet nonsignifying, unmarked body are the beginnings of the sign system that will give that body its cultural significance and value. But he is careful to point out that these marks can be called "maternal" only in the sense that they become so as a *result* of cultural practice.[18]

Both these theorists, in other words, return to Freud by drawing on a long rhetorical tradition of thinking about language as force rather than as merely representation or system. This return may give us a way to rethink the important figure of the maternal body at the origin of language and the world in Ovid's poem—to think of the mother-as-matter trope as a culturally persuasive one that retrospectively comes to embody Ovid's consistent thinking about language's materiality and origins. Kristeva writes about a violent expulsion that defines the not-yet maternal body and her not-yet signs as "abject"; Laplanche writes about the way the marks of maternal care impinge on a body that means, in itself, nothing. We find both these versions of what "maternity" means all over the place in the *Metamorphoses*, particularly when it turns to stories about the origin of "form"—as always, both bodily and poetic. On the one hand, Ovid invents figures of a violated maternal body at language's inaugural moments. On the other, he writes about a decidedly maternal nature that possesses the power of an artist's touch over the bodies she creates.

The idea that the maternal body lies at the origin of "form" and is, by definition, violated by it starts very early in the *Metamorphoses*. The matter of earth, slowly yet increasingly personified over the course of Book 1 as a "mother," becomes more and more maternal as she is more and more wounded. Scarred by the first mark of boundary lines (1.136), disemboweled by tools in the age of iron (138), and drenched in the blood of impious giants (157), earth becomes a speaking subject, "Alma . . . Tellus," only when she finally rises to protest that she has been hurt again, this time by the scorching flames from Phaethon's chariot (2.272). This newly personified "mother" earth's body is engendered and violated once again on the mountain of poetry. When Deucalion opposes his wife's literal interpretation of the oracle, "ossaque post tergum magnae iactate parentis" ("throw the bones of your great mother behind your back," 1.383), we leave the body of an actual mother behind to move into the world of signs, the world of metaphor and substitution. At once creative—the "action" is a reading that produces an entirely new race of human beings—and violent, the poem's leap into a new world produced by the ability of signs to be both one thing and another occurs at a certain cost. At least one party, Pyrrha, fears that obeying this command to touch her dead mother's body is an outrage. Deucalion tries to reassure her that what he has in mind is not "unspeakable" ("nefas," 1.392) but something else instead. In Book 5, a strikingly similar representation occurs that associates the emergence of significant form with a violated maternal body. In the Muses' account of the birth of the fountain of poetry ("origo/fontis"), we learn that the fountain arose when a winged horse was born from the blood flowing out of Medusa's decapitated body; the beating of his feet (both real feet and metrical feet) carved out the fountain. The Heliconian fountain therefore sprang "from the blood of the mother," Medusa ("materno sanguine nasci," 5.259). A crucial material presence, a mother's damaged body haunts Ovid's thinking about the origins of language—and that language, in turn, is consistently represented as at once material and exercising considerable force in the world. But at the same time, both stories tell us that there is a certain price exacted from the body of the mother left behind by the "birth" of such linguistic force.

The materialist mixing of words and matter behind Ovid's metalinguistic puns on "form" and "figure" subtends the poem, but it emerges with renewed power in Book 15 when nature itself is represented as both a poetic and a maternal principle. In Pythagoras's final speech, Ovid represents the inaugural work of the maternal body as a kind of force that gives significant form to whatever it touches. When bringing the poem's metarhetorical preoccupations in line with a theory of metempsychosis, Pythagoras makes mother nature into an artist who works with bodies as "figures": "Nothing retains its own form; but Nature, the great renewer, ever makes up figures from other figures" ("Nec species sua cuique manet, *rerumque nouatrix* / ex aliis alias reparat *natura* figuras," 15.252–53). Another mother emerges in Pythagoras's speech to depict the endless permutations of matter into new forms—this time, the touch of a mother bear's tongue:

nec catulus, partu quem reddidit ursa recenti,
sed male uiua caro est; lambendo mater in artus
fingit et in formam, quantam capit ipse, reducit.

Nor is a cub, recently brought forth by a she-bear, more than a scarcely living thing; but the mother makes its limbs by licking it and brings out the proper shape. (379–81)

Mother nature's fecund touch, however, is strangely divided against itself. Pythagoras represents the renewing power of nature through the figure of the artist's "moving" hand—a rhetorical touch that creates significant human form by releasing bodies from the "womb" of matter:

Nostra quoque ipsorum semper requieque sine ulla
corpora uertuntur, nec quod fuimusue sumusue,
cras erimus; fuit illa dies, qua semina tantum
spesque hominum *primae matris* latauimus aluo:

artifices natura manus admouit et angi
corpora uisceribus distentae condita matris
noluit eque domo uacuas emisit in auras.

Our own bodies always go through rounds of change without rest, nor will we be to-morrow what we have been or are today. There was a time when we lay in the womb of *our first mother*, mere seeds and hopes of men. Then nature *moved her artful hands* and willed not that our bodies should lie in the interior of our strained mother's body, and from our home sent us forth into the open air. (214–20)

Unlike Pygmalion, whose rhetorical power touches matter outside himself, mother nature's "artful hands" do their work by leaving a bit of herself behind. This birth of significant form from matter, from "the womb of our first mother," seems to me reminiscent of Kristeva's view that western cultures have regularly designated the not-yet significant as "maternal" and "abject," and hence to be abandoned and repudiated. It is also reminiscent of Laplanche's notion that material practice means that bodies come into significance and value through the "marks of maternal care."

In Ovid's poem, mother nature's touching rhetoric speaks to the mate-riality of corporeal and linguistic form and at the same time to the deeply cultural, hierarchical way language's material force can become engendered. That a poem as important as the *Metamorphoses* to early modern representa-tions of embodied subjectivity anticipates psychoanalytic speculation about the relationship between language and the maternal body suggests how im-portant it is for feminists to resist the tendency to divorce historicist and psy-choanalytic inquiry. Ovid's metarhetorical scenes about nature's maternal touch tell us that such a reductive critical binarism unnecessarily limits our ability to describe, much less understand, the practices and discourses that helped give such a distinctly gendered shape to early modern experiences of embodiment.

Notes

Introduction

1. George Chapman, *Ovid's Banquet of Sense*, in *The Poems of George Chapman: Poems and Minor Translations*, ed. Algernon Charles Swinburne (London: Chatto and Windus, 1875), 30.

2. Jerome Bylebyl considers the place of the five senses in clinical teaching in the Renaissance in "The Manifest and the Hidden in the Renaissance Clinic," in *Medicine and the Five Senses*, ed. W. F. Bynum and Roy Porter (Cambridge: Cambridge University Press, 1993), 40–60, esp. 47. Vivian Nutton compares Galen's stated principles for examination and his actual practice (revealed in his case histories), and he argues that for Galen, while sight is the most important sense, it is closely followed by touch. Nonetheless, all the senses are implicated in the diagnostic process for Galen and his followers. "Galen at the Bedside," in *Medicine and the Five Senses*, ed. Bynum and Porter, 7–16.

3. In *Downcast Eyes: The Denigration of Vision in Twentieth-Century French Thought* (Berkeley: University of California Press, 1993), Martin Jay analyzes the Platonic legacy and the subsequent cultural pressures that feed this visual primacy.

4. The intertwining of vision and tactility is at work in sonnet 9 of Sir Philip Sidney's *Astrophil and Stella*, in *The Poems of Sir Philip Sidney*, ed. W. A. Ringler (Oxford: Clarendon Press, 1962). As an architectural blazon, the poem participates in the allegorical tradition of body as castle, and each of the kinds of stone (marble, alabaster, porphyry) used to construct Stella's face signals its beauty and preciousness. The third quatrain describes the "windowes" through which the "heav'nly guest" surveys the world; these eyes are constructed of "touch." Sidney punningly refers to the fine-grained black stone (*OED*: quartz or jasper), which was used to test the quality of a gold or silver alloy, but he also attributes to Stella's eyes the property of tactility: "Of touch they are that without touch doth touch." That touch is a stone capable of producing a magnetic attraction generates the multi-layered analogy of the final couplet, which joins the power of Stella's gaze to touch with the properties of the stone: "Which *Cupid's* self from Beautie's myne did draw: / Of touch they are, and poore I am their straw." The helplessness of the lover's attraction replicates the familiar early modern

hierarchy of sensory seduction evident in Michael Drayton's sonnet "To the Senses," in which sight leads to hearing, smell, taste, and finally to touch, but Sidney's sonnet collapses the intervening senses and makes vision and tactility versions of each other.

5. See Jean-François Lyotard's posthumous and unfinished *The Confession of Augustine*, trans. Richard Beardsworth (Stanford, Calif.: Stanford University Press, 2000) and Gilles Deleuze, *The Logic of Sense*, trans. Mark Lester with Charles Stivale, ed. Constantin V. Boundas (Paris: Editions de Minuit, 1969; reprint New York: Columbia University Press, 1990).

6. Margreta de Grazia, Maureen Quilligan, and Peter Stallybrass, eds. *Subject and Object in Renaissance Culture* (Cambridge: Cambridge University Press, 1996); Patricia Fumerton and Simon Hunt, eds., *Renaissance Culture and the Everyday* (Philadelphia: University of Pennsylvania Press, 1998): Lena Cowen Orlin, *Material London, ca. 1600* (Philadelphia: University of Pennsylvania Press, 2000).

7. Gail Kern Paster, *The Body Embarrassed: Drama and the Disciplines of Shame in Early Modern England* (Ithaca, N.Y.: Cornell University Press, 1993): Louise Fradenburg and Carla Freccero, eds., *Premodern Sexualities* (London: Routledge, 1996): Jonathan Sawday, *The Body Emblazoned: Dissection and the Human Body in Renaissance Culture* (London: Routledge, 1995).

8. Michael Drayton, *Works,* ed. John William Hebel (Oxford: Shakespeare Head Press by Blackwell, 1961).

9. Marsilio Ficino, *Commentary on Plato's Symposium on Love*, trans. Sears Jayne (Dallas, Tex.: Spring Publications, 1985), Spenser, Edmund, *The Faerie Queene*, ed. Thomas P. Roche (New Haven, Conn.: Yale University Press, 1981); subsequent references to *The Faerie Queene* are to this edition.

10. Aristotle, *De Sensu* (*On Sense and Sensible Objects*), trans. W. S. Hett, *Aristotle*, vol. 8, Loeb Classical Library (Cambridge, Mass.: Harvard University Press, 1936), 436b; *De Anima*, in *The Basic Works of Aristotle*, ed. Richard McKeon (New York, Random House, 1941), 533–603, 434b; subsequent references are to these editions.

11. Lucretius, *On the Nature of Things*, trans. W. H. D. Rouse, rev. Martin F. Smith, Loeb Classical Library (Cambridge, Mass.: Harvard University Press, 1924; 1992), 2: 434–37. Pierre Gassendi's mid-seventeenth-century revival of Lucretius and Epicurean philosophy provided a countering movement to the dualism of Cartesian thought, thus setting up a philosophical legacy that endorsed the senses (and tactility) as essential. Hugh de Quehen's edition of Lucy Hutchinson's translation of *De rerum natura* (Ann Arbor: University of Michigan Press, 1996) discusses the English context for this influence. See also Louise Vinge, *The Five Senses: Studies in a Literary Tradition* (Lund: Royal Society of Letters at Lund, 1975), 31.

12. Phineas Fletcher, *The Purple Island*, in *Giles and Phineas Fletcher: Poetical Works*, ed. Fredrick S. Boas (Cambridge: Cambridge University Press, 1909), 5: 55.

13. This intuition is corroborated by the discovery of such touch receptors as Meissner's corpuscles, which lie between the dermis and epidermis, the Pacinian corpuscles, which are located near joints and respond to pressure, Merkel's disk's, and Ruffini endings. See Diane Ackerman, *A Natural History of the Senses* (New York: Vintage, 1990), 67–123.

14. The Five Senses are personified as male, perhaps partly because the Latin

words for the senses are of masculine gender. Carl Nordenfalk says that a shift in the gender of the personification takes place around 1500, and this change may be attributed in part to the linkage between sensuality and femininity. "The Five Senses in Late Medieval and Renaissance Art, " *Journal of the Warburg and Courtauld Institutes* 48 (1985): 1–22, 7.

15. This phrase may derive from the descriptions that St. Thomas Aquinas uses in his commentary on Aristotle's *De Anima,* where "Tactus est primus sensuum et quodammodo radix et fundamentum omnium sensum" (Touch is the first sense and in a certain way the root of all the senses) partly because of its closeness to the "fontalem radicem omnium sensuum" (the originary root of all the senses). Gino Casagrande and Christopher Kleinhenz, "Literary and Philosophical Perspectives on the Wheel of the Five Senses in Longthorpe Tower," *Traditio* 41 (1985): 311–27, 318.

16. Carl Nordenfalk discusses a frontispiece in a late fifteenth-century copy of Harderwyck's *Epitoma, seu reparationes totius philosophiiae naturalis,* in which tactility is depicted as a figure putting his hand into a stove with an open fire. He describes this image as the earliest example of touch as represented through the sensation of heat and pain. Pain as touch is accentuated in the snake biting the figure's arm, "aiming," as Nordenfalk observes, "at the nerves inside it [the elbow] which are labelled *interiores tactus,* in a remarkably modern conception of the nervous system of the human body"("Five Senses," 5–6). Touch is frequently depicted as a woman who is pierced or bitten (by a snake or bird), a blending of the painful and the sexual. Sander Gilman analyzes this conjunction in "Touch, Sexuality and Disease," in *Medicine and the Five Senses,* ed. Bynum and Porter, 198–224, especially 206ff. A version of the hand in the fire image appears as a woodcut (1664) in Descartes's *The Treatise on Man,* showing a man holding his hand over an open fire; the side of his head demonstrates the action of touch on the brain by exhibiting the nerve tubes and their connection to the pineal gland. The image is reproduced and discussed in Clair Richter Sherman's catalogue, *Writing on Hands: Memory and Knowledge in Early Modern Europe* (Carlisle, Pa.: Trout Gallery, Dickinson College and Folger Shakespeare Library, 2000), 141–42.

17. Didier Anzieu, *The Skin Ego* (*Le Moi-peau,* 1985), trans. Chris Turner (New Haven, Conn.: Yale University Press, 1989). See also Anzieu et al., *Psychic Envelopes* (1987), trans. Daphne Nash Briggs (London: Karnac, 1990) and Anzieu, *A Skin for Thought: Interviews with Gilbert Tarrab on Psychology and Psychoanalysis* (1991), trans. Daphne Nash Briggs (London: Karnac, 1990).

18. Speculum refers most obviously to the Latin word for mirror, but also, of course, to a medical instrument designed to dilate and examine the body's orifices. The *OED* records the first English use of the term in the 1597 translation of Jacques Guillemeau's treatise on surgery, where the instrument used to dilate the eyelids is called "the speculum of the eye." By 1693, the translation of Steven Blankaart's *Physical Dictionary* uses the analogous terms "dilatorium" or "speculum" to describe the surgeon's instrument that was used to open the mouth or the womb in order to render it accessible to the eye. Speculum is associated with interiority and vision in this sense, but it is a word closely linked to the history of optics as well, especially with respect to the development of magnifying lenses and telescopes. See also Toril Moi's

discussion in *Sexual/Textual Politics: Feminist Literary Theory* (London: Methuen, 1985), 129–31 of the architecture of Irigaray's *Speculum of the Other Woman* (1974), trans. Gillian C. Gill (Ithaca, N.Y.: Cornell University Press, 1985).

19. See Susan Bordo's gendered analysis of Cartesian thought and gender in "The Cartesian Masculinization of Thought and the Seventeenth-Century Flight from the Feminine," in *The Flight to Objectivity: Essays on Cartesianism and Culture* (Albany: State University of New York Press, 1987).

20. Luce Irigaray, *An Ethics of Sexual Difference* (1984), trans. Carolyn Burke and Gillian C. Gill (Ithaca, N.Y.: Cornell University Press, 1993); *Sexes and Genealogies* (1987), trans. Gillian C. Gill (New York: Columbia University Press, 1993).

21. Irigaray has, of course, been charged with essentialism for statements like these, and it is thus important to read her in the contexts of her overarching project, which sets out to expose patriarchy's structures and operations. Her central target is Western philosophical thought, or, as Margaret Whitford puts it, the *"passional foundations of reason." Luce Irigaray: Philosophy in the Feminine* (London: Routledge, 1991), 10.

22. She asks in *An Ethics of Sexual Difference* whether sensation is not for Merleau-Ponty structured like language (158). For a brilliant treatment of the complexities of Irigaray's endeavor, see Whitford, *Luce Irigaray,* especially the chapters "Feminism and Utopia"and "Woman and/in the Social Contract."

23. Maurice Merleau-Ponty *The Visible and the Invisible* (1964), ed. Claude Lefort, trans. Alphonso Lingis (Evanston, Ill.: Northwestern University Press, 1968). Elizabeth Grosz explicates Merleau-Ponty's idea of the "double sensation" and Irigaray's reading of it in *Volatile Bodies: Toward a Corporeal Feminism* (Bloomington: Indiana University Press, 1994), 97–111.

24. For a discussion of the place of metonymy in Irigaray's philosophy, see Whitford, *Luce Irigaray,* 178ff.

25. Julia Kristeva *Time and Sense: Proust and the Experience of Literature* (1994), trans. Ross Guberman (New York: Columbia University Press, 1996), 232–39.

26. Kristeva, *Powers of Horror: An Essay on Abjection* (1980), trans. Leon S. Roudiez (New York: Columbia University Press, 1982).

27. Norbert Elias, *The Civilizing Process: The History of Manners and State Formation and Civilization,* trans. Edmund Jephcott (London: Blackwell, 1939; rpt, 1994). Subsequent references appear in the text.

28. Lynn Enterline, "Touching Rhetoric," this volume, 250.

29. Chapman, *Ovid's Banquet of Sense,* 36.

30. Casagrande and Kleinhenz, "Literary and Philosophical Perspectives," Nordenfalk, "Five Senses," and F. Mütherich, "An Illustration of the Five Senses in Medieval Art," *Journal of the Warburg and Courtauld Institutes,* 18 (1955): 140–41 give specific examples. See also Sherman's *Writing on Hands* for a fuller discussion of the history of the hand, Katherine's Rowe's essay, "God's Handy Worke" in *The Body in Parts: Fantasies of Corporeality in Early Modern Europe,* ed. David Hillman and Carla Mazzio (London: Routledge, 1997) for an excellent analysis of the hand in anatomical discourse, and Marjorie O'Rourke Boyle, *Senses of Touch: Human Dignity and Deformity from Michelangelo to Calvin* (Leiden: E.J. Brill, 1998) for a study of the tradition that linked the instrumentality of the hand with erect bipedal posture.

31. For a survey of the various traditions associated with the hand, including the mnemonic and the musical, see Sherman, *Writing on Hands.*

32. Helkiah Crooke, *Microcosmographia: A Description of the Body of Man Together with the Controversies Thereto Belonging* (London, 1615), 648, 730.

33. Rowe, "God's Handy Worke," 287.

34. For a discussion of the anatomist's need to displace the mortality of the cadaver he dissected, see Valerie Traub, "Gendering Mortality in Early Modern Culture" in *Feminist Readings of Early Modern Culture: Emerging Subjects*, ed. Valerie Traub, M. Lindsay Kaplan, and Dympna Callaghan (Cambridge: Cambridge University Press, 1996), 44–92.

35. Quoted in Vinge, *Five Senses,* 39.

36. See Elizabeth Sears, "Sensory Perception and Its Metaphors in the Time of Richard of Fournival," in *Medicine and the Five Senses*, ed. Bynum and Porter, 17–39. Vinge discusses Pliny and the medieval animal imagery, and Casagrande and Kleinhenz analyze the wall paintings of Longthorpe Tower.

37. Gilman, "Touch, Sexuality, and Disease," 206–11.

38. Gilman provides a fully contextualized reading of these animals and the other elements in the engraving. Of particular interest is his discussion of the scorpion as a figure for sexually transmitted disease and for Jewish sexuality (210–12).

39. Casagrande and Kleinhenz, "Literary and Philosophical Perspectives," 22.

40. Casagrande and Kleinhenz, "Literary and Philosophical Perspectives," 321.

41. John Davies, *The Complete Poems*, ed. Alexander B. Grosart (London: Chatto and Windus, 1876), 1: 70.

42. Ovid, *Metamorphoses*, 2 vols., trans. Frank Justus Miller, Loeb Classical Library (Cambridge, Mass.: Harvard University Press, 1916; rpt 1977), book 6, 1–145.

43. Edmund Spenser, *Muipotmos: Or the Fate of the Bvtterflie*, in *Spenser: Poetical Works*, ed. J. C. Smith and Ernest de Sélincourt (London: Oxford University Press, 1970), ll. 353, 364–76.

44. Frances A. Yates, *The French Academies of the Sixteenth Century*, Studies of the Warburg Institute 15 (London: Jarrold and Sons, 1947), 111.

45. This illustration is reproduced in Sherman's catalogue, *Writing on Hands*, 31. For a discussion of Delbene's allegory, its medieval roots, and its relation to the sixteenth-century French Academies, see Yates, *French Academies*, 111–18.

46. Nordenfalk. "Five Senses, 19–20.

47. See Valerie Traub, "Gendering Mortality in Early Modern Anatomies," in *Feminist Readings*, ed. Traub, Kaplan, and Callaghan, 44–92.

48. Carla Mazzio and Douglas Trevor, eds., *Historicism, Psychoanalysis, and Early Modern Culture* (London: Routledge, 2000), 5.

Chapter 2. Anxious and Fatal Contacts: Taming the Contagious Touch

1. Between 1486 and 1604 twenty-three books exclusively concerned with the plague were published: see Paul Slack, *The Impact of Plague in Tudor and Stuart*

England (1985; Oxford: Clarendon Press, 1990), 23. More general books of medical regimen dwelt increasingly on contagion, and religious tracts dealing with God's "scourges" for sin mushroomed in the second half of the sixteenth century.

2. See below, p. 25.

3. See, for example, Raymond Anselment, *The Realms of Apollo: Literature and Healing in Seventeenth-Century England* (Newark: University of Delaware Press, 1995), which is entirely premised on the idea of the "healing," "transforming" properties of words, especially poetry (11–19). Christopher Ricks, "Doctor Faustus and Hell on Earth," *Essays in Criticism* 35 (1985): 101–20, has similarly accorded plague a positive, enabling function in relation to art: "art—in the face of the greatest horrors (plague, the slave-trade, the death-camps)—may be obliged by indirections to find directions out" (118). Raymond Stephanson, "The Plague Narratives of Defoe and Camus," *Modern Language Quarterly* 48 (1987): 224–41, suggests that "the plague in a sense compels an imaginative response" (227). The "white plague" of tuberculosis was mythically associated with Romanticism and increased creativity in the nineteenth century; see Jeffrey Meyers, *Disease and the Novel, 1880–1960* (New York: St. Martin's Press, 1985), 4–11.

4. All citations are from *Fracastoro's "Syphilis"*, ed. and trans. Geoffrey Eatough (1530; Liverpool: Francis Cairns, 1984).

5. All citations are from Shakespeare, *Venus and Adonis,* in *The Poems,* ed. F. T. Prince, Arden Shakespeare (London: Methuen, 1960), 1–62.

6. Thomas Dekker, *The Blacke and White Rod* (London, 1630), sig. A4v.

7. Thomas Lodge, *A Treatise of the Plague* (London, 1603), sig. B2v.

8. Thomas Paynell, *A Moche Profitable Treatise Against the Pestilence* (London, 1534) sigs. A3r, A5r.

9. Thomas Phayre, *The Regiment of Life, wherunto is added a treatise of the pestilence* (London, 1545), sig. L3r. Lodge, *A Treatise,* sig. L3r.

10. Cited in Slack, *Impact of Plague,* 203.

11. Fracastorius, *De Contagionibus et Contagiosis morbis,* discussed by Eatough in *Fracastoro's "Syphilis"*, Introduction, 16–17.

12. R. Bostocke, *Auncient and Later Physicke* (London, 1585), 6, 27.

13. Lodge, *A Treatise,* sig. L3r.

14. Thomas Cogan, *The Haven of Health* (London, 1584), 261, 265.

15. Simon Kellwaye, *A Defensative against the Plague* (London, 1593), sig. B1r.

16. William Vaughan, *Naturall and artificial directions for health* (London, 1600), 70.

17. Thomas Dekker's pamphlets frequently allude to his fellow Londoners' fears of buying new clothing or even passing by wool merchants' premises during epidemics.

18. Francis Bacon, *The Advancement of Learning, Book* 2, in *A Critical Edition of the Major Works,* ed. Brian Vickers (Oxford: Oxford University Press, 1996), 216.

19. Bacon, *Advancement,* 216–17.

20. Levinus Lemnius, trans. Thomas Newton in *The Touchstone of Complexions* (London, 1576), f. 22r.

21. Newton, *The Touchstone,* f. 20r.

22. Henry Holland, *Spiritual Preservatives against the Pestilence* (London, 1593), f. 26v.

23. John Cotta, *A Short Discoverie* (London, 1612).

24. Robert Burton, *The Anatomy of Melancholy* (1621; London: J.M. Dent, 1932, 1972), 188.

25. Burton, *Anatomy,* 180. On the demonic cultural imaginary of this period, see Stuart Clark, *Thinking with Demons: The Idea of Witchcraft in Early Modern Europe* (Oxford: Oxford University, 1997).

26. Bacon, *Advancement,* 216–17.

27. As the papers from the notorious Mary Glover case reveal, in the early seventeenth century medical practitioners were important arbitrators in disputes about witchcraft and possession, see Michael MacDonald, *Witchcraft and Hysteria in Elizabethan London: Edward Jordan and the Mary Glover Case* (London: Routledge, 1991).

28. James Balmford, *A Short Dialogue Concerning the Plague's Infection* (London, 1603), 15.

29. W. Muggins, *Londons Mourning Garment* (London, 1603), sig. D3v.

30. Abraham Holland, *London Looke Backe* (London, 1625), 61.

31. John Davies, *The Triumph of Death,* cited in Anselment, *Realms of Apollo,* 116.

32. John Tabor, *Seasonable thoughts in sad times, . . . reflections on the pestilence* (London, 1667), 15.

33. John Toy, *Worcester's Elegie & Eulogie* (London, 1638), sig. B1v.

34. Sander Gilman, *Disease and Representation: Images of Illness from Madness to AIDS* (Ithaca, N.Y.: Cornell University Press, 1988), 1.

35. Bacon, *Advancement,* 209.

36. Sir Philip Sidney, *The Defence of Poesy,* in *A Critical Edition of the Major Works,* ed. Katherine Duncan-Jones (Oxford: Oxford University Press, 1989), 207, 185.

37. Frances Quarles, Emblem No. 88, *Emblemes* (1635), in C.W.R.D. Moseley, *A Century of Emblems: An Introductory Anthology* (Brookfield, Vt.: Scolar Press, 1989), 261–62.

38. Moseley, *Emblems,* 262.

39. See especially Thomas Dekker, *Worke for Armorours* (London, 1609), sig. D1v.

40. See Gilman, *Disease and Representation,* 2–3: "in some cases, the fearful is made harmless though being made comic; in some cases it looms as a threat, controlled only by being made visible."

41. See Margaret Healy, "Bronzino's London 'Allegory' and the Art of Syphilis," *Oxford Art Journal* 20, 1 (1997): 3–11.

42. U. Naich, "Per Dio, Tu Sei Cortese," in *The Anthologies of Black-Note Madrigals,* ed. Don Harrán, Corpus Mensurabilis Musicae 73, i, 2 (Stuttgart: Hännsler-Verlag, 1978), lxi.

43. Peter Lowe, *An Easie, certaine, and perfect method, to cure and prevent the Spanish sickness* (London, 1596), sig. B1v.

44. Lowe, *An Easie,* sig. B1v.

45. Lowe, *An Easie,* sig. B1v.

46. Claude Quetel, *History of Syphilis,* trans. Judith Braddock and Brian Pike (1986; Cambridge: Polity Press, 1990), 33.

47. M. A. Waugh, "Venereal Diseases in Sixteenth-Century England," *Medical History* 17 (1973): 192–99, 192.

48. Cited in Charles Creighton, *A History of Epidemics in Britain*, rev. ed., 2 vols. (London: Frank Cass, 1965), 1: 417.

49. Creighton, *A History of Epidemics*, 418.

50. Creighton, *A History of Epidemics*, 417.

51. Andrew Boord, *The Breviary of Helthe* (London, 1547), f. 15v. "Burnynge" is associated with a multitude of venereal infections and is not specific to the pox in Boord's account.

52. Ulrich Von Hutten, *De Morbo Gallico*, trans. Thomas Paynell (London, 1533), f. 5v.

53. Lowe, *An Easie*, sig. B2v.

54. William Clowes, *A short and profitable Treatise touching the cure of the disease called Morbus Gallicus*, sig. B3v.

55. Clowes, "To the Frendly Reader," *Morbus Gallicus*, unpag.

56. W. Myer recounts this myth in "Syphilis and the Poetic Imagination," *Renaissance Papers* 3 (1955): 39–67; he quotes from Jean Lemaire de Belges, *Oeuvres* (1525; Louvain, 1885).

57. See Eatough, Introduction to *Fracastoro's "Syphilis"*, 17–19. Eatough draws his information from Fracastoro's *Poetics* (published in *Opera Omnia*, 1555) and from his notebooks; see Introduction, 8.

58. Desiderius Erasmus, "De Utilitate Colloquiorum" quoted in the Introduction to *The Young Man and the Harlot* in *The Colloquies of Erasmus*, ed. and trans. C. R. Thompson (Chicago: University of Chicago Press, 1965). See also Montaigne, *Essais*, I, cited in Quetel, *History of Syphilis*, 66.

59. Eatough, Introduction to *Fracastoro's "Syphilis"*, 1.

60. On the social function of medicine see Meyer Fortes, Foreword, *Social Anthropology and Medicine*, ed., J. B. Loudon (1976; London: Academic Press, 1979).

61. On the function of myths, see Claude Lévi-Strauss, *Myth and Meaning* (Toronto: University of Toronto Press, 1978), esp. 12–13, 17.

62. , See Gilman, *Disease and Representation*, chap. 1, "Depicting Disease."

63. Philip Barrough, *The Method of Physick* (London, 1652), 372.

64. John Lyly, *Euphues: The Anatomy of Wit Verie Pleasant for all Gentlemen to reade and most necessary to remember* (London, 1595), sig. A4r.

65. Richard Ames, *The Folly of Love; or, An Essay upon Satyr against Woman* (London, 1691), cited in Anselment, *Realms of Apollo*, 160.

66. Anselment, *Realms of Apollo*, 18.

Chapter 3. "Handling Soft the Hurts": Sexual Healing and Manual Contact in Orlando Furioso, The Faerie Queene, *and* All's Well That Ends Well

1 Richard Braithwait, *The Good Wife: Or, a Rare One amongst Women* (London, 1618), B2v–B3.

2. *The Diary of Lady Margaret Hoby, 1599–1605*, ed. Dorothy M. Mead (Boston: Houghton Mifflin, 1930), entry for August 26, 1601. See also Barbara Ehrenreich and

Deirdre English, *Witches, Midwives, and Nurses: A History of Women Healers* (Old Westbury, N.Y.: Feminist Press, 1973).

3. *Newes from Scotland,* ed. G. B. Harrison (London: Bodley Head, 1924).

4. Lodovico Ariosto, *Orlando Furioso,* trans. Sir John Harington, ed. Robert McNulty (Oxford: Clarendon Press, 1972). Edmund Spenser, *The Faerie Queene,* ed. A. C. Hamilton (London: Longman, 1977). William Shakespeare, *All's Well That Ends Well,* ed. G. K. Hunter, Arden ed., 2nd ser. (London: Methuen, 1959). All are cited parenthetically. Citations from other plays by Shakespeare are to *The Riverside Shakespeare,* ed. G. Blakemore Evans et al. (Dallas: Houghton Mifflin, 1974).

5. Jacques Derrida, *Of Grammatology* (*De la grammatologie*), trans. Gayatri Chakravorty Spivak (Baltimore: John Hopkins University Press, 1990), 145, 147, 150.

6. James I, *Daemonologie,* ed. G. B. Harrison (London: Bodley Head, 1924), 44, 8–9.

7. Quoted by William Kerwin, "Where Have You Gone, Margaret Kennix? Seeking the Tradition of Healing Women in English Renaissance Drama," in *Women Healers and Physicians: Climbing a Long Hill,* ed. Lilian R. Furst (Lexington: University of Kentucky Press: 1997), 93.

8. Kate Hurd-Mead, *A History of Women in Medicine* (New York: AMS Press, 1977), 348. See also Sir George Clark, *A History of The Royal College of Physicians of London,* vol. 1 (Oxford: Clarendon Press, 1966); Hilda Smith, "Gynecology and Ideology in Seventeenth-Century England," in *Liberating Women's History,* ed. Berenice Carroll (Urbana: University of Illinois Press, 1976), 97–114; Audrey Eccles, *Obstetrics and Gynaecology in Tudor and Stuart England* (Kent, Ohio: Kent State University Press, 1982).

9. Betty S. Travitsky, "Placing Women in the English Renaissance," in *The Renaissance Englishwoman in Print* (Amherst: University of Massachusetts Press, 1990), 13.

10. Smith, "Gynecology and Ideology," 109–10.

11. Katharine Park, "The Rediscovery of the Clitoris," in *The Body in Parts: Fantasies of Corporeality in Early Modern Europe,* ed. David Hillman and Carla Mazzio (London: Routledge, 1999), 171–94.

12. Thomas Laqueur, *Making Sex: The Body and Gender from the Greeks to Freud* (Cambridge, Mass.: Harvard University Press, 1990), 136.

13. Ambroise Paré, *Workes,* trans. Thomas Johnson (London, 1634), 889.

14. Park, "Rediscovery," 186.

15. Helkiah Crooke, ΜΙΚΡΟΚΟΣΜΟΓΡΑΦΙΑ *[Microcosmographia]: A Description of the Body of Man* (London, 1615), X5v.

16. See Roy Porter, "A Touch of Danger: The Man-Midwife as Sexual Predator," in *Sexual Underworlds of the Enlightenment,* ed. G. S. Rousseau and Roy Porter (Chapel Hill: University of North Carolina Press, 1988), 206–32, and David Cressy, *Birth, Marriage, and Death: Ritual, Religion, and the Life-Cycle in Tudor and Stuart England* (Oxford: Oxford University Press, 1997).

17. Lodovico Ariosto, *Orlando Furioso,* trans. Guido Waldman (Oxford: Oxford University Press, 1991), 219.

18. Deanna Shemek, "That Elusive Object of Desire: Angelica in the *Orlando Furioso,*" *Annali d'Italianistica* 7 (1989): 136.

19. Linda Woodbridge, *Women in the English Renaissance: Literature and the Nature of Womankind, 1540–1620* (Urbana: University of Illinois Press, 1984), 184.

20. Derrida, *Of Grammatology,* 145.

21. *The Early Modern English Dictionaries Database* (EMEDD), ed. Ian Lancashire (On-line, GALILEO, University of Georgia, March 24, 2000), search-term "panace" <www.chass.utoronto.ca/english/emed/emedd.html>.

22. Sonnet 9, *The Passionate Pilgrim,* in *Shakespeare: The Poems,* ed. John Roe (Cambridge: Cambridge Univesity Press, 1992).

23. John Donne, "The Extasie," in *Donne: Poetical Works,* ed. Herbert Grierson (Oxford: Oxford University Press, 1987), 21.

24. Mary Villeponteaux, "*Semper Eadem*: Belphoebe's Denial of Desire," in *Renaissance Discourses of Desire,* ed. Claude S. Summers and Ted-Larry Pebworth (Columbia: University of Missouri Press, 1994), 40.

25. Jonathan Goldberg, *Endlesse Worke: Spenser and the Structures of Discourse* (Baltimore: Johns Hopkins University Press, 1981), 79.

26. Elizabeth J. Bellamy, "Waiting for Hymen: Literary History as 'Symptom' in Spenser and Milton," *ELH* 64, 2 (1997): 410, 408.

27. See Harry Berger, Jr., "Busirane and the War Between the Sexes: An Interpretation of *The Faerie Queene* III.xi.xii," *ELR* 26 (1959): 171–87, and Donald Cheney, "Spenser's Hermaphrodite and the 1590 *Faerie Queene,*" *PMLA* 87 (1972): 192–200.

28. Lauren Silberman, however, argues that Spenser transforms hermaphroditic sexlessness into "androgynous" role-reversal. *Transforming Desire: Erotic Knowledge in Books III and IV of* The Faerie Queene (Berkeley: University of California Press, 1995), 70.

29. Publius Ovidius Naso, *Metamorphoses,* trans. Frank Justus Miller, Loeb Classical Library (Cambridge, Mass.: Harvard University Press, 1999), 457.

30. Norman Nathan suggests that "Fontybell" is a euphemism for "beautiful vagina," an attribution rejected by the chaste Diana. "Fontibell and Fountains," *Names: Journal of the American Name Society* 39 (1991): 39–41.

31. John Arderne, *Treatise of Fistula in Ano,* ed. D'Arcy Power, EETS 139 (London: Trübner, 1910), 20.

32. Andrew Boorde, *The Breuiary of Healthe* (London, 1542), H1.

33. *An Account of the Causes of Some Particular Rebellious Distempers* (London, 1547), fol. 58. In *Medicine and Shakespeare in the English Renaissance* (Newark: University of Delaware Press, 1992), F. David Hoeniger argues that Shakespeare might be playing a practical joke on his audience, implying that the King has *fistula in ano* when in fact he is suffering from a whitlow (nail-bed infection), mistakenly called *fistula in mano.* This diagnosis would account for the King's "healthful hand" (2.3.48). Hoeniger admits that this joke would necessitate hiding the King's presumably bandaged hand earlier in the scene and also that a figurative reading of the line ("hand" as a metonym for royal power) is possible.

34. On Helena's "performance," see David McCandless, "Helena's Bed-Trick:

Gender and Performance in *All's Well That Ends Well*," *Shakespeare Quarterly* 45 (1994): 449–68.

35. Gary Taylor, "Inventing Shakespeare," *Jahrbuch der Deutschen Shakespeare-Gesellschaft West* (1986): 26–44.

36. Janet Adelman, "Bed Tricks: On Marriage as the End of Comedy in *All's Well That Ends Well* and *Measure for Measure*," in *Shakespeare's Personality*, ed. Norman J. Holland, Sidney Homan, and Bernard Paris (Berkeley: University of California Press, 1989), 151–74.

37. Ann Lecercle, "Anatomy of a Fistula, Anomaly of a Drama," in *All's Well That Ends Well: Nouvelles perspectives critiques*, ed. Jean Fuzier and François Laroque (Montpellier: Université de Paul Valéry, 1985), 105–24.

38. Boccaccio, *The Decameron*, 3.9, trans. as "Giletta of Narbona," in *The Palace of Pleasure*, by William Painter, 3rd printing (London, 1575), reprinted in Shakespeare, *All's Well That Ends Well*, Appendix 1, ed. Hunter, 146.

39. Lorraine Daston and Katharine Park, "The Hermaphrodite and the Orders of Nature: Sexual Ambiguity in Early Modern France," *GLQ* 1 (1995): 419–38; Park, "Rediscovery," 184.

40. My own translation; original quoted in *Henri III: A Maligned or Malignant King? Aspects of the Satirical Iconography of Henri III*, ed. Keith Cameron (Exeter: Exeter University Printing Unit, 1978), 82.

41. "[T]he spectacle of gay male sex," Lee Edelman argues, is literally in-visible and unstageable: "any representation of sodomy between men is a threat to the epistemological security of the observer . . . a spectacle that, from the perspective of castration, can only be seen as a 'catastrophe.' " "Seeing Things: Representation, the Scene of Surveillance, and the Spectacle of Gay Male Sex," in *Inside/Out: Lesbian Theories, Gay Theories*, ed. Diana Fuss (New York: Routledge, 1991), 113.

42. See, however, Jeffrey Masten, who reads the successful cure of the fistula (in, for example, Arderne's *Treatise on Fistula in Ano*) as another example of the ways that the anus figures in early modern culture not as Leo Bersani's "grave" but as the productive site for healthy evacuation ("Is the Fundament a Grave?" in *The Body in Parts*, 129–46).

43. Patricia Parker, "Gender Ideology, Gender Change: The Case of Marie-Germain," *Critical Inquiry* 19 (1993): 337–65.

44. Boorde, *Breuiary of Healthe*, 92–93.

45. See Stephen Orgel, *Impersonations* (Cambridge: Cambridge University Press, 1996).

46. Adelman, "Bed tricks," 160.

Chapter 4. The Subject of Touch: Medical Authority in Early Modern Midwifery

My thanks to Susan Greenfield, who always knows, far better than I, what it is I'm trying to say.

1. Edmund Chapman, *Essay on the Improvement of Midwifery* (London, 1733), 89. Further citations are given in the text.

2. James H. Aveling typifies this style. He has this to say about four men who practiced midwifery in the seventeenth century. William Harvey, Peter Chamberlen, William Sermon, and Percival Willughby were, he asserts, "men of high social and medical position. Had they considered the study and practice of midwifery beneath their dignity, how disastrous would it have been to English mothers, and who can say how much longer the dark ages of midwifery would have continued in this country" *English Midwives: Their History and Prospects* (London, 1872; rpt. London: Hugh K. Elliott, 1967), 46. More recently, see Edward Shorter, *Women's Bodies: A Social History of Women's Encounter with Health, Ill-Health, and Medicine* (New Brunswick, N.J.: Transaction Publications, 1990; first published 1982 as *A History of Women's Bodies*).

3. Typical of this mode is Barbara Ehrenreich and Deirdre English, *Witches, Midwives, and Nurses* (Old Westbury N.Y.: Feminist Press, 1973). For brief summaries of the extensive scholarship, see the introduction in Doreen Evenden, *The Midwives of Seventeenth-Century London* (Cambridge: Cambridge University Press, 2000), and the chapter on "Doctors and Women" in Dorothy Porter and Roy Porter, *Patient's Progress: Doctors and Doctoring in 18th-Century England* (Stanford, Calif.: Stanford University Press, 1989).

4. Lisa Cody, "The Politics of Reproduction: From Midwives' Alternative Public Sphere to the Public Spectacle of Man Midwifery," *ECS* 32, 4 (1999): 478.

5. Adrian Wilson, *The Making of Man-Midwifery: Childbirth in England, 1660–1770* (Cambridge, Mass.: Harvard University Press, 1995). See especially chap. 14.

6. Wilson, *Making of Man-Midwifery*, 181.

7. Evenden, *Midwives of Seventeenth-Century London*, 175.

8. Jane Sharp, *The Midwives Book* (1671), ed. Elaine Hobby (Oxford: Oxford University Press, 1999), 11–12. See also Eve Keller, "Mrs. Jane Sharp: Midwifery and the Critique of Medical Knowledge in Seventeenth-Century England" *Women's Writing* 2, 2 (1995): 101–11.

9. Sarah Stone, *A Complete Practice of Midwifery* (London, 1737), vii, x. Further citations are given in the text.

10. On the limited exposure of most male practitioners to normal deliveries, see Wilson, *Making of Man-Midwifery*, 47–59. This changed dramatically only after the mid-eighteenth century.

11. Percival Willughby, *Observations in Midwifery*, ed. Henry Blenkinsop (Warwick, 1863); facsimile reprint ed. John L. Thornton (Wakefield: S. R. Publishers, 1972), 88. Willughby's *Observations* was not published until the nineteenth century, but

it probably circulated in manuscript during Willughby's lifetime, and transcripts were likely made after his death. See Thornton's introduction to the facsimile edition, x–xiii.

12. For a detailed description of the role of male practitioners in the birthing room through the early eighteenth century, see Wilson, *Making of Man-Midwifery,* 47–59.

13. Stone, *Complete Practice,* xv.

14. Helen King, " 'As If None Understood the Art That Cannot Understand Greek': The Education of Midwives in Seventeenth-Century England," in *The History of Medical Education in Britain,* ed. Vivian Nutton and Roy Porter (Amsterdam: Rodopi, 1995), 189.

15. See, for example, Nicolas Culpeper, *A Directory for Midwives* (London, 1656), which includes prefaces by both Culpeper and his wife that testify to the authenticity of the many books he wrote and translated. On Culpeper generally, see F. N. L. Poynter, "Nicolas Culpeper and his Books," *Journal of the History of Medicine* 17 (1962): 152–67 and Poynter, "Nicolas Culpeper and the Paracelsians," in *Science, Medicine, and Society in the Renaissance,* ed. Allen Debus, 2 vols. (New York: American Elsevier, 1972), 1: 201–20.

16. See Susan Lawrence, *Charitable Knowledge: Hospital Pupils and Practitioners in Eighteenth-Century London* (Cambridge: Cambridge University Press, 1996), which explores the "interconnections among medical teaching, medical knowledge, and medical authority in eighteenth-century London" (n.p.).

17. For analyses of the vernacular medical texts of the period that attend in some way to matters of structure and style, see Robert Erickson, " 'The Books of Generation': Some Observations on the Style of the British Midwife Books, 1671–1764," in *Sexuality in Eighteenth-Century Britain,* ed. Paul-Gabriel Bouce (Manchester: Manchester University Press, 1982), 74–94; Mary E. Fissell, "Readers, Texts, and Contexts: Vernacular Medical Works in Early Modern England," in *The Popularization of Medicine 1650–1850,* ed. Roy Porter (London: Routledge, 1992), 72–97; Mary E. Fissell, "Gender and Generation: Representing Reproduction in Early Modern England," *Gender and History* 7, 3 (November 1995): 433–56; Isobel Grundy, "Sarah Stone: Enlightenment Midwife," in *Medicine in the Enlightenment,* ed. Roy Porter (Amsterdam: Rodopi, 1995), 128–145. Of these articles, Grundy's is the only one that examines an author's constructed persona.

18. Roy Porter, "The Rise of Physical Examination," in *Medicine and the Five Senses,* ed. W. F. Bynum and Roy Porter (Cambridge: Cambridge University Press, 1993), 182.

19. Porter, "Rise," 183.

20. Another reason physical examination was not deemed necessary for accurate diagnosis is that, within the context of humoral medicine, disease was understood to be caused by an imbalance of an individual's idiosyncratic humoral complexion, which itself was best determined by considering a person's complete lifestyle. See Lucinda Beier, *Sufferers and Healers: The Experience of Illness in Seventeenth-Century England* (New York: Routledge, 1987), 31ff.

21. On the permeability of boundaries between learned and popular medicine, see Andrew Wear, "Popularization of Medicine in Early Modern England," in *Popularization of Medicine*, ed. Roy Porter, 17–41. This list of kinds of practitioners comes from p. 19.

22. On the absence of physical contact between physician and patient, see Nicolson, "The Art of Diagnosis: Medicine and the Five Senses," in *Companion Encyclopedia of the History of Medicine*, ed. W. F. Bynum and Roy Porter, 2 vols. (London: Routledge, 1993) 2: 801–25, and S. J. Reiser, *Medicine and the Reign of Technology* (Cambridge: Cambridge University Press, 1978), 5–6. Also, Porter, "Rise," 180.

23. W. F. Bynum, "Health, Disease and Medical Care," in *The Ferment of Knowledge: Studies in the Historiography of Eighteenth-Century Science*, ed. G. S. Rousseau and Roy Porter (Cambridge: Cambridge University Press, 1980), 211–54.

24. Henry van Deventer, *The Art of Midwifery Improv'd*, trans. Robert Samber (London, 1716), A3v.

25. Adrian Wilson, "Participant Versus Patient: Seventeenth-Century Childbirth from the Mother's Point of View," in *Patients and Practitioners: Lay Perceptions of Medicine in Pre-Industrial Society*, ed. Roy Porter (Cambridge: Cambridge University Press, 1985), 129–44.

26. Although podalic version was known in ancient times, it was a technique apparently lost to the West until the sixteenth century, when Ambroise Paré reintroduced it into medical texts, but even after that, it only slowly entered vernacular medical literature.

27. On the association of male-midwifery and obscenity, especially in the later eighteenth century, see Roy Porter, "A Touch of Danger: The Man-Midwife as Sexual Predator," in *Sexual Underworlds of the Enlightenment*, ed. G. S. Rousseau and Roy Porter (Manchester: Manchester University Press, 1987), 206–32.

28. On Willughby's practice and that of his daughter, see Adrian Wilson, "A Memorial of Eleanor Willughby, a Seventeenth-Century Midwife," in *Women, Science and Medicine, 1500–1700: Mothers and Sisters of the Royal Society*, ed. Lynette Hunter and Sarah Hutton (Phoenix Mill: Sutton Publishing, 1997), 138–78. For details about the extant manuscripts and their publication, see Wilson, "A Memorial" and John L. Thornton's introduction to the facsimile reprint of Willughby's *Observations*.

29. William Giffard, *Cases in Midwifery*, ed. Edward Hody, MD (London, 1734), 47–49.

30. For additional women's responses in the eighteenth century to the rise of male-midwifery, see Elizabeth Nihell, *A Treatise on the Art of Midwifery* (London, 1766) and Martha Mears, *The Pupil of Nature* (London, 1797). On the accusation that male-midwifery was a lecher's sport, see Porter, "Touch of Danger."

Chapter 5. The Touching Organ: Allegory, Anatomy, and the Renaissance Skin Envelope

1. Helkiah Crooke, *Microcosmographia: A Description of the Body of Man Together with the Controversies Thereto Belonging* (London, 1615).

2. Valerie Traub has explored in compelling ways the confrontation between the anatomist and abjected cadaver he dissects. "Gendering Mortality in Early Modern Anatomies" in *Feminist Readings of Early Modern Culture: Emerging Subjects,* ed. Traub, M. Lindsay Kaplan, and Dympna Callaghan (Cambridge: Cambridge University Press, 1996), 44–92. In her examination of anatomical illustrations, she contends that anxieties about death and the dead body that the anatomist touches (and with which he may be identified) contribute to the gendering of knowledge. That the object of epistemological examination is feminized through a variety of aesthetic strategies works to secure the relative empowerment of the subject of investigation, the male anatomist. As she says, "early modern anatomical illustrations demonstrate the extent to which gender is reciprocally *manufactured* in order to defend against the vulnerability to mortality that all bodies share" (45). As we will see, this gendering of embodiment in anatomical representation is shared by allegorical theory, for both displace anxieties about the abjected, mortal, and material body onto a female principle.

3. Although Mondino dei Luizzi was said to have taught from a cadaver in Bologna in the early fourteenth century, the goal of his dissection was to illustrate Galen, and it is Andreas Vesalius who is credited with bringing together the hitherto distinct roles of *ostentor* and *sector* in the practice of anatomy. The title page of the *Fabrica* depicts for the first time in the history of anatomical illustration the teacher (Vesalius) dissecting the corpse. As this illustration and the portrait of Vesalius (the verso of the title page) demonstrate, the anatomist must be versed in both partitioning the cadaver and in describing what he reveals. See Andrea Carlino's analysis of anatomical iconography in *Books of the Body: Anatomical Ritual and Renaissance Learning* (1994; trans. John Tedeschi and Anne C. Tedeschi, Chicago: University of Chicago Press, 1999).

4. Crooke quotes the stanza from Spenser's Castle of Alma episode that describes the body in mathematical terms (2.9.22) in the twelfth book of the *Microcosmographia*; he describes his anatomical project as a mirror-image of the Spenser's knights' exploration of the body, and there are frequent allusions throughout his text. See Jonathan Sawday, *The Body Emblazoned: Dissection and the Human Body in Renaissance Culture* (London: Routledge, 1995), esp. 159–70.

5. Recurrent in the history of Western culture is the sometimes submerged but nevertheless enduring idea that touch is the "root" of the other senses, and further, that tactility is somehow synonymous with life itself. See Aristotle's discussion of touch in *De Anima,* 435b, *The Basic Works of Aristotle,* ed. Richard McKeon (New York: Random House, 1941), 533–603, and Gino Casagrande and Christopher Kleinhenz's analysis of St. Thomas Aquinas's reading of Aristotle in "Literary and Philosophical Perspectives on the Wheel of the Five Senses in Longthorpe Tower," *Traditio* 41 (1985): 311–27, 318.

6. Aristotle speculated on where the sensors of touch were located, whether subcutaneous or lying closer to the surface, and we might thus see touch not just as a property of skin but also of the flesh (*De Anima*, 422b–423a).

7. One of the notable studies on this topic is Katharine Eisaman Maus's book, *Inwardness and Theater in the English Renaissance* (Chicago: University of Chicago Press, 1995), which astutely examines the trope of the interior, its relation to a sense of self and to various dialectics of revelation and concealment in the subject (29). Michael Schoenfeldt in *Bodies and Selves in Early Modern England: Physiology and Inwardness in Spenser, Shakespeare, Herbert, and Milton* (Cambridge: Cambridge University Press, 1999) locates the notion of inwardness more resolutely in the body and in relation to a set of discourses about the body. His important book is in a sense corrective, for he sees the alimentary system and the trope of digestion at once as indicative of the Galenic regime and as governing the organization of the humoral body.

8. David Hillman, "Visceral Knowledge," in *The Body in Parts: Fantasies of Corporeality in Early Modern Europe*, ed. Hillman and Carla Mazzio (London: Routledge, 1997).

9. Hillman is of course correct in calling attention to the visual dimension of early modern anatomies. Vesalius speaks in the preface to the *Fabrica* about placing the parts of the bodies "before the eyes," but while he and other Renaissance anatomists do repeatedly invoke vision, this sense is crucially paired with touch from Galen to Crooke. Berengario da Carpi, for instance, says that what is required of a good anatomist is "*sight and touch*" (quoted in Carlino, *Books of the Body*, 25). Marjorie O'Rourke Boyle discusses Galen's description of touch in anatomy in *Senses of Touch: Human Dignity and Deformity from Michelangelo to Calvin* (Leiden: E.J. Brill, 1998, 143; as her analysis demonstrates, Galen both acknowledges the importance of tactility and locates its powers in the hand. This is a tradition that, as I will suggest, Crooke invokes, even as he also draws upon another, apparently contradictory tradition of tactility.

10. Andrea Carlino in *Books of the Body* analyzes this image as well as the title page of the *Fabrica*. In both, he emphasizes the novelty of the Vesalian method, which, contra Galen, insists on bringing together practical dissection and theoretical elaboration. In the foreground of the portrait both surgical instruments and writing materials are displayed, the two components essential to the production of the anatomical text (39–53).

11. Didier Anzieu, *The Skin Ego*, trans. Chris Turner (*Le Moi-peau*, 1985; New Haven, Conn.: Yale University Press, 1989, 13.

12. Casagrande and Kleinhenz point to a passage in *De Anima* where Aristotle makes touch the "paradigm and structure of the intellect" (321). If thought and perception are analogous, as Aristotle claims, then "We know the world around us because the mind is able to through touch to *grasp* the form of things" (321).

13. This is a translation of the Vulgate's "bitumen,"which appears in the Coverdale Bible (1535) and subsequently. There are six occurrences of "slime" in *The Faerie Queene*; all are found in the first three books, and all are used in relation to sexuality and procreation.

14. David Lee Miller discusses slime in *The Faerie Queene* in ways that emphasize disgust and misogyny, but he focuses on Errour and the resulting discourse of monstrosity. *The Poem's Two Bodies: The Poetic of the 1590 Faerie Queene* (Princeton, N.J.: Princeton University Press, 1988), 246–53. James W. Broaddus sees slime, as I do here, in its more generally beneficent fertility. *Spenser's Allegory of Love: Social Vision in Books III, IV, and V of* The Faerie Queene (London: Associated University Presses, 1995), 66–67.

15. Spenser, Edmund. *The Faerie Queene,* ed. Thomas P. Roche (New Haven, Conn.: Yale University Press, 1981).

16. See my discussion of the spider and web in the iconographic tradition in my introduction to this volume, "The 'Sense of All Senses.' "

17. Boyle, *Senses of Touch,* 159, n. 359.

18. Crooke tells us that Plato compares the system of pores in the skin to a fish net (*Microcosmographia,* 73).

19. Michael C. Schoenfeldt, *Bodies and Selves in Early Modern England: Physiology and Inwardness in Spenser, Shakespeare, Herbert, and Milton* (Cambridge: Cambridge University Press, 1999), 53.

20. To all these, Crooke assigns an essentially protective function. The "Scarfeskin" or cuticle defends the skin beneath from violence of injury, sucks up sweat, and turns the roughness of the skin into "one of the principall beauties of the body" (61). The skin beneath is "the wall of the Castle," the "*cutis*" (71), an "unseamed garment covering the whole bodie" (72), and it regulates temperature (a crucial function for the humoral body, whose health depends on its caloric economy) and cleanses superfluities. Next is the fat, which, like a pillow, plumps up the body, cushions the vessels, and acts as a storage system for nourishment in times of necessity. The innermost layer is the fleshy membrane or "avant Mure," a second defense system (61).

21. For a survey of the various traditions associated with the hand, including the mnemonic and the musical, see Claire Richter Sherman, *Writing on Hands: Memory and Knowledge in Early Modern Europe* (Carlisle, Pa.: Trout Gallery, Dickinson College and Folger Shakespeare Library, 2000).

22. The conjunction of instrumental hands and erect bipedality, an ancient commonplace, is the subject of Marjorie O'Rourke Boyle's study, *Senses of Touch.* She examines the vitality of this tradition in the Renaissance and Reformation with a particular emphasis on the visual arts. Her study is immensely valuable and learned, but the emphasis on the hand is, as I suggest, only one aspect (which, of course, comes to be the dominant signifier for touch after the Renaissance, and contributed to the primacy of vision) of the history of tactility.

23. As Katherine Rowe puts it, "the hand becomes the prominent vehicle for integrating sacred mystery with corporeal mechanism. . . . The dissection of the hand in particular, from Galen to the seventeenth century, persists as one of the central *topoi* of anatomy demonstrations: celebrated for its difficulty and beauty, it reveals God's intentions as no other part can." " 'God's Handy Worke' " in *Body in Parts,* ed. Hillman and Mazzio (London: Routledge, 1997), 287.

24. For a history of the representation of the body as house or castle, see Leonard Barkan, *Nature's Work of Art: The Human Body as Image of the World* (New

Haven, Conn.: Yale University Press, 1975). He cites exemplars of the body-castle trope that range from Plato's *Timaeus,* Lactantius, *Piers Plowman,* and most important, the New Testament (151–74). See also Louise Vinge, *The Five Senses: Studies in a Literary Tradition* (Lund: Royal Society of Letters at Lund, 1975), which surveys the figure in relation to the depiction of the five senses.

25. Kenelm Digby in his 1624 commentary on this stanza attempts to understand the ligature between the body and the soul in terms of Aristotelian generation: "as in corporall generations the female affords but grosse and passive matter, to which the Male gives active heat and prolificall vertue. . . . So there is betweene the bodie and soul of Man, but what ligament they have, our Author defineth not." *The Works of Edmund Spenser: A Variorum Edition, The Faerie Queene Book Two,* ed. Edwin Greenlaw et al. (Baltimore: Johns Hopkins University Press, 1933), 2: 475. See Michael Schoenfeldt's discussion of Digby's interpretation in *Bodies and Selves in Early Modern England* (55–57).

26. Gordon Teskey," Allegory, Materialism, Violence," in *The Production of English Renaissance Culture,* ed. David Lee Miller, Sharon O'Dair, and Harold Weber (Ithaca, N.Y.: Cornell University Press, 1994), 293–318; see also his *Allegory and Violence* (Ithaca, N.Y.: Cornell University Press, 1996).

27. See Schoenfeldt, *Bodies and Selves in Early Modern England,* 62–67 and Miller, *The Poem's Two Bodies,* 164–91.

28. Miller, *The Poem's Two Bodies,* 174–83, esp. 170, 174, 178.

29. For a discussion of the relationship between the skin and weaving, see my Introduction to this volume, " 'The 'Sense of All Senses.' "

30. Monica Green discusses the convergence of this tradition with treatises on the diseases of women in "From 'Diseases of Women' to 'Secrets of Women': The Transformation of Gynecological Literature in the Later Middle Ages," *Journal of Medieval and Early Modern Studies* 30, 1 (Winter 2000), 5–39.

31. John Banister, *The Historie of Man, sucked from the sappe of the most approve Anathomistes.* (London, 1578), fol. 88v.

32. Sawday, *The Body Emblazoned,* 176.

33. Marta Poggesi, "The Wax Figure Collection in 'La Specola' in Florence," in *Encyclopeaedia Anatomica* (Florence: Taschen for the Museo La Specola, 1999), 6–25, 21.

34. The three statues are allegorical representations of Painting, Sculpture, and Architecture. Vasari designed the monument, and each statue was completed by a Florentine sculptor (Battista, Giovanni dell' Opera, and Valerio Cioli). See Vasari's description of the monument in *Lives of the Artists,* trans. George Bull (New York: Penguin, 1965), 441–42.

35. His treatise on technical method was originally published as an introduction to his *Lives of the Artists* in 1550. My references are to *Vasari on Technique,* trans. Louisa S. Maclehose, ed. G. Baldwin Brown (New York: Dover, 1960).

36. Vasari says in his "Life of Michelangelo Buonarotti" that, when Michelangelo's corpse was carried to Santa Croce where it was to be interred, the coffin was opened. Although Michelangelo had then been dead for twenty-five days, his body showed no sign of decomposition, but was as "clean and intact" "as if he had died

only a few hours before." *Lives of the Artists,* 438. By contrast, Zumbo's open coffin reveals a rotting corpse.

37. Georges Didi-Huberman, "Wax Flesh, Vicious Circles," in *Encyclopeaedia Anatomica,* 64.

38. Poggesi, "The Wax Figure Collection," 12, 13.

39. Pliny, *Naturalis Historiae* 35.41–14; Polybius 6.53–54, quoted in Harriet I. Flower, *Ancestor Masks and Aristocratic Power in Roman Culture* (Oxford: Clarendon Press, 1996), 302–6, 308–10. See also J. M. C. Toynbee, *Death and Burial in the Roman World* (Ithaca, N.Y.: Cornell University Press, 1971). I am grateful to Michael Koortbojian for supplying references on this topic.

40. B. Lanza et al., "Historical Notes on Wax Modelling," in Rumy Hilloowala et al., *The Anatomical Waxes of La Specola,* trans. Joseph Renahan (Florence: Arnaud, 1995), 45–49, 45.

41. Sigmund Freud, "A Note upon the 'Mystic Writing-Pad'," in *On Metapsychology: The Theory of Psychoanalysis,* gen. ed. James Strachey, Penguin Freud Library, 11, ed. Angela Richards (Harmondsworth: Penguin, 1991), 428–34, 430. This observation is expanded in *Civilization and Its Discontents* to include the camera and gramophone as mnemonic extensions of the visual and auditory senses.

42. For a brief history of the use of anatomical models, see Rumy Hilloowala, "Anatomical Dissection and Models," in *Anatomical Waxes of La Specola.*

43. Ovid, *Metamorphoses,* trans. Frank Justus Miller, 2 vols., Loeb Classical Library (Cambridge, Mass.: Harvard University Press, 1916. rpt, 1977), 6: 385.

44. See Ludmilla Jordanova, *Sexual Visions* (Madison: University of Wisconsin Press, 1989) for a discussion of wax anatomical models in relation to art history and eighteenth-century gender politics.

Chapter 6. As Long as a Swan's Neck? The Significance of the "Enlarged" Clitoris for Early Modern Anatomy

An earlier version of this chapter was given at the conference, Virile Women, Consuming Men: Gender and Monstrous Appetite in the Middle Ages and the Renaissance, University of Wales, Aberystwyth, 25–27 April 2000. I am grateful to the participants for their comments, especially to Bettina Bildhauer, Ruth Evans, and Mary Nyquist. I thank Christina von Braun for inspiration.

The writing was supported by a research grant from the Senatsverwaltung für Arbeit, Soziales und Frauen, Berlin. Unless otherwise indicated, all translations are my own.

1. Thomas Bartholin, *Anatomia Reformata: ex Caspari Bartholini parentis Institutionibus, omnique recentiorum & propriis observationibus tertium ad sanguinis circulationem reformata* (Hagae-Comitis: Vlacq, 1660), 186; copy in Staatsbibliothek zu Berlin, Stiftung Preußischer Kulturbesitz.

2. Stephen Blancaert, *Reformirte Anatomie oder Zerlegung des Menschlichen*

Leibes, trans. Tobias Peucer (Leipzig: Moritz Georg Weidmann, 1691); copy in Staats-bibliothek zu Berlin, Stiftung Preußischer Kulturbesitz.

3. Bartholin, *Anatomia,* 186.

4. Adrianus Spieghelius, *Fabrica Corporis Humani Libri Decem* (Venice: E. Deuchin, 1627), 278; copy in Humboldt-Universität zu Berlin, Zweigbibliothek Wissenschaftsgeschichte.

5. Spieghelius, *Fabrica Corporis,* 278.

6. Valerie Traub, "The Psychomorphology of the Clitoris," *GLQ* 2 (1995): 81–113, 94. The reemergence of the "Tribade" in Europe is much more complicated and complex than I have suggested here. For a thorough discussion see Traub's essay and Katharine Park, "The Rediscovery of the Clitoris: French Medicine and the Tribade, 1570–1620," in *The Body in Parts: Fantasies of Corporeality in Early Modern Europe,* ed. H. David Hillman and Carla Mazzio (New York: Routledge, 1997), 171–93.

7. Bartholin, *Anatomia,* 186. Bartholin refers to the apostle Paul's remarks in Romans 1: 26: "Unde haec pars contemptus virorum dicitur." For the use of the term as synonym for clitoris see Park, "Rediscovery," 186.

8. Park, "Rediscovery," 186.

9. Traub, "Psychomorphology," 94.

10. See Park, "Rediscovery," 173 and Traub, "Psychomorphology," 98.

11. Park, "Rediscovery," 184.

12. Jane Davidson Reid, *Classical Mythology in the Arts, 1300–1990s* (New York: Oxford University Press, 1993), 2: 628–35.

13. Although anatomists did not relate their findings to contemporary art, there are in fact numerous invisible ties and negotiations between art and anatomy, especially concerning the representation of the female genitals; for a discussion of these negotiations see Bettina Mathes, "From Nymph to Nymphomania: 'Linear' Perspectives on Female Sexuality," in *The Arts of Science: Representations of the Natural World in Seventeenth-Century European and American Culture,* ed. Claire Jowitt and Diane Watt (Aldershot: Ashgate, 2002).

14. Bartholin, *Anatomia,* 149.

15. Thomas Bartholin, *Neu-verbesserte Kuenstliche Zerlegung deß Menschlichen Leibes,* trans. Elias Wallner (Nürnberg: Johann Hoffmann, 1677), 255; copy in Staats-bibliothek zu Berlin, Stiftun Preußischer Kullturbesitz, Abt. Historische Drucke.

16. Giulio Casserio, *Tabulae Anatomicae LXXIIX, omnes novae nec ante hac visae* (Venice: E. Deuchin, 1627); copy in Humboldt-Universität zu Berlin, Zweigbibliothek Wissenschaftsgeschichte.

17. The tables are grouped into ten books, each book dealing with the representation of a different bodily system. The well over a hundred figures—many plates contain more than one illustration—are accompanied by short verbal descriptions in Latin on the opposite pages. Casserio's volume was published together with Adrian Spieghel's *Fabrica corpore humani libri decem,* an anatomy book describing the function of the human body parts. Spieghel's book does not contain any illustrations. Although gathered in one volume, Spieghel's verbal descriptions and Casserio's engravings are separate works altogether, without references to one another.

18. Sander L. Gilman, *Sexuality, an Illustrated History: Representing the Sexual in Medicine and Culture from the Middle Ages to the Age of AIDS* (New York: Wiley, 1989), 127. On the popularity and meaning of metaphors of male motherhood in the early modern period see Elizabeth D. Harvey, "Matrix as Metaphor: Midwifery and the Conception of Voice," in *John Donne*, ed. Andrew Mousley (New York: St. Martin's Press, 1999), 135–56. See also Bettina Mathes, "Die Schönste der Nymphen: Verwandlungen weiblicher (Homo-)Sexualität," in *Geschlecht weiblich*, ed. Carmen Franz and Gudrun Schwibbe (Berlin: Edition Ebersbach, 2002). On the possibility of giving birth through the anus, see Eve Keller's chapter in this volume.

19. For a discussion of hermaphrodites in early modern medicine, see Lorraine Daston and Katharine Park, "The Hermaphrodite and the Orders of Nature: Sexual Ambiguity in Early Modern France," in *Premodern Sexualities*, ed. Louise Fradenburg and Carla Freccero (New York: Routledge, 1996), 117–36.

20. Jacques Lacan, "The Signification of the Phallus," in *Écrits: A Selection*, ed. and trans. Alan Sheridan (London: Tavistock, 1977), 281–91, 287.

21. For a feminist discussion of the phallus, see Jane Gallop, *Thinking Through the Body* (New York: Columbia University Press, 1988) and Elizabeth Grosz, *Jacques Lacan: A Feminist Introduction* (New York: Routledge, 1990).

22. Anna Bergmann discusses the different steps of abstraction that led to the emergence of this new rational body: "Töten, Opfern, Zergliedern und Reinigen in der Entstehungsgeschichte des Körpermodells," *metis: Zeitschrift für historische Frauenforschung und feministische Praxis* 11 (1997): 45–64.

23. Lacan, "Phallus," 283.

24. Christina von Braun, *Versuch über den Schwindel: Religion, Schrift, Bild, Geschlecht* (Zürich: Pendo, 2001), 140–42.

25. In her pathbreaking study *Nicht ich: Logik, Lüge, Libido* (Frankfurt am Main: Neue Kritik, 1985), Christina von Braun describes how the symbolic order created by the alphabet translated into real gendered bodies.

26. K. B. Roberts and J. D. W. Tomlinson, *The Fabric of the Body: European Traditions of Anatomical Illustrations* (Oxford: Clarendon Press, 1992), 128.

27. Ibid.

28. Andreas Vesalius, *De humani corpore fabrica Epitome: Von des menschen coerpers anatomey / ein kurtzer / aber fast nützer außzug*, trans. Albanus Torinus (Basel: Oporinus, 1543), 2.

29. Ibid.

30. Quoted in Katharine Rowe, " 'God's Handy Worke': Divine Complicity and the Anatomist's Touch," in *The Body in Parts*, ed. Hillman and Mazzio, 285–309, 293.

31. Roberts and Tomlinson, *Fabric*, 133.

32. Quoted in Rowe, "Handy Worke," 293. Helkiah Crooke, *Microkosmographia: A Description of the Body of Man Together with the Controversies Thereto Belonging* (London: John Clarke, 1615); copy in SUB Göttingen. References to Crooke in the text will be to Rowe's work.

33. Rowe, "Handy Worke," 285. Rowe has argued that the hand is embedded in a complex net of meanings. It is used to "signify effective, voluntary action and the

unity of parts" (299) as well as to fashion anatomy into a divine undertaking. She has also suggested that the treatment of the hand confounds the split between agent (anatomist) and anatomized cadaver.

34. Gilman, *Sexuality*, 148–60.

35. Cf. Rowe, "Handy Worke," 290.

36. Roberts and Tomlinson, *Fabric*, 208.

37. Ibid., 126.

38. Ibid., 137, 263.

39. Ibid., 104–11.

40. Quoted in ibid., 101.

41. Ibid.,104.

42. For a discussion of the cultural and corporeal implications of linear perspective and the perspectival gaze, see Norman Bryson, *Vision and Painting: The Logic of the Gaze* (London: Macmillan, 1983) and Martin Jay, *Downcast Eyes: The Denigration of Vision in Twentieth-Century French Thought* (Berkeley: University of California Press, 1993).

43. John Berger, *Ways of Seeing* (Harmondsworth: Penguin, 1972), 16.

44. On the practice of anatomical dissection in medieval medicine, see Nancy Siraisi, *Medieval and Early Renaissance Medicine: An Introduction to Knowledge and Practice* (Chicago: University of Chicago Press, 1990). For a more thorough discussion of the influence of linear perspective on anatomy, see Bettina Mathes, *Verhandlungen mit Faust: Geschlechterverhältnisse in der Kultur der Frühen Neuzeit* (Königstein/Ts.: Ulrike Helmer Verlag, 2001), 95–130.

45. The term "culture of dissection" was coined by Jonathan Sawday, *The Body Emblazoned: Dissection and the Human Body in Renaissance Culture* (London: Routledge, 1995), 3.

46. Sergei Lobanow-Rostovsky, "Taming the Basilisk," in *The Body in Parts*, ed. Hillman and Mazzio, 195–217, 200.

47. Berger, *Ways of Seeing*, 88.

48. Berger, *Ways of Seeing*, 90.

49. Christina von Braun, "Ceci n'est pas une femme: Betrachten, Begehren, Berühren—Von der Macht des Blicks," *Lettre International* 80 (1994): 80–84, 82.

50. Quoted in Sawday, *Body Emblazoned*, 196.

51. Sawday, *Body Emblazoned*, 197.

52. Gilman, *Sexuality*, 127.

53. Braun, "Ceci n'est pas une femme," 82.

54. Quoted in Thomas W. Laqueur, "Amor Veneris, vel Dulcedo Appeletur," in *Fragments for a History of the Body*, ed. Michel Feher, Ramona Nadaff, and Nadia Tazi (New York: Zone, 1989), 3: 90–131, 103.

55. Bartholin, *Anatomia*, 186.

56. Leo, Steinberg, *The Sexuality of Christ in Renaissance Art and Modern Oblivion*, 2nd ed., rev. and exp. (Chicago: University of Chicago Press, 1996), 86.

57. For an elaboration of this context see Mathes, *Verhandlungen mit Faust*, 91–94.

58. Spieghelius, *Fabrica*, 278; Crooke, *Microkosmographia*. See also Laqueur, "Amor Veneris," 110.

59. Crooke, *Mikrokosmographia*, 238.

60. Bartholin, *Zerlegung*, 254.

61. Laqueur writes: "It [the discovery of the clitoris] does not matter . . . because the dominant medical paradigm of his day held that there was only one sex anyway, differing only in the arrangement of a common set of organs. The problem in Columbus's day well into the seventeenth century was not finding the organic signs of sexual opposition but understanding heterosexual desire in the world of one sex. . . . But the clitoris was only a very small part of the problem, if a problem at all, when the entire female genitalia were construed as a version of the male's" ("Amor Veneris," 113). For a critique see Park, "Rediscovery," 187 and Traub, "Psychomorphology," 84.

62. Cf. Thomas Laqueur, *Making Sex: Body and Gender From the Greeks to Freud* (Cambridge, Mass.: Harvard University Press, 1990). The *two-sexed male body* is also visible in the common representation of vagina and uterus as penis. Thus, these images do not so much illustrate the prevalence of the one-sex body—as Laqueur suggests in *Making Sex*. Rather, they attest to the deeply rooted fantasy that man and woman become "one flesh"—with the male body serving as the role model for this "oneness." It would therefore be more accurate to talk about a *two-sexed male body*. Especially the images in anatomy books prove how much early modern anatomy was indebted to Christian ideas and traditions; cf. Gilman, *Sexuality*, passim.

63. Roberts and Tomlinson, *Fabric*, 246.

64. Park, "Rediscovery," 173.

Chapter 7. New World Contacts and the Trope of the "Naked Savage"

I wish to acknowledge both the generous support of the Ford Foundation, which made possible my research at the John Carter Brown Library, and the help and advice of Dr. Norman Fiering and the library staff.

1. Walter Ong, " 'I See What You Say': Sense Analogues of Intellect," in Ong, *Interfaces of the Word: Studies in the Evolution of Consciousness and Culture* (Ithaca, N.Y.: Cornell University Press, 1977), 121–44.

2. Ibid., 136.

3. Debora Shuger, *Habits of Thought in the English Renaissance: Religion, Politics, and the Dominant Culture* (Berkeley: University of California Press, 1990), 16.

4. Edward Morick, "Introduction," *Wittgenstein and the Problem of Other Minds*, ed. Edward Morick (New York: McGraw-Hill, 1967), xiv.

5. Hayden White, "The Noble Savage: Theme as Fetish," in *First Images of America*, ed. F. Chiappelli (Berkeley: University of California Press, 1976), 133.

6. Sir Thomas Browne attempts to dispel this belief in his comments on the subject in the *Pseudodoxia Epidemica*, bk. VI, chaps. 10, 11.

7. Aristotle, *Politics*, 1254b; quoted by Tzvetan Todorov in *The Conquest of America*, trans. Richard Howard (New York: Harper and Row, 1985), 152.

8. Stephen Greenblatt, *Marvelous Possessions* (Chicago: University of Chicago Press, 1991), 46.

9. Columbus, *The Four Voyages*, ed. and trans. J. M. Cohen (London: Penguin, 1969), 55.

10. Todorov, *The Conquest of America*, 36.

11. For an overview on the contested significance of nakedness in the western tradition see Margaret Miles, *Carnal Knowing: Female Nakedness and Religious Meaning in the Christian West* (Boston: Beacon Press, 1989) and Judy Kronenfeld, *King Lear and the Naked Truth: Rethinking the Language of Religion and Resistance* (Durham, N.C.: Duke University Press, 1998).

12. See John Moffitt and Santiago Sebastián, *O Brave New People: The European Invention of the American Indian* (Albuquerque: University of New Mexico Press, 1996), esp. 112–26 and Karen Kupperman, *Indians and English: Facing Off in Early America* (Ithaca, N.Y.: Cornell University Press, 2000), esp. 41–76.

13. See Kathleen Brown, "Native Americans and Early Modern Concepts of Race," in *Empire and Others: British Encounters with Indigenous Peoples, 1600–1850*, ed. Martin Daunton and Rick Halpern (Philadelphia: University of Pennsylvania Press, 1999), esp. 87–95. In this essay Brown discusses the often favorable reaction of the English to the physical characteristics of the Native Americans.

14. Quoted by Richard Halpern, " 'The Picture of Nobody': White Cannibalism," in *The Production of English Renaissance Culture*, ed. David Lee Miller, Sharon O'Dair, and Harold Wilson (Ithaca, N.Y.: Cornell University Press, 1994), 268.

15. William Brandon, *New Worlds for Old: Replofrts from the New World and Their Effect on the Development of Social Thought in Europe, 1500–1800* (Athens: Ohio University Press, 1986), 13.

16. Brandon, *New Worlds for Old*, 38.

17. Brandon, *New Worlds for Old*, 42.

18. See Margaret Healy, "Anxious and Fatal Contacts: Taming the Contagious Touch," this volume.

19. James Axtell, *Beyond 1492: Encounters in Colonial North America* (Oxford: Oxford University Press, 1992), 72. See also Jared Diamond, *Guns, Germs, and Steel: The Fate of Human Societies* (New York: W.W. Norton, 1997).

20. Claude Quétel, *History of Syphilis*, trans. Judith Braddock and Brian Pike (Cambridge: Polity Press, 1990).

21. Quétel. *History of Syphilis*, 35.

22. Roger Williams, *A Key into the Language of America* (1643), ed. John Teunissen and Evelyn Hinz (Detroit: Wayne State University Press, 1973), 185.

23. In regard to this seemingly double meaning we should note that a peasant standing shirtless before his lord might easily be described as "naked" without the implication that he is "stark naked." Such a distinction may offer a way of explaining the seeming paradox discussed by Margaret Ferguson in her engaging essay, "Feathers

and Flies: Aphra Behn and the Seventeenth-Century Trade in Exotica," in *Subject and Object in Renaissance Culture*, ed. Margreta de Grazia, Maureen Quilligan, and Peter Stallybrass (Cambridge: Cambridge University Press, 1996), 243.

24. Laurent Joubert, *Popular Errors*, trans. Gregory de Rocher (Tuscaloosa: University of Alabama Press, 1989), 102.

25. William Wood, *New England's Prospect* (1634), ed. A. T. Vaughan (Amherst: University of Massachusetts Press, 1977), 41. Cf. with Montaigne's statement in "Of Cannibals," "Those people are wild, just as we call wild the fruits that Nature has produced by herself and in her normal course; whereas really it is those that we have changed artificially and led astray from the common order, that we should rather call wild." *The Complete Essays of Montaigne*, trans. Donald Frame (Stanford, Calif.: Stanford University Press, 1958), 152.

26. Mary Fuller, *Voyages in Print: English Travel to America, 1576–1624* (Cambridge: Cambridge University Press, 1995), 122.

27. Majorie O'Rourke Boyle, *Senses of Touch: Human Dignity and Deformity from Michelangelo to Calvin* (Leiden: E.J. Brill, 1998), 67.

28. Michel de Montaigne, *The Essayes of Montaigne*, trans. John Florio (1603; New York: Modern Library, 1933), 1: xxxv, 178. "Je devisoy, en cette saison frileuse, si la façon d'aller tout nud de ces nations dernierement trouvée est une façon forcée par la chaude tempreture de l'air, . . . , ou si c'est l'originele des homes." Montaigne, *Œuvres complètes*, ed. Albert Thibaudet and Maurice Rat (Paris: Gallimard, 1962), 1: xxxvi, 221.

29. Montaigne, *Œuvres complètes*, 1: xxxvi, 221.

30. See Elizabeth D. Harvey, " 'The Sense of All Senses,' " this volume.

31. Montaigne, *Essayes*, trans. Florio, 1: xxxv, 179: "car, de ces nations qui n'ont aucune connoissance de vestements, il s'en trouve d'assises environs soubs mesme ciel que le nostre, et puis la plus delicate partie de nous est celle qui tient tousjours descouverte: les yeux, la bouche, le nez, les oreilles; à nos contadins, comme à nos ayeulx, la partie pectorale et le ventre." *Essais*, 1: xxxvi, 222.

32. For a broad ranging discussion of Native Americans brought to Europe and interest in their presence there, see Christian Feest, "Indians and Europe? Editor's Postscript," in *Indians and Europe: An Interdisciplinary Collection of Essays*, ed. Feest (Aachen: Rader-Verlag, 1987), 609–19.

33. Peter Martyr, *Decades*, trans. Richard Eden (London, 1577), vol. 1, bk. vi, fol. 31.

34. Henry Warner Bowden, *American Indians and Christian Missions: Studies in Cultural Conflicts* (Chicago: University of Chicago Press, 1981), 86–87.

35. Stephen Greenblatt, "Remnants of the Sacred in Early Modern England," in *Subject and Object*, ed. de Grazia et al., 344.

36. Tzvetan Todorov, *On Human Diversity*, trans. Catherine Porter (Cambridge, Mass.: Harvard University Press, 1993), 32–43.

37. Montaigne, *Essayes*, trans. Florio, 1: xxx, 167: "ill n'y avoit aucun mal de se servir de nostre charoigne à quoy que ce fut pour nostre besoin, et d'en tirer de la nouriture." *Essais*, 1: xxxi, 208.

38. Hiram Haydn makes an important distinction between what he calls the Classicists' Golden Age and the Naturalists' Golden Age. The former, he argues, is "al-

most exclusively interested in a picture of the courtly paradise, close to Spenser's Bower of Bliss in its ideal of unending sensual love and beauty," whereas the latter "is seriously concerned with presenting arguments for, and examples of, cultural, technological, economic, marital, juristic, and ethical primitivism." Hiram Haydn, *The Counter-Renaissance* (New York: Grove Press, 1950), 461–544, 505.

39. Montaigne, *Essayes,* trans. Florio, "The Author to the Reader," xxvii: "Mes defauts s'y liront au vif, et ma forme naïfve, autant que la reverence publique me l'a permis. Que si j'eusse esté entre ces nations qu'on dict vivre encore sous la douce liberté des premieres loix de nature, je t'asseure que je m'y fusse très-volontiers peint tout entier, et tout nud." *Essais,* "Au Lecteur," 2.

40. Montaigne, *Essayes,* trans. Florio, 3: viii, 840: "C'est toujours à l'homme que nous avons affaire, duquel la condition est merveilleusement corporelle." *Essais,* 3: viii, 909.

Chapter 8. Noli me tangere: *Colonialist Imperatives and Enclosure Acts in Early Modern England*

The authors wish to acknowledge the generous support of the Social Sciences and Humanities Research Canada Council. Lisa M. Smith would also like to thank Mary Nyquist, whose seminar on "Republicanism and Revolution" was an inspiration for this essay.

1. Genesis 3: 3, *The Geneva Bible: A Facsimile of the 1560 Edition,* intro. Lloyd E. Berry (Madison: University of Wisconsin Press, 1969).

2. Stephen Greenblatt, *Marvelous Possessions: The Wonder of the New World* (Chicago: University of Chicago Press, 1991).

3. Anthony Pagden, *Lords of All the World: Ideologies of Empire in Spain, Britain and France c. 1500–c.1800* (New Haven, Conn.: Yale University Press, 1995), 76–79.

4. Cristina Malcolmson, "The Garden Enclosed/The Woman Enclosed: Marvell and the Cavalier Poets," in *Enclosure Acts: Sexuality, Property, and Culture in Early Modern England,* ed. Richard Burt and John Michael Archer (Ithaca, N.Y.: Cornell University Press, 1994), 252.

5. Bruce McLeod, *The Geography of Empire in English Literature, 1580–1745* (Cambridge: Cambridge University Press, 1999), 123.

6. Edward W. Said, *Culture and Imperialism* (New York: Random House, 1993), 9.

7. On Milton and imperialism, see David Quint, *Epic and Empire: Politics and Generic Form from Virgil to Milton* (Princeton, N.J.: Princeton University Press, 1993), 268–324; for competing views on Milton's imperialism, see Balachandra Rajan and Elizabeth Sauer, eds., *Milton and the Imperial Vision* (Pittsburgh: Duquesne University Press, 1999).

8. John Milton, *Complete Poems and Major Prose,* ed. Merritt Y. Hughes (New York: Odyssey, 1957), 10: 303.

9. Philo Judaeus, *Questions and Answers in Genesis 1:35,* quoted in James L.

Kugel, "An Extra Proviso," *Traditions of the Bible: A Guide to the Bible as It Was at the Start of the Common Era* (Cambridge, Mass.: Harvard University Press, 1998), 102. Calvin, *Commentaries on the First Book of Moses Called Genesis* (c. 1555). Also see Arnold Williams, *The Common Expositor: An Account of the Commentaries on Genesis, 1527–1633* (Chapel Hill: University of North Carolina Press, 1948), 121.

10. Milton, *The Christian Doctrine*, in *Complete Prose Works of John Milton*, ed. Don M. Wolfe et al., 8 vols. (New Haven, Conn.: Yale University Press, 1953–82), 6: 353. All quotations to Milton's prose are taken from this edition, hereafter abbreviated *CPW*. As we indicate below, Ralph Austen in *A Treatise of Fruit-Trees* underscores this typological association in a seventeenth-century justification of land enclosures.

11. Rowland Watkyns, "The Gardener," *Flamma sine fumo* (1662), ed. Paul C. Davies (Cardiff: University of Wales Press, 1968), 98; "Chastity," 109.

12. Though many Catholic as well as Protestant writers assumed the destruction of Eden, Protestants were ready to assail the views of those writers who insisted on its existence. Joseph Ellis Duncan, *Milton's Earthly Paradise: Historical Study of Eden* (Minneapolis: University of Minnesota Press, 1972), 190–93.

13. Stephen Greenblatt, "Learning to Curse: Aspects of Linguistic Colonialism in the Sixteenth Century," in *First Images of America: The Impact of the New World on the Old*, ed. Fredi Chiappelli et al., 2 vols. (Berkeley: University of California Press, 1976), 2: 561–80; Greenblatt, *Learning to Curse: Essays in Early Modern Culture* (New York: Routledge, 1990).

14. Mary Douglas, *Purity and Danger: An Analysis of Concepts of Pollution and Taboo* (London: Routledge, 1966), 3.

15. Simon Schama, *The Embarrassment of Riches: An Interpretation of Dutch Culture in the Golden Age* (New York: Knopf, 1988), 104.

16. Paul Stevens, " 'Leviticus Thinking' and the Rhetoric of Early Modern Colonialism," *Criticism* 35, 3 (1993): 441–61, 458.

17. Stevens, " 'Leviticus Thinking', " 457.

18. See Patricia Seed's explication of the different cultural codes which were accepted by particular European nations as indicators of possession, *Ceremonies of Possession in Europe's Conquest of the New World, 1492–1640* (Cambridge: Cambridge University Press, 1995), 4–5, 9–10, 16–40.

19. J. R. Wordie persuasively argues that England became a mainly enclosed country during the seventeenth and not the eighteenth century. "Chronology of English Enclosure, 1500–1914," *Economic History Review* 36, 4 (November 1983): 494. The enclosure of royal lands in particular links the Christic *noli me tangere* with an exaltation of private property.

20. Andy Wood, *Riot, Rebellion, and Popular Politics in Early Modern England* (New York: Palgrave, 2002), 43, 83. John E. Martin notes that enclosures did not go unopposed, and cautions us against assuming that seventeenth-century enclosures were less oppressive than earlier ones. Martin, *Feudalism to Capitalism: Peasant and Landlord in English Agrarian Development*, Studies in Historical Sociology (London: Macmillan, 1983; reprint 1986), 139. See also Joan Thirsk, *Tudor Enclosures* (London: Historical Association, 1958; reprint 1965).

21. See E. C. K. Gonner, *Common Land and Inclosure*, intro. G. E. Mingay, 2nd

ed. (London: Frank Cass, 1966), 53–55. In the interregnum years, H. Halhead and John Moore were numbered among those who denounced enclosures; see H. Halhead, *Inclosure Thrown Open; or, Depopulation Depopulated* (1650), 8, 9; John Moore, *The Crying Sin of England of not Caring for the Poor, wherein Inclosure . . . is Arraigned . . .* (1653), 13, both quoted in Gonner, *Common Land and Enclosure*, 168.

22. Christopher Hill, *The World Turned Upside Down: Radical Ideas During the English Revolution* (London: Temple Smith, 1972), 16; J. A. Yelling, *Common Field and Enclosure in England, 1450–1850* (London: Macmillan, 1977), 233.

23. Karl Marx, *Capital: A Critique of Political Economy*, trans. Ben Fowkes, intro. Ernest Mandel (New York: Penguin, 1976), 1: 879.

24. *Light shining in Buckingham-shire, or, A discovery of the main grounds; originall cause of all the slavery in the world . . . Printed in the year 1648*, In *The Works of Gerrard Winstanley*, ed. George H. Sabine (Ithaca, N.Y.: Cornell University Press, 1941), 612, 611.

25. William C. Carroll, "The Nursery of Beggary": Enclosure, Vagrancy, and Sedition in the Tudor-Stuart Period," in *Enclosure Acts: Sexuality, Property, and Culture in Early Modern England*, ed. Richard Burt and John Michael Archer (Ithaca, N.Y.: Cornell University Press, 1994), 36.

26. McLeod, *Geography of Empire*, 80.

27. Henri Lefebvre, *The Production of Space*, trans. Donald Nicholson-Smith (Oxford: Blackwell, 1991), 36.

28. Malcolmson, "Garden Enclosed," 259.

29. Seed, *Ceremonies of Possession*, 24–25; Seed also notes that an obsolete meaning for "improve" is closely associated with enclosure acts. The term was "especially used of the lord's inclosing and bringing into cultivation of waste land" (*OED*).

30. Robert Gray, *A Good Speed to Virginia* (London, 1609), reprinted in *Early Accounts of Life in Colonial Virginia*, ed. Wesley F. Craven (New York: Scholars' Facsimiles and Reprints, 1937), sig. C3v–C4r.

31. John Winthrop, "General Considerations for the Plantation in New England . . ." (1629), in *Winthrop Papers*, ed. Allyn B. Forbes, 5 vols. (Boston: Massachusetts Historical Society, 1929–47), 2: 118, quoted in Gary B. Nash, *Red, White, and Black: The Peoples of Early America* (Englewood Cliffs, N.J.: Prentice-Hall, 1974), 80.

32. Warren M. Billings, *The Old Dominion in the Seventeenth Century: A Documentary History of Virginia, 1606–1689*, quoted in Seed, *Ceremonies of Possession*, 23.

33. Francis Bacon, "Of Gardens," in *The Essayes or Counsels, Civill and Morall* (1625; New York: Thomas Y. Crowell, 1901), 194, 190, 190, 189.

34. See Ralph Austen, *A Treatise of Fruit-Trees Together with The Spirituall Use of an Orchard* (Oxford, 1653), ed. John Dixon Hunt, The English Landscape Garden (New York: Garland, 1982).

35. Tom Williamson, "The Triumph of Geometry: c. 1680 to c. 1735," *Polite Landscapes: Gardens and Society in Eighteenth-Century England* (Stroud, Gloucestershire: Allan Sutton; Baltimore: Johns Hopkins University Press, 1995), 19–47, 19. Various designs for knots are depicted in John Marriott, *Certaine excellent and new inuented Knots and Mazes, for plots for Gardens . . .* (1618), ed. John Dixon Hunt, The English Landscape Garden (New York: Garland, 1982).

36. Gerrard Winstanley, *A declaration from the poor oppressed people of England . . . Printed in the yeer, 1649*, *The Works of Gerrard Winstanley*, ed. George H. Sabine (Ithaca, N.Y.: Cornell University Press, 1941), 276.

37. See John Milton, *Considerations Touching the Likeliest Means to Remove Hirelings . . .* , *CPW* 7: 296. In *Proposalls of Certaine Expedients for the Preventing of a Civill War*, Milton advised that the government provide for "the just division of wast Commons" (7: 338).

38. William Cronon, *Changes in the Land: Indians, Colonists, and the Ecology of New England* (New York: Hill and Wang, 1983), 22.

39. Chris Fitter, *Poetry, Space, Landscape: Toward a New Theory* (Cambridge: Cambridge University Press, 1995), 236.

40. J. M. Evans, *Paradise Lost and the Genesis Tradition* (Oxford: Clarendon Press, 1968), 249.

41. McLeod, *Geography of Empire*, 121.

42. *Reason of Church-Government*, *CPW* 1: 752.

43. Fitter, *Poetry*, 301.

44. See A. Bartlett Giamatti, *The Earthly Paradise and the Renaissance Epic* (Princeton, N.J.: Princeton University Press, 1966); Barbara Lewalski, *"Paradise Lost" and the Rhetoric of Literary Form* (Princeton, N.J.: Princeton University Press, 1985), chap. 7; Douglas Chambers, *The Planters of the English Landscape Garden: Botany, Trees and the Georgics* (New Haven, Conn.: Yale University Press, 1993); John Dixon Hunt, *Garden and Grove: The Italian Renaissance Garden in the English Imagination, 1600–1750* (1986; reprint Philadelphia: University of Pennsylvania Press, 1996).

45. Poetry itself was intended at this time to reproduce a "paradisal consciousness." Diane Kelsey McColley, *A Gust for Paradise: Milton's Eden and the Visual Arts* (Urbana: University of Illinois Press, 1993), 12.

46. Michael Drayton, "To the Virginian Voyage," in *The Works of Michael Drayton*, ed. J. William Hebel, 5 vols. (Oxford: Blackwell, 1961), 2: 363, line 24.

47. *Purchas His Pilgrimage* (London, 1613), 754.

48. James R. Siemon, "Landlord Not King: Agrarian Change and Interarticulation," in *Enclosure Acts: Sexuality, Property, and Culture in Early Modern England*, ed. Richard Burt and John Michael Archer (Ithaca, N.Y.: Cornell University Press, 1994), 24. The partitioning of space is not limited to the construction of Eden but becomes a cosmic principle defining God's act of creation. Acts of enclosure were justified by the principle of creating order from disorder and reforming "wild" "waste." The world comes into being, too, through a reformation of Chaos. God's creation is not ex nihilo but is accomplished through banishing Chaos and through circumscribing space. See PL 3.708–21; 7.216–75.

49. J. Martin Evans, *Milton's Imperial Epic: "Paradise Lost" and the Discourse of Colonialism* (Ithaca, N.Y.: Cornell University Press, 1996), 96.

50. Catherine Gimelli Martin, *The Ruins of Allegory* (Durham, N.C.: Duke University Press, 1998), 270–71.

51. Jeremy Cohen, *"Be Fertile and Increase, Fill the Earth and Master It": The Ancient and Medieval Career of a Biblical Text* (Ithaca, N.Y.: Cornell University Press, 1989), 310.

52. Seed, *Ceremonies of Possession,* 34.

53. Georgia Christopher, *Milton and the Science of the Saints* (Princeton, N.J.: Princeton University Press, 1982), 154.

54. Maureen Quilligan, "Freedom, Service, and the Trade in Slaves: The Problem of Labor in *Paradise Lost,*" in *Subject and Object in Renaissance Culture,* ed. Margreta de Grazia, Maureen Quilligan, and Peter Stallybrass (Cambridge: Cambridge University Press, 1996), 225.

55. Peter Stallybrass, "Patriarchal Territories: The Body Enclosed," in *Rewriting the Renaissance: The Discourses of Sexual Difference in Early Modern Europe,* ed. Margaret W. Ferguson, Maureen Quilligan, and Nancy J. Vickers (Chicago: University of Chicago Press, 1986), 127. The term "husband/ry" is significant in forging a link between men's marital and proprietary relations.

56. McLeod, *Geography of Empire,* 126.

57. Philip Gallagher, *Milton, the Bible, and Misogyny,* ed. Eugene R. Cunnar and Gail L. Mortimer (Columbia: University of Missouri Press, 1990), 92.

58. Paul Stevens, "*Paradise Lost* and the Colonial Imperative," *Milton Studies* 34 (1996): 7.

59. Douglas, *Purity,* 55–57; Lev. 11: 20–26.

60. Keith W. F. Stavely, *Puritan Legacies: "Paradise Lost" and the New England Tradition. 1630–1890* (Ithaca, N.Y.: Cornell University Press, 1987), 90–91. Also see Evans, *Imperial,* 232–34.

61. Evans, *Imperial Epic,* 232, 234.

62. Greenblatt, *Marvelous Possessions,* 20.

63. Wayne Franklin, *Discoverers, Explorers, Settlers: The Diligent Writers of Early America* (Chicago: University of Chicago Press, 1979), 22.

64. Patricia A. Parker, *Literary Fat Ladies: Rhetoric, Gender, Property* (London: Methuen, 1987), 148.

65. Williams, *Common Expositor,* 89; James Grantham Turner, *One Flesh: Paradisal Marriage and Sexual Relations in the Age of Milton* (Oxford: Oxford University Press, 1987), 299.

66. Elizabeth Sauer, *Barbarous Dissonance and Images of Voice in Milton's Epics* (Montreal: McGill-Queen's University Press, 1996), 122–23. On this passage, also see Balachandra Rajan, "Banyan Trees and Fig Leaves: Some Thoughts on Milton's India," in *Of Poetry and Politics: New Essays on Milton and His World,* ed. P. G. Stanwood (Binghamton, N.Y.: Medieval and Renaissance Texts and Studies, 1995), 223.

67. The idea for this essay was also inspired by the example of people who fight for justice today. At a conference on feminist spirituality, Maude Barlow (Chair of the Council of Canadians) presented "Will Women Save the Commons?" (London, Ontario, May 2000), in which she diagnosed the disease of our society—the privatization and the enclosure of the commons by a global economy. Ms Barlow expressed an urgent appeal to take back the commons from their enclosure.

Chapter 9. Acting With Tact: Touch and Theater in the Renaissance

I am deeply grateful for the thoughtful responses of William Ingram, Steven Mullaney, Joshua Scodel, Richard Strier, and Margaret Walsh. The English faculty at the University of Chicago and the Renaissance Colloquium at Northwestern University also provided helpful comments on an early draft, and the staff at the Huntington Library, where I researched the topic of touch, were a dream.

1. Jean-Luc Nancy, "Corpus," in *Thinking Bodies*, ed. Juliet Flower MacCannell and Laura Zakarin (Stanford, Calif.: Stanford University Press, 1994), 24.

2. William Perkins, *A direction for the government of the tongue according to Gods word* (Cambridge, 1593), 36.

3. On "interpretive literalism" and somatic symbolism, see Gail Kern Paster, "Nervous Tension," in *The Body in Parts: Fantasies of Corporeality in Early Modern Europe*, ed. David Hillman and Carla Mazzio (New York: Routledge, 1997), xx, 107–25.

4. Thomas Cooper, *Thesavrvs lingvae romanae & britannicae* (London, 1578), sv "Tango."

5. Didier Anzieu, *The Skin Ego*, trans. Chris Turner (*Le Moi-peau*, 1995; New Haven, Conn.: Yale University Press, 1989), 13.

6. Much recent scholarship on the symbolics of the hand in Renaissance literature has emphasized the hand as an instrument of reading (Peter Stallybrass), writing (Jonathan Goldberg), gesture (David Bevington), memory (Claire Richter Sherman), of labor, political agency, and contractual negotiation (Katherine Rowe). But the hand as an instrument often looks quite different when it is represented as a receptor of touch. See especially Katherine Rowe, *Dead Hands: Fictions of Agency, Renaissance to Modern* (Stanford, Calif: Stanford University Press, 1999), Jonathan Goldberg, *Writing Matter: From the Hands of the English Renaissance* (Stanford, Calif.: Stanford University Press, 1990); David Bevington, *Action Is Eloquence: Shakespeare's Language of Gesture* (Cambridge, Mass.: Harvard University Press, 1984); Claire Richter Sherman, *Writing on Hands: Memory and Knowledge in Early Modern Europe*, exhibition catalogue (Carlisle, Pa.; Trout Gallery, Dickinson College, and Folger Shakespeare Library, 2001); Peter Stallybrass, "How Many Hands Does It Take to Read (or Write) a Book," essay in progress.

7. Shakespeare, *Romeo and Juliet*, in *The Riverside Shakespeare*, 2nd ed., ed. G. Blakemore Evans (Boston: Houghton Mifflin, 1997), I.v.91–106.

8. Susan Stewart, *Poetry and the Fate of the Senses* (Chicago: University of Chicago Press, 2002), 165.

9. Stewart, *Poetry*, 165.

10. Anne Carson, *Eros the Bittersweet* (Normal, Ill.: Dalkey Archive Press, 1998), 136.

11. On hearing, see Bruce Smith, *The Acoustical World of Early Modern England* (Cambridge: Cambridge University Press, 1999). On vision, see Michael O'Connell, *The Idolatrous Eye: Iconoclasm and Theater in Early Modern England* (New York: Oxford University Press, 2000); Jonathan Sawday, *The Body Emblazoned:* (London: Routledge, 1995); Martin Jay, *Force Fields: Between Intellectual History and Cultural Critique* (New York: Routledge, 1993); and Barbara Freedman, *Staging the Gaze:*

Postmodernism, Psychoanalysis, and Shakespearean Comedy (Ithaca, N.Y.: Cornell University Press, 1991). On "audience" and "spectator," see Andrew Gurr, *Playgoing in Shakespeare's London* (Cambridge: Cambridge University Press, 1996), 86–105, and Jonathan Baldo, *The Unmasking of Drama: Contested Representation in Shakespeare's Tragedies* (Detroit: Wayne State University Press, 1997). On the interanimation (as opposed to the isolation) of vision and hearing in this period, see Elizabeth L. Eisenstein, *The Printing Press as an Agent of Change: Communications and Cultural Transformations in Early Modern Europe* (Cambridge: Cambridge University Press, 1979). For an earlier approach to the senses in Shakespeare, see Caroline Spurgeon, *Shakespeare's Imagery* (Cambridge: Cambridge University Press, 1935), which devotes twenty-two pages to vision and hearing, compared to one and a half on touch (57–78, 82–83).

12. Aristotle, *Nicomachean Ethics*, trans. J. A. K. Thomson, ed. Jonathan Barnes (London: Penguin, 1955), 1976. Touch and taste, writes Aristotle, are "are concerned with such pleasures as are shared by animals too (which makes them regarded as low and brutish)" (137). Touch is worthy of "reproach . . . because it attaches to us not as men but as animals. So to enjoy such sensations and find the greatest satisfaction in them is brutish" (137). For a recapitulation of vision as the "most precious, and the best . . . by it we learn and discern all things" and touch as the "most ignoble," see Robert Burton, *The Anatomy of Melancholy*, ed. Floyd Dell and Paul Jordan-Smith (London: Routledge, 1931), 138–39.

13. Much recent work on the body in contemporary literature and thought has integrated "touch" as a technology of body, mind, and culture: while Anzieu maps out a kind of thermal and tactual unconscious, other theorists of the body such as Jean Luc-Nancy and Elizabeth Gross have turned to "touch" as a rich and largely neglected technology of perception. See, for example, Elizabeth Grosz, *Volatile Bodies: Toward a Corporeal Feminism* (Bloomington: Indiana University Press, 1994); Luce Irigaray's seminal "The Sex Which Is Not One," in *New French Feminisms: An Anthology* (Amherst: University of Massachusetts Press, 1980); and Stewart, *Poetry and the Fate of the Senses*.

14. The editors, Margreta de Grazia, Maureen Quilligan, and Peter Stallybrass, ask a simple question that aims to complicate histories of the subject in Renaissance studies: "in the period that has from its inception been identified with the emergence of the subject: where is the object?" *Subject and Object in Renaissance Culture* (Cambridge: Cambridge University Press, 1996), 2.

15. Helkiah Crooke, *Mikrokosmographia: A Description of the Body of Man* (London, 1615). Citations will be given in the text.

16. This issue is still fully alive when Alexander Ross responds to ancient and contemporary medical writing in the mid-seventeenth century: "The sense of tact either hath no medium, or else we must make the skin the medium; and the flesh, membranes and nerves the organ." *Arcana microcosmi: or, The hid secrets of man's body discovered; in an anatomical duel between Aristotle and Galen* (London, 1651), 66. The singular use of "organ" to encapsulate such complex and individuated parts of the body speaks to the extent to which the triad of organ, object and medium, though insufficient, was nonetheless continually invoked to organize the sensory modes.

17. Burton, *The Anatomy of Melancholy,* 139.

18. The representation of the palace of touch in Phineas Fletcher's *The Purple Island* is relatively brief and vague in comparison with the other senses. Abram Barnett Langdale suggests that "Fletcher had no opportunity to be more courteous [in elaborating the specifics of both touch and taste], because touch and taste had to await Malpighi's microscope and genius," *Phineas Fletcher, Man of Letters, Science, and Divinity* (New York: Columbia University Press, 1937), 194; cited in Louise Vinge, *The Five Senses: Studies in a Literary Tradition* (Lund: Berlingska Boktryckeriert, 1975), 97.

19. For details on this morality drama, attributed to Jean Gerson and written between 1377 and 1384, see Vinge's text and informative note, *Five Senses,* 60, n.27.

20. Thomas Tomkis, *Lingua, or the Combat of the Tongue and the five Senses for Superiority* (London, 1607), ed. John Farmer (Amersham: Tudor Facsimile Reprints, 1913). Farmer alludes to the tradition of linking Tactus with Cromwell and notes the other editions that surfaced in 1610, 1617, 1622, 1623, and 1657. For a more reliable discussion of Cromwell as Tactus, interesting as a recasting of Cromwell's politics in terms of the character of touch, see Michael Russell, *The Life of Oliver Cromwell* (Edinburgh: Constable, 1829). A newly edited and annotated edition of *Lingua* is now underway.

21. See, for example, Leonard Hutton, *Bellum Grammaticale* (Oxford, 1583). Hutton's drama was based on Andreas Guarna's *Bellum Grammaticale* (Cremona, 1511), which was translated into English by William Hayward as *Bellum Grammaticale: A Discourse of Gret War and Dissention betweene Two Worthy Princes, the Noune and the Verbe* (London, 1576). For "Pathopolis," see *Pathomachia: or, The Battel of Affections* (London, 1630), which is about the banishment of affection, and *Fallacy; or, The Troubles of Great Hermenia* (Oxford, 1610).

22. "A Twellfe Night Merriment. Anno 1602," was renamed *Narcissus* by its nineteenth-century editor, Margaret L. Lee. For details about the play, see Frederick S. Boas, *University Drama in the Tudor Age* (Oxford: Clarendon Press, 1914).

23. Boas, *University Drama,* 281.

24. Patricia Parker, "On the Tongue: Cross Gendering, Effeminacy, and the Art of Words," *Style* 23 (1989): 445–63.

25. On touch in Aristotle as a "contact" sense, see Richard Sorabji, "Aristotle on Demarcating the Five Senses,"in *Articles on Aristotle,* ed. Jonathan Barnes, Malcolm Schofield, and Richard Sorabji, vol. 4, *Psychology and Aesthetics* (New York: St. Martin's Press), 76–92.

26. On the medium as the message, see Marshall McLuhan, *The Gutenburg Galaxy* (Toronto: University of Toronto Press, 1962).

27. Malcolm McCullough, *Abstracting Craft: The Practiced Digital Hand* (Cambridge, Mass: MIT Press, 1996), 130.

28. David Howes, "Sensorial Anthropology," in *Varieties of Sensory Experience: A Sourcebook in the Anthropology of the Senses,* ed. Howes (Toronto: University of Toronto Press, 1971), 167–91, 185. As Howes points out, sight and hearing have taken up most of the conceptual space in theories of sense perception in American and European societies. This is due not simply to the famed denigration of touch in the Western philosophical tradition, but also, I want to suggest, to the particular analytic

lens within which systems of sensory dominance are often detected. As the term "sense-ratio" might imply (*ratio* meaning "a count"), this model is implicitly biased against, at the very least one of the senses, the sense of touch. If touch it resists quantification, how could it possibly measure up to the standards of rational inquiry? "Touch," despite its minimal quantitative content, *did* mean in the Renaissance, "to test" (hence "touchstone" as a commonplace for locus of meaning or truth). What I want to do here is to put touch back into the test, and see what happens when touch is factored into the "ratio" of sense, particularly in the domain of theater. For if, as theorists of communications have often suggested, the English Renaissance witnessed a shift of "sense ratios" from a predominantly audile-tactile model of orality to a predominantly visual-analytic model of writing and print, one might consider the place of the theater at this particular moment in the history of mediation. On the shifting sensorium as a measure of communications, see Walter Ong, "The Shifting Sensorium," in *Varieties of Sensory Experience*, ed. Howes, 25–30.

29. On the conceptual structure of the senses in relation to these basic analogical systems, see Vinge, *Five Senses*, 11. Interestingly, in Aristotle's *De sensu*, the disequilibrium between the elements of sense (five) and the elements of the natural world (four) is of some concern to Aristotle, but, as Vinge notes, he quickly reconciles this by simply conflating taste and touch, which are both aligned with the earth (17).

30. This infinite divisibility of the senses dramatizes a classical paradox whereby indivisible properties of thinking and judging are inextricably linked with infinitely divisible sensory perceptions. See Aristotle, *De Anima* (esp. 427a–b).

31. Marshall Grossman, *The Story of All Things: Writing the Self in English Renaissance Narrative Poetry* (Durham, N.C.: Duke University Press, 1998), 154.

32. As Aristotle writes, "For if touch is not one sense, but several, there must be several kinds of tangibles. It is difficult to say whether touch is one sense or more than one, and also what the organ is which is perceptive of the object of touch.... For every sensation appears to be concerned with one pair of contraries, e.g., vision is of white and black, hearing of high and low pitch, and taste of bitter and sweet; but in the tangible there are many pairs of contraries, hot and cold, wet and dry, hard and soft, and all other like qualities" (*De Anima*, 422b, 18–28). This, the touch that is not one, clearly complicates matters of classification. As such, despite Aristotle's analytical attempts to find the necessary "solution" for this problematic sense, he finds more and more "problems" posed by the protean and mysterious tactual realm. Ultimately, the sense of touch for Aristotle is the one sense necessary for all the others to function.

33. Phineas Fletcher, *The Purple Island* (1633), in *The Poems of Phineas Fletcher*, ed. Alexander B. Grosart (London: 1869), Canto 2, st. 31. On the dual sense of "lingua" in *The Purple Island* and other Renaissance texts concerned with the material dimensions of language, see my "Sins of the Tongue," in *The Body in Parts*, ed. Hillman and Mazzio, 52–79.

34. Aristotle, *Nicomachean Ethics*, 137.

35. In fact, Aristotle ultimately affirmed the senses of taste and touch "are proved two, because they are not convertible" (*De Anima*, 423a 21–22).

36. Aristotle, *Nicomachean Ethics*, 137.

37. On the relationship between tasting and touching the fruit, see Marjorie O'Rourke Boyle, "Eve's Palm," in *Senses of Touch: Human Dignity and Deformity from Michelangelo to Calvin*, Studies in Medieval and Reformation Thought 71 (Leiden: E.J. Brill, 1998), 90–171.

38. In slightly different terms, that optic window to the soul was also, of course, a particularly vulnerable muscle subject to involuntary motion: to describe the glazy look of love, Jaques Ferrand draws on Andre du Laurens, nothing that "our Moderne Anatomists call that Muscle, which is the Instrument by which this Love-looke is caused, *Musculus Amorosus*." Ferrand, *Erotomania, A Treatise Discoursing of the Essence, Causes, Sumptomes, Prognosticks, and Cure of Love or Erotique Melancholy* (Oxford, 1640), 107.

39. John Davies, *Nosce Teipsum*, in *The Complete Poems of Sir John Davies*, ed. A. B. Grosart (London, 1876), 67. In *The Purple Island*, Fletcher writes of the faculty of selective hearing that "Admits what best he likes, shuts out the rest," but this sense is vulnerable nonetheless to "oylie flatteries" that physically affect and caress the interior of the otherwise rational and discriminating man. On the symbolic and material dimensions of the ear, see Joel Fineman, "Shakespeare's Ear," *Representations* 28 (1985): 6–13 and Vinge, *Five Senses*, 97.

40. Francis Bacon, "Against Duelling," in *The Philosophical Works of Francis Bacon, Baron of Verulam, &c. Methodized and made English from the Originals*, ed. Peter Shaw, 2nd ed. (London, 1737), 1: 397.

41. Shakespeare, *The Winter's Tale*, in *The Arden Shakespeare*, ed. J. H. P. Pafford (London: Methuen, 1963).

42. The passage continues: "And that vast gaping of the Firmament, / Vnder the Southerne pole, is nothing else, / But the great hazzard of their Tennis Court; / The Zodiack is the line; The shooting Starres, / Which in an eye-bright euening seem'd to fall, /Are nothing but the Balls they loose at Bandy" (Sig. E2).

43. David Hillman, "Visceral Knowledge," in *The Body in Parts*, ed. Hillman and Mazzio, 81–105.

44. For a series of these "self-figuring" anatomical figures, see Sawday, *Body Emblazoned*, 38–39. On the optical fantasies of knowing oneself, see Sawday's opening chapter, "The Autopic Vision," 1–15.

45. Sawday, *Body Emblazoned*, 18.

46. Burton, *Anatomy of Melancholy*, 137.

47. Francis Bacon, *Sylva Sylvarum* (London, 1627), 198.

48. This shift in imagination from the body as a perceptive organism to a body subject to hurt, with pain now defining individuated parts, is parodied in a stage direction where hearing and smelling enter at each others "throats": enter "Avditvs, *pulling* Olfactvs *by the nose*, and Olfactvs *wringing* Auditvs *by the eares*": "AVD: Oh mine eares, mine eares, mine eares. / OLF: Oh my nose, my nose, my nose "(Sig. K3). Even "*Visus* hath broke his fore-head against the oake yonder" (Sig. K3). In a flash these disintegrating senses are "bound" by Somnus, the immobilizing force of sleep and dream. Indeed, any merit to Tactus's resistance to rational, quantitative, and in-

deed scopic regimes is undermined by the localization of touch in the manifestly vulnerable body. When Tactus sobers up, he explains to Common Sense that it was the
wine that "made our braynes, somewhat irregular" (Sig. M3).

49. Stephen Gosson, *The Schoole of Abuse* (London, 1579); reprinted in *Early Treatises on the Stage* (London: Shakespeare Society, 1853), 22.

50. From the French "*flatar;* the primary meaning of this word is believed to be 'to flatten down, smooth'; hence 'to stroke with the hand, caress' " (*OED,* sv. "Flatter").

51. Gosson, *Schoole of Abuse,* 22.

52. Ibid., 25.

53. Aristotle, *Nicomachean Ethics,* 137.

54. George Chapman, *The Iliads of Homer prince of poets Neuer before in any languag truely translated. With a co[m]ment vppon some of his chiefe places; donne according to the Greeke by Geo: Chapman* (London, 1611), xix, 77 (see *OED, sv.* "Touch," 17a).

55. Browne, Sir Thomas. *Pseudodoxia Epidemica,* 2nd ed. (London, 1650), 224.

56. Smith, *Acoustical World,* 101.

57. Thomas Blount, *Glossographia: or A Dictionary Interpreting the Hard Words of Whatsoever Language, now used in our refined English Tongue,* 4th ed. (London, 1674).

58. Thomas Cooper, *Thesaurus linguae Romanae et Britannicae* (London, 1578), *sv.* "Os."

59. Richard Brathwait, *Essaies vpon the five senses, revived by a new supplement; with a pithy one upon detraction. Continued vvith sundry Christian resolves, and divine contemplations, full of passion and devotion; purposely composed for the zealously-disposed* (London, 1635), 37.

60. Gosson, *Schoole of Abuse,* 25.

61. John Northbrooke, *A Treatise Against Dicing, Dancing, Plays, and Interludes* (c. 1577), in *Early Treatises on the Stage* (London: Shakespeare Society, 1853), 94–95.

62. Northbrooke, *Treatise,* 88.

63. Aristotle, *Nicomachean Ethics,* 137.

64. John Milton, *Paradise Lost,* ed. G. K. Hunter (Boston: Allen and Unwin, 1982), 8.579–82.

65. Lactantius, *Divinae Institutiones,* in *Caeli Firmiani Lactani Opera Omnia,* ed. Samuel Brandt and Georgius Laubmann (1893), chap. 23, cited in Vinge, *Five Senses,* 36. The "touch of death" might be located in moral and religious context, but also in the structure of language itself. Early etymologies of tactile pleasure fore-grounded mortal danger as both a moral and material phenomenon. As Varro writes, "*Lubere,* 'to be pleasing' is said from *labi* 'to slip,' because the mind is *lubrica* 'slippery' and *prolabitur* 'slips forward,' as of old they used to say. From *lubere* 'to be pleasing' comes *libido* 'lust,' *libidinosus* 'lustful,' and Venus *Libentina* 'goddess of sensual plea-sure' and *Libitina* 'goddess of the funeral equipment.' " The lexical root of pleasure is slippery, where at the mere slip of the tongue the venereal becomes the funereal. Varro, *De Lingua Latina,* trans. Roland C. Kent (Cambridge, Mass: Harvard Univer-sity Press, 1951), 215.

66. Thomas Lodge, "The Causes and Cures of the Plague" (1605), in *The Complete Works of Thomas Lodge* (New York: Russell and Russell, 1963), 4: 12.

67. Shakespeare, *The Tragicall Historie of Hamlet Prince of Denmarke, As it hath beene diuerse times acted by his Highnesse seruants in the Cittie of London: as also in the two Vniuersities of Cambridge and Oxford, and else-where* (London, 1603), Sig. D3. Other citations from *Hamlet* are from the Arden Edition, ed. Harold Jenkins (London: Routledge, 1982).

68. For an illustrated history of the relationship between hands, books, and memory systems, see Sherman, *Writing on Hands.*

69. On the possibility that this soliloquy is *read* from a book, see Margreta de Grazia, "Soliloquies and Wages in the Age of Emergent Consciousness," *Textual Practice* 9, 1 (1995): 67–92, 74.

70. "Touching" was used interchangeably with terms for "concerning" and "of," as in Bacon's *A Briefe Discovrse, Touching the Happie Vnion of the Kindomes of England, and Scotland (1603),* or his *Considerations Touching A Warre With Spaine* (1629). The contemporary analogue to this use of "touching" is now generally "with regard to" or "with respect to," both visual rather than tactile metaphors of cognitive contact or relevance more generally.

71. Thomas Kyd, *The Spanish Tragedy,* ed. J. R. Mulryne (London: A & C Black, 1989), see 1602 additions, 129.

72. This shift is in many ways analogous to what Rosalie Colie termed the process of "unmetaphorization" in Shakespearean drama, where cliches and symbols become animated as part of the theatrical action. What is striking is the attention in Renaissance drama to the specifically sensory dimensions of this process: unmetaphorization is also a form of tactually imagined materialization. Indeed, it might well be said that tragic drama itself is marked by a trajectory of "touch" from a metaphoric, mobile and emotional phenomenon to touch as acute bodily pain. See Colie, *Shakespeare's Living Art* (Princeton, N.J.: Princeton University Press, 1974).

73. Shakespeare, *King Lear,* ed. Kenneth Muir, Arden Shakespeare (London: Methuen, 1964).

74. John Goodman, *The penitent pardoned, or, A discourse of the nature of sin, and the efficacy of repentance: under the parable of the prodigal son* (London, 1679).

75. Nicholas Ling, *Politeuphia. Wits Common wealth* (London, 1598).

76. Thomas Cooper, *Thesaurus,* sv. "Tango."

77. Alexander Ross, *Arcana microcosmi.* As the epigraph to this essay reads: Of all the creatures, the sense of tact is most exquisite in man."

Chapter 10. Living in a Material World: Margaret Cavendish's The Convent of Pleasure

1. Jonathan Bennett, "Locke's Philosophy of Mind," in *The Cambridge Companion to Locke,* ed. Vere Chappell (Cambridge: Cambridge University Press, 1994).

2. Margaret Cavendish, *Philosophical and Physical Opinions* (London, 1655) let-

ter 36. I cite from the following editions of Cavendish's works: *The Philosophical Opinions, Written by Her Excellency the Lady Marchionesse of Newcastle* (London: J. Martin and J. Allestrye, 1655); *The Worlds Olio, Written by the Right Honorable, the Lady Margaret Newcastle* (London: J. Martin and J. Allestrye, 1655); *Philosophical Letters, or, Modest reflections upon some opinions in natural philosophy maintained by several famous and learned authors of this age, expressed by way of letters, By theThrice Noble, Illustrious, and Excellent Princess the Lady Marchioness of Newcastle* (London: A. Warren for J. Martyn, 1664); *Observations on Experimental Philosophy to which is added The Description of a NewBlazing World* (London: A. Maxwell, 1666); *Poems and Fancies Written by the Right Honourable, the Lady Margaret Newcastle* (London: J. Martin and J. Allestrye, 1653); *Sociable Letters,* ed. James Fitzmaurice (New York: Garland, 1997); *The Description of a New World, called the Blazing World and Other Writings,* ed. Kate Lilley (New York: New York University Press, 1992); and *The Convent of Pleasure and Other Plays,* ed. Anne Shaver (Baltimore: Johns Hopkins University Press, 1999). I have used the three modern editions for references to *Sociable Letters, The New World, called the Blazing World,* and *The Convent of Pleasure;* all other references come from the first editions cited above.

3. René Descartes, *Meditations on First Philosophy,* ed. Stanley Tweyman (New York: Routledge, 1993), 6.91. Citations are from this edition.

4. Carolyn Merchant's *The Death of Nature: Women, Ecology, and the Scientific Revolution* (San Franscico: Harper and Row, 1980) traces the demise of "organic cosmology" in which a feminine world of matter as described in Platonic and later Aristotelian terms gives way to a mechanized, passive, and inanimate matter which nonetheless retains its feminine associations in this modern world view. See also Susan Bordo, *Flight to Objectivity: Essays on Cartesianism and Culture* (Albany: State University of New York Press, 1987), 97–118.

5. My argument here is informed by Bordo's more psychoanalytically nuanced reading of gender in Cartesian thought. See esp. chap. 6, "The Cartesian Masculinization of Thought and the Seventeeth-Century Flight from the Feminine."

6. On June 10, 1643, Princess Elizabeth wrote "il est pourtant très difficile à comprendre qu'une âme, comme vous l'avez décrite, après avoir eu la faculté et l'habitude de bien raisonner, peut perdre tout cela par quelques vapeurs, et que pouvant subsister sans le corps et n'ayant rien de commun avec lui." See *Correspondance, publiée, avec une introduction et des notes,* vol. 5, ed. Ch. Adam and G. Milhaud (Paris: Presses Universitaires de France, 1951), 316.

7. I am endebted to the work of Albert A. Johnstone for drawing the correspondence of Elizabeth of Bohemia to my attention. See Johnstone, "The Bodily Nature of the Self, or What Descartes Should Have Conceded Princess Elizabeth of Bohemia," in *Giving the Body Its Due,* ed. Maxine Sheets-Johnstone (Albany: State University of New York Press, 1992), 16–47.

8. Jay Stevenson, "The Mechanist-Vitalist Soul of Margaret Cavendish," *SEL* 36, 3 (1996): 527–43, 532.

9. Eve Keller, "Producing Petty Gods: Margaret Cavendish's Critique of Experimental Science," *ELH* 64, 2 (Summer 1997): 457, 451.

10. Peter A. Schouls, *The Imposition of Method: A Study of Descartes and Locke* (Oxford: Oxford University Press, 1980), 5.

11. *The Conway Letters: The Correspondence of Anne, Viscountess of Conway, Henry More, and Their Friends, 1642–1684,* ed. Marjorie Hope Nicolson (New York: Oxford University Press, 1992).

12. Quoted in Douglas Grant, *Margaret the First: A Biography of Margaret Cavendish, Duchess of Newcastle, 1623–1673* (London: Hart-Davis, 1957), 24, from Public Records Office document SPD 29/450.

13. Valerie Traub, "The (In)significance of Lesbian Desire in Early Modern England," in *Erotic Politics: Desire on the Renaissance Stage,* ed. Susan Zimmerman (New York: Routledge, 1992), 156. For a perspective on the political and social issues of male cross-dressing and the emergence of sexual identity in British society through molly house culture, see Randolph Trumbach, "The Birth of the Queen: Sodomy and the Emergence of Gender Equality in Early Modern Culture, 1660–1750," in *Hidden from History: Reclaiming the Gay and Lesbian Past,* ed. Martin Bauml Duberman, Martha Vicinus, and George Chauncey, Jr. (New York: New American Library, 1989) and "Sodomitical Subcultures, Sodomitical Roles, and the Gender Revolution of the Eighteenth Century," in *'Tis Nature's Fault: Unauthorized Sexuality During the Enlightenment,* ed. Robert Maccubin (New York: Cambridge University Press, 1987), 109–21.

14. Cavendish, "To the Readers," *Playes* (London: J. Warren for John Martyn, James Allestry, and Tho. Dicas, 1662), A5.

15. Michael McKeon, building on analyses of gender from Thomas Laqueur, Michel Foucault, and Nancy Armstrong, elaborates this line of argument in "Historicizing Patriarchy: The Emergence of Gender Difference in England, 1660–1760" *Eighteenth-Century Studies* 28, 3 (Spring 1995): 295–322.

16. Judith Drake, *An Essay in Defense of the Female Sex* (London: A. Roper and E. Wilkinson, 1696; reprint New York: Source Book Press, 1970), and Mary Astell, "Reflections on Marriage," (London, 1700), reprinted in *Astell: Political Writings,* ed. Patricia Springborg (Cambridge: Cambridge University Press, 1996).

17. Michael McKeon's "Historicizing Patriarchy," which works from very different material to the same theoretical conclusion, maps the persistence of the structures of patriarchy through the development of the modern sex/gender system and modern sexual identities, in particular the construction of the "sodomite" as a category of being.

18. Catherine Stimpson, "Zero Degree Deviance: The Lesbian Novel in English," *Critical Inquiry* 3 (1981): 365, and, in response, Valerie Traub, "The (In)Significance" and Lisa Moore, *Dangerous Intimacies: Toward a Sapphic History of the British Novel* (Durham, N.C.: Duke University Press, 1997).

19. Laura Rosenthal, *Playwrights and Plagiarists in Early Modern England* (Ithaca, N.Y.: Cornell University Press, 1996), 58–104, and Theodora A. Jankowski, "Pure Resistance: Queer(y)ing Virginity in William Shakespeare's *Measure for Measure* and Margaret Cavendish's *The Convent of Pleasure,*" *Shakespeare Studies* 26 (1998): 218–55; see also Jankowski, *Pure Resistance: Queer Virginity in Early Modern English Drama* (Philadelphia: University of Pennsylvania Press, 2000).

20. Luce Irigaray, "The Mechanics of Fluids," 111 and "When Our Two Lips Speak Together," 205–18 in *This Sex Which Is Not One,* trans. Catherine Porter with Carolyn Burke (Ithaca, N.Y.: Cornell University Press, 1985).

21. For further information on the life of Margaret Cavendish, see Grant, *Margaret the First;* Kathleen Jones, *A Glorious Fame: The Life of Margaret Cavendish, Duchess of Newcastle, 1623–1673* (London: Bloomsbury, 1988), and Anna Battigelli, *Margaret Cavendish and the Exiles of the Mind* (Lexington: University Press of Kentucky, 1998).

22. The duchess identified deeply with Newcastle's military persona, conflating it with Plutarch's life of Caesar, which led her to wish "that Nature and Fate had made me such a one as he was; and sometimes I have the Courage, as to think I should not be afraid of his Destiny, so I might have as great a Fame" (*Sociable Letters,* 52). She dedicated her highly imaginative *Life* of Newcastle to Charles II as a reproach for exiling Newcastle from the court.

23. Cavendish, *Playes, Never Before Printed* (London: A. Maxwell, 1668).

24. See Catherine Gallagher, "Embracing the Absolute: The Politics of the Female Subject in Seventeenth-Century England," *Genders* 1 (Spring 1988): 24–39.

25. Battigelli, *Margaret Cavendish,* 11–14.

26. My thanks to Julie Crawford for graciously sharing her work on Henrietta Maria and Margaret Cavendish. For additional historical documentation of Henrietta Maria's involvement with the convent, see Runar Strandberg, "Études et Documents: Sainte-Marie de Chaillot d'après des documents inédits," *Bulletin de la Société de l'Histoire de l'Art Français* (1970): 189–201, and Marie-Ange Duvignacq-Glessgen, "La Visitation de Chaillot au XVIIe siècle: Splendeurs et tribulations d'un monastère dans le siècle," *Dix-Septième Siècle* 41, 4 (1989): 383–400, and Crawford's forthcoming "Convents and Pleasures: Margaret Cavendish and the Drama of Property."

27. Merchant, *Death of Nature,* 169–70, and Bordo, *Flight to Objectivity,* 81, 109.

28. Victoria Kahn, "Margaret Cavendish and the Romance of Contract," *Renaissance Quarterly* 50, 2 (1997): 526–66, 557.

29. Maria Lynn Cioni discusses this influence in *Women and the Law in Elizabethan England with Particular Reference to the Court of Chancery,* Garland Economic History Series (New York: Garland, 1985). See also Amy Louise Erickson, *Women and Property in Early Modern England* (London: Routledge, 1993) and Susan Staves, *Married Women's Separate Property in England, 1660–1833* (Cambridge, Mass.: Harvard University Press, 1990), 29–37, 196–230.

30. Rosenthal, *Playwrights and Plagiarists,* 92–94.

31. For example, *Love's Adventures* flouts convention in its 33 scenes without subdivisions.

32. Cavendish, Notice to Readers in *Playes.*

33. Kahn, in "Margaret Cavendish," argues that Cavendish's preoccupation with marriage did not reflect merely (or even necessarily) heterosexual ends so much as the political stop-gap to the Hobbsean exchange of obedience for protection, which dissolves if the sovereign can no longer provide protection.

34. Linda R. Payne, "Dramatic Dreamscapes: Women's Dreams and Utopian Vi-

sion in the Works of Margaret Cavendish, Duchess of Newcastle," in *Curtain Calls: British and American Women and the Theater, 1660–1820,* ed. Mary Anne Schofield and Cecilia Macheski (Athens: Ohio University Press, 1991).

35. Mihoko Suzuki makes a similar point in "Margaret Cavendish and the Female Satirist," *SEL* 37 (1997): 483–500, 494.

36. Keller, "Producing Petty Gods," 458.

37. Thomas Laqueur makes this argument in his influential *Making Sex: Body and Gender from the Greeks to Freud* (Cambridge, Mass.: Harvard University Press, 1990).

38. In "Historicizing Patriarchy," McKeon summarizes the implications of his argument: "the difference between men and women, although complex and problematic, is nonetheless understood as what renders the system systematic" (301). And later, "the empiricist insistence on a radical separation of subject from object enacts its wholesale repudiation of tacit knowledge. The separation isolates what is known from the familiar and customary matrix of its intelligibility" (303).

39. Donoghue points out the Ovidian echo from the story of Iphis and Ianthe in *Passions Between Women: British Lesbian Culture, 1668–1701* (New York: Harper-Collins, 1995), 229.

40. On the inscription of female same-sex desire as a legal/critical lack in Renaissance culture, see Traub, "The (In)Significance," 150–69.

41. Jacqueline Pearson, *The Prostituted Muse: Images of Women and Women Dramatists, 1642–1737* (New York: Harvester Wheatsheaf, 1988), 142.

42. Gilbert and Gubar use her as a madwoman figure in *The Madwoman in the Attic: The Woman Writer and the Nineteenth-Century Literary Imagination* (New Haven, Conn.: Yale University Press, 1979), 62–63. Douglas Grant (1957) Marjorie Nicolson (1948), Angeline Goreau (1983), and, most famously, Virginia Woolf (1929) have all intimated that Cavendish was insane or became insane over the course of her life. Payne overviews their positions in "Dramatic Dreamscapes."

43. See Johnstone, "The Bodily Nature of the Self" and Carol Pateman, *The Sexual Contract* (Stanford, Calif.: Stanford University Press, 1988).

Chapter 11. Touch in the Hypnerotomachia Poliphili: *The Sensual Ethics of Architecture*

1. See Liane Lefaivre, *Leon Battista Alberti's Hypnerotomachia Poliphili: Re-Cognizing the Architectural Body in the Early Italian Renaissance* (Cambridge, Mass.: MIT Press, 1997), 12–18. See also Marco Ariani and Mino Gabriele, "Le illustrazioni," in their critical edition and commentary, Francesco Colonna, *Hypnerotomachia Poliphili* (Milan: Adelphi Edizion, 1998), 2: xcv-cix. This is the edition used in the present study; it is cited by their page numbering.

2. See Lefaivre, *Alberti's Hypnerotomachia,* 10–12. And see Maurizio Calvesi, *Il sogno di Polifilo prenestino* (Roma: Officina, 1980), 71, 314; see also Peter Dronke, "Introduction," *Hypnerotomachia Poliphili,* ed. Dronke (Zaragoza: Ediciones del Por-

tico, 1981), 18ff; Giovanni Pozzi and L. A. Ciapponi, eds., *Hypnerotomachia Poliphili* (Padova: Editrice Antenore, 1980), vol. 2 for the classical texts cited in the *Hypnerotomachia Poliphili*.

3. See Lefaivre, *Alberti's Hypnerotomachia*, 34–40. See also Stefano Borsi, *Polifilo architetto: cultura architettonica e teoria artistica nell'Hypnerotomachia Poliphili di Francesco Colonna* (Roma: Officina, 1995), 9.

4. See Lefaivre, *Alberti's Hypnerotomachia*, 10.

5. Lefaivre, *Alberti's Hypnerotomachia*, 76.

6. See Lefaivre, *Alberti's Hypnerotomachia*, 262, n. 39.

7. The eroticism of the *Hypnerotomachia Poliphili* has generally been regarded as typical of the "paganized" Neoplatonism of the late fifteenth century. See, for example, Edgar Wind, *Pagan Mysteries of the Renaissance* (London: Faber, 1958), 45. Ariani recognizes, however, that the sensualism of the *Hypnerotomachia Poliphili* goes beyond that of the Neoplatonism of Plotinus or Proclus because there is no Platonic abandonment of sensual knowledge in the *Hypnerotomachia Poliphili*. See Marco Ariani, "Il sogno filosofico," in *Hypnerotomachia Poliphili*, ed. Ariani and Gabriele, 2: l, lii–liii. Though he regards Aristotelian ethics as an important source for the *Hypnerotomachia Poliphili*, Ariani sees the book's sensualism as the combined result of two influences specific to the Renaissance, Lucretian naturalism and late antique mystery literature (see xv, xxxvii, lvi–lxi). There are those who have noted the scholastic character of the *Hypnerotomachia Poliphili*'s spiritual quest, including Ariani. However, it is not generally linked to the book's eroticism. See Pozzi, 45–46 and Ariani, lviii–lxi and Pozzi, *Hypnerotomachia Poliphili*, ed. Pozzi and Ciapponi, 45–46.

8. See Ariani, "Il sogno filosofico," lix; Wind, *Pagan Mysteries*, 45; see also Leonard Barkan, *The Gods Made Flesh* (New Haven, Conn.: Yale University Press, 1986), 171–72, 226–28, who goes on to note that this sensualism was grounded in systems of thought already established during the later Middle Ages, an approach that tempers the impulse to overinterpret the uniqueness of Renaissance eroticism. See, for example, Lefaivre, *Alberti's Hypnerotomachia*, 76.

9. Jill Kraye, "Moral Philosophy," in *Cambridge History of Renaissance Philosophy*, ed. C. B. Schmitt and Quentin Skinner (Cambridge: Cambridge University Press, 1988), 303–4.

10. For the influence of the *Nicomachean Ethics* on Dante, see A. J. Minnis and A. B. Scott, *Medieval Literary Theory and Criticism, c.1100–c.1375: The Commentary Tradition* (Oxford: Oxford University Press, 1988), 380; for its influence on the tradition of the allegorical dream vision, see Rosamond Tuve, *Allegorical Imagery: Some Medieval Books and Their Posterity* (Princeton, N.J.: Princeton University Press, 1966), 67–77; Ernest Sirluck, "The *Faerie Queene*, Book II and the *Nicomachean Ethics*," *Modern Philology* 49, 2 (1951): 73–95; Louise Vinge, *The Five Senses: Studies in a Literary Tradition* (Lund: CWK Gleerup, 1975), 81; for its influence on the *Hypnerotomachia Poliphili*, see Ariani, "Ilsogno filosofico," xxxviii. See also Frances Yates, *The French Academies of the Sixteenth Centuries* (London: Warburg Institute, 1947), 110–16.

11. See A. C. Spearing, *Medieval Dream Poetry: Sources and Analogies* (Cambridge: Cambridge University Press, 1976); K. L. Lynch, *The High Medieval Dream Vision* (Stanford, Calif.: Stanford University Press, 1988).

12. See Ariani, "Il sogno filosofico," xlix and Dronke, "Introduction," 26.

13. See Jonathan Barnes, *Aristotle* (Oxford: Oxford University Press, 1982), 57–58; David Summers, *The Judgment of Sense: Renaissance Naturalism and the Rise of Aesthetics* (Cambridge: Cambridge University Press, 1987), 75–89. See also Lynch, *Dream Vision*, 29, 57–60.

14. Gordon Leff, *Medieval Thought, St. Augustine to Ockham* (Harmondsworth: Penguin, 1958), 47–50.

15. See Lynch, *Dream Vision*, 52–64.

16. See Lynch, *Dream Vision*, 57–60, 77. See also Winthrop Wetherbee, *Platonism and Poetry in the Twelfth Century* (Princeton, N.J.: Princeton University Press, 1972), 74ff; Paul Piehler, *The Visionary Landscape: A Study in Medieval Allegory* (Montreal: McGill-Queen's University Press, 1971), 46.

17. See Lynch, *Dream Vision*, 26–34 and Étienne Gilson, *The Philosophy of St. Thomas Aquinas*, trans. Edward Bullough (Cambridge: Cambridge University Press, 1924), 9. Also see Lynch, 60–64 for a discussion of the general move toward a more precise psychology in allegorized literature of the period.

18. Aquinas, *Summa theologiae*, Blackfriar's ed. and trans. (New York: McGraw-Hill, 1964–76), Ia, 79, 2. See also Ia, 88, 3 and Frederick C. Copleston, *Aquinas: An Introduction to the Life and Work of the Great Medieval Thinker* (1955; rpt. London: Penguin, 1991), 27–29.

19. "Ma sta cu laeto aio & da opa apiacer, cb la tua dilecta Polia la ritroverai" (1: 84). See also 1: 128, where Reason explains to Poliphilo that sensual perception gives enjoyment to the intellect.

20. See 1: 367, where Poliphilo describes himself dying after being physically unified with Polia. See also 1: 455, where Poliphilo describes his own death because of Polia's cruelness.

21. Barnes, *Aristotle*, 65–68; Copleston, *Aquinas*, 30, 156–63.

22. See Copleston, *Aquinas*, 166–78; Herbert McCabe, "The Immortality of the Soul," in *Aquinas: A Collection of Critical Essays*, ed. Anthony Kenny (Notre Dame, Ind.: University of Notre Dame Press, 1969), 297–306; Kraye, "Moral Philosophy," 349ff. And see Caroline Walker Bynum, *The Resurrection of the Body in Western Christianity, 200–1336* (New York: Columbia University Press, 1995).

23. For the difference between Thomistic thought and Platonic mysticism on the possibility of divine knowledge, see Steven Payne, *John of the Cross and the Cognitive Value of Mysticism* (Dordrecht: Kluwer Academic Publishers, 1990), 27–29, 47, n. 19. For the position of Averroes and Avicenna on direct knowledge of universals, see Mary Carruthers, *The Book of Memory: A Study of Memory in Medieval Culture* (Cambridge: Cambridge University Press, 1990), 56, 303, n.39. See also Anthony Kenny, "Intellect and Imagination in Aquinas," in *Aquinas*, ed. Kenny, 273–96; Edward Mahoney, "Sense, Intellect, and Imagination in Albert, Thomas, and Siger," in *The Cambridge History of Late Medieval Philosophy* (Cambridge: Cambridge University Press, 1982), 611. I would like to thank Robert Sweetman for alerting me to his article "Love, Understanding, and the Mystical Knowledge of God," in *Saints and the Sacred*, ed. Joseph, Geering, Francesco Guardiani, and Giulio Silano, St. Michael's College Series 3 (New York: Legas, 2001).

24. See, for example, Lynch, *Dream Vision,* 46–112; Minnis and Scott, *Medieval Literary Theory and Criticism,* 373–82; Mark Musa "Introduction," Dante Alighieri, *The Divine Comedy,* trans. Musa (Harmondsworth: Penguin, 1984), 28; Étienne Gilson, *Dante and Philosophy* (New York: Harper and Row, 1963).

25. Copleston, *Aquinas,* 199–219; Alan Donagan, "Thomas Aquinas on Human Action," in *Cambridge History of Late Medieval Philosophy,* ed. Norman Kretzmann, Anthony Kenny, and Jan Pinbourg (Cambridge: Cambridge University Press, 1982), 642–54. For the recovery of the *Nicomachean Ethics* in the later Middle Ages, see George Wieland, "The Reception and Interpretation of Aristotle's *Ethics,*" in *Cambridge History of Late Medieval Philosophy,* 657–72; also articles by Wieland, "Happiness: The Perfection of Man," 673–86; J. B. Korolec, "Free Will and Free Choice," 629–41. See also Kraye, "Moral Philosophy," 326–29.

26. Aristotle, *Nicomachean Ethics,* trans. Terence Irwin (Indianapolis: Hackett, 1985), 1177a10–1178a5.

27. See T. J. Tracy, *Physiological Theory and the Doctrine of the Mean in Plato and Aristotle* (The Hague: Mouton, 1969), 228.

28. Aristotle, *Nicomachean Ethics,* 1104b14–15; Tracy, *Physiological Theory,* 227–37. See also Kraye, "Moral Philosophy," 330–42 and Martha Nussbaum, *The Fragility of Goodness: Luck and Ethics in Greek Tragedy and Philosophy* (Cambridge: Cambridge University Press, 1986), 264–89.

29. Aristotle, *Nicomachean Ethics,* 1103a15–1107a; Tracy, *Physiological Theory,* 227–29.

30. See 1: 30, where Poliphilo describes having his emotions overly aroused by the sensual stimulation received from various artworks and buildings. See also 1: 57, 74, 78, 101, 110.

31. See 1: 57, where Poliphilo describes being overcome with the sensual pleasure he feels when looking at ancient ruins. See also 1: 61, 67, 101, 109. And see Lefaivre, *Alberti's Hypneromachia,* 63, who notes the extremes of Poliphilo's attractions and avoidances in the book; and Ariani, "Il sogno filosofico," xlvii.

32. See 1: 151, where Poliphilo describes suppressing his voluptuous urgings. See also 1: 150–52.

33. See, for example, 1: 136, where Poliphilo's Will tells him that he is not yet ready for the path of pure contemplation; also 1: 134, where Poliphilo's Reason interprets hieroglyphs that read "Blessed are those who hold to the mean."

34. See Lynch, *Dream Vision,* 148–60. See also Dronke, "Introduction," 18; Ariani, "Il sogno filosofico," xxxvi, xxxviii.

35. "Offuscare gia principiato havendo el mio intellecto, de non potere cognoscere, & nubilare gli sentimenti, quale optione eligere dovesse, over la odibile morte oppetere, overe nellombrifeo & opaco luco nutante sperare salute" (1: 15)

36. Aristotle, *De Anima,* trans. D. W. Hamlyn (Oxford: Clarendon Press, 1968), 413b4–9, 434b11–24, 435b3–25.

37. See Tracy, *Physiological Theory,* 194–212.

38. Aristotle, *De partibus animalium,* trans. William Ogle (New York: Garland, 1987), 650b35, 665a11–13, 667a4–7; Tracy, *Physiological Theory,* 188–96, 245–61.

39. This kind of equilibrium is also the model for the function of all the sense

organs, another reason touch had a particular value in Aristotelian physiology. See Tracy, *Physiological Theory*, 207–12.

40. "Et postala nella sua, strengerla sentiva tra calda neve, & in fra coagulo lacteo. Et parve ad me imo cusi era de attingere & attrectare pur altro che cosa di coditione humana" (1: 149).

41. See 1: 151–52; see also Barnes, *Aristotle*, 32–36, 68.

42. R. D. Hale, " 'Taste and See, for God Is Sweet': Sensory Perception and Memory in Medieval Christian Mystical Experience," in *Vox Mystica: Essays on Medieval Mysticism in Honour of Professor Valerie M. Lagorio*, ed. A. C. Bartlett (Cambridge: D.S. Brewer, 1995), 5.

43. "Quivi fervida mete tacto di piacevoli ardori, paulatini vegetantese in cominciorono di riscaldare & succendere la frigida paura & lalterato calore ad uno amore sincero dispositivamente adaptare" (1: 150).

44. Aristotle, *De partibus animalii*, 650b35; Tracy, *Physiological Theory*, 254–21.

45. See Anthony Kenny, *Aristotle's Theory of the Will* (London: Duckworth, 1979); T. H. Irwin, "Aristotle on Reason, Desire and Virtue," *Journal of Philosophy* 72 (1975): 567–78.

46. See Tracy, *Physiological Theory*, 183–90; Anthony Kenny, *Aquinas on Mind* (London: Routledge, 1993), 59–74; Paul Wadell, *The Primacy of Love: An Introduction to the Ethics of Thomas Aquinas* (New York: Paulist Press, 1992), 57–62, 79–92.

47. See Copleston, *Aquinas*, 202–4.

48. Carruthers, *Book of Memory*, 49–60; Kenny, "Intellect and Imagination," 273–96; Kenny, *Aquinas on Mind*, 89–99.

49. Aquinas also followed Aristotle in his idea that these syntheses are turned into universal concepts through the activity of two distinct intellects, the active and passive intellects. See *Summa*, Ia, 84, 6–a, 85, 1.

50. See Carruthers, *Book of Memory*, 17–18, 22, 27–28, 73, 78, 94–95, 242, 281, 292. Also see Summers, *Judgment of Sense*, 32–41.

51. See Aquinas, *De Malo*, trans. John Oesterle (Notre Dame, Ind.: University of Notre Dame Press, 1995) 16, 8, ad 3. See also M. D. Chenu, *La Théologie au douzième siècle* (Paris: J. Vrin, 1957), 159–90 and *Nature, Man and Society: Essays on New Theological Perspectives in the Latin West*, trans. Jerome Taylor and L. K. Little (Chicago: University of Chicago Press, 1968), 99–145.

52. Aquinas, *Summa*, IaIIae, 28, 1.

53. Aquinas, *Summa*, IaIIae, 4, 5.

54. Aquinas, *Summa*, IaIIae, 28, 1.

55. Copleston, *Aquinas*, 88–97.

56. See Wadell, *Primacy of Love*, 63–105; see also Josef Pieper, *Guide to Thomas Aquinas* (New York: Pantheon Books, 1962).

57. See J. P. Levina, *A Philosophy and Psychology of Sensation, with Special Reference to Vision According to the Principles of St. Thomas Aquinas* (Washington, D.C.: Catholic University of America, 1941), 38–49. See also Carruthers, *Book of Memory*, 304, n. 49 and Kenny, *Aquinas on Mind*, 31–40.

58. Aquinas, *Summa*, Ia, 78, 1.

59. Aquinas, *Summa*, Ia, 78, 1. See also Carruthers, *Book of Memory*, 54. For how

this was not the case for the other lower senses, hearing, smelling, or tasting, see again Aquinas, *Summa,* Ia, 78, 1.

60. See 1: 361, where Poliphilo describes his union with Polia. For another case where touch is the turning point in a journey of knowledge, see Vinge, *Five Senses,* 109 and Vinge's discussion of George Chapman's *Ovid's Banquet of Sence.* See also Vigne, "Chapman's *Ovid's Banquet of Sense:* Its Sources and Themes," *Journal of the Warburg and Courtauld Institutes* 38 (1975): 249–50. Vinge also notes in *Five Senses,* 104 that, according to Mario Equicola's *Di Natura d'Amore,* touch yields the highest pleasure of all the senses, the pleasure of coition. See also Lactantius, *Divinae institutiones,* VI, in his *Opera omnia,* vol. 1, PL (Paris, 1844), col. 705 for an early medieval example of touch as the sense of the libido, as cited in Sander Gilman, "Touch, Sexuality and Disease," in *Medicine and the Five Senses,* ed. W. F. Bynum and Roy Porter (Cambridge: Cambridge University Press, 1993), 201.

61. Aquinas, *Summa Contra Gentiles,* trans. A. C. Pegis (Notre Dame, Ind.: University of Notre Dame Press, 1975), 1: 91; Aquinas, *In Dionysii De divinis nominibus* (Taurini: Marietti, 1950), IV, lect. 12. See also Evelyn Underhill, *Mysticism: A Study in the Nature and Development of Man's Spiritual Consciousness* (1930; rpt. London: Methuen, 1967), 413–43; R. Garrigou-Lagrange, *Christian Perfection and Contemplation According to St. Thomas Aquinas and St. John of the Cross,* trans. Timothea Doyle (St. Louis: Herder, 1937).

62. Aquinas, *Summa,* IaIIae, 28, 2, 3, 3, 5.

63. Wieland, "Reception," 680.

64. "Perche no lice, ne permesso e ad gli ochii corporali diva formositate debbi apparere" (1: 122).

65. Aristotle, *Nicomachean Ethics,* 1096b; Aquinas, *Summa,* Ia, IIae, 1, 7. See also Copleston, *Aquinas,* 202–4.

66. See, for example, Ariani, "Il sogno filosofico," 2: xl, xli, and Ariani and Gabriele, notes 724, n. 4, 764–69, n. 5, who regard Poliphilo's choice of the way of love as a choice opposed to the intellectualism of Aristotelian, Stoic, and Christian/ scholastic ethics. They rather regard Poliphilo's choice of *voluptas* as Epicurean, an interpretation that supports the idea that Colonna was introducing something new and of an especially "Renaissance" nature, since the rediscovery of Epicurus was a Renaissance phenomenon most often associated with the thought of Lorenzo Valla. Ariani also recognizes that there were precedents for Poliphilo's choice of love in the courtly tradition. However, he does not consider how this tradition might have fitted with the scholastic conception of love as an ethical necessity or how Poliphilo's choice of love as the middle way is able to reflect the scholastic recognition of the necessity of striking the mean in our appetites as a way of approaching God. Striking the appropriate balance in love is again represented in the *Hypnerotomachia Poliphili* in the painting of the lovers who love either too much or too little; see 1: 249–51. Those who love too little are too cold to move in the direction of goodness. Those who love too much are too hot to act with reason. See also Dronke, "Introduction," 37.

67. See Lefaivre, *Alberti's Hypnerotomachia,* 76.

68. See D. M. Ferrara, *Imago Dei: Knowledge, Love, and Bodiliness in the Summa Theologiae of St. Thomas Aquinas* (Ann Arbor, Mich.: University Microfilms, 1989).

69. E. R. Curtius, *European Literature and the Latin Middle Ages*, trans. Willard Trask (Princeton, N.J.: Princeton University Press, 1953), 126.

70. See Copleston, *Aquinas*, 204–5.

71. See Summers, *Judgment of Sense*, 42–49.

72. "Lequale non crasso, non gemino, non disfracto, non breve il cythereo corpo reddedendo, Ma integerrimo & simplice, quale era cusi in ipso perfectamente se cerniva" (1: 362).

73. "Cum facteze & mirando composito tra gli humani ne viduto ne unque meditato" (1: 362)

74. See 1: 365–67, where Poliphilo describes the exhalation of his spirit through the wound made by Cupid's arrow when Cupid went to fix the image of Polia in Poliphilo's soul.

75. The exact meaning of Polia's name is much discussed. See Lefaivre, *Alberti's Hypnerotomachia*, 65. And see Ariani, "Il sogno filosofico," 2: xlii, liv–lvi, and Ariani and Gabriele, 10, 683–86. See also Dronke, "Introduction," 18 who notes the influence of Martianus Capella's allegorical encyclopedia, *The Marriage of Philology and Mercury*, on the *Hypnerotomachia Poliphili*. And for a *locus classicus* for the importance of "manysidedness" in educational knowledge see Cicero, *De Oratore*, iii, 32, 127. See also Carruthers, *Book of Memory*, 147.

76. See Vitruvius, *De Arch*, I, 1, 12.

77. A. Preminger, O. B. Hardison and Kevin Kerrane, eds., *Classical and Medieval Literary Criticism: Translations and Interpretations* (New York: Frederick Ungar, 1974), 14; Summers, *Judgment of Sense*, 258.

78. Deborah Black, *Logic and Aristotle's Rhetoric and Poetics in Medieval Arabic Philosophy* (Leiden: E.J. Brill, 1990); Summers, *Judgment of Sense*, 235–65; Preminger et al., *Classical and Medieval Literary Criticism*, 14; Minnis and Scott, *Medieval Literary Theory and Criticism*, 9; C. C. Greenfield, *Humanist and Scholastic Poetics, 1250–1500* (Lewisburg, Pa.: Bucknell University Press, 1981).

79. Bernard Weinberg, *A History of Literary Criticism in the Italian Renaissance* (Chicago: University of Chicago Press, 1961), 1.

80. Preminger et al., *Classical and Medieval Literary Criticism*, 15. Though it is beyond the scope of this study to outline the process of memory formation, Dante's specific task as a poet was to create memory images (*fantasie*) that would incite his readers to virtue. See Carruthers, *Book of Memory*, 156–88. See also Frances Yates, *The Art of Memory* (London: Routledge and Kegan Paul, 1966) for her discussion of memory and prudence.

81. The comparison between architecture and the human body has a long history in western thought. Tied to discussions of proportion that understood the human form to offer a proportional standard for architecture, the association gained particular strength in the Middle Ages. See Leonard Barkan, *Nature's Work of Art* (New Haven, Conn: Yale University Press, 1975); David Summers, *Michelangelo and the Language of Art* (Princeton, N.J.: Princeton University Press, 1981), 424–46; Rudolf

Wittkower, *Architectural Principles in the Age of Humanism* (New York: W.W. Norton, 1971). The comparison of the walls of the body to the human skin, however, was more likely the result of another intellectual tradition that was able to incorporate the tradition of the *homo quadratus*, the medieval moral allegory. Dependent on Prudentius's portrayal in his *Psychomachia* of the internal battle between the virtues and vices, this tradition developed more specific comparisons of the parts of the body and the various parts of a building after the Aristotelian renaissance and its assimilation of Aristotelian psychology. See Barkan, *Nature's Work of Art*, 160; Carruthers, *Book of Memory*, 46–79; R. D. Cornelius, *The Figurative Castle* (Bryn Mawr, Pa.: Bryn Mawr College, 1930); Lynch, *Dream Vision*, 21–45; Pozzi and Ciapponi, *Hypnerotomachia*, 46; Ariani and Gabriele, *Hypnerotomachia*, 2: 697, n. 6.

82. Aristotle, *De Anima*, Book II, cap. 11. Also see Elizabeth D. Harvey's chapter in this volume, "The Touching Organ: Allegory, Anatomy, and the Renaissance Skin Envelope," 81–102.

83. See, for example, 1: 358, when Poliphilo and Polia are finally brought to the fountain of Venus. Poliphilo's experience of the fountain is one where he is literally invaded by a sweetness that is not perceptible, i.e., not subject to the processes of perception. See also Lefaivre, *Alberti's Hypnerotomachia*, 239–49 for a listing of the various occasions when Poliphilo experiences buildings voluptuously.

84. See Payne, *John of the Cross*, 41–44 for a discussion of what were known in the writing of the mystics as "substantial touches of the soul," communications that did not take the form of an image and aroused a more fervent love. Also see Marjorie O'Rourke, *Senses of Touch: Human Dignity from Michelangelo to Calvin* (Leiden: E.J. Brill, 1998), 5–6.

85. It is worth comparing the *Hypnerotomachia Poliphili*'s promotion of architecture with Alain de Lille's case for music, and thus the sense of hearing, in his *Anticlaudianus*. See Alain de Lille, *Anticlaudianus or the Good and Perfect Man*, trans. J. Sheridan (Toronto: Pontifical Institute of Mediaeval Studies, 1973), 109–12. A greater adherence to Pythagorean notions concerning the harmony of the spheres than to Thomistic ideas about the centrality of touch is likely responsible for this difference. See M. De Wulf, *History of Medieval Philosophy*, trans. E. C. Messenger (London: Longmans, Green and Co., 1935), 222–25.

Chapter 12. The Touch of the Blind Man: The Phenomenology of Vividness in Italian Renaissance Art

1. Bernard Berenson, *The Florentine Painters of the Renaissance, with an Index to Their Works* (New York: G.P. Putnam's Sons, 1896). Citations are taken from the edition *The Italian Painters of the Renaissance* (London: Phaidon Press, 1967), here 41.

2. Berenson, *Florentine Painters*, 42–43.

3. Mary Ann Calo, *Bernard Berenson and the Twentieth Century* (Philadelphia: Temple University Press, 1994), 69; Hayden B. J. Maginnis, "Reflections of Formalism: The Post-Impressionists and the Early Italians," *Art History* 19, 2 (June 1996): 191–207.

For a brief discussion of the importance of the haptic for late nineteenth-century theorists, including Bernard Berenson, Aloïs Riegl, and Adolf Hildebrand, see Margaret Olin, "Tactile Verification," in *Forms of Representation in Aloïs Riegl's Theory of Art* (University Park: Pennsylvania State University Press, 1992), 132–37.

4. The bibliography on the sense of touch in Renaissance art, both representations of the sense and the role of touch in the phenomenology of the arts, includes the following: Carl Nordenfalk, "The Sense of Touch in Art," in *The Verbal and the Visual: Essays in Honor of William Sebastian Heckscher,* ed. Karl-Ludwig Selig and Elizabeth Sears (New York: Italica Press, 1990), 109–33; Nordenfalk, "The Five Senses in Late Medieval and Renaissance Art," *Journal of the Warburg and Courtauld Institutes* 48 (1985): 1–22; Marjorie O'Rourke Boyle, *Senses of Touch: Human Dignity and Deformity from Michelangelo to Calvin* (Leiden: E.J. Brill, 1998); Mary Pardo, "Artifice as Seduction in Titian," in *Sexuality and Gender in Early Modern Europe: Institutions, Texts, Images,* ed. James Grantham Turner (Cambridge: Cambridge University Press, 1993), 55–89; Fredrika H. Jacobs, "Aretino and Michelangelo, Dolce and Titian: *Femmina, Mascolo, Grazia,*" *Art Bulletin* 82, 1 (March 2000): 51–67; Andrea Bolland, "*Desiderio* and *Diletto*: Vision, Touch, and the Poetics of Bernini's *Apollo and Daphne,*" *Art Bulletin* 82, 2 (June 2000): 309–30. See also Jonathan Crary, *Techniques of the Observer* (Cambridge, Mass.: MIT Press, 1990), and *Suspensions of Perception: Attention, Spectacle, and Modern Culture* (Cambridge, Mass.: MIT Press, 1999).

5. BN 2038, 19r. Leonardo da Vinci, *Leonardo on Painting,* ed. Martin Kemp, trans. Kemp and Margaret Walker (New Haven, Conn.: Yale University Press, 1989), 20.

6. *Codex Urbinas* 13r, 15r–v; *Leonardo on Painting,* 21–22. For the comparison between the arts, see Irma A. Richter, ed., *Paragone: A Comparison of the Arts by Leonardo da Vinci* (London: Oxford University Press, 1949); Claire Farago, *Leonardo da Vinci's "Paragone": A Critical Interpretation with a New Edition of the Text in the "Codex Urbinas"* (Leiden: E.J. Brill, 1992).

7. *Codex Urbinas* 7r–v; *Leonardo on Painting,* 22.

8. *Codex Urbinas* 14v–15r; *Leonardo on Painting,* 25–26.

9. Bruno Maier, ed., *Il Cortegiano con una scelta delle opere minori* (Turin: Unione Tipografico, 1964), 598; David Rosand, "The Portrait, the Courtier, and Death," in *Castiglione: The Ideal and Real in Renaissance Culture,* ed. Robert W. Hanning and David Rosand (New Haven, Conn.: Yale University Press, 1983), 91–129.

10. Mary Rogers, "Sonnets on Female Portraits from Renaissance North Italy," *Word and Image* 2 (1986): 291–304; John Shearman, *Only Connect . . . Art and the Spectator in the Italian Renaissance* (Princeton, N.J.: Princeton University Press, 1992), 108–48. See also Lodovico Dolce, *Dialogo della Pittura* (1557), in Mark Roskill, *Dolce's "Aretino" and Venetian Art Theory of the Cinquecento* (New York: New York University Press, 1968), 97–99, 157–59.

11. Jaynie Anderson, "The Giorgionesque Portrait: From Likeness to Allegory," in *Giorgione: Atti del convegno internazionale di studio per il 5° centenario della nascita* (Castelfranco Veneto: Banco Popolare di Asolo e Montebelluna, 1979), 153–58; Anderson, *Giorgione: The Painter of "Poetic Brevity"* (New York: Flammarion, 1997); Carlo Pedretti, "Ancora sul rapporto Giorgione-Leonardo e l'origine del ritratto di spalla," in *Giorgione: Atti del convegno,* 181–85; Wendy Steadman Sheard, "Giorgione's Portrait

Inventions c.1500: Transfixing the Viewer (with Observations on Some Florentine Antecedents)," in *Reconsidering the Renaissance*, ed. Mario A. Di Cesare (Binghamton, N.Y.: Medieval and Renaissance Texts and Studies, 1992), 171–76; Jodi Cranston, *The Poetics of Portraiture in the Italian Renaissance* (Cambridge: Cambridge University Press, 2000).

12. Much of the scholarship on this painting centers on the identification of the precise story represented. For a summary of the bibliography (pre-1990) see *Tiziano*, Exhibition Catalog, Palazzo Ducale, Venice (Venice, 1990), 178–80. Marco Boschini, *La carta del navegar pitoresco* . . . (Venice, 1660), ed. A. Pallucchini (Venice: Istituto per la collaborazione culturale, 1966), 1, 256, significantly describes the painting not in terms of a recognizable narrative, but as a *contrapposto* of *affetti* and vividness: "e chi non vede la semplicità di quel giovinetto spaventato dal timore non sa cosa sia afflizione d'animo, ne spavento di Morte: affetto vivamente espresso, benche si vegga semivivo l'assalito, all incontro Claudio così rigido, così crudele, così furioso, che rende terrore alle stesse Furie. Due opposti d'affetti che formano un concerto pittoresco, che più non puo far l'Arte." Cf. Titian's so-called *Concert* (Florence, Galleria Palatina di Palazzo Pitti).

13. Raphael's *Self-Portrait with His Fencing Master* (Louvre, Paris) offers an example of a touch on the shoulder that depicts the elicited turn from the designated.

14. Baldassare Castiglione, *The Book of the Courtier*, trans. Charles S. Singleton (New York: Doubleday, 1959), 50.

15. Castiglione, *Book of the Courtier*, 56. "Talor vorrei che pigliasse alcune parole in altra significazione che la lor propria e, trasportandole a proposito, quasi le inserisse come rampollo d'albero in più felice tronco, per farle più vaghe e belle, e quasi per accostar le cose al senso degli occhi proprii e, come si dice, farle toccar con mano, con diletto di chi ode o legge." *Il cortegiano*, ed. Amedeo Quondam and Nicola Longo (Milan: Garzanti, 1992), 76. Significantly, Lodovico Dolce employs in his *Dialogo della Pittura* (1557) the phrase "ci fa toccar con mano (98) to describe vividness in painting. I am currently researching the larger rhetorical and poetical context of these Renaissance discussions and their relationship to contemporary paintings.

16. Cicero, *De Oratore*, trans. H. Rackham (Cambridge, Mass.: Loeb Classical Library, 1968), III. xxxvii, 149–50.

17. Cicero, *De Partitione Oratoriae*, trans. H. Rackham (Cambridge, Mass.: Loeb Classical Library, 1968), vi. 20.

18. Aristotle, "Rhetoric," in *On Poetry and Style*, trans. G. M. A. Grube (Indianapolis, Ind.: Hackett, 1989), 1412a.

19. Giorgio Vasari, *Le vite de'più eccellenti pittori scultori ed architettori*, ed. G. Milanesi (Florence, 1906), vii, 724 ; also cited and discussed in Philip Sohm, *Pittoresco: Marco Boschini, His Critics, and Their Critiques of Painterly Brushwork in Seventeenth-Century and Eighteenth-Century Italy* (Cambridge: Cambridge University Press, 1991), 27.

20. Luigi Grassi, "I concetti di schizzo, abbozzo, macchia, "non-finito" e la costruzione dell'opera d'arte," in *Studi in onore di Pietro Silva* (Florence: Monnier, 1957), 99–100; Sohm, *Pittoresco*, 28–31; Paola Barocchi, "Finito e non-finito nella critica vasariana," *Arte antica e moderna* 1 (1958): 221–35.

21. "Quella prima fatica, che fanno I Pittori sopra le tele o tavole, cominciando a colorire così alla grossa le figure, per poi tornarvi sopra con altri colori." *Vocabolario toscano dell'arte del Disegno* (Florence, 1681);also cited in Grassi, "I concetti," 99–100.

22. Giorgio Vasari, *La vita di Michelangelo nelle redazioni del 1550 e del 1568*, ed. Paola Barocchi (Milan and Naples: Riccardo Ricciardi, 1962), 1: 44.

23. *De'veri precetti della pittura* (Ravenna, 1587). Cited in Sohm, *Pittoresco*, 29. Leonardo da Vinci frequently employs the term "ritocca" when he describes the application of paint. See, for example, *Codex Urbinas* 1270, f. 161v.

24. Cited in Grassi, "I concetti," 101.

25. Thomas Brachert, "A Distinctive Aspect in the Painting Technique of the *Ginevra de'Benci* and of Leonardo's Early Works," *Report and Studies in the History of Art, 1969* (Washington, D.C.: National Gallery of Art, 1970), 89–104. For related observations after the 1990 restoration, see Eric Gibson, "Leonardo's *Ginevra de'Benci*: The Restoration of a Renaissance Masterpiece," *Apollo* 133 (1991): 161–65; David Bull, "Two Portraits by Leonardo: *Ginevra de'Benci* and the *Lady with an Ermine*," *Artibus et Historiae* 13, (1992): 67–83; David Alan Brown, *Leonardo da Vinci: Origins of a Genius* (New Haven, Conn.: Yale University Press, 1998), 114. Other painters to use their fingers are Giovanni Bellini, who uses his hands exclusively in the flesh areas.

26. John Shearman, "Leonardo's Color and Chiaroscuro," *Zeitschrift für Kunstgeschichte* 25 (1962): 22–26.

27. On the differences between tempera and oil paint and the corresponding aesthetics, see David Rosand, *Painting in Sixteenth-Century Venice: Titian, Veronese, Tintoretto* (Cambridge: Cambridge University Press, 1997), 10–25, 33–34.

28. See Dolce, *Dialogo della Pittura*, 153.

29. Rona Goffen articulates similar effect in the inscription in Giovanni Bellini's *Woman with a Mirror*.

30. Brachert, "A Distinctive Aspect," 93.

31. David Rosand, "Titian and the Critical Tradition," in *Titian: His World and His Legacy*, ed. Rosand (New York: Columbia University Press, 1982), 1–39.

32. David Rosand, *Titian* (New York: Harry Abrams, 1978), 33.

33. Sperone Speroni, "Discorso in lode della pittura," in *Scritti d'arte del Cinquecento*, ed. Paola Barocchi (Milan: Riccardo Ricciardi Editore, 1971), 998.

34. Speroni, "Discorso," 998.

35. Speroni, "Discorso," 2002.

36. Giorgio Vasari, *Letter to Benedetto Varchi* (Florence, February 12, 1547), in Barocchi, *Scritti d'Arte del Cinquecento*, 499–500. For a discussion of Vasari's letter to Varchi, see Leatrice Mendelsohn, *Paragoni: Benedetto Varchi's "Due Lezzioni" and Cinquecento Art Theory* (Ann Arbor, Mich.: UMI Research Press, 1982), 148–49.

37. Vasari, *Letter*, 499.

38. David Summers, *Michelangelo and the Language of Art* (Princeton, N.J.: Princeton University Press, 1981), 207–9.

39. Bernardino Daniello, *Della poetica* (1536), in *Trattati di poetica e retorica del '500*, ed. Bernard Weinberg (Bari: G. Laterza, 1970), 1: 272.

40. Benedetto Varchi, *Lezzione sopra il sottoscritto sonetto di Michelagnolo*

Buonarroti in *Le rime di Michelangelo Buonarroti,* ed. Cesare Guasti (Florence: Monnier, 1863), xcix. For a discussion of this passage, see Summers, *Michelangelo,* 209–11.

41. Benedetto Varchi, "Della maggioranza delle arti—Disputa II," in *Trattati d'arte del Cinquecento fra Manierismo e Controriforma,* ed. Paola Barocchi (Bari: G. Laterza, 1960), 1: 43.

42. Charles De Tolnay, *Michelangelo: The Tomb of Julius II* (Princeton, N.J.: Princeton University Press, 1954), vol. 4. See also James M. Saslow, " Michelangelo: Sculpture, Sex, and Gender," in *Looking at Italian Renaissance Sculpture,* ed. Sarah Blake McHam (Cambridge: Cambridge University Press, 1998), 223–45.

43. Michelangelo's sonnet is a response to another sonnet written by Giovanni Battista Strozzi. For the earliest record of the exchange, see Giorgio Vasari, *Le vite de' più eccellenti pittori, scultori, ed architettori,* ed. G. Milanesi (Florence, 1906), 7: 197. See also Leonard Barkan, *Unearthing the Past: Archaeology and Aesthetics in the Making of Renaissance Culture* (New Haven, Conn.: Yale University Press, 1999), 243–44.

44. For a brief discussion of this drawing in the context of blindness and the art of drawing, see Jacques Derrida, *Memoirs of the Blind: The Self-Portrait and Other Ruins,* trans. Pascale-Anne Brault and Michael Naas (Chicago: University of Chicago Press, 1993), 43–44, 133.

45. Cranston, *Poetics of Portraiture,* 134–35.

46. *Cours de peinture par principes,* ed. Jacques Thullier (Paris, 1989), 161ff. Also cited in Charles Dempsey and Elizabeth Cropper, *Nicholas Poussin: Friendship and the Love of Painting* (Princeton, N.J.: Princeton University Press, 1996), 213.

Afterword: Touching Rhetoric

1. Elizabeth Harvey, Introduction to this volume, 1–21.

2. Much of this essay condenses a more detailed analysis of sexuality and rhetoric in Ovid's *Metamorphoses* and the impact of this relationship on Renaissance representations of subjectivity and gender in my *The Rhetoric of the Body from Ovid to Shakespeare* (Cambridge: Cambridge University Press, 2000).

3. Jodi Cranston, "The Touch of the Blind Man," this volume. For a complete discussion of Pygmalion's career as a central figure in the debates of the *paragone,* see Leonard Barkan, *The Gods Made Flesh: Metamorphosis and the Pursuit of Paganism* (New Haven, Conn.: Yale University Press, 1986), passim.

4. Quando giunse a Simon l'alto concetto
   ch'a mio nome gli pose in man lo stile,
   s'avesse dato a l'opera gentile
   colla figura voce ed intelletto,

   di sospir molti mi sgombrava il petto
   che ciò ch'altri à più caro a me fan vile.
   Però che'n vista ella si monstra umile,
   promettendomi pace ne l'aspetto,

ma poi ch' i' vengo a ragionar con lei,
benignamente assai par che m'ascolte:
se risponder savesse a' detti miei!

Pygmaliòn, quanto lodar ti dei
de l'imagine tua, se mille volte
n'avesti quel ch' i' sol una vorrei!

5. From Petrarch, *Petrarch's Lyric Poems,* ed. and trans. Robert M. Durling (Cambridge, Mass.: Harvard University Press, 1976), no. 78. Translation mmodified.

6. Poems nos. 78, 79, trans. William H. Draper in *Petrarch's Secret* (London: Chatto, 1911), 134.

7. Kenneth Gross, *The Dream of the Moving Statue* (Ithaca, N.Y.: Cornell University Press, 1992).

8. For further comment on the Ovidian subject as the embodied subject of linguistic crisis and the poem's corollary metarhetorical reflection that engenders such crisis, see my *Rhetoric of the Body.*

9. Roland Barthes, "L'ancienne rhétorique," *Communications* 16 (1970): 172–223. For the systematic way in which Ovid's poem plays with this fusion between poetry and rhetoric, see Simone Viarre, *Ovide: Essai de lecture poétique* (Paris: Société d'Édition les Belles Lettres, 1957), 55–69. See also F. J. E. Raby, *A History of Secular Latin Poetry in the Middle Ages* (Oxford: Clarendon Press, 1957), 1: 28.

10. Ovid, *Metamorphoses,* 10.249–86. All subsequent citations are to Ovid, *Metamorphoses,* trans. F. J. Miller (Cambridge, Mass.: Harvard University Press, 1968).

11. *Oxford Latin Dictionary, imago,* senses 1 and 7. In rhetorical treatises like Cicero's *De Oratore, imago* can also signify a comparison or simile.

12. For further comment on the importance of the wax simile to Ovid's programmatic reflection on the poem's scene of writing, see my *Rhetoric of the Body.*

13. Carla Mazzio, "Acting with Tact," this volume.

14. Michel Foucault, *The Order of Things: An Archaeology of Human Sciences* (New York: Vintage Books, 1973), 55; Timothy Reiss, *The Discourse of Modernism* (Ithaca, N.Y.: Cornell University Press), 132.

15. Shoshana Felman, *The Literary Speech Act: Don Juan with J. L. Austin, or Seduction in Two Languages* (Ithaca, N.Y.: Cornell University Press, 1980).

16. Elizabeth Grosz, *Volatile Bodies: Toward a Corporeal Feminism* (Bloomington: Indiana University Press, 1994), 192.

17. For further comment on this retrospective organization for what only appears as a story of origins in Kristeva, see my *The Tears of Narcissus: Melancholia and Masculinity in Early Modern Writing* (Stanford, Calif.: Stanford University Press, 1995), 28–38.

18. Jean Laplanche, *Life and Death in Psychoanalysis,* trans. Jeffrey Mehlman (Baltimore: Johns Hopkins University Press, 1976), chapters 2 and 3.

Contributors

MISTY G. ANDERSON is a member of the English Department at the University of Tennessee, Knoxville, where she also teaches in the Women's Studies program. The author of *Female Playwrights and Eighteenth-Century Comedy: Negotiating Marriage on the London Stage*, she has published articles in *Textual Practice, Eighteenth Century: Theory and Interpretation, Jane Austen and Discourses of Feminism*, and journals and other collections.

JODI CRANSTON is the author of *The Poetics of Portraiture in the Italian Renaissance*, has published articles on portraiture, and is currently working on a book on touch and the hand in Italian Renaissance art, focusing in particular on Michelangelo and Titian. She teaches art history at Boston University.

LYNN ENTERLINE is Professor of English at Vanderbilt University. Her work explores the connections between Renaissance texts and their classical antecedents, moving between Greek, Latin, Italian, and English literary traditions. Her books, *The Rhetoric of the Body from Ovid to Shakespeare* and *The Tears of Narcissus: Melancholia and Masculinity in Early Modern Writing*, examine foundational texts from these traditions in light of contemporary literary and feminist theory. She is currently writing a book on the erotics of early modern pedagogy entitled *Imitating Schoolboys: An Essay in Shakespeare's Emotions*.

ELIZABETH D. HARVEY is the author of *Ventriloquized Voices: Feminist Theory and Renaissance Texts* and coeditor of *Women and Reason* and *Soliciting Interpretation: Literary Theory and Seventeenth-Century English Poetry*. She is completing a book on literature and medicine, *The Inscrutable Womb: Issues of Interiority and Femininity in Early Modern England*. She is Associate Professor of English at the University of Toronto.

MARGARET HEALY is a lecturer in English at the University of Sussex. She is the author of *Richard II* (1998), *Fictions of Disease in Early Modern England: Bodies, Plagues and Politics* (2001), and many articles on literature, medicine, and art.

SUJATA IYENGAR is Assistant Professor of English Literature at the University of Georgia. Her current research historicizes bodily differences and their literary or theatrical representations. "Shakespeare in HeteroLove" appeared in *Literature/Film Quarterly*, a comparison of racial representation in early modern translations of Heliodorus's novel *Aithiopika* and a critique of black-face make-up in twentieth-century productions of *Othello* are forthcoming in edited collections. "Royalist, Romancist, Racialist," the last chapter of her current book project (tentatively titled *Mythologies of Color*) is forthcoming in *English Literary History* ; it analyzes the relationship between race, gender and labor in Margaret Cavendish's seventeenth-century utopia, *Blazing World*.

EVE KELLER is Associate Professor of English at Fordham University. She has published on Milton *(Milton Quarterly)*, Hobbes *(Prose Studies)*, Cavendish *(English Literary History)*, William Harvey *(Women's Studies)*, Jane Sharp, and embryology theory and early modern subjectivity *(Eighteenth-Century Studies)*. She is working on a book called *Generating Subjectivity: The Rhetorics of Reproduction in Early Modern England*.

CARLA MAZZIO teaches English at the University of Chicago. She is coeditor of *Social Control and the Arts: An International Perspective, The Body in Parts: Fantasies of Corporeality in Early Modern Europe,* and *Historicism, Psychoanalysis, and Early Modern Culture*. She is currently completing a book entitled *The Inarticulate Renaissance* and has begun a new book entitled *Calculating Minds: Literature and Mathematics in Early Modern England*.

BETTINA MATHES teaches early modern culture at Humboldt-University Berlin. She has published essays on torture, masculinity, and the male body, and a study of Faust, *Verhandlungen mit Faust: Geschlechterverhältnisse in der Kultur der Frühen Neuzeit*. Her research favors transdisciplinary approaches and focuses on the construction and representation of genders, bodies, and sexualities.

ELIZABETH SAUER, Professor of English at Brock University, Canada, is author of *Barbarous Dissonance and Images of Voice in Milton's Epics* (1996), and coeditor of *Agonistics: Arenas of Creative Contest, Milton and the Imperial Vision*, winner of the Milton Society of America Irene Samuel Memorial Award, *Books and Readers in Early Modern England: Textual Studies*, and *Reading Early Women: Texts in Manuscript and Print, 1500–1700*. A Social Sciences and Humanities Research Council-funded book on seventeenth-century textual communities is in progress, as is a coedited volume, *Comparative Imperialisms: Early Modern to Late Romantic*.

REBEKAH SMICK has taught at the University of Toronto, Queen's University, and the Université Canadienne en France. She is coeditor of and a contributing author to *Antiquity and Its Interpreters*. She is the author of essays on the themes of feminine mercy and the Renaissance comparison of the arts. She was a Social Sciences and Humanities Research Council of Canada Postdoctoral Fellow at the Warburg Institute in 1995–97 and is currently a Senior Fellow at the Centre for Reformation and Renaissance Studies in Toronto, working on a book on the Renaissance reception of Michelangelo's Vatican *Pieta*.

LISA M. SMITH is a doctoral candidate in the Department of English at the University of Toronto. Her dissertation focuses on George Eliot's fiction and the epistemology of empiricism.

SCOTT MANNING STEVENS teaches English literature and Indigenous Studies at the State University of New York at Buffalo. He contributed a chapter to *The Body in Parts: Fantasies of Corporeality in Early Modern Europe* and works in the fields of early modern British culture and the literature of the Encounter. He is currently completing a book on the encounter narratives of the Amerindian and European communities of New England and New France.

Index

Acknowledgments

This book had its inception in a series of conversations with Heather Meakin. Although she decided ultimately not to participate in the collection, I would like to record here her integral presence in the initial stages, her shaping role in its conception, and her collaboration in gathering the essays. I am also grateful to her organization of a session on touch at the Renaissance Society of America, in which she, I, Elizabeth Sauer, and Carla Mazzio took part. I am indebted to Nicholas Watson and Mary Nyquist, who provided help in making initial contact with contributors, to Barbara McLean, who patiently read multiple drafts of my essays, to Spring Hurlbut for her photographic contacts, to Susan Valentine, who was a resourceful research assistant, to Sophia Levy, who gave wonderfully helpful editorial assistance, to Sujata Iyengar and Michael Schoenfeldt, who participated in a session on touch at the International Spenser Society meeting in Cambridge, and to Robert Barsky and Tilottama Rajan for their enabling belief in my work. A Social Sciences and Humanities Research Council of Canada internal grant from the University of Western Ontario helped with research, travel, and the preparation of the essays. I completed some of the writing while on a fellowship at the Sterling and Francine Clark Art Institute, and the library and the community of colleagues there provided a stimulating intellectual environment. Peter Erickson, in particular, was immensely supportive at a crucial stage, and Jerome Singerman's wise advice and vision throughout the process have been instrumental. The contributors were heroically patient; special thanks go to Carla Mazzio and Lynn Enterline for intellectual companionship and friendship, and for sustaining me during moments of crisis. My graduate students and colleagues at the University of Toronto have given me a generous and nourishing intellectual community. John Astington supplied superb references to prints and paintings of the Five Senses, and Mark Levene listened to my ideas, read my essays, and furnished a ready store of wit. I am especially grateful to Brian Corman, David Galbraith, and Linda Hutcheon.

This book is dedicated to Nicholas and Anthea, whose lives touch mine in every way, and to Mark Cheetham, who makes all things possible.